CHRISTIAN THEISM
AND THE PROBLEMS OF PHILOSOPHY

LIBRARY OF RELIGIOUS PHILOSOPHY

Thomas V. Morris, editor

Volume 5

Christian Theism
and the Problems of Philosophy

EDITED BY MICHAEL D. BEATY

UNIVERSITY OF NOTRE DAME PRESS
NOTRE DAME   LONDON

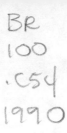

The following articles are reprinted from *Faith and Philosophy* by permission of the editors:

"Advice to Christian Philosophers" by Alvin Plantinga from vol. 1, no. 3, July 1984.
"Justification and Theism" by Alvin Plantinga from vol. 4, no. 4, October 1987.
"A Theistic Conception of Probability" by Richard Otte from vol. 4, no. 4, October 1987.
"Nomo(theo)logical Necessity" by Del Ratzsch from vol. 4, no. 4, October 1987.
"Theism, Platonism, and the Metaphysics of Mathematics" by Christopher Menzel from vol. 4, no. 4, October 1987.

Library of Congress Cataloging-in-Publication Data

    Christian theism and the problems of philosophy / edited by
    Michael D. Beaty.
        p.   cm. — (Library of religious philosophy ; v. 5)
    Essays in response to Alvin Plantinga's Advice to Chris-
    tian philosophers, which is included as the prologue.
    ISBN 0-268-00778-0
    1. Christianity—Philosophy. 2. Theism. 3. Plantinga,
    Alvin. 4. Philosophy and religion. I. Beaty, Michael D.
    II. Plantinga, Alvin. Advice to Christian philosophers. 1990.
    III. Series.
    BR100.C54 1990
    190—dc20   90-33341
                                           CIP

Contents

III. MORAL THEORY AND THEISM

Acknowledgments

While most of the papers in this collection were written specially for it, some of them have been published previously in *Faith and Philosophy,* the official journal of the Society of Christian Philosophers. In my judgment these essays were especially suited for this collection. I would like to thank the editor of *Faith and Philosophy* for permitting us to include them in this book.

The idea for this project came to me at a National Endowment for the Humanities Summer Institute in the Philosophy of Religion, co-directed by Alvin Plantinga and William Alston and held during the summer of 1986 at Western Washington University in Bellingham, Washington. The setting for the institute was picturesque and the participants were a marvelous group of people, both in philosophical abilities and in character. I thank a number of the philosophers who attended that institute for encouraging me to initiate and carry through this project. Among them are William Alston, Richard Creel, Alvin Plantinga, and Charles Taliaferro. A very special thanks goes to Thomas V. Morris for his guidance and for his confidence in the project. Finally, I thank both Baylor University and Ouachita Baptist University. The latter stages of the work on the book were completed after I joined the Baylor faculty. My colleagues and, in particular, our secretary, Beverly Locklin, have been very supportive and helpful. The work on the book was begun after I returned from the NEH summer institute and while I was a member of the Ouachita faculty. Ouachita provided some financial assistance toward the institute, and also provided me a rich environment for the several years I was a member, first, of the student body and then of the faculty. It is to Ouachita—its students, faculty, and staff—that I dedicate this book. May your work continue to flourish.

Introduction

The extent and intensity of recently renewed interest in philosophy of religion is well-known. Evidence of this rebirth of interest and activity abound. Numerous articles in leading philosophical journals are devoted to epistemological or conceptual assessments of religious beliefs. These days many more books by philosophers are available which address central religious concerns. Indeed, major book publishers are initiating new series devoted to philosophical issues in philosophy of religion and philosophical theology. Conferences which bring together both junior and senior members of our discipline to share their research on these matters are being sponsored by a wide range of groups, organizations, universities, and professional societies.

One of the individuals who has done much to stimulate the resurgence of interest in philosophy of religion is Alvin Plantinga. This collection of essays attempts to take seriously a provocative and important paper called "Advice to Christian Philosophers," written by Plantinga. In his essay, Plantinga issues a powerful, and inevitably controversial, challenge to religious philosophers to serve their own religious communities more faithfully. Being faithful involves, he suggests, exercising an appropriately circumspect kind of autonomy or independence of the rest of the philosophical world, having a sense of identity with the Christian community, both its philosophers and nonphilosophers, and displaying self-confidence in the philosophical service of one's own religious community. Of significant importance, Plantinga advises Christian philosophers to expend more effort on issues of importance to the Christian community in general, and, by implication, on issues of importance to the particular, concrete Christian communities of which they are members. In addition, he urges them to use their distinctively the-

1

istic and Christian perspectives in working in the many traditional areas of philosophy. Believing that the first task is well on its way, I hope to stimulate interest in the second by this collection of essays entitled Christian Theism and the Problems of Philosophy.

The book's prologue presents Plantinga's seminal essay and the essays which follow address issues in three traditional areas of interest to philosophers: epistemology, metaphysics, and ethics. If this collection is successful, it will stimulate research and writing which brings Christian beliefs and practices to bear on a wider range of issues that captivate the attention of philosophers.

The first section of the book is entitled "Epistemology and Theism." Typically, epistemology is characterized as "the theory of knowledge." Since knowledge has been conceived traditionally as, roughly, "justified true belief," epistemology has focused much attention on epistemic justification. This is true of a great number of contemporary discussions in epistemology. In "Justification and Theism" Alvin Plantinga takes his own advice and contends that Christian theism can make important contributions to our understanding of epistemic justification. According to a theistic perspective, human beings have been designed and created by God and in God's image. Reflecting God's own capacities as an intellectual being, human beings are created with capacities to attain knowledge. Our faculties work in such a way that they form the appropriate beliefs in the appropriate circumstances when they are functioning properly. According to Plantinga, epistemic justification is a matter of the degree of inclination one has toward a belief when one's epistemic faculties are functioning properly in the appropriate environment. This view, he suggests, fits most naturally with a theistic perspective and, moreover, it provides a vantage point from which one can see that none of the other main views of epistemic justification are, in the end, plausible.

Reliabilist theories have come to be very widely discussed as theories of knowledge and justification in contemporary epistemology. One of the principal features of the various versions of reliabilism available is the insistence on a very strong connection between truth and justification. A reliabilist theory of justification will insist that a justified belief is a belief that is likely to be objectively true. But more must be said so that we can distinguish probabilistic theories of justification from reliabilist theories of justification. There seem to be two ways of making this distinction. In both cases what is justified is justified because there is some specified way, it is claimed, of determining that beliefs of this sort are reliable indicators of what is true. According to process reliabilism, a belief is justified only if it was acquired by a reliable belief producing process (a process which is such that beliefs produced by it are objectively likely to be true). According to personal reliabilism, the objective likelihood that a belief is true is a function of a person's intellectual virtues, those stable dispositions to acquire truth rather than falsehood. In "Theism, Reliabilism, and the Cognitive Ideal," Jonathan Kvanvig argues that both personal reliabilism and process reliabilism are problematic because of an epistemically hostile environment. On the one hand, Kvanvig contends that process reliabilism is the more resilient and attractive version of reliabilism. On the other, he concludes that while it is inadequate as the fundamental theory of justification, one can defend process reliabilism if one is a theist, suggesting, in a Cartesian-like manner, that a nondeceptive God would not allow a systematic correlation of our cognitive equipment to epistemically hostile environments. An interesting feature of Kvanvig's essay is his reliance on the perspective of the unlimited cognitive ideal, the nature of which is discovered by an investigation of God's cognitive powers.

Probability can be understood as either a statistical concept or an epistemological concept. Epistemic probability is concerned with rational degrees of belief. However, since Pascal first applied probability to belief in God, several ways of interpreting epistemic probability have been offered. In "A Theistic Conception of Probability," Richard Otte argues that the doctrines of theism are rich enough to support a distinctively theistic conception of probability, a conception which avoids many of the problems associated with other interpretations of probability. Moreover, Otte claims that the theistic conception of probability he presents satisfies the ascertainability and applicability criteria for acceptable interpretations of probability which have been proposed by Wesley Salmon in his well-known book, *The Foundations of Scientific Inference*. While Otte concedes that his own conception of probability fails the admissibility criterion laid down by Salmon, he argues that this particular criterion is not a legitimate one for human cognizers. Finally, he contends the theistic conception of probability illuminates sources of confusion over how to understand various claims involving probabilistic arguments with respect to a variety of philosophical issues. Hence, Otte claims to have made a strong case for a theistic conception of probability.

It is not uncommon to hear someone protest that philosophy of religion, as it is practiced in the Academy, has been preoccupied with issues and arguments having little to do with "real" religious belief and practice. Ironically, this same kind of criticism has been leveled against philosophy of science—that it pays little or no attention to actual science. Such criticism has contributed, at least in part, to what is now called "a theory of scientific rationality." A theory of scientific rationality is the philosophical endeavor to articulate the norms by which theories are accepted, debated, revised, and replaced in the actual life of science, and to do so in a way that illuminates why those theories have the claim on us we take them to have. It seems natural to ask of the philosophers of religion what has been asked of philosophers of science—a "theory of religious rationality." A theory of religious rationality would be the articulation of the norms by which beliefs are accepted, revised, and replaced in the actual life of religious communities, and the theory ought to do so in a way that illuminates why those beliefs have the claim on us (the members of a believing community) we take them to have. But that's not all. Since the claim that "believing *p* is rational" (when *p* is a statement asserting some "religious truth") seems, at least in our own age, more controversial than assertions about some nonreligious subject matter, a theory of religious rationality ought to illuminate why the rational acceptability of religious assertions are more controversial than nonreligious ones and why such assertions are rationally acceptable despite being more controversial, if, indeed, they are rationally acceptable. In his essay, "Reasons, Redemption, and Realism: The Axiological Roots of Rationality in Science and Religion," Stephen Wykstra sketches a theory (in the sense suggested above) of religious rationality which, claims Wykstra, accomplishes these aims while making both religious and philosophical sense. Wykstra focuses on three questions:

(1) What is it for something to be a "good reason" for believing?
(2) What should (and should not) count as a "good reason" for believing; and why should (shouldn't) it so count?

(3) Should what counts as "good reason" be the same in religious matters as in scientific matters?

His essay consists of three sections. In section I, Wykstra presents a "historical-axiological" image of science, an image prompted by some of the recent work in the history and philosophy of science. Interestingly, though this image of science he develops owes much to Kuhn, Wykstra ultimately departs from Kuhn because of Kuhn's nonrealist commitments. In section II, utilizing resources identified and discussed in the previous section, he attempts to reconcile the historic confrontation between those who think that the request for good reasons in religion is appropriate and those who think it is not. The central idea in these two sections is this: in both science and religion "good reasons" implies norms and norms are grounded in values or aims, that is, axiological concerns. If the values governing "good reasons" are not the same, then the norms of rationality will be to some extent different for scientific and religious claims. The history of science has shown us that science is more than methodological techniques for "discovering facts." It intends to make our world predictively intelligible. On the other hand, Christian discourse aims to make our world redemptively intelligible. It is not intended to help us predict, control, and redesign the physical features of the universe. In both cases, the scientific and the religious, participants in these communities of discourse purport to refer to "realities" distinct from the discourse itself. In both cases there will be norms governing what counts as "good reasons." In neither case will these norms or rules get us from "facts" to "truth" in a manner that is guaranteed to be error free. This means that both the practicing scientist and the religious believer are in a "Pascalian" position of having to bet that these methods, rules, or beliefs work. Since we are more than merely contemplative beings, we have good reasons to value those statements which open up the possibility of prediction and of redemption. Since the norms of religious rationality are grounded in its distinctive telos, redemption, the norms of scientific rationality are not wholly appropriate as a means of evaluating the rationality of religious belief (but neither are they wholly inappropriate).

If Christian discourse does not aim principally at giving us a true picture of the universe, does this mean that one can believe whatever makes one happy or contributes in some "salvific" way to wholeness or redemption? Should we regard religious beliefs as more or less useful constructions, but not as more or less "true" (or false) accounts of how things are? In section III, Wykstra attempts to overcome this sort of objection, arguing that his theory of religious rationality is consistent with a thoroughgoing realism, just as a theory of scientific rationality is consistent with that sort of realism. Interestingly, Wykstra claims that in both cases justification for one's beliefs is a function of the convergence over time in results obtained by specifying theories in a way that can be "appropriately" tested. Moreover, since such "testing" presupposes values to which we have no independent access, such testing requires commitment and if commitment, then trust, confidence and even hope. Thus, Wykstra reminds us that "by faith" we are saved.

Providing a general characterization of metaphysics is difficult. Often we say that metaphysics is concerned with what is real, the nature and constituents of ultimate reality, and the place of human beings in the structure or structures of reality. The essays in section II, "Metaphysics and Theism," provocatively explore the implications of theistic beliefs for various metaphysical issues of these sorts. For example, on the standard semantics of counterfactual conditionals, every counterfactual with a necessarily false antecedent is trivially true. That is, according to the received view, both of the following are true:

(1) If it were both raining and not raining, then I would be the Pope.
(2) If it were both raining and not raining, then I would not be the Pope.

Linda Zagzebski in "What If the Impossible Had Been Actual?" calls any "would" counterfactual with an impossible proposition as an antecedent a "counterpossible." For many of us, accepting both (1) and (2) as trivially true may seem unproblematic. However, how should we think about the following two propositions?

(3) If God were not good, then there would be more evil in the world than there is.

(4) If God were not good, then there would be less evil in the world than there is.

Theists who maintain that God exists necessarily and is essentially good are very likely to believe that neither (3) nor (4) are merely trivially true because (3) is substantively true and (4) is just false. Zagzebski thinks that there ought to be a way of showing this by means of the general logic of counterfactual conditionals. One of the mistakes in the standard accounts of modal and counterfactual logic, Zagzebski contends, is that they treat all necessary falsehoods as logically equivalent, suggesting that each such proposition describes the same situation or state of affairs. Zagzebski explicitly rejects this assumption. Instead, she argues that the category of the impossible is an ontological category of significant interest containing some impossible propositions which are not self-contradictory and which are of considerable importance to various metaphysical arguments and issues. She also suggests a plausible way to extend the standard account of counterfactuals to include the intuition that some counterpossibles are non-trivially true and others are nontrivially false.

In another area of metaphysics, the status and nature of natural laws is widely recognized as problematic. In "Nomo(theo)logical Necessity" Del Ratzsch argues that the materials for solutions to the problems besetting the discussion of natural laws may be available and available only to the theist. Ratzsch rejects the view that statements of natural law are either material statements, categorical necessities, or arbitrary components in particular deductive systems. He contends that there is something fundamentally subjunctive about law statements. Yet, subjunctives seem to involve presuppositions about laws. Hence, we seem to be confronted with a pernicious circularity. The way out is to recognize that laws are grounded on a type of subjunctive which does not depend on prior laws. These subjunctives are counterfactuals of freedom. Hence, natural laws must be viewed as grounded in truths about an agent of a certain sort—one with a thoroughly stable character whose free choices are the sources of the constants which we experience as the natural laws of our universe. Interestingly, while many of us may have conceded that law presupposes a lawgiver only in reference to socially legislative activities, Ratzsch claims that even the natural laws of the physical universe presuppose the existence of a lawgiver.

Most theists believe that God is the creator of everything that is distinct from the divine nature. In addition to the physical and mental realms, some theists acknowledge the existence of a realm of abstract objects like numbers, sets, properties, and propositions. Because such objects are usually thought to exist necessarily, and beyond the causal reach of any agents, the inclusion of such abstract objects within God's creative activity has been seen as quite problematic. In one recent paper, Thomas V. Morris and Christopher Menzel sketch a view in which the medieval doctrine of divine ideas could be incorporated into a traditional understanding of creation in such a way as to include necessarily existing abstract objects within the range of God's creative activity. First, abstract objects are the contents of a certain kind of divine intellective activity; so, as abstract products of God's "mental life," they exist at any given moment because God is thinking them. In the essay included here, "Theism, Platonism, and the Metaphysics of Mathematics," Menzel extends that account to cover mathematical objects as well. Since numbers are properties of sets, Menzel needs an account of the nature of sets, an account which will be consistent with his claim that God is the creator of sets, though sets are in a sense a part of the divine and thus exist necessarily. While Menzel locates the origins of sets in the divine intellective activity, he does not locate their existence in the same sort of intellective activity that gives rise to properties, relations, and propositions. Sets are taken to be the product of a collecting activity on God's part, an activity analogous to the human ability to selectively direct our attention to certain objects and collect or gather them together mentally. Since sets so constructed are capable of being the objects of further collectings, this view naturally gives rise to an iterative conception of sets, according to which they are "built up" in levels from some initial collection of nonsets. At first glance, the model Menzel offers seems to suggest several troublesome paradoxes; however, he develops a picture of the abstract realm that finally appears to avoid them.

The philosophy of mind now includes a wide variety of questions, but of central concern is the nature of personhood. The principal theories about the status of human beings as persons and their relationship to the physical world include eliminative materialism, identity theory, functionalism, property dualism, substantive dualism, and idealism. When a philosopher takes up the general task of weighing these alternative answers to the fundamental question of what is a person, we may wonder whether the Christian philosopher is entitled to address the issues in a distinctive fashion. Charles Taliaferro answers affirmatively in "Philosophy of Mind and the Christian." He insists that theism can offer us independent reasons for accepting a particular theory of the person. Toward that end, Taliaferro identifies a central set of Christian convictions which have implications for the philosophy of mind. He also identifies and responds to some worries about adopting the sort of methodology he is defending, a methodology Taliaferro attributes to Plantinga in his "Advice to Christian Philosophers." Finally, despite its current philosophical and theological unpopularity, he defends a particular conception of the person based on a precisely formulated version of substantive dualism. He contends that the popular religious objections to substantive dualism are genuine concerns, but one need not defend a version of substantive dualism which is subject to them. Taliaferro points out that our prephilosophical experience about our own mind-body distinctiveness and our own mental agency, puts the presumption in favor of dualism, a presumption that is not overcome by the alternative accounts. These considerations, buttressed by plausible thought experiments and by appeal to Christian beliefs in God-world distinctiveness and divine agency, strengthen decisively the case for substantive dualism, argues Taliaferro.

Freedom, it is often claimed, presupposes the ability to do otherwise, a presupposition Harry Frankfurt calls the Principle of Alternate Possibilities (PAP). Frankfurt, and several others as well, have offered counterexamples which, they claim, show that PAP is false. Moreover, it appears that PAP is incompatible with certain traditional Christian views. For example, God is understood to be both free, in the incompatibilist sense, and incapable of doing what is morally evil. On the other hand, PAP has been considered to be an essential part of certain important Christian positions, a prominent example being the free will defense. In "Intellect, Will, and the Principle of Alternate Possibilities," Eleonore Stump addresses these concerns. Her essay discusses, in an interesting and illuminating fashion, Frankfurt's hierarchical conception of free will, John Martin Fisher's accounts of incompatibilist free will and moral responsibility, and

Thomas Aquinas's theory of the will along with his account of moral responsibility. She argues that we can consistently maintain an incompatibilist account of free will and still reject PAP. In addition, she contends that an appropriate understanding of Aquinas's theory of the will permits us to accommodate the intuitions which inclined many of us to accept PAP. What we will see, she says, is that PAP holds only for most of the situations human beings encounter in our ordinary comings and goings. The unusual Frankfurt-like examples show us this. Because the will is not merely a neutral capacity for choosing but a hunger for the good, it is possible for a person to will freely and have no alternate possibilities. Interestingly, if Professor Stump is right about this, theists are not remiss in affirming the *de re* necessity of God's moral perfection, despite the fact that it is not possible for God to do evil. Her essay, then, provides some resources for responding to, among others, Nelson Pike and Stephen Davis, who argue that God is only contingently morally perfect.

Ethics, we sometimes say, is about the good and the right. Philosophical ethics typically examines alternative views about the nature of the good and the right, the relation between the two, the ways, if any, by which we have moral knowledge, and related issues. Very often, moral philosophers are inclined to offer ethical theories, hoping, perhaps, to provide in ethics something analogous to the long sought-after Unified Field Theory in physics. The bearing of belief in God on these sorts of issues is discussed in section III, "Moral Theory and Theism."

Is truth-telling morally obligatory because it is commanded by God, or is truth-telling commanded by God because it is morally obligatory (right, what one ought to do)? Some theists have endorsed the first disjunct and embraced a divine command theory of ethics. Many have not, contending that there are quite serious philosophical objections to such a normative theory of ethics. Recently, several individuals have attempted to defend a divine command ethic by formulating clearly the basic ideas of such a normative theory and arguing that it can survive the variety of objections which have been advanced against it. Even if such attempts were successful, they would not complete the task of defending a divine command ethic. To accomplish this aim, one must also provide good reasons for accepting such a view. In his essay, "An Argument for Divine Command

Ethics," Philip Quinn turns to the task of formulating a positive case for this sort of normative theory of ethics. His aims are modest but important ones. He first attempts to construct an argument whose conclusion is one of the central claims of theological voluntarism and whose major premise is the doctrine of divine sovereignty, a version of which would be widely accepted across the diverse Christian community. He then seeks to examine and respond to one historically and philosophically substantial objection to the sort of argument he has proposed.

In the next essay, "Some Suggestions for Divine Command Theorists," William P. Alston indicates how a divine command theory of ethics can avoid being impaled on a Euthyphro-like dilemma. On the one hand, Alston presents a modified divine command theory. Two modifications are particularly important, for these modifications allow his account of a divine command ethic to overcome two very serious objections, contends Alston. The first objection insists that divine command theories do not permit an adequate understanding of the moral goodness of God. To accommodate this criticism, Alston draws a sharp distinction between goodness or value (including the moral values of actions as well as of persons, traits, and motives), and obligation, duty, moral requiredness and so on. A modified divine command theory of the sort suggested by Alston takes divine commands to be constitutive only of moral obligation and not of the moral goodness of actions, persons, and the like. Alston then argues that the concepts of duty or obligation have no application to God. Nonetheless, it is coherent to assert, as theists want to do, that God is perfectly morally good. For the moral goodness of God consists in God's dispositions to do what is morally good. Thus, a theist has a coherent account of the goodness of God. A second modification allows the theist to respond to another common objection to divine command normative theories — that they make morality arbitrary. Alston suggests that the theist understand God's dispositions to do what is morally good as necessarily fixed. Since God is essentially morally good it is impossible that God should command us to do anything except what is morally acceptable.

Having escaped from the first horn of the dilemma, are we now impaled on the second horn of the dilemma? That is, must we hold that God commands us to do *A* because it is good that we do *A*, with the theistically unwelcome implication that goodness, or standards of value, exist independently of God, which appears to be a violation of divine sovereignty? Interestingly, Alston suggests that we can escape this horn of the dilemma by taking the supreme standard of value to be God, a concrete individual, rather than the Platonic Idea of the Good.

In contrast to both Alston and Quinn, "Egoistic Rationalism: Aquinas's Basis for Christian Morality," Scott MacDonald suggests that Christian philosophers ought not to prefer divine command normative theories. He argues that something like Aquinas's naturalistic and rationalistic moral theory provides an appropriate understanding of Christian morality. He devotes the major part of the essay to explicating Aquinas's metaethics, arguing that it is plausible in its own right. Of significant interest in MacDonald's account of Aquinas is the reminder that Aquinas's metaphysics of goodness provides the foundation, both conceptually and epistemically, for his moral theory. Also, MacDonald discusses some significant objections against the adequacy of a naturalistic and rationalist ethic as the basis for a Christian morality. For example, he denies that Aquinas's metaethics entails an objectable sort of psychological egoism at odds with Christian altruism. Moreover, while MacDonald concedes that Aquinas's metaethics has the appearance of making morality essentially independent of God and, thus, religion irrelevant to morality, he argues that such an appearance is in important ways a misconception. Finally, he draws attention to some of the features of Aquinas's view which make it attractive as a particularly Christian metaethical theory. For example, MacDonald contends that Aquinas's metaethics provides an explanation of the Christian belief that a life of obedience to God and of love of our neighbor is the most fulfilling life a human being can live.

Carlton Fisher, in "Because God Says So," concurs with Philip Quinn that a Christian theist and philosopher has several reasons for finding a divine command normative theory attractive, one of which is the doctrine of divine sovereignty. Nonetheless, Fisher agrees with MacDonald that a Christian moral philosopher ought to reject a divine command ethic. Thus, Fisher offers an account of the source of obligation which rejects a divine command ethic while affirming the Christian impulse to deny any moral theory which would make God's existence or nonexistence, God's will, commands, and purposes irrelevant to morality. Central to Fisher's attempt to accommodate these two aims is his location of the source of moral obligation in the creative activity of God rather than in God's will. What is right is determined on the basis of what is good for God's creatures. It follows that, while God ultimately has determined the content of morality in the actual world by creating us as we are, if God had commanded the torture of innocent babies in our actual world, then God would have done wrong. But Fisher argues that admitting this does no real damage whatsoever to God's sovereignty. Finally, he contends that though his view of the epistemology of ethics makes moral knowledge available to nonbelievers as well as believers, the Christian metaphysics of morality provides an adequate foundation for moral obligation which is unavailable to a noncreationist metaphysics.

These essays take seriously Plantinga's advice. While addressing traditional philosophical issues, each of the authors, in his or her own way, has attempted to think hard about certain fundamental human beliefs, and in a manner which is faithful to particular, deeply held religious convictions. In doing so, our authors have exhibited the robust health of philosophy, of philosophy of religion, and of philosophical theology. May their work stimulate additional efforts of this sort.

Prologue: Advice to Christian Philosophers

Alvin Plantinga

1. INTRODUCTION

Christianity, these days, and in our part of the world, is on the move. There are many signs pointing in this direction: the growth of Christian schools, of the serious conservative Christian denominations, the furor over prayer in public schools, the creationism/ evolution controversy, and others.

There is also powerful evidence for this contention in philosophy. Thirty or thirty-five years ago, the public temper of mainline establishment philosophy in the English speaking world was deeply non-Christian. Few establishment philosophers were Christian; even fewer were willing to admit in public that they were, and still fewer thought of their being Christian as making a real difference to their practice as philosophers. The most popular question of philosophical theology, at that time, was not whether Christianity or theism is *true*; the question, instead, was whether it even *makes sense* to say that there is such a person as God. According to the logical positivism then running riot, the sentence "there is such a person as God" literally makes no sense; it is disguised nonsense; it altogether fails to express a thought or a proposition. The central question wasn't whether theism is *true*; it was whether there is such a thing as theism — a genuine factual claim that is either true or false — *at all*. But things have changed. There are now many more Christians and many more unabashed Christians in the professional mainstream of American philosophical life. For example, the foundation of the

14

Society for Christian Philosophers, an organization to promote fellowship and exchange of ideas among Christian philosophers, is both
an evidence and a consequence of that fact. Founded some six years
ago, it is now a thriving organization with regional meetings in every
part of the country; its members are deeply involved in American
professional philosophical life. So Christianity is on the move, and
on the move in philosophy, as well as in other areas of intellectual life.

But even if Christianity is on the move, it has taken only a few
brief steps; and it is marching through largely alien territory. For
the intellectual culture of our day is for the most part profoundly
nontheistic and hence non-Christian—more than that, it is anti-
theistic. Most of the so-called human sciences, much of the non-
human sciences, most of nonscientific intellectual endeavor and even
a good bit of allegedly Christian theology is animated by a spirit
wholly foreign to that of Christian theism. I don't have the space
here to elaborate and develop this point; but I don't have to, for it
is familiar to you all. To return to philosophy: most of the major
philosophy departments in America have next to nothing to offer
the student intent on coming to see how to be a Christian in philosophy—how to assess and develop the bearing of Christianity on
matters of current philosophical concern, and how to think about
those philosophical matters of interest to the Christian community.
In the typical graduate philosophy department there will be little
more, along these lines, than a course in philosophy of religion in
which it is suggested that the evidence for the existence of God—
the classical theistic proofs, say—is at least counterbalanced by the
evidence against the existence of God—the problem of evil, perhaps;
and it may then be added that the wisest course, in view of such
maxims as Ockham's Razor, is to dispense with the whole idea of
God, at least for philosophical purposes.

My aim, in this talk, is to give some advice to philosophers
who are Christians. And although my advice is directed specifically
to Christian philosophers, it is relevant to all philosophers who believe in God, whether Christian, Jewish or Moslem. I propose to
give some advice to the Christian or theistic philosophical community:
some advice relevant to the situation in which in fact we find ourselves. "Who are you," you say, "to give the rest of us advice?" That's
a good question. I shall deal with it as one properly deals with good
questions to which one doesn't know the answer: I shall ignore it.

My counsel can be summed up on two connected suggestions, along with a codicil. First, Christian philosophers and Christian intellectuals generally must display more autonomy—more independence of the rest of the philosophical world. Second, Christian philosophers must display more integrity—integrity in the sense of integral wholeness, or oneness, or unity, being all of one piece. Perhaps 'integrality' would be the better word here. And necessary to these two is a third: Christian courage, or boldness, or strength, or perhaps Christian self-confidence. We Christian philosophers must display more faith, more trust in the Lord; we must put on the whole armor of God. Let me explain in a brief and preliminary way what I have in mind; then I shall go on to consider some examples in more detail.

Consider a Christian college student—from Grand Rapids, Michigan, say, or Arkadelphia, Arkansas—who decides philosophy is the subject for her. Naturally enough, she will go to graduate school to learn how to become a philosopher. Perhaps she goes to Princeton, or Berkeley, or Pittsburgh, or Arizona; it doesn't much matter which. There she learns how philosophy is presently practiced. The burning questions of the day are such topics as the new theory of reference; the realism/anti-realism controversy; the problems with probability; Quine's claims about the radical indeterminacy of translation; Rawls on justice; the causal theory of knowledge; Gettier problems; the artificial intelligence model for the understanding of what is to be a person; the question of the ontological status of unobservable entities in science; whether there is genuine objectivity in science or anywhere else; whether mathematics can be reduced to set theory and whether abstract entities generally—numbers, propositions, properties—can be, as we quaintly say, "dispensed with"; whether possible worlds are abstract or concrete; whether our assertions are best seen as mere moves in a language game or as attempts to state the sober truth about the world; whether the rational egoist can be shown to be irrational, and all the rest. It is then natural for her, after she gets her Ph.D., to continue to think about and work on these topics. And it is natural, furthermore, for her to work on them in the way she was taught to, thinking about them in the light of the assumptions made by her mentors and in terms of currently accepted ideas as to what a philosopher should start from or take for granted, what requires argument and defense, and what a satisfying philosophical explanation or a proper resolution to a philosophical question is like. She will be uneasy about departing widely from these topics and assumptions, feeling instinctively that any such departures are at best marginally respectable. Philosophy is a social enterprise; and our standards and assumptions—the parameters within which we practice our craft—are set by our mentors and by the great contemporary centers of philosophy.

From one point of view this is natural and proper; from another, however, it is profoundly unsatisfactory. The questions I mentioned are important and interesting. Christian philosophers, however, are the philosophers of the Christian community; and it is part of their task as *Christian* philosophers to serve the Christian community. But the Christian community has its own questions, its own concerns, its own topics for investigation, its own agenda and its own research program. Christian philosophers ought not merely take their inspiration from what's going on at Princeton or Berkeley or Harvard, attractive and scintillating as that may be; for perhaps those questions and topics are not the ones, or not the only ones, they should be thinking about as the philosophers of the Christian community. There are other philosophical topics the Christian community must work at, and other topics the Christian community must work at philosophically. And obviously, Christian philosophers are the ones who must do the philosophical work involved. If they devote their best efforts to the topics fashionable in the non-Christian philosophical world, they will neglect a crucial and central part of their task as Christian philosophers. What is needed here is more independence, more autonomy with respect to the projects and concerns of the nontheistic philosophical world.

But something else is at least as important here. Suppose the student I mentioned above goes to Harvard; she studies with Willard van Orman Quine. She finds herself attracted to Quine's programs and procedures: his radical empiricism, his allegiance to natural science, his inclination towards behaviorism, his uncompromising naturalism, and his taste for desert landscapes and ontological parsimony. It would be wholly natural for her to become totally involved in these projects and programs, to come to think of fruitful and worthwhile philosophy as substantially circumscribed by them. Of course she will note certain tensions between her Christian belief and her way of practicing philosophy; and she may then bend her efforts to putting the two together, to harmonizing them. She may devote her time and energy to seeing how one might understand or reinterpret Christian belief in such a way as to be palatable to the Quinean. One philosopher I know, embarking on just such a project, suggested that Christians should think of God as a *set* (Quine is prepared to countenance sets): the set of all true propositions, perhaps, or the set of right actions, or the union of those sets, or perhaps their Cartesian product. This is understandable; but it is also profoundly misdirected. Quine is a marvelously gifted philosopher: a subtle, original and powerful philosophical force. But his fundamental commitments, his fundamental projects and concerns, are wholly different from those of the Christian community— wholly different and, indeed, antithetical to them. And the result of attempting to graft Christian thought onto his basic view of the world will be at best an unintegral *pastiche;* at worst it will seriously compromise, or distort, or trivialize the claims of Christian theism. What is needed here is more wholeness, more integrality.

So the Christian philosopher has her own topics and projects to think about; and when she thinks about the topics of current concern in the broader philosophical world, she will think about them in her own way, which may be a *different* way. She may have to reject certain currently fashionable assumptions about the philosophic enterprise—she may have to reject widely accepted assumptions as to what are the proper starting points and procedures for philosophical endeavor. And—and this is crucially important—the Christian philosopher has a perfect right to the point of view and prephilosophical assumptions she brings to philosophic work; the fact that these are not widely shared outside the Christian or theistic community is interesting but fundamentally irrelevant. I can best explain what I mean by way of example; so I shall descend from the level of lofty generality to specific examples.

2. THEISM AND VERIFIABILITY

First, the dreaded "Verifiability Criterion of Meaning." During the palmy days of logical positivism, some thirty or forty years ago, the positivists claimed that most of the sentences Christians characteristically utter—"God loves us," for example, or "God created the heavens and the earth"—don't even have the grace to be false;

they are, said the positivists, literally meaningless. It is not that they express *false* propositions; they don't express any propositions at all. Like that lovely line from *Alice in Wonderland,* "T'was brillig, and the slithy toves did gyre and gymbol in the wabe," they say nothing false, but only because they say nothing at all; they are "cognitively meaningless," to use the positivist's charming phrase. The sorts of things theists and others had been saying for centuries, they said, were now shown to be without sense; we theists had all been the victims, it seems, of a cruel hoax—perpetrated, perhaps, by ambitious priests and foisted upon us by our own credulous natures.

Now if this is true, it is indeed important. How had the positivists come by this startling piece of intelligence? They inferred it from the Verifiability Criterion of Meaning, which said, roughly, that a sentence is meaningful only if either it is analytic, or its truth or falsehood can be determined by empirical or scientific investigation—by the methods of the empirical sciences. On these grounds not only theism and theology, but most of traditional metaphysics and philosophy and much else besides was declared nonsense, without any literal sense at all. Some positivists conceded that metaphysics and theology, though strictly meaningless, might still have a certain limited value. Carnap, for example, thought they might be a kind of *music.* It isn't known whether he expected theology and metaphysics to supplant Bach and Mozart, or even Wagner; I myself, however, think they could nicely supersede *rock.* Hegel could take the place of The Talking Heads; Immanuel Kant could replace The Beach Boys; and instead of The Grateful Dead we could have, say, Arthur Schopenhauer.

Positivism had a delicious air of being *avant garde* and with-it; and many philosophers found it extremely attractive. Furthermore, many who didn't endorse it nonetheless entertained it with great hospitality as at the least extremely plausible. As a consequence many philosophers—both Christians and non-Christians—saw here a real challenge and an important danger to Christianity: "The main danger to theism today," said J. J. C. Smart in 1955, "comes from people who want to say that 'God exists' and 'God does not exist' are equally absurd." In 1955 *New Essays in Philosophical Theology* appeared, a volume of essays that was to set the tone and topics for philosophy of religion for the next decade or more; and most of this

volume was given over to a discussion of the impact of Verificationism on theism. Many philosophically inclined Christians were dis-
turbed and perplexed and felt deeply threatened; could it really be
true that linguistic philosophers had somehow discovered that the
Christian's most cherished convictions were, in fact, just meaningless? There was a great deal of anxious hand wringing among philosophers, either themselves theists or sympathetic to theism. Some
suggested, in the face of positivistic onslaught, that the thing for
the Christian community to do was to fold up its tents and silently
slink away, admitting that the verifiability criterion was probably
true. Others conceded that strictly speaking, theism really *is* nonsense, but is *important* nonsense. Still others suggested that the
sentences in question should be reinterpreted in such a way as not
to give offense to the positivists; someone seriously suggested, for
example, that Christians resolve, henceforth, to use the sentence "God
exists" to mean "some men and women have had, and all may have,
experiences called 'meeting God'"; he added that when we say "God
created the world from nothing" what we should mean is "everything we call 'material' can be used in such a way that it contributes
to the well-being of men." In a different context but the same spirit,
Rudolph Bultmann embarked upon his program of demythologiz-
ing Christianity. Traditional supernaturalistic Christian belief, he said,
is "impossible in this age of electric light and the wireless." (One
can perhaps imagine an earlier village skeptic taking a similar view
of, say, the tallow candle and the printing press, or perhaps the pine
torch and the papyrus scroll.)

By now, of course, Verificationism has retreated into the ob-
scurity it so richly deserves; but the moral remains. This hand wringing and those attempts to accommodate the positivist were wholly
inappropriate. I realize that hindsight is clearer than foresight and
I do not recount this bit of recent intellectual history in order to
be critical of my elders or to claim that we are wiser than our fa-
thers: what I want to point out is that we can *learn* something from
the whole nasty incident. For Christian philosophers should have
adopted a quite different attitude towards positivism and its verifiability criterion. What they should have said to the positivists is:
"Your criterion is mistaken: for such statements as 'God loves us'
and 'God created the heavens and the earth' are clearly meaningful;
so if they aren't verifiable in your sense, then it is false that all and

only statements verifiable in that sense are meaningful." What was needed here was less accommodation to current fashion and more Christian self-confidence: Christian theism is true; if Christian theism is true, then the verifiability criterion is false; so the verifiability criterion is false. Of course, if the verificationists had given cogent *arguments* for their criterion, from premises that had some legitimate claim on Christian or theistic thinkers, then perhaps there would have been a problem here for the Christian philosophers; then we would have been obliged either to agree that Christian theism is cognitively meaningless, or else revise or reject those premises. But the Verificationists never gave any cogent arguments; indeed, they seldom gave any arguments at all. Some simply trumpeted this principle as a great discovery, and when challenged, repeated it loudly and slowly; but why should *that* disturb anyone? Others proposed it as a *definition*—a definition of the term "meaningful." Now of course the positivists had a right to use this term in any way they chose; it's a free country. But how could their decision to use that term in a particular way show anything so momentous as that all those who took themselves to be believers in God were wholly deluded? If I propose to use the term 'Democrat' to mean 'unmitigated scoundrel,' would it follow that Democrats everywhere should hang their heads in shame? And my point, to repeat myself, is that Christian philosophers should have displayed more integrity, more independence, less readiness to trim their sails to the prevailing philosophical winds of doctrine, and more Christian self-confidence.

3. THEISM AND THEORY OF KNOWLEDGE

I can best approach my second example by indirection. Many philosophers have claimed to find a serious problem for theism in the existence of *evil,* or of the amount and kinds of evil we do in fact find. Many who claim to find a problem here for theists have urged the *deductive argument from evil*: they have claimed that the existence of an omnipotent, omniscient, and wholly good God is *logically incompatible* with the presence of evil in the world—a presence conceded and indeed insisted upon by Christian theists. For their part, theists have argued that there is no inconsistency here. I think the present consensus, even among those who urge some form

of the argument from evil, is that the deductive form of the argument from evil is unsuccessful.

More recently, philosophers have claimed that the existence of
God, while perhaps not actually *inconsistent* with the existence of
the amount and kinds of evil we do in fact find, is at any rate *unlikely* or *improbable* with respect to it; that is, the probability of
the existence of God with respect to the evil we find, is less than
the probability, with respect to that same evidence, that there is no
God—no omnipotent, omniscient and wholly good Creator. Hence
the existence of God is improbable with respect to what we know.
But if theistic belief is improbable with respect to what we know,
then, so goes the claim, it is irrational or in any event intellectually
second rate to accept it.

Now suppose we briefly examine this claim. The objector holds
that

(1) God is the omnipotent, omniscient and wholly good creator of the world

is improbable or unlikely with respect to

(2) There are 10^{13} turps of evil

(where the *turp* is the basic unit of evil).

I've argued elsewhere[1] that enormous difficulties beset the claim
that (1) is unlikely or improbable given (2). Call that response "the
low road reply." Here I want to pursue what I shall call the *high
road* reply. Suppose we stipulate, for purposes of argument, that
(1) is, in fact, improbable on (2). Let's agree that it is unlikely, given
the existence of 10^{13} turps of evil, that the world has been created
by a God who is perfect in power, knowledge and goodness. What
is supposed to follow from that? How is that to be construed as an
objection to theistic belief? How does the objector's argument go
from there? It doesn't follow, of course, that theism is false. Nor
does it follow that one who accepts both (1) and (2) (and let's add,
recognizes that (1) is improbable with respect to (2)) has an irrational system of beliefs or is in any way guilty of noetic impropriety;
obviously there might be pairs of propositions *A* and *B*, such that
we *know* both *A* and *B*, despite the fact that *A* is improbable on
B. I might know, for example, both that Feike is a Frisian and 9
out of 10 Frisians can't swim, and also that Feike can swim; then

I am obviously within my intellectual rights in accepting both these propositions, even though the latter is improbable with respect to the former. So even if it were a fact that (1) is improbable with respect to (2), that fact, so far, wouldn't be of much consequence. How, therefore, can this objection be developed?

Presumably what the objector means to hold is that (1) is improbable, not just on (2) but on some appropriate body of *total evidence* — perhaps all the evidence the theist has, or perhaps the body of evidence he is rationally obliged to have. The objector must be supposing that the theist has a relevant body of total evidence here, a body of evidence that includes (2); and his claim is that (1) is improbable with respect to this relevant body of total evidence. Suppose we say that T_s is the relevant body of total evidence for a given theist T; and suppose we agree that a belief is rationally acceptable for him only if it is not improbable with respect to T_s. Now what sorts of propositions are to be found in T_s? Perhaps the propositions he *knows* to be true, or perhaps the largest subset of his beliefs that he can rationally accept without evidence from other propositions, or perhaps the propositions he knows *immediately* — knows, but does not know on the basis of other propositions. However exactly we characterize this set T_s, the question I mean to press is this: why can't belief in God be itself a member of T_s? Perhaps for the theist — for many theists, at any rate — belief in God is a member of T_s, in which case it obviously won't be improbable with respect to T_s. Perhaps the theist has a right to *start from* belief in God, taking that proposition to be one of the ones probability with respect to which determines the rational propriety of *other* beliefs he holds. But if so, then the Christian *philosopher* is entirely within his rights in starting from belief in God to his philosophizing. He has a right to take the existence of God for granted and go on from there in his philosophical work — just as other philosophers take for granted the existence of the past, say, or of other persons, or the basic claims of contemporary physics.

And this leads me to my point here. Many Christian philosophers appear to think of themselves *qua* philosophers as engaged with the atheist and agnostic philosopher in a common search for the correct philosophical position *vis à vis* the question whether there is such a person as God. Of course the Christian philosopher will have her own private conviction on the point; she will believe, of course, that indeed there is such a person as God. But she will think, or be inclined to think, or half inclined to think that as a *philosopher* she has no right to this position unless she is able to show that it follows from, or is probable, or justified with respect to premises accepted by all parties to the discussion — theist, agnostic and atheist alike. Furthermore, she will be half inclined to think she has no right, as a philosopher, to positions that presuppose the existence of God, if she can't show that belief to be justified in this way. What I want to urge is that the Christian philosophical community ought *not* to think of itself as engaged in this common effort to determine the probability or philosophical plausibility of belief in God. The Christian philosopher quite properly *starts from* the existence of God, and presupposes it in philosophical work, whether or not she can show it to be probable or plausible with respect to premises accepted by all philosophers, or most philosophers, or most philosophers at the great contemporary centers of philosophy.

Taking it for granted, for example, that there is such a person as God and that we are indeed within our epistemic rights (are in that sense justified) in believing that there is, the Christian epistemologist might ask what it is that confers justification here: by virtue of what is the theist justified? Perhaps there are several sensible responses. One answer he might give and try to develop is that of John Calvin (and before him, of the Augustinian, Anselmian, Bonaventurian tradition of the Middle Ages): God, said Calvin, has implanted in humankind a tendency or nisus or disposition to believe in him:

> "There is within the human mind, and indeed by natural instinct, an awareness of divinity." This we take to be beyond controversy. To prevent anyone from taking refuge in the pretense of ignorance, God himself has implanted in all men a certain understanding of his divine majesty. . . . Therefore, since from the beginning of the world there has been no region, no city, in short, no household, that could do without religion, there lies in this a tacit confession of a sense of deity inscribed in the hearts of all.[2]

Calvin's claim, then, is that God has so created us that we have by nature a strong tendency or inclination or disposition towards belief in him.

Although this disposition to believe in God has been in part smothered or suppressed by *sin,* it is nevertheless universally present. And it is triggered or actuated by widely realized conditions:

> Lest anyone, then, be excluded from access to happiness, he not only sowed in men's minds that seed of religion of which we have spoken, but revealed himself and daily disclosed himself in the whole workmanship of the universe. As a consequence, men cannot open their eyes without being compelled to see him (p. 51).

Like Kant, Calvin is especially impressed in this connection, by the marvelous compages of the starry heavens above:

> Even the common folk and the most untutored, who have been taught only by the aid of the eyes, cannot be unaware of the excellence of divine art, for it reveals itself in this innumerable and yet distinct and well-ordered variety of the heavenly host (p. 52).

And now what Calvin says suggests that one who accedes to this tendency and in these circumstances accepts the belief that God has created the world — perhaps upon beholding the starry heavens, or the splendid majesty of the mountains, or the intricate, articulate beauty of a tiny flower — is quite as rational and quite as justified as one who believes that he sees a tree upon having that characteristic being-appeared-to-treely kind of experience.

No doubt this suggestion won't convince the skeptic; taken as an attempt to convince the skeptic it is circular. My point is just this: the Christian has his own questions to answer, and his own projects; these projects may not mesh with those of the skeptical or unbelieving philosopher. He has his own questions and his own starting point in investigating these questions. Of course, I don't mean to suggest that the Christian philosopher must accept Calvin's answer to the question I mentioned above; but I do say it is entirely fitting for him to give to this question an answer that presupposes precisely that of which the skeptic is skeptical — even if this skepticism is nearly unanimous in most of the prestigious philosophy departments of our day. The Christian philosopher does indeed have a responsibility to the philosophical world at large; but his fundamental responsibility is to the Christian community, and finally to God.

Again, a Christian philosopher may be interested in the relation between faith and reason, and faith and knowledge: granted that we hold some things by faith and know other things; granted that we believe that there is such a person as God and that this belief is true; do we also *know* that God exists? Do we accept this belief by faith or by reason? A theist may be inclined towards a *reliabilist* theory of knowledge; she may be inclined to think that a true belief constitutes knowledge if it is produced by a reliable belief producing mechanism. (There are hard problems here, but suppose for now we ignore them.) If the theist thinks God has created us with the *sensus divinitatis* Calvin speaks of, she will hold that indeed there is a reliable belief producing mechanism that produces theistic belief; she will thus hold that we *know* that God exists. One who follows Calvin here will also hold that a capacity to apprehend God's existence is as much part of our natural noetic or intellectual equipment as is the capacity to apprehend truths of logic, perceptual truths, truths about the past, and truths about other minds. Belief in the existence of God is then in the same boat as belief in truths of logic, other minds, the past, and perceptual objects; in each case God has so constructed us that in the right circumstances we acquire the belief in question. But then the belief that there is such a person as God is as much among the deliverances of our natural noetic faculties as are those other beliefs. Hence we *know* that there is such a person as God, and don't merely believe it; and it isn't by *faith* that we apprehend the existence of God, but by reason; and this whether or not any of the classical theistic arguments is successful.

Now my point is not that Christian philosophers must follow Calvin here. My point is that the Christian philosopher has a right (I should say a duty) to work at her own projects — projects set by the beliefs of the Christian community of which she is a part. The Christian philosophical community must work out the answers to *its* questions; and both the questions and the appropriate ways of working out their answers may presuppose beliefs rejected at most of the leading centers of philosophy. But the Christian is proceeding quite properly in starting from these beliefs, even if they are so rejected. She is under no obligation to confine her research projects to those pursued at those centers, or to pursue her own projects on the basis of the assumptions that prevail there.

Perhaps I can clarify what I want to say by contrasting it with a wholly different view. According to the theologian David Tracy,

In fact the modern Christian theologian cannot ethically do other than challenge the traditional self-understanding of the theologian. He no longer sees his task as a simple defense of or even as an or- thodox reinterpretation of traditional belief. Rather, he finds that his ethical commitment to the morality of scientific knowledge forces him to assume a critical posture towards his own and his tradition's beliefs. . . . In principle, the fundamental loyalty of the theologian *qua* theologian is to that morality of scientific knowledge which he shares with his colleagues, the philosophers, historians and social sciences. No more than they can he allow his own—or his tradition's —beliefs to serve as warrants for his arguments. In fact, in all prop- erly theological inquiry, the analysis should be characterized by those same ethical stances of autonomous judgment, critical judgment and properly skeptical hard-mindedness that characterizes analysis in other fields.[3]

Furthermore, this "morality of scientific knowledge insists that each inquirer start with the present methods and knowledge of the field in question, unless one has evidence of the same logical type for rejecting those methods and that knowledge," Still further, "for the new scientific morality, one's fundamental loyalty as an analyst of any and all cognitive claims is solely to those methodological pro- cedures which the particular scientific community in question has developed" (6).

I say *caveat lector*. I'm prepared to bet that this "new scientific morality" is like the Holy Roman Empire: it is neither new nor scien- tific nor morally obligatory. Furthermore the "new scientific moral- ity" looks to me to be monumentally inauspicious as a stance for a Christian theologian, modern or otherwise. Even if there were a set of methodological procedures held in common by most philoso- phers, historians and social scientists, or most secular philosophers, historians, and social scientists, why should a Christian theologian give ultimate allegiance to them rather than, say, to God, or to the fundamental truths of Christianity? Tracy's suggestion as to how Christian theologians should proceed seems at best wholly unprom- ising. Of course I am only a philosopher, not a modern theologian; no doubt I am venturing beyond my depths. So I don't presume to speak for modern theologians; but however things stand for them,

the modern Christian *philosopher* has a perfect right, as a philosopher, to start from his belief in God. He has a right to assume it,
take it for granted, in his philosophical work—whether or not he
can convince his unbelieving colleagues either that this belief is true
or that it is sanctioned by those "methodological procedures" Tracy
mentions.

And the Christian philosophical community ought to get on
with the philosophical questions of importance to the Christian community. It ought to get on with the project of exploring and developing the implications of Christian theism for the whole range of questions philosophers ask and answer. It ought to do this whether or
not it can convince the philosophical community at large either that
there really is such a person as God, or that it is rational or reasonable to believe that there is. Perhaps the Christian philosopher *can*
convince the skeptic or the unbelieving philosopher that indeed there
is such a person as God. Perhaps this is possible in at least some
instances. In other instances, of course, it may be impossible; even
if the skeptic in fact accepts premises from which theistic belief follows by argument forms he also accepts, he may, when apprised of
this situation, give up those premises rather than his unbelief. (In
this way it is possible to reduce someone from knowledge to ignorance
by giving him an argument he sees to be valid from premises he knows
to be true.)

But whether or not this is possible, the Christian philosopher
has other fish to fry and other questions to think about. Of course
he must listen to, understand, and learn from the broader philosophical community and he must take his place in it; but his work
as a philosopher is not circumscribed by what either the skeptic or
the rest of the philosophical world thinks of theism. Justifying or
trying to justify theistic belief in the eyes of the broader philosophical community is not the only task of the Christian philosophical
community; perhaps it isn't even among its most important tasks.
Philosophy is a communal enterprise. The Christian philosopher who
looks exclusively to the philosophical world at large, who thinks
of himself as belonging primarily to *that* world, runs a two-fold risk.
He may neglect an essential part of his task as a Christian philosopher; and he may find himself adopting principles and procedures
that don't comport well with his beliefs as a Christian. What is
needed, once more, is autonomy and integrality.

4. THEISM AND PERSONS

My third example has to do with philosophical anthropology: how should we think about human persons? What sorts of things, fundamentally, *are* they? What is it to be a person, what is it to be a *human* person, and how shall we think about personhood? How, in particular, should Christians, Christian philosophers, think about these things? The first point to note is that on the Christian scheme of things, *God* is the premier person, the first and chief exemplar of personhood. God, furthermore, has created man in his own image; we men and women are image bearers of God, and the properties most important for an understanding of our personhood are properties we share with him. How we think about God, then, will have an immediate and direct bearing on how we think about humankind. Of course we learn much about ourselves from other sources— from everyday observation, from introspection and self-observation, from scientific investigation and the like. But it is also perfectly proper to start from what we know as Christians. It is not the case that rationality, or proper philosophical method, or intellectual responsibility, or the new scientific morality, or whatever, requires that we start from beliefs we share with everyone else—what common sense and current science teach, e.g.— and attempt to reason to or justify those beliefs we hold as Christians. In trying to give a satisfying philosophical account of some area or phenomenon, we may properly appeal, in our account or explanation, to anything else we already rationally believe—whether it be current science or Christian doctrine.

Let me proceed again to specific examples. There is a fundamental watershed, in philosophical anthropology, between those who think of human beings as *free*—free in the libertarian sense—and those who espouse determinism. According to determinists, every human action is a consequence of initial conditions outside our control by way of causal laws that are also outside our control. Sometimes underlying this claim is a picture of the universe as a vast machine where, at any rate at the macroscopic level, all events, including human actions, are determined by previous events and causal laws. On this view every action I have in fact performed was such that it wasn't within my power to refrain from performing it; and if, on a given occasion I did *not* perform a given action, then it wasn't then within my power to perform it. If I now raise my arm, then, on the view in question, it wasn't within my power just then not to raise it. Now the Christian thinker has a stake in this controversy just by virtue of being a Christian. For she will no doubt believe that God holds us human beings responsible for much of what we do — responsible, and thus properly subject to praise or blame, approval or disapproval. But how can I be responsible for my actions if it was never within my power to perform any action I didn't in fact perform and never within my power to refrain from performing any I did perform? If my actions are thus determined, then I am not rightly or justly held accountable for them; but God does nothing improper or unjust, and he holds me accountable for some of my actions; hence it is not the case that all of my actions are thus determined. The Christian has an initially strong reason to reject the claim that all of our actions are causally determined — a reason much stronger than the meager and anemic arguments the determinist can muster on the other side. Of course if there *were* powerful arguments on the other side, then there might be a problem here. But there aren't; so there isn't.

Now the determinist may reply that freedom and causal determinism are, contrary to initial appearances, in fact compatible. He may argue that my being free with respect to an action I performed at a time *t,* for example, doesn't entail that it was then within my power to refrain from performing it, but only something weaker — perhaps something like *if I had chosen not to perform it, I would not have performed it.* Indeed, the clearheaded compatibilist will go further. He will maintain, not merely that freedom is *compatible* with determinism, but that freedom *requires* determinism. He will hold with Hume that the proposition *S is free with respect to action A* or *S does A freely* entails that S is causally determined with respect to *A* — that there are causal laws and antecedent conditions that together entail either that S performs A or that S does not perform A. And he will back up this claim by insisting that if S is not thus determined with respect to *A,* then it's merely a matter of *chance* — due, perhaps, to quantum effects in S's brain — that S does A. But if it is just a matter of chance that S does A, then either S doesn't really do A at all, or at any rate S is not responsible for doing A. If S's doing A is just a matter of chance, then S's doing A is something that just *happens* to him; but then it is not really the case that he *performs* A—at any rate it is not the case that he is *respon-sible* for performing A. And hence freedom, in the sense that is re-quired for responsibility, itself requires determinism.

But the Christian thinker will find this claim monumentally implausible. Presumably the determinist means to hold that what he says characterizes actions generally, not just those of human be-ings. He will hold that it is a *necessary* truth that if an agent isn't caused to perform an action then it is a mere matter of chance that the agent in question performs the action in question. From a Chris-tian perspective, however, this is wholly incredible. For God per-forms actions, and performs free actions; and surely it is not the case that there are causal laws and antecedent conditions outside his control that determine what he does. On the contrary: God is the author of the causal laws that do in fact obtain; indeed, perhaps the best way to think of these causal laws is as records of the ways in which God ordinarily treats the beings he has created. But of course it is not simply a matter of *chance* that God does what he does—creates and upholds the world, let's say, and offers redemption and renewal to his children. So a Christian philosopher has an extremely good reason for rejecting this premise, along with the determinism and compatibilism it supports.

What is really at stake in this discussion is the notion of agent causation: the notion of a person as an ultimate source of action. According to the friends of agent causation, some events are caused, not by other events, but by substances, objects—typically personal agents. And at least since the time of David Hume, the idea of agent causation has been languishing. It is fair to say, I think, that most contemporary philosophers who work in this area either reject agent causation outright or are at the least extremely suspicious of it. They see causation as a relation among *events*; they can understand how one event can cause another event, or how events of one kind can cause events of another kind. But the idea of a *person*, say, causing an event, seems to them unintelligible, unless it can be analyzed, somehow, in terms of event causation. It is this devotion to event causation, of course, that explains the claim that if you perform an action but are not caused to do so, then your performing that action is a matter of chance. For if I hold that all causation is ultimately event causation, then I will suppose that if you perform an action but are not caused to do so by previous events, then your perform-

ing that action isn't caused at all and is therefore a mere matter of
chance. The devotee of event causation, furthermore, will perhaps
argue for his position as follows. If such agents as persons cause
effects that take place in the physical world—my body's moving in
a certain way, for example—then these effects must ultimately be
caused by volitions or *undertakings*—which, apparently, are immaterial, unphysical events. He will then claim that the idea of an
immaterial event's having causal efficacy in the physical world is puzzling or dubious or worse.

But a Christian philosopher will find this argument unimpres-
sive and this devotion to event causation uncongenial. As for the
argument, the Christian already and independently believes that acts
of volition have causal efficacy; she believes indeed, that the physical
universe owes its very existence to just such volitional acts—God's
undertaking to create it. And as for the devotion to event causation,
the Christian will be, initially, at any rate, strongly inclined to reject
the idea that event causation is primary and agent causation to be
explained in terms of it. For she believes that God does and has done
many things: he has created the world; he sustains it in being; he
communicates with his children. But it is extraordinarily hard to
see how these truths can be analyzed in terms of causal relations
among events. What events could possibly cause God's creating the
world or his undertaking to create the world? God himself institutes
or establishes the causal laws that do in fact hold; how, then, can
we see all the events constituted by his actions as related to causal
laws to earlier events? How could it be that propositions ascribing
actions to him are to be explained in terms of event causation?

Some theistic thinkers have noted this problem and reacted by
soft pedalling God's causal activity, or by impetuously following Kant
in declaring that it is of a wholly different order from that in which
we engage, an order beyond our comprehension. I believe this is the
wrong response. Why should a Christian philosopher join in the
general obeisance to event causation? It is not as if there are cogent
arguments here. The real force behind this claim is a certain philosophical way of looking at persons and the world; but this view has
no initial plausibility from a Christian perspective and no compelling argument in its favor.

So on all these disputed points in philosophical anthropology
the theist will have a strong predilection for resolving the dispute

in one way rather than another. She will be inclined to reject compatibilism, to hold that event causation (if indeed there is such a thing) is to be explained in terms of agent causation, to reject the idea that if an event isn't caused by other events then its occurrence is a matter of chance, and to reject the idea that events in the physical world can't be caused by an agent's undertaking to do something. And my point here is this. The Christian philosopher is within her rights in holding these positions, whether or not she can convince the rest of a philosophical world and whatever the current philosophical consensus is, if there is a consensus. But isn't such an appeal to God and his properties, in this philosophical context, a shameless appeal to a *deus ex machina*? Surely not. "Philosophy," as Hegel once exclaimed in a rare fit of lucidity, "is thinking things over." Philosophy is in large part a clarification, systematization, articulation, relating and deepening of pre-philosophical opinion. We come to philosophy with a range of opinions about the world and humankind and the place of the latter in the former; and in philosophy we think about these matters, systematically articulate our views, put together and relate our views on diverse topics, and deepen our views by finding unexpected interconnections and by discovering and answering unanticipated questions. Of course we may come to change our minds by virtue of philosophical endeavor; we may discover incompatibilities or other infelicities. But we come to philosophy with pre-philosophical opinions; we can do no other. And the point is: the Christian has as much right to her pre-philosophical opinions as others have to theirs. She needn't try first to 'prove' them from propositions accepted by, say, the bulk of the non-Christian philosophical community; and if they are widely rejected as naive, or pre-scientific, or primitive, or unworthy of "man come of age," that is nothing whatever against them. Of course if there were genuine and substantial arguments against them from premises that have some legitimate claim on the Christian philosopher, then she would have a problem; she would have to make some kind of change somewhere. But in the absence of such arguments—and the absence of such arguments is evident—the Christian philosophical community quite properly starts, in philosophy, from what it believes.

But this means that the Christian philosophical community need not devote all of its efforts to attempting to refute opposing claims and or to arguing for its own claims, in each case from premises accepted by the bulk of the philosophical community at large. It ought to do this, indeed, but it ought to do more. For if it does only this, it will neglect a pressing philosophical task: systematizing, deepening, clarifying Christian thought on these topics. So here again: my plea is for the Christian philosopher, the Christian philosophical community, to display, first, more independence and autonomy: we needn't take as our research projects just those projects that currently enjoy widespread popularity; we have our own questions to think about. Secondly, we must display more integrity. We must not automatically assimilate what is current or fashionable or popular by way of philosophical opinion and procedures; for much of it comports ill with Christian ways of thinking. And finally, we must display more Christian self-confidence or courage or boldness. We have a perfect right to our pre-philosophical views: why, therefore, should we be intimidated by what the rest of the philosophical world thinks plausible or implausible?

These, then, are my examples; I could have chosen others. In ethics, for example: perhaps the chief theoretical concern, from the theistic perspective, is the question how are right and wrong, good and bad, duty, permission and obligation related to God and to his will and to his creative activity? This question doesn't arise, naturally enough, from a nontheistic perspective; and so, naturally enough, nontheist ethicists do not address it. But it is perhaps the most important question for a Christian ethicist to tackle. I have already spoken about epistemology; let me mention another example from this area. Epistemologists sometimes worry about the confluence or lack thereof of epistemic *justification,* on the one hand, and *truth,* or *reliability,* on the other. Suppose we do the best that can be expected of us, noetically speaking; suppose we do our intellectual duties and satisfy our intellectual obligations: what guarantee is there that in so doing we shall arrive at the truth? Is there even any reason for supposing that if we thus satisfy our obligations, we shall have a better chance of arriving at the truth than if we brazenly flout them? And where do these intellectual obligations come from? How does it happen that we have them? Here the theist has, if not a clear set of answers, at any rate clear suggestions towards a set of answers. Another example: creative antirealism is presently popular among philosophers; this is the view that it is human behavior—in particular, human thought and language—

that is somehow responsible for the fundamental structure of the world and for the fundamental kinds of entities there are. From a theistic point of view, however, universal creative antirealism is at best a mere impertinence, a piece of laughable bravado. For *God,* of course, owes neither his existence nor his properties to us and our ways of thinking; the truth is just the reverse. And so far as the created universe is concerned, while it indeed owes its existence and character to activity on the part of a person, that person is certainly not a *human* person.

One final example, this time from philosophy of mathematics. Many who think about *sets* and their nature are inclined to accept the following ideas. First, no set is a member of itself. Second, whereas a property has its extension contingently, a set has *its* membership essentially. This means that no set could have existed if one of its members had not, and that no set could have had fewer or different members from the ones it in fact has. It means, furthermore, that sets are contingent beings; if Ronald Reagan had not existed, then his unit set would not have existed. And thirdly, sets form a sort of iterated structure: at the first level there are sets whose members are non-sets, at the second level sets whose members are non-sets or first level sets; at the third level, sets whose members are non-sets or sets of the first two levels, and so on. Many are also inclined, with Georg Cantor, to regard sets as *collections* — as objects whose existence is dependent upon a certain sort of intellectual activity — a collecting or "thinking together" as Cantor put it. If sets were collections of this sort, that would explain their displaying the first three features I mentioned. But if the collecting or thinking together had to be done by *human* thinkers, or any finite thinkers, there wouldn't be nearly enough sets — not nearly as many as we think in fact there are. From a theistic point of view, the natural conclusion is that sets owe their existence to *God's* thinking things together. The natural explanation of those three features is just that sets are indeed collections — collections collected by God; they are or result from God's thinking things together. This idea may not be popular at contemporary centers of set theoretical activity; but that is neither here nor there. Christians, theists, ought to understand sets from a *Christian* and *theistic* point of view. What they believe as theists affords a resource for understanding sets not available to the nontheist; and why shouldn't they employ it? Perhaps here we *could* proceed without appealing to what we believe as theists; but why *should* we, if these beliefs are useful and explanatory? I could probably get home this evening by hopping on one leg; and conceivably I could climb Devil's Tower with my feet tied together. But why should I want to?

The Christian or theistic philosopher, therefore, has his own way of working at his craft. In some cases there are items on his agenda — pressing items — not to be found on the agenda of the non-theistic philosophical community. In others, items that are currently fashionable appear of relatively minor interest from a Christian perspective. In still others, the theist will reject common assumptions and views about how to start, how to proceed, and what constitutes a good or satisfying answer. In still others the Christian will take for granted and will start from assumptions and premises rejected by the philosophical community at large. Of course I don't mean for a moment to suggest that Christian philosophers have nothing to learn from their non-Christian and nontheist colleagues: that would be a piece of foolish arrogance, utterly belied by the facts of the matter. Nor do I mean to suggest that Christian philosophers should retreat into their own isolated enclave, having as little as possible to do with nontheistic philosophers. Of course not! Christians have much to learn and much of enormous importance to learn by way of dialogue and discussion with their nontheistic colleagues. Christian philosophers must be intimately involved in the professional life of the philosophical community at large, both because of what they can learn and because of what they can contribute. Furthermore, while Christian philosophers need not and ought not to see themselves as involved, for example, in a common effort to determine whether there is such a person as God, we are all, theist and nontheist alike, engaged in the common human project of understanding ourselves and the world in which we find ourselves. If the Christian philosophical community is doing its job properly, it will be engaged in a complicated, many-sided dialectical discussion, making its own contribution to that common human project. It must pay careful attention to other contributions; it must gain a deep understanding of them; it must learn what it can from them and it must take unbelief with profound seriousness.

All of this is true and all of this is important; but none of it runs counter to what I have been saying. Philosophy is many things. I said earlier that it is a matter of systematizing, developing and deepening one's pre-philosophical opinions. It is that; but it is also an arena for the articulation and interplay of commitments and allegiances fundamentally religious in nature; it is an expression of deep and fundamental perspectives, ways of viewing ourselves and the world and God. The Christian philosophical community, by virtue of being Christian, is committed to a broad but specific way of looking at humankind and the world and God. Among its most important and pressing projects are systematizing, deepening, exploring, articulating this perspective, and exploring its bearing on the rest of what we think and do. But then the Christian philosophical community has its own agenda; it need not and should not automatically take its projects from the list of those currently in favor at the leading contemporary centers of philosophy. Furthermore, Christian philosophers must be wary about assimilating or accepting presently popular philosophical ideas and procedures; for many of these have roots that are deeply anti-Christian. And finally the Christian philosophical community has a right to its perspectives; it is under no obligation first to show that this perspective is plausible with respect to what is taken for granted by all philosophers, or most philosophers, or the leading philosophers of our day.

In sum, we who are Christians and propose to be philosophers must not rest content with being philosophers who happen, incidentally, to be Christians; we must strive to be Christian philosophers. We must therefore pursue our projects with integrity, independence, and Christian boldness.[4]

NOTES

1. "The Probabilistic Argument from Evil," *Philosophical Studies,* 1979, pp. 1–53.

2. *Institutes of the Christian Religion,* trans. Ford Lewis Battles (Philadelphia: Westminster Press, 1960), Bk. 1, chap. III, pp. 43–44.

3. *Blessed Rage for Order* (New York: Seabury Press, 1978), p. 7.

4. Delivered November 4, 1983, as the author's inaugural address as the John A. O'Brien Professor of Philosophy at the University of Notre Dame.

PART I

Epistemology and Theism

Justification and Theism

ALVIN PLANTINGA

According to an ancient and honorable tradition, knowledge is justified true belief. But what is this "justification"? Theologians of the Protestant Reformation (however things may stand with their contemporary epigoni) had a clear conception of justification; justification, they held, is by faith. Contemporary epistemologists, sadly enough, do not thus speak with a single voice. They don't often subject the concept in question — the concept of epistemic justification — to explicit scrutiny; while there are many discussions of the conditions under which a person is justified in believing a proposition, there are few in which the principle topic is the *nature* of justification. But when they do discuss it, they display a notable lack of unanimity. Some claim that justification is by *epistemic dutifulness,* others that it is by *coherence,* and still others that it is by *reliability.*[1] The differences among these views are enormous; this is by no means a case of variations on the same theme. Indeed, disagreement is so deep and radical it is sometimes hard to be sure the various disputants are discussing approximately the same issue. Now what should a Christian, or more broadly, a theist, make of this situation? How should such a person react to this baffling welter of conflict, this babble or Babel of confusion? In what follows I shall try to get a clearer look at epistemic justification and allied conceptions. In particular, I propose to examine this topic from an explicitly Christian, or more broadly, theistic point of view: how shall we think of epistemic justification from a theistic perspective? What can Christianity or theism contribute to our understanding of epistemic justification?

But here we need a preliminary word as to what it is, more

exactly, I mean to be talking about. How shall we initially locate epistemic justification? First, such terms as 'justification' and 'justified' are, as Roderick Chisholm[2] suggests, terms of epistemic appraisal; to say that a proposition is *justified* for a person is to say that his believing or accepting it (here I shall not distinguish these two) has *positive epistemic status* for him. What we appraise here are a person's *beliefs*: more exactly, his *believings*. Someone's belief that there is such a person as God may be thus appraised, as well as her belief that human life evolved from unicellular life by way of the mechanisms suggested by contemporary evolutionary theory, and the less spectacular beliefs of everyday life. We may speak of a person's beliefs as *warranted,* or *justified,* or *rational,* or *reasonable,* contrasting them with beliefs that are unwarranted, unjustified, irrational, or unreasonable. The evidentialist objector to theistic belief, for example, argues that those who believe in God without evidence are unjustified in so doing, and are accordingly somehow unreasonable—guilty of an intellectual or cognitive impropriety, perhaps, or, alternatively and less censoriously, victims of some sort of intellectual dysfunction. Secondly, epistemic justification or positive epistemic status clearly comes in degrees: at any rate some of my beliefs have more by way of positive epistemic status for me than others.

And thirdly, among the fundamental concepts of epistemology, naturally enough, we find the concept of *knowledge*. It is widely agreed that true belief, while necessary for knowledge, is not sufficient for it. What more is required? It is widely agreed, again, that whatever exactly this further element may be, it is either epistemic justification or something intimately connected with it. Now it would be convenient just to *baptize* that quantity as 'justification', thus taking that term as a proper name of the element, whatever exactly it is, enough of which (Gettier problems, perhaps, aside) distinguishes knowledge from mere true belief. The term 'justification', however, has a deontological ring; it is redolent of duty and permission, obligation and rights. Furthermore, according to the long and distinguished tradition of Cartesian internalism (represented at its contemporary best by Roderick Chisholm's work),[3] aptness for epistemic duty fulfillment is indeed what distinguishes true belief from knowledge; using this term as a mere proper name of what distinguishes true belief from knowledge, therefore, can be confusing. Accordingly, I shall borrow Chisholm's term 'positive epistemic status' as my official name of the quantity in question—the quantity enough of which distinguishes mere true belief from knowledge. (Of course we cannot initially assume that positive epistemic status is a *single* or *simple* property; perhaps it is an amalgam of several others.) Initially, then, and to a first approximation, we can identify justification or positive epistemic status as a normative (possibly complex) property that comes in degrees and which is such that enough of it (ignoring Gettier problems for the moment) is what distinguishes true belief from knowledge.

1. POSITIVE EPISTEMIC STATUS AND THEISM

Now how shall we think of positive epistemic status, or, indeed, the whole human cognitive enterprise, from a Christian or theistic point of view? What bearing does theism have on the human cognitive enterprise? What features of theism bear on this topic? The central point, I think, is this: according to the theistic way of looking at the matter, we human beings, like ropes and linear accelerators, have been designed; we have been designed and created by God. We have been created by God; furthermore, according to Christian and Jewish versions of theism, we have been created by him *in his own image*; in certain crucial respects we resemble him. Now God is an actor, an agent, a creator: one who chooses certain ends and takes action to accomplish them. God is therefore a *practical* being. But he is also an *intellectual* or *intellecting* being. He has knowledge; indeed, he has the maximal degree of knowledge. He holds beliefs (even if his way of holding a belief is different from ours); and because he is omniscient, he believes every truth and holds only true beliefs. He therefore has the sort of grasp of concepts, properties, and propositions necessary for holding beliefs; and since he believes every true proposition, he has a grasp of every property and proposition.[4]

In setting out to create human beings in his image, then, God set out to create them in such a way that they could reflect something of his capacity to grasp concepts and hold beliefs. Furthermore, as the whole of the Christian tradition suggests, his aim was to create them in such a way that they can reflect something of his

capacity for holding *true* beliefs, for attaining *knowledge*. This has
been the the nearly unanimous consensus of the Christian tradition;
but it is worth noting that it is not inevitable. God's aim in creating us with the complicated, highly articulated establishment of faculties we do in fact display *could* have been something quite different; in creating us with these faculties he could have been aiming
us, not at truth, but at something of some other sort—survival, for
example, or a capacity to appreciate art, poetry, beauty in nature,[5]
or an ability to stand in certain relationships with each other and
with him. But the great bulk of the tradition has seen our imaging
God in terms (among other things) of knowledge: knowledge of
ourselves, of God himself, and of the world in which he has placed
us; and here I shall take for granted this traditional understanding
of the *imago dei.*

God has therefore created us with cognitive faculties designed
to enable us to achieve true beliefs with respect to a wide variety
of propositions—propositions about our immediate environment,
about our own interior lives, about the thoughts and experiences
of other persons, about our universe at large, about right and wrong,
about the whole realm of abstracta: numbers, properties, propositions, states of affairs, possible worlds and their like; about modality—what is necessary and possible—and about himself. These
faculties work in such a way that under the appropriate circumstances
we form the appropriate belief. More exactly, the appropriate belief
is *formed in us;* in the typical case we do not *decide* to hold or form
the belief in question but simply find ourselves with it. Upon considering an instance of *modus ponens,* I find myself believing its corresponding conditional; upon being appeared to in the familiar way,
I find myself holding the belief that there is a large tree before me;
upon being asked what I had for breakfast, I reflect for a moment
and then find myself with the belief that what I had was eggs on
toast. In these and other cases I do not *decide* what to believe; I
don't total up the evidence (I'm being appeared to redly; on most
occasions when thus appeared to I am in the presence of something
red; so most probably in this case I am) and make a decision as to
what seems best supported; I simply find myself believing. Of course
in *some* cases I may go through such a procedure. For example, I
may try to assess the alleged evidence in favor of the theory that
human life evolved by means of the mechanisms of random genetic

mutation and natural selection from unicellular life (which itself arose by substantially similar random mechanical processes from nonliving material); I may try to determine whether the evidence is in fact compelling or, more modestly, such as to make the theory plausible. Then I may go through a procedure of that sort. Even in this sort of case I still don't really *decide* anything: I simply call the relevant evidence to mind, try in some way to weigh it up, and find myself with the appropriate belief. But in more typical and less theoretical cases of belief formation nothing like this is involved.

Experience, obviously enough, plays a crucial role in belief formation. Here it is important to see, I think, that two rather different sorts of experience are involved. In a typical perceptual case there is sensuous experience: I look out at my back yard and am appeared to greenly, perhaps. But in many cases of belief formation, there is present another sort of experiential component as well. Consider a memory belief, for example. Here there may be a sort of sensuous imagery present—I may be appeared to in a certain indistinct fleeting sort of way in trying to recall what I had for breakfast, for example. But this sort of sensuous imagery is in a way (as Wittgenstein never tired of telling us) inessential, variable from person to person, and perhaps in the case of some persons altogether absent. What seems less variable is a different kind of experience not easy to characterize: it is a matter not so much of sensuous imagery as of feeling impelled, or inclined, or moved towards a certain belief—in the case in question, the belief that what I had for breakfast was eggs on toast. (Perhaps it could be better put by saying that the belief in question has a sort of experienced attractiveness about it, a sort of drawing power.) Consider an *a priori* belief: 'If all human beings are mortal and Socrates is a human being, then Socrates is mortal.' Such a belief is not, as the denomination *a priori* mistakenly suggests, formed *prior to* or in the absence of experience; it is rather formed *in response to experience.* Thinking of the corresponding conditional of *modus ponens* feels different from thinking of, say, the corresponding conditional of 'affirming the consequent'; thinking of $2+1=3$ feels different from thinking of $2+1=4$; and this difference in experience is crucially connected with our accepting the one and rejecting the other. Again, when I entertain or think of an example of *modus ponens,* there is both sensuous imagery—Descartes' clarity and distinctness, the luminous brightness of which

Locke spoke; but there is also the feeling of being impelled to believe or accept the proposition; there is a sort of inevitability about it. (As I said, this isn't easy to describe.) Of course experience plays a different role here from the role it plays in the formation of perceptual beliefs; it plays a still different role in the formation of moral beliefs, beliefs about our own mental lives, beliefs about the mental lives of other persons, beliefs we form on the basis of inductive evidence, and so on. What we need here is a full and appropriately subtle and sensitive description of the role of experience in the formation of these various types of beliefs; that project will have to await another occasion, as one says when one really has no idea how to accomplish the project.

God has therefore created us with an astonishingly complex and subtle establishment of cognitive faculties. These faculties produce beliefs on an enormously wide variety of topics — our everyday external environment, the thoughts of others, our own internal life (someone's internal musings and soliloquies can occupy an entire novel), the past, mathematics, science, right and wrong, our relationships to God, what is necessary and possible, and a host of other topics. They work with great subtlety to produce beliefs of many different degrees of strength ranging from the merest inclination to believe to absolute dead certainty. Our beliefs and the strength with which we hold them, furthermore, are delicately responsive to changes in experience — to what people tell us, to perceptual experience, to what we read, to further reflection, and so on.

Now: how shall we think of positive epistemic status from this point of view? Here is a natural first approximation: a belief has positive epistemic status for a person only if his faculties are *working properly,* working the way they ought to work, working the way they were designed to work (working the way God designed them to work), in producing and sustaining the belief in question. I therefore suggest that a necessary condition of positive epistemic status is that one's cognitive equipment, one's belief-forming and belief-sustaining apparatus, be free of cognitive malfunction. It must be functioning in the way it was designed to function by the being who designed and created us. Initially, then, let us say that a belief has positive epistemic status, for me, to the degree that my faculties are functioning properly in producing and sustaining that belief; and my faculties are working properly if they are working in the way they were designed to work by God.

The first thing to see here is that this condition — that of one's cognitive equipment functioning properly — is not the same thing as one's cognitive equipment functioning *normally,* or in normal conditions — not, at any rate, if we take the term 'normally' in a broadly statistical sense. If I give way to wishful thinking, forming the belief that I will soon be awarded a Nobel Prize for literature, then my cognitive faculties are not working properly — even though wishful thinking may be widespread among human beings. Your belief's being produced by your faculties working normally or in normal conditions — i.e., the sorts of conditions that obtain for the most part — must be distinguished from their working *properly.* It may be (and in fact is) the case that it is not at all abnormal for a person to form a belief out of pride, jealousy, lust, contrariness, desire for fame, wishful thinking, or self-aggrandizement; nevertheless, when I form a belief in this way my cognitive equipment is not functioning properly. It is not functioning the way it ought to.

I shall have more to say about the notion of proper functioning below. For the moment, let us provisionally entertain the idea that one necessary condition of a belief's having positive epistemic status for me is that the relevant portion of my noetic equipment involved in its formation and sustenance be functioning properly. It is easy to see, however, that this cannot be the whole story. Suppose you are suddenly and without your knowledge transported to an environment wholly different from earth; you awake on a planet near Alpha Centauri. There conditions are quite different; elephants, we may suppose, are invisible to human beings, but emit a sort of radiation unknown on earth, a sort of radiation that causes human beings to form the belief that a trumpet is sounding nearby. An Alpha Centaurian elephant wanders by; you are subjected to the radiation, and form the belief that a trumpet is sounding nearby. There is nothing wrong with your cognitive faculties; but this belief has little by way of positive epistemic status for you. Nor is the problem merely that the belief is false; even if we can add that a trumpet really *is* sounding nearby (in a soundproof telephone booth, perhaps, so that it isn't audible to you), your belief will have little by way of positive epistemic status for you. To vary the example, imagine that the radia-

tion emitted causes human beings to form the belief, not that a
trumpet is sounding, but that there is a large gray object in the
neighborhood. Again, an elephant wanders by; while seeing nothing of any particular interest, you suddenly find yourself with the
belief that there is a large gray object nearby. A bit perplexed at this
discovery, you examine your surroundings more closely: you still see
no large gray object. Your faculties are displaying no malfunction
and you are not being epistemically careless or slovenly; nevertheless, you don't know that there is a large gray object nearby. That
belief has little by way of positive epistemic status for you.

The reason is that your cognitive faculties and the environment
in which you find yourself are not properly attuned. The problem
is not with your cognitive faculties; they are in good working order.
The problem is with the environment. In approximately the same
way, your automobile might be in perfect working order, despite the
fact that it will not run well at the top of Pike's Peak, or under water,
or on the moon. We must therefore add another component to positive epistemic status; your faculties must be in good working order
and the environment must be appropriate for your particular reper-
toire of epistemic powers. (Perhaps there are creatures native to the
planet in question who are much like human beings but whose cognitive powers differ from ours in such a way that Alpha Centaurian
elephants are not invisible to them.)

It is tempting to suggest that positive epistemic status *just is*
proper functioning (in an appropriate environment), so that one has
warrant for a given belief to the degree that one's faculties are functioning properly (in producing and sustaining that belief) in an environment appropriate for one's cognitive equipment: the better
one's faculties are functioning, the more positive epistemic status.
But it is easy to see that this cannot be correct. Couldn't it happen
that my cognitive faculties are working properly (in an appropriate
environment) in producing and sustaining a certain belief in me, while
nonetheless that belief has very little by way of positive epistemic
status for me? Say that a pair of beliefs are (for want of a better
term) *productively equivalent* if they are produced by faculties functioning properly to the same degree and in environments of equal
appropriateness. Then couldn't it be that a pair of my beliefs should
be productively equivalent while nonetheless one of them has more
by way of positive epistemic status—even a great deal more—than

the other? Obviously enough, that could be; as a matter of fact it is plausible to think that *is* the case. *Modus ponens* has more by way of positive epistemic status for me than does the memory belief, now rather dim and indistinct, that forty years ago I owned a secondhand 16-gauge shotgun and a red bicycle with balloon tires; but both, I take it, are produced by cognitive faculties functioning properly in a congenial environment. Although both epistemic justification and 'being properly produced' come in degrees, there seems to be no discernible functional relationship between them: but then we can't see positive epistemic status as simply a matter of a belief's being produced by faculties working properly in an appropriate environment. We still have no real answer to the question of what is positive epistemic status? That particular frog is still grinning residually up from the bottom of the mug.

Fortunately there is an easy response. Not only does the first belief, the belief in the corresponding conditional of *modus ponens,* have more by way of positive epistemic status for me than the second; it is also one I accept much more firmly. It seems much more obviously true; I have a much stronger inclination or impulse to accept that proposition than to accept the other. When my cognitive establishment is working properly, the strength of the impulse towards believing a given proposition will be proportional to the degree it has of positive epistemic status — or if the relationship isn't one of straightforward proportionality, the appropriate functional relationship will hold between positive epistemic status and this impulse. So when my faculties are functioning properly, a belief has positive epistemic status to the degree that I find myself inclined to accept it; and this (again, if my faculties are functioning properly and I do not interfere or intervene) will be the degree to which I *do* accept it.

As I see it then, positive epistemic status accrues to a belief, B, for a person, S, only if S's cognitive environment is appropriate for his cognitive faculties and only if these faculties are functioning properly in producing this belief in him; and under these conditions the degree of positive epistemic status enjoyed by B is proportional to the strength of his inclination to accept B. To state the same claim a bit differently: a belief, B, has positive epistemic status for S if and only if that belief is produced in S by his epistemic faculties working properly (in an appropriate environment); and B has more positive epistemic status than B^* for S iff (1) B has positive epistemic status for S and (2) either B^* does not or else S is more strongly inclined to believe B than B^*.

2. EIGHT OBJECTIONS, QUALIFICATIONS, OR APPLICATIONS

So far, of course, what I have said is merely programmatic, just a picture. Much more needs to be said by way of qualification, development, articulation. Let me therefore respond to some objections, make some qualifications and additions, and mention some topics for further study.

(1) Aren't such ideas as that of "working properly" and related notions such as "cognitive dysfunction" deeply problematic? What is it for a natural organism — a tree, for example, or a horse — to be in good working order, to be functioning properly? Isn't "working properly" relative to our aims and interests? A cow is functioning properly when she gives the appropriate kind and amount of milk; a garden patch is as it ought to be when it displays a luxuriant preponderance of the sorts of vegetation we propose to promote. But here it seems patent that what constitutes proper functioning depends upon our aims and interests. So far as nature herself goes, isn't a fish decomposing in a hill of corn functioning just as properly, just as excellently, as one happily swimming about chasing minnows? But then what could be meant by speaking of "proper functioning" with respect to our cognitive faculties? A chunk of reality — an organism, a part of an organism, an ecosystem, a garden patch — "functions properly" only with respect to a sort of grid *we* impose on nature — a grid that incorporates *our* aims and desires.

Reply: from a *theistic* point of view, of course, there is no problem here. The idea of my faculties functioning properly is no more problematic than, say, that of a Boeing 747's working properly. Something we have constructed — a heating system, a rope, a linear accelerator — is functioning properly when it is functioning in the way in which it was designed to function. But according to theism, human beings, like ropes, linear accelerators, and ocean liners, have been designed; they have been designed and created by God. Our faculties are working properly, then, when they are working in the way they were designed to work by the being who designed and created us and them. Of course there may be considerable room for disagreement and considerable difficulty in determining just how our faculties have in fact been designed to function and consequent disagreement as to whether they are functioning properly in a given situation. There is disease, disorder, dysfunction, malfunction of the mind as well as of the body. This can range from the extreme case of Descartes's lunatics (who thought their heads were made of glass or that they themselves were gourds) to cases where it isn't clear whether or not cognitive dysfunction is present at all. I stubbornly cling to my theory, long after wiser heads have given it up as a bad job: is this a matter of cognitive dysfunction brought about by excessive pride or desire for recognition on my part? Or is it a perfectly natural and proper display of the sort of cognitive inertia built into our cognitive faculties (in order, perhaps, that we may not be blown about by every wind of doctrine)? Or a display of some other part of our cognitive design whose operation guarantees that new and unfamiliar ideas will persist long enough to get a real run for their money? Or what? So there may be great difficulty in discerning, in a particular instance, whether my faculties are or are not functioning properly; but from a theistic point of view there is no trouble in principle with the very *idea* of proper function.

But can a nontheist also make use of this notion of working properly? Is the idea of proper functioning so tightly tied to the idea of design and construction in such a way that one can use it in the way I suggest only if one is prepared to agree that human beings have been designed? This is a topic I shall have to leave for another occasion;[6] here let me say just this much. This notion of proper functioning is, I think, more problematic from a nontheistic perspective — more problematic, but by no means hopeless. Can't anyone, theist or not, see that a horse, let's say, is suffering from a disease, is displaying a pathological condition? Can't anyone see that an injured bird has a wing that isn't working properly? The notions of proper function and allied notions (sickness, dysfunction, disorder, malfunction, and the like) are ones we all or nearly all have and use. If in fact this notion is ultimately inexplicable or unacceptable from a nontheistic point of view, then there lurks in the neighborhood a powerful theistic argument — one that will be attractive to all those whose inclination to accept and employ the notion of proper function is stronger than their inclinations to reject theism.

(2) Roderick Chisholm[7] sees fulfillment of epistemic duty as crucial to positive epistemic status; in fact he analyzes or explains positive epistemic status in terms of aptness for fulfillment of epistemic duty. Must we go with him, at least far enough to hold that a belief has positive epistemic status for me only if I am appropriately discharging my epistemic duty in forming and holding that belief in the way I do form and hold it? This is a difficult question. No doubt there *are* epistemic duties, duties to the truth, duties we have as cognitive beings; but the question is whether a necessary condition of my knowing a proposition is my violating or flouting no such duties in forming the belief in question. I am inclined to doubt that there is an element of this kind in positive epistemic status. It seems that that belief may constitute knowledge even if I am flouting an intellectual duty in the process of forming and holding it. Suppose I am thoroughly jaundiced and relish thinking the worst about you. I know that I suffer from this aberration and ought to combat it; but I do nothing whatever to correct it, taking a malicious pleasure in it. I barely overhear someone make a derogatory comment about you; I can barely make out his words, and, were it not for my ill will, I would not have heard them correctly. (Others thought he said your thought was deep and rigorous; because of my ill will I correctly heard him as saying that your thought is weak and frivolous.) In this case perhaps I am not doing my cognitive duty in forming the belief in question; I am flouting my duty to try to rid myself of my inclination to form malicious beliefs about you, and it is only because I am not doing my duty that I do form the belief in question. Yet surely it seems to have positive epistemic status for me.

Consider another kind of example. Suppose I am convinced by a distinguished epistemologist that (like everyone else) I have a duty to do my best to try to bring it about that for every proposition I consider, I believe that proposition if and only if it is true. Suppose she also convinces me that on most of the occasions when we form ordinary perceptual beliefs, these beliefs are false. I therefore undergo a strenuous, difficult regimen enabling me, at considerable cost in terms of effort and energy, to inhibit my ordinary belief-forming impulses so that I am able to withhold most ordinary perceptual beliefs. Now suppose I hear a siren; I take a quick look and am appeared to in the familiar way in which one is appeared to upon perceiving a large red firetruck. The thought that I must withhold the natural belief here flashes through my mind. I have been finding the regimen burdensome, however, and say to myself: "This is entirely too much trouble; I am sick and tired of doing my epistemic duty." I let nature take its course, forming the belief that what I see is a large red firetruck. Then (assuming that my beliefs do in fact induce in me a duty to try to inhibit the natural belief) I am forming a belief in a way that is contrary to duty; but don't I nonetheless know that there is a red firetruck there? I think so. I am therefore inclined to think that I could know a proposition even if I came to believe it in a way that is contrary to my epistemic duty. The matter is delicate and unclear, however, and complicated by its involvement with difficult questions about the degree to which my beliefs are under my voluntary control. I am inclined to think that fulfillment of epistemic duty, while of course an estimable condition, is neither necessary nor sufficient for positive epistemic status; but the relationship between positive epistemic status and epistemic duty fulfillment remains obscure to me.

(3) If a belief is to have positive epistemic status for me, then my faculties must be functioning properly in producing the *degree* of belief with which I hold A, as well as the belief that A itself. I am driving down a freeway in Washington, D.C.; as I roar by, I catch a quick glimpse of what seems to be a camel in the median strip; if my faculties are functioning properly, I may believe that I saw a camel, but I won't believe it very firmly—not nearly as firmly, for example, as that I am driving a car. If, due to cognitive malfunction (I am struck by a sudden burst of radiation from a Pentagon experiment gone awry), I do believe the former as firmly as the latter, it will have little by way of positive epistemic status for me.[8]

(4) When my epistemic faculties are functioning properly, I will often form one belief *on the evidential basis of* another. The notion of proper function does not apply, of course, only to basic beliefs, that is, beliefs not formed on the evidential basis of other beliefs; my faculties are also such that under the right conditions I will believe one proposition on the basis of some other beliefs I already hold. I may know that either George or Sam is in the office; you inform me that Sam is not there; I then believe that George is in the office on the basis of these other two beliefs. And of course if my faculties are functioning properly, I won't believe a proposition

on the evidential basis of just *any* proposition. I won't, for example, believe a proposition on the evidential basis of itself (and perhaps this is not even possible). I won't believe that Homer wrote the *Iliad* on the evidential basis of my belief that the population of China exceeds that of Japan. Nor will I believe that Feike cannot swim on the basis of the proposition that 99 out of 100 Frisians can swim and Feike is a Frisian. Proper functioning here involves believing a proposition on the basis of *the right kind* of proposition.

(5) A very important notion here is the idea of *specifications,* or *design plan.* We take it that when human beings (and other creatures) function properly, they function *in a particular way.* That is, they not only function in such a way as to fulfill their purpose (in the way in which it is the purpose of the heart to pump blood), but they function to fulfill that purpose in just one of an indefinitely large number of possible ways. Our cognitive faculties have been designed, no doubt, with reliability in mind; they have been designed in such a way as to produce beliefs that are for the most part true. But they are not designed to produce true beliefs in just any old way. There is a proper way for them to work; we can suppose there is something like a set of plans for us and our faculties. A house is designed to produce shelter—but not in just any old way. There will be plans specifying the length and pitch of the rafters, what kind of shingles are to be applied, the kind and quantity of insulation to be used, and the like. Something similar holds in the case of us and our faculties; we have been designed in accordance with a specific set of plans. Better (since this analogy is insufficiently dynamic), we have been designed in accordance with a set of specifications, in the way in which there are specifications for, for example, the 1983 GMC van. According to these specifications (here I am just guessing), after a cold start the engine runs at 1500 RPM until the engine temperature reaches 140° F.; it then throttles back to 750 RPM. In the same sort of way, our cognitive faculties are designed to function in a certain specific way—a way that may include development and change over time. It is for this reason that it is possible for a belief to be produced by a belief-producing process that is *accidentally* reliable. This notion of specifications or design plan is also the source of counterexamples to the reliabilist claim that a belief has positive epistemic status if it is produced by a reliable belief-producing mechanism.[9]

(6) We do have the idea of our cognitive faculties working properly in an appropriate environment and we also have the idea of positive epistemic status as what accrues to a belief for someone whose epistemic faculties are thus functioning properly. Still, there are cases in which our faculties are functioning perfectly properly but where their working in that way does not seem to lead to truth; indeed, it may lead away from it. Perhaps you remember a painful experience as less painful than it was. (Some say it is thus with childbirth.) Or perhaps you continue to believe in your friend's honesty after evidence and objective judgment would have dictated a reluctant change of mind. Perhaps your belief that you will recover from a dread disease is stronger than the statistics justify. In all of these cases, your faculties may be functioning just as they ought to, but nonetheless their functioning in that way does not obviously seem to lead to truth.

The answer here is simplicity itself: what confers positive epistemic status is one's cognitive faculties working properly or working as designed to work *insofar as that segment of design is aimed at producing* **true** *beliefs.* Not all aspects of the design of our cognitive faculties need be aimed at the production of truth; some might be such as to conduce to survival, or relief from suffering, or the possibility of loyalty, and the like. But someone whose holding a certain belief is a result of an aspect of our cognitive design that is aimed not at truth but at something else won't properly be said to know the proposition in question, even if it turns out to be true. (Unless, perhaps, the same design would conduce both to truth and to the other state of affairs aimed at.)

(7a) Consider Richard Swinburne's "Principle of Credulity": "So generally, . . . I suggest that it is a principle of rationality that (in the absence of special considerations) if it seems (epistemically) to a subject that x is present, then probably x is present; what one seems to perceive is probably so. How things seem to be is good grounds for a belief about how things are."[10] This principle figures into his theistic argument from religious experience: "From this it would follow that, in the absence of special considerations, all religious experiences ought to be taken by their subjects as genuine, and hence as substantial grounds for belief in the apparent object— God, or Mary, or Ultimate Reality or Poseidon" (p. 254). Swinburne understands this "principle of rationality" in such a way that it relates *propositions:* the idea is that on any proposition of the form 'S seems (to himself) to be experiencing a thing that is *F,*' the corresponding proposition of the form 'S is experiencing a thing that is *F*' is more probable than not: "If it seems epistemically to S that *x* is present, then that is good reason for S to believe that it is so, in the absence of special considerations. . . . And it is good reason too for anyone else to believe that *x* is present. For if *e* is evidence for *h,* this is a relation which holds quite independently of who knows about *e*" (p. 260).

To understand Swinburne's thought here we must briefly consider how he thinks of probability. He accepts a version of the logical theory of probability developed by Jeffrey, Keynes, and Carnap; Swinburne himself develops a version of this theory in *An Introduction to Confirmation Theory.*[11] On this theory for any pair of propositions [A,B] there is an objective, logical probability relation between them: the probability of A conditional on B ($P(A/B)$). This relation is *objective* in that it does not depend in any way upon what anyone (any human being, anyway) knows or believes, it is *logical* in that if $P(A/B)$ is *n*, then it is necessary (true in every possible world) that $P(A/B)$ is *n*. (Of course logical probability conforms to the Calculus of Probability.) Carnap spoke of the probabilistic relation between a pair of propositions as *partial entailment;* we may think of the logical probability of A on B as the degree to which B entails A, with entailment *simpliciter* as the limiting case. We could also think of the logical probability of A on B as follows: imagine the possible worlds as uniformly distributed throughout a logical space; then $P(A/B)$ is the ratio between the volume of the space occupied by worlds in which both A and B hold to the volume of the space occupied by worlds in which B holds. And Swinburne's suggestion, as we have seen, is that on any proposition of the form 'S seems (to himself) to be experiencing a thing that is *F,*' the corresponding proposition of the form 'S is experiencing a thing that is *F*' is more probable (logically probable) than not.

I find this dubious. First there are notorious difficulties with the very notion of probability thought of this way. (I'll mention one a couple of paragraphs further down.) But second, even if we embrace a logical theory of probability of this kind we are still likely to have grave problems here. Why suppose that on the proposition 'It seems to Paul that Zeus is present' it is more probable than not (probability taken as logical probability) that Zeus really is present? Here we are not to rely on our having discovered that as a matter of fact most of what most people think is true; what we must consider is the probability of Zeus's presence on the proposition 'It seems to Sam that Zeus is present' *alone,* apart from any background knowledge or beliefs we might have. (Alternatively, this is the case where our background information "consists of nothing but tautologies," as it is sometimes put.) But if all we have for background information is tautologies (and other necessary truths), why think a thing like that? Wouldn't it be just as likely that Sam was mistaken, the victim of a Cartesian demon, or an Alpha Centaurian scientist, or any number of things we can't even think of? What would be a reason for thinking this? That in most possible worlds, most pairs of such propositions are such that the second member is true if the first is? But is there any reason to think that? (That is, is there any reason apart from *theism* to think that; if theism is true, then perhaps most beliefs in most possible worlds are indeed true, if only because God does most of the believing.)

But there is a quite different way in which we might think of this principle. Suppose we think of it from the perspective of the idea that positive epistemic status is a matter of the proper function of our epistemic faculties. It is of course true that when our faculties are functioning properly, then for the most part we do indeed believe what seems to us to be true. This isn't inevitable: consider the Russell paradoxes, where we wind up rejecting what seems true (and what still seems true even after we see where it leads). A madman, furthermore, might find himself regularly believing what didn't seem to him true; and an incautious reader of Kant, intent upon accentuating his free and rational autonomy might undertake a regimen at the conclusion of which he was able to reject what he finds himself inclined by nature to believe. But all else being equal, we ordinarily believe what seems to us to be true, and what seems to us true (when our faculties are functioning properly in a suitable environment) will have more by way of positive epistemic status for us than what does not. The explanation, I suggest, is not that p is logically probable on the proposition 'p seems to Paul to be true'; the explanation is much simpler: it is the fact that when my faculties are functioning properly, the degree of positive epistemic status a proposition has for me just is (modulo a constant of proportionality) the degree to which I am inclined to believe that proposition.

(7b) Similar comments apply to Swinburne's "Principle of Testimony": "the principle that (in the absence of special considerations) the experiences of others are probably as they report them" (272). Here again Swinburne apparently understands this principle in terms of his understanding of probability: the proposition 'Sam's experience is F' is more probable than not, in the logical sense, on the proposition 'Sam testifies that his experience is F'. But this seems dubious: is there any reason to think that in most possible worlds in which Sam claims to have a headache, he really does have a headache? or that the volume of 'logical space' occupied by worlds in which Sam testifies that he has a headache and in fact does, is more than half of the volume of worlds in which Sam testifies that he does? What could be the basis of such a claim? Swinburne's suggestion is that if we do not accept principles of this sort, we shall land in the "morass of skepticism." But we can avoid that morass without accepting these implausible claims about logical probability. Thomas Reid[12] speaks of "Credulity"—the tendency we display to believe what we are told by others. This tendency is of course subject to modification by experience: we learn to trust some people on some topics and distrust others on others; we learn never to form a judgment about a marital altercation until we have spoken to both parties; we learn that people's judgment can be skewed by pride, selfishness, desire to exalt oneself at the expense of one's fellows, love, lust, and much else. Nonetheless there is this tendency, and under the right circumstances when you tell me p (that your name is 'Paul', for example) then (if p is true, and I believe p sufficiently firmly and my faculties are functioning properly in the formation of this belief) I know p. And here we need not try to account for this fact in terms of the logical probability of one proposition on another; we can note instead that (1) when our faculties are functioning properly, we are typically inclined to believe what we are told and (2) if we believe what is true and what we are are sufficiently strongly inclined to believe, then if our faculties are functioning properly (and the cognitive environment is congenial) what we believe is something we know.

(7c) Finally, consider Swinburne's claim that simplicity is a prime determinant of *a priori* or intrinsic probability, at least for explanatory theories: "Prior probability depends on simplicity, fit with background knowledge, and scope. A theory is simple in so far as it postulates few mathematically simple laws holding between entities of an intelligible kind. . . . I am saying merely that a theory which postulates entities of an intelligible kind, as opposed to other entities, will have a greater prior probability, and so, *other things being equal,* will be more likely to be true. . . . For large scale theories the crucial determinant of prior probability is simplicity" (52–53). Here Swinburne is speaking of *prior* probability, not a priori or intrinsic probability: "the prior probability of a theory is the probability before we consider the detailed evidence of observation cited in its support" (52). The prior probability of a theory also depends on its fit with our background knowledge. But if we consider the *a priori* or *intrinsic* probability of the theory, then fit with background information drops out, so that we are left with content (or 'scope', as Swinburne calls it in *The Existence of God*) and simplicity as the determinants of intrinsic probability; and of these two, it is simplicity that is the more important: "sometimes it is convenient to let *e* be all observational evidence and let *k* be mere 'tautological evidence'. In the latter case the prior probability $P(h/k)$ will depend mainly on the simplicity of *h* (as well as to a lesser extent on its narrowness of scope)" (p. 65).

Now I believe there are real problems here. The chief problem, it seems to me, is with the very notion of intrinsic, logical probability. On the theory in question, as we have seen, for any pair of propositions there is an objective, logical probability relation between them. As a special case of this relation we have intrinsic probability: the probability of a proposition conditional on nothing but necessary truths. Take such a contingent proposition as 'Paul Zwier owns an orange shirt'; on this view, there is such a thing as the probability of that proposition conditional on the proposition '$7 + 5 = 12$'. And the problem here is substantially twofold. In the first place there is no reason, so far as I can see, to think that contingent propositions *do* in general have an intrinsic logical probability; and if they do, there seems to be no way to determine, even within very broad limits, what it might be.

But second and more important: there are many large classes of propositions such that there seems to be no way in which intrinsic probability can be distributed over their members in a way that accords both with the calculus of probability and with intuition.

Consider, for example, a countably infinite set S of propositions that are mutually exclusive in pairs and such that necessarily, exactly one of them is true: S might be, for example, the set of propositions such that for each natural number n (including 0), S contains the proposition 'There exist exactly n flying donkeys'. Given nothing but necessary truths, none of these propositions should be more likely to be true than any others; if there is such a thing as a logical probability on nothing but necessary truths, one number should be as probable as another to be the number of flying donkeys. But the members of this countably infinite set can have the same probability only if each has probability 0. That means, however, that the proposition 'There are no flying donkeys' has intrinsic probability 0; hence its denial—'There are some flying donkeys'—has an intrinsic probability of 1. Further, according to the Probability Calculus, if a proposition has an intrinsic probability of 1, then its probability on any evidence is also 1; hence no matter what our evidence, the probability on our evidence that there are flying donkeys is 1. Still further, it is easy to see that (under these assumptions) for any number n, the probability that there are at least n flying donkeys also has an intrinsic probability of 1 and hence a probability of 1 on any evidence.[13] And of course this result is not limited to flying donkeys; for any kind of object such that for any number n it is possible that there be n objects of that kind—witches, demons, Siberian Cheesehounds—the probability that there are at least n of them (for any n) is 1 on any evidence whatever.[14]

The only way to avoid this unsavory result is to suppose that intrinsic probabilities are distributed in accordance with some series that converges to 0: for example, 'There are no flying donkeys' has an intrinsic probability of ½, 'There is just one flying donkey' get ¼, and so on. But then we are committed to the idea that some numbers are vastly more likely (conditional on necessary truths alone) than others to be the number of flying donkeys. In fact we are committed to the view that for any number n you please, there will be a pair of natural numbers m and m^* such that m^* is n times more likely (conditional on necessary truths alone) to be the number of donkeys than m. And this seems just as counterintuitive as the suggestion that for any number n you pick, the probability (on any evidence) that there are at least n flying donkeys is 1.

It therefore seems to me unlikely that such propositions have intrinsic probability at all; but similar arguments can be brought to bear on many other classes of propositions. Accordingly, I think the whole idea of intrinsic probability is at best dubious. But even if there is such a thing, why should we suppose that *simpler* propositions, all else being equal, have more of it than complex propositions? Is there some *a priori* reason to suppose that reality prefers simplicity? Where would this notion come from? Swinburne, again, believes that if we don't accept some such principle as this, we shall fall into that skeptical bog: if we don't accept some such principle, we will have no reason for preferring simple to complex hypotheses, but in many contexts all that our favored hypotheses have going for them (as compared to others that fit the same data just as well) is simplicity.

But suppose we look at the matter from the point of view of the present conception of positive epistemic status. Despite the real problems in saying just what simplicity is (and in saying in any sort of systematic way when one theory is simpler than another) there clearly is such a thing as simplicity, and it clearly does contribute to the positive epistemic status a theory or explanation has for us. But why think of this in terms of the problematic notion of intrinsic logical probability? Why not note instead that when our faculties are functioning properly, we do opt for simple theories as opposed to complex ones (all else being equal); we can therefore see the greater positive epistemic status of simple theories (again, all else being equal) as resulting from the fact that when our faculties are functioning properly, we are more strongly inclined to accept simple theories than complex ones.

(8) There are presently three main views as to the nature of positive epistemic status: Chisholmian Internalism, Coherentism, and Reliabilism. The present conception of positive epistemic status as a matter of degree of inclination towards belief when epistemic faculties are functioning properly—the conception that seems to me to go most naturally with theism—provides a revealing perspective from which, as it seems to me, we can see that none of these three views is really viable. For each we can easily see that the proposed necessary and sufficient condition for positive epistemic status is not in fact sufficient (and in some cases not necessary either)—and not sufficient just because a belief could meet the condition in question but still have little by way of positive epistemic status because of

cognitive pathology, failure to function properly. I don't have the space here to go into the matter with the proper thoroughness;[15] I shall say just the following.

First, the Chisholmian Internalist (or at any rate its most distinguished exemplar) sees positive epistemic status as a matter of aptness for epistemic duty fulfillment. Chisholm begins by introducing an undefined technical locution: 'p is more reasonable than q for S at t' here the values for p and q will be such states of affairs as 'believing that all men are mortal' and 'withholding the belief that all men are mortal'—that is, believing neither the proposition in question nor its denial. Given 'is more reasonable than' as an undefined locution, he goes on to define a battery of "terms of epistemic appraisal" as he calls them: 'certain', 'beyond reasonable doubt', 'evident', 'acceptable', and so on. A proposition A is beyond reasonable doubt for a person at a time t, for example, if it is more reasonable for him to accept that proposition then than to withhold it; A has some presumption in its favor for him at t just if accepting it then is more reasonable than accepting its negation. Now Chisholm introduces "is more reasonable than" as an undefined locution; but of course he intends it to have a sense, and to have a sense reasonably close to the sense it has in English. In *Foundations of Knowing,* his most recent full dress presentation of his epistemology, he says that "Epistemic reasonability could be understood in terms of the general requirement to try to have the largest possible set of logically independent beliefs that is such that the true beliefs outnumber the false beliefs. The principles of epistemic preferability are the principles one should follow if one is to fulfill this requirement."[16] In his earlier *Theory of Knowledge* Chisholm is a bit more explicit about intellectual requirements: "We may assume," he says,

> that every person is subject to a purely intellectual requirement: that of trying his best to bring it about that for any proposition p he considers, he accepts p if and only if p is true;[17]

and he adds that

> One might say that this is the person's responsibility qua intellectual being. . . . One way, then of re-expressing the locution 'p is more reasonable than q for S at t' is to say this: 'S is so situated at t that his intellectual requirement, his responsibility as an intellectual being, is better fulfilled by p than by q'.

Reasonability, therefore, is a *normative* concept; more precisely, it pertains to requirement, duty, or obligation. And Chisholm's central claim here is that a certain epistemic requirement, or responsibility, or duty, or obligation lies at the basis of such epistemic notions as evidence, justification, positive epistemic status, and knowledge itself. To say, for example, that a proposition *p* is *acceptable* for a person at a time is to say that she is so situated, then, that it is not the case that she can better fulfill her epistemic duty by withholding than by accepting *p*; to say that *p* is *beyond reasonable doubt* for her is to say that she is so situated, then, that she can better fulfill her intellectual responsibility by accepting *p* than by withholding it. The basic idea is that our epistemic duty or requirement is to try to achieve and maintain a certain condition — call it 'epistemic excellence' — which may be hard to specify in detail, but consists fundamentally in standing in an appropriate relation to truth. A proposition has positive epistemic status for me, in certain circumstances, to the extent that I can fulfill my epistemic duty by accepting it in those circumstances. This duty or obligation or requirement, furthermore, is one of *trying* to bring about a certain state of affairs. It is not my requirement to *succeed* in achieving and maintaining intellectual excellence; my requirement is only to try to do so. Presumably the reason is that it may not be within my power to succeed. Perhaps I don't know how to achieve intellectual excellence; or perhaps I do know how but simply can't do it. So my duty is only to *try* to bring about this state of affairs.

This is a simple and attractive picture of the nature of justification and positive epistemic status. I think it is easy to see, however, that it is deeply flawed: for it is utterly clear that aptness for the fulfillment of epistemic duty or obligation is not sufficient for positive epistemic status. Suppose Paul is subject to cognitive dysfunction: then there could be a proposition *A* that has little by way of positive epistemic status for him, but is nonetheless such that believing it is maximally apt for epistemic duty fulfillment for him. Suppose Paul is subject to a cerebral disturbance that causes far-reaching cognitive dysfunction: when he is appeared to in one sense modality, he forms beliefs appropriate to another. When he is aurally appeared to in the way in which one is appeared to upon hearing church bells, for example, he has a nearly ineluctable tendency to believe that there is something that is appearing to him in that fashion, and that that thing is orange—bright orange. This belief, furthermore, seems utterly convincing; it has for him, all the phenomenological *panache* of *modus ponens* itself. He knows nothing about this defect in his epistemic equipment, and his lack of awareness is in no way due to dereliction of epistemic duty. As a matter of fact, Paul is unusually dutiful, unusually concerned about doing his epistemic duty; fulfilling this duty is the main passion of his life. Add that those around him suffer from a similar epistemic deficiency: Paul lives in Alaska and he and all his neighbors have suffered all their lives from similar lesions due to radioactive fallout from a Soviet missile test. Now suppose Paul is aurally appeared to in the way in question and forms the belief that he is being appeared to in that way by something that is orange. Surely this proposition is such that believing it is the right thing to do from the point of view of epistemic duty; nevertheless the proposition has little by way of positive epistemic status for him. Paul is beyond reproach; he has done his duty as he saw it; he is within his epistemic rights; he is permissively justified, and more. Nevertheless there is a kind of positive epistemic status this belief lacks—a kind crucial for knowledge. For that sort of positive epistemic status, it isn't sufficient to satisfy one's duty and do one's epistemic best. Paul can be ever so conscientious about his epistemic duties and still be such that his beliefs do not have that kind of positive epistemic status.

Clearly enough, we can vary the above sorts of examples. Perhaps you think that what goes *in excelsis* with satisfying duty is *effort*; perhaps (in a Kantian vein) you think that genuinely dutiful action must be contrary to inclination. Very well; alter the above cases accordingly. Suppose, for example, that Paul (again, due to cognitive malfunction) nonculpably believes that his nature is deeply misleading. Like the rest of us, he has an inclination, upon being appeared to redly, to believe that there is something red lurking in the neighborhood; unlike the rest of us, he believes that this natural inclination is misleading and that on those occasions there really isn't anything that is thus appearing to him. He undertakes a strenuous regimen to overcome this inclination; after intense and protracted effort he succeeds; upon being appeared to redly he no longer believes that something red is appearing to him. His devotion to duty costs him dearly. The enormous effort he expends takes its toll upon his health; he is subject to ridicule and disapprobation on the part of his fellows; his wife protests his unusual behavior and finally leaves him for someone less epistemically nonstandard. Nonetheless he persists in doing what he nonculpably takes to be his duty. It is obvious, I take it, that even though Paul is unusually dutiful in accepting, on a given occasion, the belief that nothing red is appearing to him, he has little by way of positive epistemic status for that belief.

We may therefore conclude, I think, that positive epistemic status is not or is not merely a matter of aptness for fulfillment of epistemic duty or obligation. Could it be *coherence,* as with Lehrer,[18] Bonjour,[19] and several Bayesians? Coherentism, of course, comes in many varieties; here I don't have the space to discuss any of them properly. From the present perspective, however, there is at least one crucial difficulty with them all: they all neglect the crucial feature of proper function. According to coherentism, all that is relevant to my belief's having positive epistemic status for me is a certain internal relationship among them. But surely this is not so. Consider, for example, the case of the Epistemically Inflexible Climber. Paul is climbing Guide's Wall, in the Grand Tetons; having just led the next to last pitch, he is seated on a comfortable ledge, belaying his partner. He believes that Cascade Canyon is down to his left, that the cliffs of Mt. Owen are directly in front of him, that there is a hawk flying in lazy circles 200 feet below him, that he is wearing his new Fire rock shoes, and so on. His beliefs, we may stipulate, are coherent. Now imagine that Paul is struck by a burst of high energy cosmic radiation, causing his beliefs to become fixed, no longer responsive to changes in experience. His partner gets him down the Wall and, in a last ditch attempt at therapy, takes him to the opera in Jackson, where the Metropolitan Opera on tour is performing *La Traviata* with Pavarotti singing the tenor lead. Paul is appeared to in the same way as everyone else there; he is inundated by waves of golden sound. Sadly enough, the effort at therapy fails; Paul still believes that he is on the belay ledge at the top of the next to last pitch of Guide's Wall, that Cascade Canyon is down to his left, that there is a hawk flying in lazy circles 200 feet below him, and so on. Furthermore, since he believes the very same things he believed when seated on the ledge, his beliefs are coherent. But surely they have very little by way of positive epistemic status for him. Clearly, then, coherence is not sufficient for positive epistemic status.

I turn finally to reliabilism, the last of the three chief contemporary ideas as to the nature of positive epistemic status. The view I have suggested in this paper is closer to reliabilism, especially in the form suggested by William Alston,[20] than to either of the other two; indeed, perhaps you think it *is* a form of reliabilism. I don't propose to argue about labels; still, as I see it, that would be less than wholly accurate. Of course reliability crucially enters into the account I suggest. According to that account, we implicitly think of positive epistemic status as involving our faculties' functioning properly; but clearly we wouldn't think of positive epistemic status in this way if we didn't think that when our faculties function as they ought, then for the most part they are in fact reliable. Still, there is more to a belief's having positive epistemic status than its being reliably produced. There are even more brands of reliabilism than of coherentism; and what is true of one may not be true of another. But the leading idea of at least many central brands of reliabilism is that a belief has positive epistemic status if and only if it is produced by a reliable belief-producing mechanism or process; and the degree of its positive epistemic status is determined by the degree of reliability of the process that produces it. Thus Alvin Goldman: "The justificational status of a belief," he says, "is a function of the reliability of the process or processes that cause it, where (as a first approximation) reliability consists in the tendency of a process to produce beliefs that are true rather than false."[21]

Here there are problems of several sorts; one of the most important is the dreaded *problem of generality,* developed by Richard Feldman in "Reliability and Justification."[22] But there are other problems as well, problems that arise out of the neglect of the idea of proper function. As we saw above, a crucial part of our notion of positive epistemic status is the idea of a design plan or specifications. But then not just any reliable belief-producing process can confer positive epistemic status. Suppose I am struck by a burst of cosmic rays, resulting in the following unfortunate malfunction. Whenever I hear the word "prime" in any context, I form a belief, with respect to one of the first 1000 natural numbers, that it is not prime. So you say "Pacific Palisades is prime residential area," or "Prime ribs is my favorite," or "First you must prime the pump," or "(17′) entails (14)," or "The prime rate is dropping again," or anything else in which the word occurs; in each case I form a belief, with respect to a randomly selected natural number, that it is not prime. This belief-producing process or mechanism is indeed reliable; in the vast majority of cases it produces truth. But it is only *accidentally* reliable; it just happens, by virtue of a piece of epistemic serendipity, to produce mostly true beliefs. And the force of the suggestion that the process in question is accidentally reliable, I suggest, is just that under the envisaged conditions my faculties are not working in accordance with the design plan or the specifications for human beings; that's what makes the reliability in question *accidental* reliability. Furthermore, it does not confer positive epistemic status. Here the process or mechanism in question is indeed reliable; but my belief—that, say, 41 is not prime—has little or no positive epistemic status. Nor is the problem simply that the belief is false; the same goes for my (true) belief that 631 is not prime, if it is formed in this fashion. So reliable belief formation is not sufficient for positive epistemic status.

By way of conclusion, then: from a theistic perspective, it is natural to see positive epistemic status, the quantity enough of which is sufficient, together with truth, for knowledge: positive epistemic status accrues to a belief, B, for a person, S, only if S's cognitive environment is appropriate for her cognitive faculties and only if these faculties are functioning properly in producing this belief in her—i.e., only if her cognitive faculties are functioning in the way God designed human cognitive faculties to function, and only if S is in the sort of cognitive environment for which human cognitive faculties are designed; and under these conditions the degree of positive epistemic status enjoyed by B is proportional to the strength of her inclination to accept B. Alternatively: a belief B has positive epistemic status for S if and only if that belief is produced in S by her epistemic faculties working properly (in an appropriate environment); and B has more positive epistemic status than B^* for S iff B has positive epistemic status for S and either B^* does not or else S is more strongly inclined to believe B than B^*. Still another way to put the matter: a belief, B, has degree d of positive epistemic status for a person, S, if and only if the faculties relevant to producing B in S are functioning properly (in an appropriate environment), and S is inclined to degree d to believe B.

There remains, of course, an enormous amount to be said and an enormous amount to be thought about. For example: (1) What about *God's* knowledge? God is the premier example of someone who knows; but of course his faculties are not designed either by himself or by someone else. So how shall we think of his knowledge? The answer, I think, lies in the following neighborhood: "Working properly" is used *analogically* when applied to God's cognitive faculties and ours, the analogy being located in the fact that a design plan for a *perfect* knower would specify cognitive powers of the very sort God displays. But of course this notion needs to be developed and worked out in detail. (2) Our spiritual forebears at Princeton used to speak of the *noetic effects of sin.* Clearly (from a Christian perspective) sin has had an important effect upon the function of our cognitive faculties; but just how does this work and how does it bear on specific questions about the degree of positive epistemic status enjoyed by various beliefs? (3) This way of thinking of positive epistemic status, I believe, makes it much easier to understand the degree of positive epistemic status enjoyed by *moral* beliefs and by *a priori* beliefs; but just what sort of account is correct here? (4) How, from this perspective, shall we think of the dreaded Gettier problem? (5) The present account is clearly an *externalist* account of positive epistemic status; but how do internalist factors fit in? (6) From the present perspective, how shall we think about skepticism? (7) How is the present account related to the broadly Aristotelian account of knowledge to be found in medieval thinkers? (8) How shall we construe *epistemic probability*—more exactly, how shall we construe the relationship between *A* and *B* when *A* is a good nondeductive reason for *B,* or where *B* is epistemically probable with respect to *A?* Here the present account of positive epistemic status is clearly suggestive;[23] but how, precisely, does it work? (9) Over the last few years several philosophers[24] have been arguing that rational belief in God does not require propositional evidence or argument, that it can be properly basic; how shall we think of that claim from the present perspective? These and many others are questions for another occasion.

NOTES

1. See my "Positive Epistemic Status and Proper Function" in *Philosophical Perspectives,* vol. 2: *Epistemology,* ed. James Tomberlin (Northridge: California State University), 1988.

2. See R. Chisholm, *Theory of Knowledge* (New York: Prentice Hall, 2nd ed., 1977), pp. 5ff.

3. See my "Chisholmian Internalism" in *Philosophical Analysis: A Defense by Example,* ed. David Austin (Dordrecht: Reidel, 1988).

4. Indeed, it is ludicrous understatement to say that God has a grasp of every proposition and property: from a theistic point of view the natural way to view propositions and properties is as God's thoughts and concepts. (See my "How to Be an Anti-realist," *Proceedings of the American Philosophical Association,* vol. 56, no. 1, 1983.)

5. In C. S. Lewis's novel *Out of the Silent Planet* the creatures on Mars are of several different types, displaying several different kinds of cognitive excellences: some are particularly suited to scientific endeavors, some to poetry and art, and some to interpersonal sensitivity.

6. See my "Positive Epistemic Status and Proper Function."

7. See his *Theory of Knowledge,* p. 14, and *Foundations of Knowing* (Minneapolis: University of Minnesota Press, 1982), p. 7. See also my "Chisholmian Internalism" in *Philosophical Analysis: A Defense by Example.*

8. Must all of my cognitive faculties be functioning properly for any belief to have positive epistemic status for me? Surely not. And what about the fact that proper function comes in degrees? How well must the relevant faculties be working for a belief to have positive epistemic status for me? On these questions see my "Positive Epistemic Status and Proper Function."

9. See below, pp. 66.

10. *The Existence of God* (Oxford: at the Clarendon Press, 1979), p. 254. Subsequent references to Swinburne's work will be to this volume.

11. See R. Swinburne, *An Introduction to Confirmation Theory* (London: Methuen, 1973).

12. My whole account of positive epistemic status, not just this example, owes much to Thomas Reid with his talk of faculties and their functions and his rejection of the notion (one he attributes to Hume and his predecessors) that self-evident propositions and propositions about one's own immediate experience are the only properly basic propositions.

13. The proposition 'There are at least n flying donkeys' is equivalent to the denial of (a) 'There are 0 flying donkeys', or 'There is just 1 flying donkey', or 'There are just 2 flying donkeys,' or 'There are just n-1 flying donkeys'. By hypothesis, the probability of each disjunct of (a) is 0; hence by the Additive Axiom the probability of the disjunction is 0, so that the probability of its denial is 1.

14. See my "The Probabilistic Argument from Evil," *Philosophical Studies,* 1979.

15. See my "Chisholmian Internalism" for detailed criticism of Chisholmian Internalism; see my "Coherentism and the Evidentialist Objection to Theistic Belief" in *Rationality, Religious Belief, and Moral Commitment,* ed. William Wainwright and Robert Audi (Ithaca: Cornell University Press, 1986) for detailed criticism of Coherentism, and see my "Positive Epistemic Status and Proper Function," p. 7.

16. P. 7.

17. P. 14.

18. Keith Lehrer, *Knowledge* (Oxford: Oxford University Press, 1974).

19. Lawrence Bonjour, *The Structure of Empirical Knowledge* (Cambridge, Mass.: Harvard University Press, 1986).

20. See his "Concepts of Epistemic Justification," *The Monist* 68, no. 1 (Jan. 1985) and "An Internalist Externalism," forthcoming in *Synthese*.

21. "What Is Justified Belief?" in *Justification and Knowledge: New Studies in Epistemology,* ed. George Pappas (Dordrecht: D. Reidel, 1979), p. 10.

22. *The Monist* 68, no. 2 (April 1985), pp. 159ff.

23. See Richard Otte's "Theistic Conception of Probability," in the present volume.

24. See, for example, William Alston's "Christian Experience and Christian Belief," Nicholas Wolterstorffs "Can Belief in God be Rational If It Has No Foundations?" and my "Reason and Belief in God," all in *Faith and Rationality,* ed. N. Wolterstorff and A. Plantinga (Notre Dame, Ind.: University of Notre Dame Press, 1983).

Theism, Reliabilism, and the Cognitive Ideal

Jonathan Kvanvig

In recent years, reliabilist theories have come to be, if not the most widely held, at least the most widely discussed theories of knowledge and justification. Here I shall limit discussion to two kinds of reliabilist theories of justification, which I shall call 'personal reliabilism' and 'process reliabilism'.[1] As is often the case with powerful philosophical theories, it is quite difficult to give a general characterization of reliabilism. Two necessary conditions for being a reliabilist theory emerge in the literature, however. One is that there be an objective connection between justification and truth, so a reliabilist theory of justification will hold that a justified belief is one objectively likely to be true (on some appropriate construal of objective likelihood). This requirement distinguishes reliabilist theories from theories which emphasize weaker connections to the truth: connections such as those involved in the claim that a justified belief is one to hold in the attempt to find the truth and avoid error,[2] one sanctioned by epistemic norms,[3] one which coheres with what one would believe if one's only interests were in finding the truth and avoiding error,[4] or one in which one's degree of belief matches the subjective probability of the content of the belief for the person in question.[5] The second necessary condition for being a reliabilist theory has to do with the way in which the objective likelihood of a belief is grounded. I know of no general way to eliminate the vagueness of this condition, but it is necessary in order to distinguish reliabilism from purely probabilistic theories of justification which hold that a belief is justified just in case the content of the belief is ob-

71

jectively likely to be true. The difficulty with such a theory of justification is that what makes the content of a belief objectively likely may be wholly unrelated to the belief itself: it might be that it is objectively likely that there is a planet beyond Neptune in our solar system and yet a person may believe this, not on the basis of that which makes the claim objectively likely, but rather because nine is his favorite number and he likes the thought that there should be just that number of planets. The second condition for being a reliabilist theory aims at eliminating improperly based beliefs of the sort just described. Though I cannot give a general account of the ways open to reliabilist to address this issue, it is easy enough to say how process and personal reliabilism address the problem. According to process reliabilism, the objective likelihood of a belief must derive from features of the process or method by which the belief was acquired or is sustained. Personal reliabilism claims that the objective likelihood of a belief must derive from characteristics of the person involved in the holding of the belief, from those intellectual virtues exemplified in the formation and sustenance of the belief.

There is a dialectic between these forms of reliabilism and theism, a dialectic issuing in a surprising union of reliabilism with theism. The dialectic begins with an investigation of the cognitive ideal, and a proper appreciation of the cognitive ideal for humans will show that personal reliabilism must be abandoned and will lay the foundation for my claim that the adequacy of reliabilism requires a union with theism.

1. RELIABILISM AND THE COGNITIVE IDEAL

Our question in this section concerns the relationship between knowledge, justification, and the cognitive ideal. Now, there are different cognitive ideals for different kinds of beings, since the ideal for a kind of being depends on the capacities that being has (or could develop). Yet, some common thread should be able to be found among the variety of cognitive ideals, and thus it should be fruitful to examine the unrestricted cognitive ideal if we are interested in the cognitive ideal for human beings. A natural assumption here is that if we understand the unrestricted cognitive ideal, an awareness of the limitations to which human beings are naturally subject will allow us to replace the unrestricted cognitive ideal with an appropriately restricted cognitive ideal for human beings. Thus, let us begin by investigating the unrestricted cognitive ideal.

Quite clearly, the unrestricted cognitive ideal is that ideal satisfied by God: since it is a necessary truth that God is maximally perfect, it is also a necessary truth that he is maximally cognitively perfect. Thus, we can explore the unrestricted cognitive ideal by considering the constitution of God's cognitive perfection. An initial hypothesis is that God's cognitive perfection consists in his omniscience, but it is not difficult to see that this position is too weak. The concept of omniscience does not preclude a being's having omniscience in one world and lacking it in another; yet, clearly, any being who was only contingently omniscient would be less perfect than a being who was omniscient in a modally stronger fashion. Thus, at the very least, we must affirm a stronger account of God's cognitive perfection, one on which his cognitive perfection is taken to consist in being essentially omniscient.

Both of these accounts share the claim that the unrestricted cognitive ideal is clarified solely in terms of knowledge; they differ concerning which possible worlds are to be investigated in determining whether a being satisfies the ideal. There is an objection which shows that trans-world omniscience, no matter how extensive, does not exhaust the concept of the cognitive ideal and hence does not exhaust God's cognitive perfection; thus, this objection shows that the feature the two views share in common (that the unrestricted cognitive ideal is to be clarified solely in terms of knowledge) must be abandoned. First, imagine two omniscient beings, the first of whom knows everything on its own, so to speak, and the second of whom knows everything by being told the truth by the first being; nothing in the concept of omniscience itself implies that this scenario is impossible. Yet, if the concept of omniscience itself is not incompatible with this scenario, neither is the concept of essential omniscience; so imagine two beings, each of whom is essentially omniscient, where the first knows everything on its own and the second by being told by the first. Adding that each being necessarily exists yields no contradiction, hence the concept of two necessarily existent, essentially omniscient beings is coherent,[6] where the first has independent knowledge and the second has only dependent knowledge. Obviously, though, the first being is cognitively superior to the second; hence, God's cognitive perfection cannot be characterized solely by his essential omniscience.

Some have taken this scenario to imply that omniscience should not be clarified in terms of knowing all truths, but rather in terms of knowing all truths on the basis of one's own cognitive powers.[7] However, this evaluation of the case is mistaken; there is a sense in which when any being acquires knowledge, it is moving closer to omniscience, regardless of how the knowledge is acquired. Yet, if omniscience is clarified in terms of knowing all truths on the basis of one's own cognitive powers, one could not be closer to omniscience merely by coming to know something—one would have to have acquired the knowledge on the basis of one's own cognitive powers. What goes wrong in taking the scenario in question to imply that a new understanding of omniscience is needed is a kind of tunnel vision about the cognitive ideal: it is assumed that God's cognitive ideality is exhausted by God's essential omniscience, and hence it is assumed that omniscience cannot be clarified in terms of knowledge across possible worlds. This assumption that God's cognitive ideal is exhausted by his omniscience is false, and that is the lesson of the multiple omniscient beings example, not that a new definition of omniscience is called for.

Thus, we must abandon the account of God's cognitive perfection which clarifies that perfection solely in terms of God's essential omniscience. Clearly, the kinds of changes required concern the way in which the knowledge is acquired: through the use of one's own cognitive powers or dependent on another's. Now, one might think that it is not necessary that God use only his own cognitive powers in being omniscient; it might be suggested that all that is required is that he be able to do so. We should reject this account, though, for God's cognitive perfection is absolute in the sense that it would be wholly superfluous for anyone to attempt to inform him of anything. Thus, the account of God's cognitive perfection we should accept clarifies that perfection in terms of his essential omniscience deriving from the use of his own cognitive powers.

These cognitive powers, since they are character traits which are dispositions toward, or abilities to find, the truth, are intellectual virtues. Though, as we shall see, a character trait need not have those characteristics in order to be an intellectual virtue, a character trait which in every world has that characteristic will certainly count as an intellectual virtue. Thus, the account of God's cognitive perfection above clarifies that perfection in terms of God's essential omniscience grounded in, or deriving from the use of, his intellectual virtues.

This investigation of the unrestricted cognitive ideal can be used to show that personal reliabilism must be abandoned, for two reasons. The first is that the natural source for the view of personal reliabilists is to be found in an unacceptable account of the unrestricted cognitive ideal. The second is that to the extent that personal reliabilism is developed through an appreciation of the correct account of the unrestricted cognitive ideal, it fails adequately to take into account the differences between the epistemic situation relevant when the unrestricted cognitive ideal applies and the situation which applies when a restricted cognitive ideal applies, as is the case when considering the intellectual ideality of any human being.

Let us take each point in turn. The first is that personal reliabilism rests on an inadequate construal of the unrestricted intellectual ideal. In particular, personal reliabilism has as its natural source the account of the unrestricted intellectual ideal on which intellectual ideality is clarified solely in terms of essential omniscience. If we accept such an account of the unrestricted intellectual ideal, it will be natural to think that possession and realization of the intellectual virtues is intrinsically connected with having knowledge. This inadequate view of the unrestricted cognitive ideal, in order to handle the case of the two omniscient beings discussed earlier, must hold that omniscience is to be understood in terms of finding the truth on the basis of one's own intellectual virtues. If it does not maintain this claim, it will have to claim that a being who is omniscient by being told the truth by another omniscient being is as intellectually ideal as a being who is omniscient by its own cognitive power. But if omniscience is clarified in this way, it is natural to clarify knowledge itself in the same way: knowledge is then construed to be that which arises when and only when the employment of the intellectual virtues results in finding the truth.

Since the understanding of the unrestricted intellectual ideal is inadequate, we should expect that there may be problems with a view which finds its natural source in such an understanding. One

such view which is obviously inadequate claims that knowledge requires finding the truth solely on the basis of one's own intellectual
virtues. Such a view should be rejected because it dismisses the possibility of knowledge based on testimony. Now, personal reliabilism
is not committed to this rejection of testimonial knowledge, but it
is committed to the rejection of the possibility of knowledge arising
apart from the virtues. The difficulty with such a view is that it fails
to appreciate how intellectual development is crucial to the epistemic
life. In the case of human beings, some virtues are methodological
in nature and require intentional effort to develop; in the case of
God, of course, his insight is of such power that it need not proceed
toward the truth via individually specifiable steps nor is it subject
to the particular kind of becoming found in developmental efforts.
God has no methodological virtues—virtues involving the habitual
following a particular series of steps which constitute a method of
arriving at the truth—for his insight is so great that he intuitively
perceives what the truth is apart from following any such method.
Thus, in the divine case, there is no analogue of a common phenomenon in the human case, that of following a particular method
prior to, and on the road to, the inculcation of the habit of following that method. In such a case, it is clear that the only intellectual
virtue relevant to the epistemic standing of the resulting beliefs would
be the habitual following of that method; however, given that the
habit is only the process of inculcation, there is no such virtue present yet. Thus, personal reliabilism requires that there be such a virtue in which to ground the knowledge which can result from following an appropriate method of inquiry when the virtue in question
does not yet exist. It does not yet exist because it comes to be possessed by a human being only through the process of repeatedly
forming justified beliefs and repeatedly coming to have knowledge
on the basis of following the method in question. Hence, personal
reliabilism is false.

So, personal reliabilism is plagued by a certain kind of circularity. Personal reliabilism requires virtues to be present while still
in the process of formation, for the kind of virtues under discussion
are just those which are developed through repeatedly forming justified beliefs or by repeatedly arriving at knowledge through the use
of a certain method. This inadequacy can be traced to a reliance
on an inadequate account of the unrestricted cognitive ideal. On

that account of the unrestricted cognitive ideal, the possession and realization of the intellectual virtues is assumed to be a requirement for omniscience; taking into account the restrictions which apply in the human epistemic situation, omniscience would not be required, but one would still assume that the possession and realization of the intellectual virtues is required for knowledge. On the other hand, if it is noted that, even at the level of the unrestricted cognitive ideal, the role of omniscience and the role of cognitive powers is distinct, this inference would not be made. For, if it is one thing to be omniscient and another thing to be omniscient in virtue of one's cognitive powers, it would be natural to assume that, in the human epistemic situation, it is one thing to have knowledge or justified belief and quite another to have knowledge or justification grounded in the intellectual virtues.

The second objection to personal reliabilism is that personal reliabilism fails to appreciate the differences between the epistemic situations in which the unrestricted cognitive ideal applies and a restricted one applies. Recall that, for an essentially omniscient being, cognitive powers cannot fail to be dispositions toward, or abilities to find, the truth; once this feature of divine cognitive powers is noticed, however, it is natural to assume that the virtues (including cognitive powers such as perception and memory) are to be defined as dispositions toward, or abilities to find, the truth. That is, if one is insufficiently attentive to the differences between the features of the epistemic situation in which the unrestricted ideal applies and the human situation in which only a restricted ideal applies, one will be tempted to infer that the intellectual virtues or excellences are to be given a truth-conducive construal.

Of course, very few if any contemporary epistemologists will make the mistake of inferring that the intellectual virtues are characteristics which are maximally efficacious dispositions toward the truth from the claim that this is the nature of God's intellectual virtues. Such an inference would require that nothing be a virtue unless it was incapable of generating false beliefs. A construal more cognizant of the fallibility of human beings would insist that in accepting a truth-conducive construal of the virtues, one is not requiring that virtues are *infallible dispositions* toward the truth, but only *dispositions* toward it. Hence it might be thought the difference in terms of fallibility between God and humans could not undermine the truth-conducive construal of the virtues. Yet, a slippery slope lurks in the neighborhood, for if it is possible to have some justified yet false beliefs grounded in the virtues, it is not clear why one could not have mostly false beliefs grounded in the virtues.

There are two reasons for thinking that this is a possibility. The first centers on the role the environment plays in getting to the truth once one is considering fallible instead of infallible beings. With an infallible being, no environment is epistemically hostile, i.e., no environment could be resistant to the formation of true beliefs by such an individual. Once a being is fallible, such a possibility is introduced. When error is the result of cognitive endeavors for such a being, two explanations are thus possible. The first is that one's intellectual faculties are deficient in certain respects; the other is that the environment is especially hostile to fallible equipment (or to the particular fallible equipment in question). Descartes's evil demon world is just a maximal example of an epistemically hostile environment; more specifically, evil demon worlds are examples of environments which are essentially epistemically hostile to fallible cognitive equipment. For as long as a being has fallible equipment, a demon world can be described so that error is the normal result of the operation of the cognitive equipment in question. The second reason for thinking that it may be possible to have mostly false beliefs grounded in the virtues is that we identify the virtues in terms of characteristics which are admirable; for example, courage is a virtue even in those who achieve bad ends (either intentionally or through the "luck of the draw") because even in the pursuit of evil there is something admirable about facing danger to achieve one's goals instead of abandoning the goals. Now, if the proper explanation of why error is the consistent product of the operation of one's cognitive equipment is that the environment is epistemically hostile, the proper conclusion to draw is that one's equipment can still be virtuous even though not truth-conducive. To draw the conclusion that the equipment fails to count as an intellectual virtue or excellence in such a case would be like concluding that one who consistently get in car accidents because of the careless driving of others is really not a safe driver at all.

One is tempted to appeal to relevantly close counterfactual circumstances to solve the problem facing a truth-conducive account of the virtues. One is tempted to say, for example, that a safe driver might have such bad luck that he consistently gets in accidents because of the carelessness of others. But, it might be claimed it may still be true that a safe driver is one who *would* avoid accidents.

The difficulty here is easy to appreciate. *Under what conditions* would a safe driver avoid accidents? Obviously, under some conditions she would and in others she would not. The point is that the environment itself can be responsible for the gap between what a virtue aims at and what it achieves. In such a case, the characteristic in question is still virtuous; what follows in the case of the intellectual virtues is that a truth-conducive account must be abandoned.

If virtues are not truth-conducive, how are they to be understood? A justification-conducive account is suggested by the following vague, but instructive, considerations. What is important and admirable in investigating an epistemically hostile environment is the way in which one pursues the truth, not just whether one actually discovers the truth (after all, the fact that one does not discover the truth will be due to the hostility of the environment and not to any lack in the agent, her equipment or procedures). But a natural and intuitive starting point in clarifying what epistemic justification amounts to is the following: justification is a property a belief comes to have when that belief is an ideal one to form in the pursuit of the truth. Of course, more needs to be said, for a quick objection to this claim is that the ideal belief to form in the pursuit of the truth is a true one or one objectively likely to be true. What this objection shows is that some clarification of the notion of ideality is being assumed which bars true beliefs from counting as ideal, solely in virtue of being true or objectively likely to be true, in the pursuit of truth. There are ways to do this,[8] but it is not relevant to our task here to pursue them. The point to be made instead is that this rough, intuitive construal of the notion of epistemic justification gives credence to the claim that the virtues are best thought of as justification-conducive rather than truth-conducive, for even in an epistemically hostile environment, a person can be virtuous by aiming in the best way possible to get to the truth, and that is just to form justified, though perhaps false, beliefs.

This account of the virtues has disastrous implications for personal reliabilism. For, according to personal reliabilism, justification is the sort of thing arising out of the employment of the virtues. This account makes some sense if the virtues are thought to be truth-conducive; if, however, one is aware that they are only justification-conducive, the account is self-evidently false, for it now claims that justification is a property arising out the employment of a characteristic which is conducive to the formation of that property. Unless 'conducive' here is read as "infallibly conducive" the account is false, and if we read the term in this way, the view is false for a different reason, for there are degrees of virtuosity.

Thus, consideration of the relationship between the unrestricted cognitive ideal and the restricted one applying to the human epistemic situation reveals a double inadequacy on the part of personal reliabilism. First, it is relevant to the circularity objection to which personal reliabilism is subject, for if a proper appreciation of the unrestricted cognitive ideal is achieved, the temptation toward personal reliabilism will be seen as a temptation in the wrong direction. Second, it reveals an inadequate construal of the notion of an intellectual virtue or excellence on which personal reliabilism depends. If one thinks of the virtues as truth-conducive (a natural construal when one considers the nature of the virtues of a being who satisfies the unrestricted cognitive ideal), then it is natural to think of cases in which such a characteristic is realized in forming a belief as resulting in a belief which is objectively likely to be true and hence justified. However, if we think of virtues as justification-conducive in some way (the account which fits better with an awareness of the differences between the epistemic situation of the divine being and the epistemic situation of human beings), there will be no special temptation arising out of the construal of the virtues for thinking that the realization of a virtue in the activity of believing results in a justified belief. Thus, it would seem that, once we clearly appreciate the relationship between the cognitive ideal for God and the cognitive ideal for humans, instancing the virtues is neither necessary nor sufficient for justification. Such characteristics are important in that they dispose us toward a desirable end, but what disposes one toward an end and what guarantees achieving that end are quite distinct.

2. THEISM AND PROCESS RELIABILISM

Personal reliabilism must therefore be abandoned, and so we turn to the other major kind of reliabilism—process reliabilism. Process reliabilism grounds the objective likelihood of a belief, not in the intellectual virtues or excellences of the individual in question, but rather in the "virtues" of the process or method by which the person formed the belief in question. Because of this difference, it is not susceptible to the charge that it is most analogous to a defective account of the unrestricted cognitive ideal, and therefore avoids the circularity charge which is generated for personal reliabilism because of its relationship to just such a defective account. Further, since process reliabilism grounds justification in the process or method by which a belief is formed or sustained, it is committed to no account of the intellectual virtues and thus is not committed to the inadequate truth-conducive account of the virtues.

Yet, it might seem that, once we see the problem with a truth-conducive account of the intellectual virtues, we have found a source for an objection to process reliabilism as well. For the difficulty with a truth-conducive account of the intellectual virtues centers on the fact that a failure to find the truth can be owing to an epistemically hostile environment rather than to defective equipment, and it would seem to be true as well that the "virtues" that a process or method might have could be undermined in much the same way. Namely, a process or method could be completely adequate for generating justifications for beliefs and yet exist and operate in such an epistemically hostile environment that it is not truth-conducive and hence does not make the beliefs which it justifies objectively likely to be true. An evil demon world is just a maximal version of such an epistemically hostile environment, and it is one in which, for example, perceptual processes almost always mislead. Hence, it might seem, the very same considerations which undermined personal reliabilism undermine process reliabilism as well.

There are some attempts which can be made to respond to this objection. A first attempt is to ignore evil demon worlds by claiming that the theory being offered is one intended to apply only to the actual world.[9] The difficulty with this response, construed as an attempt to solve evil demon world objections, is that it misses the point of alternative world considerations. If alternative world considerations were only ruminations about distant peoples in distant lands, it would be appropriate to respond that we are not attempting to give an account which applies to them. But this misconceives what a possible world is and how possible world considerations are to be taken. A possible world, for present purposes, is just a way the actual world might have been, and the point of possible world considerations is that the world in question might be this one.[10] The point is that, unless we can definitively fix the character of the world we are presently in, it will be of no epistemological value to give an account of justification which applies only to the actual world. If the actual world is as we believe it to be, the account perhaps would be acceptable; if however it is not—if, for example, it is a demon world—the account is clearly not acceptable, for it would then imply that we have almost no justified beliefs, and that claim is false.

Another attempt to overcome the problem of evil demon worlds denies that such worlds are possible worlds. In this endeavor, one may appeal to Davidsonian semantic conservatism: that, in order for the ascription of beliefs to a person to be possible, most of those beliefs must be true.[11] Even if some such argument is successful so that it is concluded that evil demon worlds are not possible worlds, problems will still remain. For such a response only addresses a small portion of those epistemically hostile environments which plague reliabilist views in general; in particular, such a response only deals with maximally hostile environments. Perhaps there is no such maximum in the arena in question, just as there is no largest number. However, that only eliminates the threat coming from the tip of the iceberg, for the substance of the objection remains intact. Instead of describing globally hostile environments, as is purportedly found in the demon worlds, the objector can describe locally hostile environments: environments which are hostile to the particular process or method employed (in the particular kind of circumstances in question): perhaps the demon only undermines perceptual beliefs of a certain kind, or only memorial beliefs about close relatives, for example. Notice that in order to escape such possibilities, processes will have to be individuated according to an appropriate environment of operation in such a way that it is simply impossible for such a process to fail to produce mostly true beliefs. Clearly, such a requirement on process individuation is overwhelming, and it would seem that process reliabilists would be better off seeking a different way around the objection.

Another way to respond to this objection is to build epistemic friendliness of environment into the process reliabilist account (without, of course, making the resulting account circular). Goldman attempts to do this through the concept of a normal world. The rough contours of his account are as follows: a belief is justified just in case it is produced by a belief-producing mechanism which is reliable in normal worlds. A world is normal just in case it is one which accords with our general beliefs about the world. For the moment at least, let us assume that our general beliefs about the world imply that it is an epistemically friendly environment,[12] i.e., that it is such that getting to the truth is the ordinary achievement when our cognitive equipment is employed.

One should note the virtues of this account before criticizing it, and this account has one essential virtue. One quite trivial version of process reliabilism claims that a justified belief is one formed by a process which is reliable in environments which are epistemically friendly to that process, i.e., environments in which the process in question is adequate for finding the truth and avoiding error. Of course, it is analytically true that any process is truth-conducive in an environment which is so related to that process; thus, the challenge for the process reliabilist is to present an account which implies epistemic friendliness without making this implication an analytic one. Goldman's account succeeds where the above account fails, for Goldman's account involves a clarification of the concept of a normal world which allows it to be a substantive claim that a process is reliable in an epistemically friendly environment.

The appeal to a normal world is inadequate in spite of its virtues. We need not know much about how our beliefs are formed for them to be justified, and the appeal to a normal world violates this truth. It is possible that some of our beliefs are formed by processes regarding which we are entirely ignorant: none of our general beliefs imply anything at all about the reliability of the particular process in question in our world. It will be compatible with the operation of such a process that it produce mostly false beliefs in a normal world, and it will be compatible with the operation of such a process that it produce mostly true beliefs in a normal world. If so, however, there will be normal worlds in which the process is truth-conducive and normal worlds in which it is not. It is therefore indeterminate, on Goldman's account, whether beliefs formed by such a process are justified. Just as clearly, should the process turn out to be actually reliable, anyone inclined toward reliabilism should not want to rule out the possibility of the operation of such a process producing justification for the beliefs which result.

Thus, employing the concept of a normal world to specify a relevant environment for determining reliability will not work. The difficulty is that there is a contingent connection at best between what we believe our world to be like and the fact that it is epistemically friendly. The contingency of the connection shows up most clearly when considering the possibility of belief-forming processes unknown to us at present. What is needed, instead, is a specification of an environment in which to determine the reliability of a belief-forming process or method which necessarily implies, though not analytically so, that the environment in question is a friendly one.

One might think a theist has a manuever unavailable to non-theists, given that God's purposes in creating persons includes anything linked to our finding the truth and avoiding error. For example, it is plausible to hold that God intends us to image his nature, and if so, it is plausible to think that part of imaging his nature involves finding the truth and avoiding error. If such a plan exists, then there will be a link between certain kinds of cognitive equipment and particular types of environments in the plan of God so that the following kind of reliabilist theory could be developed: a belief is justified just in case it would be reliable were it formed by the process or method in question in a world God might create.[13] Here it may appear that we have the specification of an environment appropriate to the evaluation of the reliability of processes and methods which implies, though not analytically so, that those environments are epistemically friendly, for it may appear to be a necessary truth on this account that an environment is epistemically friendly to certain cognitive equipment just in case God might create beings with that equipment in that environment.

Appearances are deceiving here, however, for even if God's intentions in creating include that persons image his nature, it is far from obvious that his intentions *must* include this feature. Further, unless his intentions must include this feature, we will not have any necessary implication from environments in which God creates to environments which are epistemically friendly, and thus what appeared to be an advantage for theistically inclined reliabilists is in fact not an advantage.

Suppose, though, that a theistically inclined reliabilist attempts to build God's actual purposes into the account. Now, one cannot simply say that a belief is justified just in case it is produced by equipment in an environment such that God might, given his actual purposes, create beings with that equipment in that environment. This account suffers from the same defect that undermines attempts to avoid evil demon world objections to reliabilism by claiming that one's account applies only to the actual world. In both cases, the fact that we are fallible human beings implies that we have no guarantee as to what the actual world or the actual purposes of God are, and the account of justification is jeopardized by this fact. But the theistic reliabilist has an advantage over the nontheistic reliabilist for he can specify how God's intentions are to be construed; he can offer an account of justification analogous to the defective one above. He might claim that a belief is justified just in case it is produced by equipment in an environment such that God might, for the purpose of having a creation which images his nature, create beings with that equipment in that environment.

One sticky point for such a view is whether some specification of the notion of imaging God's nature can be given which implies, though not analytically so, that imaging God's nature involves coming to find the truth and avoid error. It is not at all obvious that this can be done; in fact, there seem to be obvious counterexamples to it. Suppose God creates a world in which persons become completely morally good and virtuous. Clearly, such beings image God's nature. Perhaps though the theorist will insist that such beings do not fully image God's nature. Well, that would seem to require persons becoming omniscient, omnipotent, and omnipresent in addition to becoming completely morally good and virtuous.

Is there an intermediate position between these two which has just the desired implications? The answer to this question hinges on how a theistic reliabilist is to account for the possibility of error. There are two routes that can be taken here. The first is to cite the possibility of conflict among the purposes of God for humans; the second is to hold that some uses of our cognitive equipment are outside the purview of God's intentions; the last is that error is within the purview of God's intentions. This last alternative reduces to the first, for if God intends us to be in error, it must be to satisfy some more important purpose than finding the truth. So, we are left with two possible explanations of error.

Let us consider the second explanation first, the one on which God's intentions regarding the use of our cognitive equipment are held not to be universal in scope; in particular, it is held that his purposes extend to no cases in which false beliefs are formed. One way to maintain this thesis is to hold with Descartes that error is the result of the inappropriate use of our freedom. This explanation, though, is not especially attractive, for the domain of belief, even if within our indirect control, is not susceptible enough to our will to explain every case of false belief in terms of the inappropriate use of freedom. Further, there seems to be an in principle objection to restricting the scope of God's intentions in this way. For God could not be unaware of how any cognitive equipment would operate in any environment; and if he knew that error would be the result in certain areas, had other alternatives which would not achieve error, and yet created the equipment which allows for error, it is not plausible to hold that the error-producing capacity was outside the purview of the divine purposes.

This consideration leads naturally back to the first alternative, the one on which error is the result of conflict between an interest in the truth and more important practical (or other) interests. But this explanation is inadequate in two respects. The first is that when such conflict is experienced regarding the formation of a particular belief, the fact that God's purposes are satisfied implies that the belief is justified on the theory in question. Yet, that implication is unfortunate; when interests other than the truth infect and dominate the formation of a belief, the belief may be pragmatically justified or warranted for practical purposes, but it is not epistemically justified. The second reason the explanation of error is inadequate is that many cases of error seem incapable of explanation in the desired fashion. Cases of hallucination, for example, seem to be cases which do not contribute to some greater purpose for human beings.

What other ways a theistic reliabilist might attempt are unclear; thus, a fair conclusion is that the problem of individuation is as severe for theistic as for nontheistic reliabilism, and so a theistic reliabilist has no advantage in solving the problems facing reliabilism. I conclude that there is no obvious way to offer a reliabilist account on which reliability is specified relative to an environment which is epistemically friendly which does not trivialize the account of justification or render it obviously false.

There is, however, one other response available to the reliabilist to deal with the problem of epistemically hostile environments. That way is to insist that there is more than one sense of the notion of epistemic justification, and hold that in the sense reliabilism intends to clarify, beliefs are not justified in epistemically hostile environments. An assumption we have made to this point is that beliefs are justified in such environments, and the motivation for this assumption would seem to be something like the following principle: if two persons are in the same "seeming-states" and have the same background beliefs and awarenesses, then the first person's belief that p is justified if and only if the second person's belief that p is justified. This principle is obviously an *internalist* principle, for it claims that only what is "in the head" of the individual is relevant to the justificatory status of belief. In particular, what factors exist in the external environment — including the degree of epistemic hostility it displays — is irrelevant to whether a belief is justified. Now, a reliabilist might insist that there are at least two senses of the notion of justification, one internalist in nature and a different one externalist in certain ways. In particular, she might claim that when the environment is hostile, this external factor undermines the possibility of justification obtaining, when one is thinking of this more externalistic kind of justification. What goes wrong with evil demon world objections, then, is that a conflation occurs between the internalist's sense of justification and that sense which reliabilism intends to clarify.

Such a response succeeds in preserving reliabilism in the face of evil demon world objections, but when facing the more general problem of epistemically hostile environments, such a response again trivializes reliabilism. An epistemically hostile environment is one in which our cognitive equipment is not likely to get us to the truth. Now, if a reliabilist claims to be explicating that notion of justification only for beliefs formed in environments which are not epistemically hostile, the theory begins to look trivial: it claims that a belief is justified in the truth-conducive sense of justification just in case it is formed or sustained in some truth-conducive manner or other.

This point can be put in another way. Perhaps there is a sense of justification on which the inhabitants of evil demon worlds have few justified beliefs. Even if this is so, it is quite another thing to claim that there is a sense of justification on which no beliefs formed in epistemically hostile environments are justified. And, in particular, it will not do first to develop a theory of justification on which only beliefs objectively likely to be true (read: "formed in environments which are epistemically friendly") are justified, and then in the face of counterexamples to the theory, claim that one is only offering this theory as a theory of that sort of justification which cannot obtain for beliefs formed in epistemically hostile environments (read: "beliefs which are not objectively likely to be true").

So, even if there are a multitude of senses of justification, it is not clear that this fact can absolve reliabilism of the problem of epistemically hostile environments; and it may begin to appear that process reliabilism succumbs with personal reliabilism in the face of facts about epistemically hostile environments. I wish to argue that this appearance is deceiving, too. I want to suggest that the reliabilist can take a lesson here from Descartes and thereby preserve the truth of reliabilism, though in a somewhat qualified form.

Descartes holds that knowledge obtains when and only when a candidate for knowledge is produced by the faculty of clear and distinct perception, and, if his arguments are sound, he is entitled to hold that this account of knowledge is necessarily true and not just contingently true. Yet, if there were no God, this account of knowledge would be in jeopardy, for Descartes employs the fact of the existence of God to argue for the adequacy of the above account of knowledge: since God exists and is not a deceiver, whatever we clearly and distinctly perceive to be the case must be so. In accord with this view, Descartes holds that error is not to be attributed to any inadequacy of our cognitive equipment, but rather to the fact that our will can operate in domains our understanding has not reached.

A contemporary reliabilist need not have quite so high an opinion of our cognitive equipment, for we, unlike Descartes, appreciate how fallibility is endemic to the epistemic life, even when knowledge is achieved. The lesson to be learned from Descartes concerns, not the quality of our equipment, but the way in which a general account of knowledge is to be defended. In particular, Descartes does not appeal to the general account of knowledge given above in defending the existence of God; or, at the very least, it would be best for methodological purposes if he did not. Instead, Descartes can speak of inference patterns which preserve metaphysical certainty, and generate a proof for the existence of God from an account of knowledge on which any inference pattern preserving metaphysical certainty can yield knowledge if the resulting belief is based on an awareness of the virtuous nature of the inference pattern. Of course, this manner of defending the general account of knowledge in terms of the faculty of clear and distinct perception implies that there is a more fundamental account of knowledge than the one being defended, but that does not bar the account from being true. As long as the arguments are sound, it will have been shown that knowledge is necessarily the product of clear and distinct perception.

Reliabilism can be defended in a similar fashion. If one can show that God exists and essentially is not a deceiver, then one can defend reliabilism by arguing that a nondeceptive God would not allow the coincidence of cognitive equipment with environments which are epistemically hostile to it. Of course, such a defense bars reliabilism from being the fundamental theory of justification, but if the arguments are sound, they will show that reliabilism is nonetheless true. Reliabilism is no longer the fundamental theory of justification here, because there is no attempt to suggest that the elements by which we become epistemically entitled to believe the proposition: 'God is nondeceptive and would not, even could not, allow the coincidence of equipment with environments which consistently frustrate attemps to find the truth', are elements described by an adequate version of reliabilism. The way in which these beliefs become part of the corpus of beliefs from which further inferences may be drawn is quite distinct from reliabilism; but if these beliefs count as knowledge (the showing of which is the aim of the Cartesian defense of reliabilism), then reliabilism is true, indeed, even necessarily true.

3. CONCLUSION

Thus, the lesson of epistemically hostile environments is not so much that reliabilism is false, but only that it cannot be a fundamental theory of justification. The problem with the inadequate attempts to escape the problem of epistemically hostile environments canvassed above is that they implicitly attempt to preserve reliabilism as a fundamental theory of justification. Once this implicit assumption is abandoned, a solution to the problem of epistemically hostile environments is in view. The lesson of such hostile environments, then, is this: if one wants to be a reliabilist, be a theist.

NOTES

1. A paradigm example of a personal reliabilist is Ernest Sosa. See, for example, "The Raft and the Pyramid: Foundationalist versus Coherence Theories of Justification," *Midwest Studies in Philosophy* 5. A paradigm example of a process reliabilist is Alvin Goldman. The most complete expression of his views is contained in *Epistemology and Cognition* (Cambridge, Mass., 1986).

2. See, for example, Richard Foley, *The Theory of Epistemic Rationality* (Cambridge, Mass., 1986).

3. See, for example, John Pollock, *Contemporary Theories of Knowledge* (Totowa, N.J., 1986).

4. See, for example, Keith Lehrer, *Knowledge* (Oxford, 1977).

5. This position about construal of 'justification' has come to be associated with the title of Bayesian epistemology. For an example, see Henry E. Kyburg, Jr., *Probability and Inductive Logic* (London, 1970).

6. The concept of coherence here is a somewhat technical one. For a concept to be coherent, it is not necessary that it is possibly exemplified. Instead, all that is required is that the concept be such that the claim that the concept is exemplified, the proper analysis of the concept in question, plus the axioms of quantification theory (second-order will do for present purposes) yield no contradiction. When a concept is coherent, we might say it is logically possible that it is exemplified, where a logical possibility need not be a metaphysical possibility. The two can diverge if there are other metaphysical possibilities, which, in conjunction with the information which accounts for the coherence of a concept, imply that the concept metaphysically could not be exemplified.

7. For a defense of this view, see Charles Taliaferro, "Divine Cognitive Power," *International Journal for Philosophy of Religion* 18 (1985), 133–40.

8. I explore some of these ways in "How to Be a Reliabilist," *American Philosophical Quarterly* 23, no. 2 (1986), 189–98.

9. See, for example, Alvin Goldman, "What Is Justified Belief?" *Knowledge and Justification,* ed. George Pappas (Boston, 1981), p. 17; William P. Alston, "Epistemic Circularity," *Philosophy and Phenomenological Research* 47, no. 1 (1986), 2.

10. Of course, we shall have to read the two 'might's here differently; the first is the 'might' of logical possibility and the second is the 'might' of

what we cannot infallibly rule out. This fact is irrelevant to the argur,
however.

11. See Donald Davidson, "Thought and Talk," in *Mind & Langua*,
ed. Samuel Guttenplan (Oxford, 1975), pp. 20–21.

12. If Goldman's account lacks this implication, the account will fai
to meet the objection. For if our general beliefs fail to imply that our environment is epistemically friendly, then there will be no reason to think it true that
the processes in question are reliable in normal worlds. After all, if the implication were lacking, there would be normal worlds where any particular
process is reliable and normal worlds where it is not; and we have no reason,
given Goldman's account, to choose one such world or group of worlds over
any other.

13. There are deep similarities between this attempt at avoiding the problem of epistemically hostile environments and Plantinga's design theory of justification. See his "Epistemic Justification," *Noûs* 20, no. 1 (1986), 3–18 and
his "Justification and Theism," in the present volume.

A Theistic Conception of Probability

RICHARD OTTE

Our modern probability calculus was developed in the seventeenth century by thinkers such as Pascal. But although there was one probability calculus, there were two dominant interpretations of what probability was. On one view probability was an aleatory notion. Probability was a statistical concept and was used for the purposes of life insurance and annuities. The other major position considered probability to be an epistemological concept. According to this view, probability was a measure of rational degree of belief and was useful for the purposes of decision theory and wagering in games of chance. Both of these interpretations of probability shared a common probability calculus, and both of them were called "probability." These two basic interpretations of probability have survived the test of time and are still the primary ways of interpreting probability. Although these original interpretations of probability have evolved, and new ones have been developed, the distinction between aleatory and epistemological interpretations of probability is still useful.

The first epistemological interpretation of probability was the classical interpretation. According to this view, which was promoted by Laplace, epistemic probability is the ratio of favorable to equally possible cases. Due to difficulties this interpretation faced, it became less popular and was eventually replaced by more sophisticated epistemological interpretations. Logical theories grew out of the classical theory and retained a modification of the central idea of the classical interpretation. The logical interpretation, as developed by Harold Jeffreys, J. M. Keynes, and Rudolf Carnap, construed epistemic probability as a logical relation. The amount of support a hypothesis received from some evidence was logically related to the hypothesis and the evidence. It was believed that the rational degree of belief in a hypothesis on the basis of some evidence should be equal to the logical probability of the hypothesis given the total available evidence. One serious problem with this interpretation has been finding a logical relation which can plausibly be thought to be epistemic probability. Although it is not difficult to find a logical relation which satisfies the probability calculus, a logical relation that can be equated with rational degrees of belief has proven much more elusive. For example, upon Carnap's logical theory all universal generalizations receive probability 0, and all existential statements receive probability 1. But surely these logical probabilities cannot be identified with rational degrees of belief. As a result, many philosophers have adopted subjective theories of epistemic probability.

According to the interpretation of probability developed by F. P. Ramsey and B. de Finetti, epistemic probability is to be explicated in terms of an individual's degrees of belief. A person's degrees of belief constitute that person's subjective probability function. However, we are interested in *rational* degrees of belief, and not all subjective probability functions are rational, because people have irrational systems of beliefs. A necessary condition for a person's degrees of belief to be rational is that they be internally consistent. Many subjectivists claim that internal consistency is also a sufficient condition of rationality. A set of degrees of belief are considered to be internally consistent if and only if they are coherent, which means that they satisfy the probability calculus. Thus epistemic probability is a measure of an individual's coherent degrees of belief. This interpretation of probability has been called 'personal probability' by L. J. Savage, although many philosophers refer to it as 'Bayesianism'.[1]

Bayesianism faces difficulties because it does not appear that the constraint of coherence which is placed upon degrees of belief is adequate to characterize rational degrees of belief. The requirement that rational degrees of belief satisfy the probability calculus is both too strong and too weak. There are rational sets of beliefs which do not satisfy the probability calculus as well as sets of belief that satisfy the probability calculus but which are irrational. For example, the probability calculus requires that every necessary proposition have probability 1. This implies that all mathematical truths, which are necessary, receive probability 1. But it is rational for a human to believe true mathematical propositions to a degree less than 1; hence some rational degrees of belief do not satisfy the probability calculus. Furthermore, it would be irrational for any human to believe all necessarily true propositions to degree 1. For example, Goldbach's conjecture is either necessarily true or necessarily false. If it is necessarily true, it would be incoherent to believe it to any degree other than 1. And if it is necessarily false, coherence requires it be believed to degree 0. But we would consider it irrational for a person to believe Goldbach's conjecture to degree 1 or 0. Hence subjective probability functions which satisfy the probability calculus are irrational. Bayesianism is a normative interpretation of epistemological probability in the sense that it attempts to characterize *rational* degrees of belief. However, the requirement of coherence does not characterize rational degrees of belief. Thus we still lack anything like a deep understanding of epistemic probability.

Historically there have been close connections between epistemic probability and theism. The first application of probability to decision theoretical contexts other than games of chance was Pascal's wager. Teleological arguments are often stated in probabilistic terms, and more recent discussions of the rationality of belief in God have relied on probabilistic confirmation theory. However, even though theists have been quick to employ the concept of probability in their reasoning, they have had very little to say about probability itself. Theists have usually adopted some currently popular interpretation of probability for use in their arguments. A good example of this is Thomas Reid. Reid's discussion of "the probability of chances" is a typical discussion in terms of the classical interpretation of probability.[2] This is unfortunate since the doctrines of theism are rich enough to support a radically different view of epistemic probability.

In this paper I will investigate how a theist might view epistemic probability. I will then show that a certain conception of probability naturally follows from ideas central to theism, and explain how this theistic conception of epistemic probability is quite different from the other traditional epistemological interpretations of probability. Finally, I will argue that this theistic conception of probability avoids many of the problems besetting the other interpretations of probability.

THEISTIC CONSIDERATIONS ON RATIONALITY

Since epistemic probability is concerned with rational degrees of belief, the theistic doctrines relevant to epistemic probability will be those connected with the formation of rational beliefs. One relevant theistic doctrine is that humans are created in the image of God. God is a being that has knowledge, and humans were created with the capacity for knowledge and the ability to know certain propositions. Furthermore, human beings were placed in an environment in which it is possible for them to have knowledge and rational beliefs. Just as the environment we live in was designed to be habitable by creatures with bodies such as ourselves, our cognitive faculties and the environment were designed in such a way that humans can have rational beliefs and knowledge about this environment. This is not a necessary situation, because it is possible that our cognitive faculties and the environment could have been unsuited for each other. Those irreconcilable differences might have prevented us from obtaining knowledge about the environment. For example, there are possible environments in which humans would consistently produce false beliefs about the external world. Skeptics are fond of pointing out that these are possible environments. Or our senses might consistently give rise to conflicting beliefs, and we might be quite confused. However, according to theism, there is a compatability between our cognitive faculties and our environment. The cognitive faculties of human beings did not arise by chance, but were designed to function in such a way that knowledge would be produced. For example, our cognitive faculties may be designed in such a way that we form the belief that we see a tree when we are appeared to in a treely sort of way. In such a situation, our belief that a tree is present may be rational and count as knowledge, even though there is no good inductive or deductive argument from our experience to the existence of the tree. The belief is rational and counts as knowledge because our cognitive faculties were designed to produce that belief in those circumstances.

According to this theistic perspective, a person S's belief is rational if it is produced in S by cognitive faculties that are functioning properly.[3] However, our minds do not always operate in the way in which they were designed to function; there are such things as cognitive dysfunction and mental illness. In the *First Meditation*

Descartes gives examples of men who believe that their heads are made of clay, or that their bodies are made of glass. Our cognitive faculties can malfunction and fail to produce the beliefs they were designed to produce. In instances such as these the beliefs formed may not be rational beliefs. The crucial idea is that our minds and cognitive faculties have ways of functioning properly and ways of malfunctioning. Our beliefs are rational when our cognitive faculties function properly. We will say that a person with properly functioning cognitive faculties is a properly functioning cognizer. Two philosophers who have stressed this aspect of rationality are Thomas Reid and Alvin Plantinga. According to Reid, our minds are designed to produce certain beliefs in certain situations, and minds that fail to form those beliefs are defective (p. 565). Plantinga goes further and claims that epistemic warrant or justification is best thought of as the result of a properly functioning mind.[4] Both Reid and Plantinga connect rationality with a mind forming beliefs in the way it was designed to form beliefs.

In considering epistemic probability we are interested in rational degrees of belief. According to a theistic view of rationality, our minds are designed in such a way that in appropriate circumstances we will believe a given proposition to a certain, possibly vague, degree. In other words, a person with a properly functioning mind will have beliefs of varying degrees.[5] These degrees of belief provide the basis for a theistic conception of epistemic probability. This view of probability was vaguely anticipated by Reid. In his discussion of probabilistic reasoning, he claimed that "in most cases, we measure the degrees of evidence by the effect they have upon a *sound understanding,* when comprehended clearly and without prejudice" (p. 691, emphasis mine). It is these ideas about rational belief that will be developed into a theistic interpretation of probability.

PROBABILITY

The above considerations on rationality indicate that the epistemic probability of a proposition can be interpreted in terms of the degree to which a person with a properly functioning mind would believe the proposition. But, of course, the degree to which a person with a properly functioning mind would believe a proposition will be dependent upon the circumstances the person is in. For example, if my faculties are functioning properly and I am appeared to in a treely sort of way, I may believe that a tree is present. But if I am not being appeared to treely, I may not believe that a tree is present. One cannot legitimately speak of what a person with a properly functioning mind would believe without specifying the circumstances that the person is in. A proposition might be very believable relative to some circumstances and yet without warrant relative to other circumstances. Rationality is relative to a mind's epistemic situation. Accordingly, we will relativize epistemic probability to the circumstances that a person can be in. The circumstances are states of affairs that can include what situation the epistemic agent is in, as well as what he senses, remembers, and believes. For example, the state of affairs that the agent is appeared to treely, knows that $7 + 5 = 12$, and remembers having eggs for breakfast might be included in some sorts of circumstances. We will write $P_C(A)$ for the probability of A relative to circumstances C.

Although the above considerations about probability present the general picture of probability from a theistic perspective, much more detail is needed in order to have an adequate conception of probability. As a first approximation, let us define probability as follows:

> $P_C(A) = r$ iff r is the degree to which a person with a properly functioning mind would believe proposition A in circumstances C.

Although this is a useful first approximation of the analysis of probability we are developing, it requires modification in several directions. One immediate problem is that there may be no real number r such that r is the degree to which a person with properly functioning cognitive faculties would believe A in circumstances C. A person in circumstances C might have several different possible rational degrees of belief in a certain proposition. Rationality may also allow different properly functioning persons in the same circumstances to believe the same proposition to different degrees. In this case, there would be no single real number which is the degree to which all properly functioning cognizers would believe the proposition in the circumstances, but rather there would be a range of several rationally permissible degrees of belief. We need to modify

the above account of probability to allow different persons with properly functioning minds in the same circumstances to believe the same
proposition to different degrees, as well as allow a single individual
several possible rational degrees of belief. One way to do this is to
use an interval to represent rationally permissible degrees of belief:

> $P_C(A) = <x,y>$ iff $<x,y>$ is the smallest interval which con-
> tains all of the degrees to which a person with a properly func-
> tioning mind could believe proposition A in circumstances C.[6]

According to this account, epistemic probability is an interval which
includes all of the degrees to which a rational person could believe
the proposition. It does not require that a rational person in circumstances C have only one possible rational degree of belief in a
proposition, nor does it require that all rational people in the same
circumstances believe the proposition to the same degree.

One problem with this revised account of probability is that
it requires each individual with a properly functioning mind to believe the proposition in question to some precise degree, which is
represented by a real number. However, a properly functioning cognizer may not have precise degrees of belief in all propositions. Perhaps some rational degrees of belief are vague and cannot be represented by a single real number. For example, my degree of belief
that I can ski down Mt. Shasta without falling is vague. There is
no single real number which represents this probability, but rather
my degree of belief in that proposition falls within a certain range.
We can capture this idea by representing vague or uncertain degrees
of belief by intervals instead of real numbers.[7] Since different intervals may represent different properly functioning persons' vague degrees of belief, we let the probability of a proposition be the small-
est interval that includes all of those vague degrees of belief:

> $P_C(A) = <x,y>$ iff $<x,y>$ is the smallest interval which con-
> tains all of the intervals which represent the degree that a per-
> son with a properly functioning mind could believe proposi-
> tion A in circumstances C.

This analysis of probability allows for the possibility that properly
functioning cognizers may have vague degrees of belief. Of course,
it also allows them to have precise degrees of belief. A precise degree
of belief in a proposition equal to a real number r will be represented by the interval $<r,r>$.

In addition to the notion of probability simpliciter, the idea of conditional probability plays an important role in probability theory. The basic idea behind conditional probability is that belief in certain propositions can affect the probability of other propositions. For example, the epistemic probability of a randomly drawn card being a diamond is affected by knowledge that it is not a club. The probability of a card being a diamond is not equal to the probability of a card being a diamond conditional on it not being a club. The intuitive idea behind the epistemic conditional probability of A given B, written as $P_C(A/B)$, is that of how strongly A should be believed if B were fully believed. Upon our theistic conception of rationality, this intuitive conception of the conditional probability of A given B is interpreted in terms of how strongly a person with a properly functioning mind would believe A if he believed B. We can make this more precise as follows:

> $P_C(A/B) = <x,y>$ iff $<x,y>$ is the smallest interval which contains all of the intervals which represent the degree that a properly functioning cognizer could believe proposition A if he fully believed proposition B, in circumstances C.

According to this account, the notion of conditional probability is explicated subjunctively in terms of how strongly a person with a properly functioning mind who fully believed the information conditionalized on could believe the proposition in question. If it is impossible for a person with a properly functioning mind to believe the proposition conditionalized on, then the conditional probability is undefined.[8]

Although the above account of conditional probability is close to our intuitive understanding of conditional probability, it is quite different from traditional analyses of conditional probability. Most theories of epistemic probability define conditional probability as follows:

> $P(A/B) = P(A\&B) \div P(B).$

This definition of conditional probability has the advantage that conditional probability is defined in terms of unconditional probability without relying on additional counterfactual elements. But this advantage is illusory. One problem that immediately arises is that this definition depends upon probability being a real number and not an interval. Although it may be possible to modify this definition to account for probabilities that are intervals, it is not obvious that this definition or any modifications of it account for our intuitive understanding of conditional probability. The traditional account defines conditional probability in terms of the probability of a conjunction. But we are usually more certain about the conditional probability of one proposition on another than we are about the probability of the conjunction of those two propositions. I intuitively know what the probability of passing a test conditional on not studying is, but I am less certain about the probability of passing the test and not studying. Since we are usually clearer about conditional probability than we are about the probability of conjunctions, it is a mistake to analyze conditional probability in terms of the probability of conjunctions. Another problem is that the traditional proposal reduces the analysis of conditional probability to that of the probability of conjunctions, but no independent analysis of the probability of conjunction is given. The probability of conjunctions is usually defined in terms of conditional probability. Our analysis is to be preferred because it gives an independent analysis of conditional probability.[9] Conditional probability and the probability of conjunctions may be related in the manner described by the traditional analysis, but this should be used to give an analysis of the probability of conjunctions in terms of conditional probability instead of the other way around. However, the traditional analysis of conditional probability may be adequate for statistical probability, for which we can give an independent account of the probability of conjunctions. But statistical probability and epistemic probability are quite different, and we have good reason to think that an adequate analysis of conditional probability will be different for the two of them.

I believe that the above account of epistemic probability is basically correct, but perhaps we can test it by considering some problems. These problems deal with what all persons with properly functioning minds would believe, or with what certain specific properly functioning cognizers would believe. Consider the probabilities of the following, relative to some circumstances C:

(a) B is true but S doesn't believe it
(b) at least one person believes B, conditional on B is true[10]
(c) at least one mind exists.

The problem with (a) is that it does not appear possible for person S to believe it to a high degree. It may not be possible for person S to believe both B and that person S does not believe B. Therefore the lower bound of the interval for the probability of (a) will be very low, regardless of what proposition B is. This is problematic, because there do appear to be circumstances in which (a) is probably true and the lower bound of the interval is not low. It may be irrational for someone to have a low degree of belief in (a). The solution to this problem is to pay close attention to what the circumstances are. The circumstances C may include the state of affairs of being person S. If so, then the probability of (a) would be low, and it would be false to say that a person with a properly functioning mind in those circumstances could believe it strongly. It is rational for person S in those circumstances to have a low degree of belief in (a). Now suppose the circumstances C include the state of affairs of not being person S. In this case we have no reason to think that it will be rational to have a low degree of belief in (a), and the circumstances may be such that it would be irrational to have a low degree of belief in (a). If the circumstances are general enough to permit the person to either be person S or not be person S, then the range of rational degrees of belief in (a) may vary from very low to very high. But this is the correct result in this example. In those circumstances it is rational for person S to believe (a) to a low degree and it may be rational for some other person to believe (a) to a high degree. Since probability is degree of rational belief, the probability of (a) must allow both person S and others to be rational. The only way this is possible is for the interval to be large enough to contain everyone's rational degrees of belief in (a).[11] Thus the circumstances C is very important to what the probability of (a) is.

The considerations raised by (b) and (c) indicate that upon the theory of epistemic probability presented here some propositions are very probable, even though they may be neither necessary nor likely to be true in the statistical sense. I believe that a person with a properly functioning mind would believe that she exists, and thus the epistemic probability of (c) would be very close to $<1,1>$. (b) is also very probable upon this theory, because any person with a properly functioning mind that fully believes R will also believe that at least one person believes R. Hence its probability will also be very high, if not $<1,1>$. Although these results may appear strange, I do not think they are evidence against the theory presented here. We are dealing with rational belief, and it is well known that necessary truth and what can or cannot be believed do not coincide. For example, some philosophers have claimed that the proposition expressed by the sentence 'I do not exist' cannot be rationally believed, even though it is not necessarily false. For similar reasons, it may be that some propositions must be strongly believed, if believed at all, even though they may be very improbable in the statistical sense. Hence I do not find propositions (b) and (c) to be problematic for this theory.

COMPARISON WITH OTHER THEORIES

The theory of epistemic probability presented above is similar to other theories of probability in some respects, but in many ways it is quite different. One obvious difference is that upon this view probability if relativized to a set of circumstances. On this view, in contrast to Bayesianism or logical theories, probability is relativized to the person's epistemic situation. Both Bayesianism and logical theories allow for probability conditional on other propositions, but neither allow for probability relativized to a person's experiences and epistemic situation. This is significant because even if we assume that a person's epistemic situation can be adequately described by a proposition, it is possible that a proposition is highly probable given a certain set of circumstances, and yet is not highly probable conditional only on a proposition describing those circumstances. It may be rational to form certain beliefs in certain epistemic situations whereas believing a proposition describing that epistemic situation does not provide enough support for the beliefs to be rationally formed.[12] This is especially true given a theistic framework. Our minds may be designed to function in such a way that we form the belief in question when we have a certain experience; we may not be designed to form the belief just on the basis of believing we have the experience. A proposition may receive more epistemic support from certain circumstances than from believing a proposition describing those circumstances. Thus it is necessary to relativize probability to a set of circumstances in order to adequately characterize rational degree of belief.

To illustrate the problems that arise for the logical and subjective theories, consider a simple perceptual belief. Suppose a person is in the circumstances of being appeared to in a treely sort of way and forms the belief that a tree is present. Neither the logical nor subjective theories of probability are relativized to a person's epistemic situation; therefore the rationality of believing that a tree is nearby is dependent upon a belief describing the person's experience of the tree. For this reason there are serious problems that the logical and personal theories face in connection with this example. According to the logical theory, the probability of a tree being present given a person's experience of seeing the tree will depend on the degree to which a proposition describing the person's experience partially entails that the tree exists. But there is no reason to think that this degree of partial entailment is high. The history of philosophy teaches us that we have no reason to believe that a description of my experience entails or partially entails that the external world exists. One might attempt to argue that the ratio of possible worlds in which people have tree experiences and trees exist to the worlds in which people have tree experiences is high. However, I see no reason to be optimistic about the success of such an argument. Hence, according to the logical theory we have no reason to believe that the person should have a high degree of belief that a tree exists given a description of his or her experiences.

The situation is not any better for the subjective theories. According to Bayesianism, the probability of the tree existing given the description of the experience could be infinitesimally low or extremely high. Since it is a subjective theory, wildly different degrees of belief are tolerated as being rational. I find this counterintuitive. In the absence of overriding considerations it is rational for the person looking at the tree to believe that a tree is present, and it is irrational to disbelieve that the tree is present. Neither personal probability nor the logical theory can account for what we consider to be a rational degree of belief in this example, but the theory based upon proper functioning appears to give the correct answers.

There are further problems that any theory which avoids relativizing probability to a set of circumstances by conditionalizing on a proposition describing those circumstances will face. Suppose our epistemic agent takes a philosophy class and becomes convinced that a malicious demon deceives us on our perceptual beliefs about trees.

She also believes that this demon is so competent at deceiving us that we are deceived when and only when we firmly believe that we are appeared to in a treely sort of way. That is, the demon does not deceive us if we just look at a tree and believe a tree is there; we are deceived only when we form the strong belief that we are appeared to treely. Hence she believes the following proposition:

Q: If I firmly believe that I am appeared to treely, then a tree is not present (I am deceived).

Now suppose that our epistemic agent looks at a tree and is appeared to in a treely sort of way. We are interested in the probability of a tree being present in those circumstances. Since believing proposition Q is part of the epistemic situation, it will be included in the set of circumstances C. Assuming there are no other abnormal features about the epistemic situation, I propose that P_C(a tree is present) is fairly high. Our epistemic agent naturally forms the belief that a tree is present without forming any beliefs about how she is appeared to. In particular, she does not firmly believe that she is appeared to treely. Thus her belief in Q does not provide a reason to disbelieve that a tree is present. Since she does not firmly believe she is appeared to treely, she has no reason to think that the demon is deceiving her about the presence of the tree. In those circumstances it is rational to believe strongly that a tree is present, which is consistent with the analysis of probability based on proper functioning.

Now suppose that we attempt to avoid relativizing probability to a set of circumstances by conditionalizing on a proposition describing those circumstances. According to these theories, we are interested in P(a tree is present / description of circumstances C). For our purposes the relevant part of the circumstances is that the epistemic agent is appeared to treely and believes Q. Hence we are interested in P(a tree is present / I am appeared to treely and I believe that if I firmly believe I am appeared to treely, then a tree is not present). I propose that this probability is not high. If the epistemic agent fully believes the propositions conditionalized on, it would seem improper for her to strongly believe that a tree is present. Since she fully believes she is appeared to treely, she would believe that the demon was deceiving her; therefore she should not strongly believe that a tree is present. But this seems to be the wrong result for this example. In the example given, the epistemic agent does not form any beliefs about how she is appeared to. Hence it is rational for her to believe that a tree is present.[13]

The reason this proposal gives the wrong result is that it is telling us what it would be rational to believe in circumstances different from the one given in the example. It correctly claims that it is irrational to believe the tree is present if she fully believes she is being appeared to treely, but it is incorrect to claim it is irrational to believe the tree is present if she does not form that belief about how she is appeared to. Conditionalizing on propositions describing the epistemic situation instead of relativizing probability to the epistemic situation fails because it does not distinguish between two different epistemic situations. The epistemic situation of being appeared to treely and believing Q is very different from the epistemic situation of fully believing that one is being appeared to treely and believing Q. It is rational to believe a tree is present in the former epistemic situation, but not in the latter. The theory based on proper functioning is sensitive to these distinctions and gives the correct result because it relativizes probability to an epistemic situation. Simply conditionalizing on propositions describing those situations will give unintuitive results, because very different epistemic situations will not be distinguished.

Theories of rational belief can usefully be divided into two types: internalist and externalist theories. According to internalist theories of rationality, whether or not a belief is rational depends only upon the individual epistemic agent and not upon any factors external to the agent. Two prominent versions of this are Chisholmian and Cartesian internalism. According to these positions, whether a belief is rational is within the control of the epistemic agent. If the epistemic agent is responsible and fulfills all his intellectual obligations, then his beliefs are rational regardless of what the agent is unaware of or how the beliefs were formed. Rationality consists in how the epistemic data is used, and since that is within the control of the epistemic agent, rationality is also within the epistemic agent's control.

In contrast to internalism, externalism holds that factors outside the agent's control are relevant to the rationality of a belief. The rationality of a belief does not consist only in whether the agent applies correct epistemic principles to the data he or she had, but it may also depend upon factors that the epistemic agent is unaware of. According to externalism, a person could diligently and responsibly fulfill all intellectual obligations and still form an irrational belief, since not all the requirements for rationality are under our control. Clearly the theistic view of rationality based on proper functioning is an externalist theory. Other externalist theories base rationality on causal connections between a state of affairs and a belief, or upon reliable belief-producing mechanisms.

From an externalist point of view rationality is not dependent only upon what the epistemic agent believes, but also upon properties of the epistemic situation of which the agent may be unaware. Hence, even if our experiences and epistemic situation could be adequately described by a proposition, and even if a proposition received as much support from believing the proposition describing the experience as it does from the experience, it would still be necessary to relativize probability to the agent's epistemic situation. The reason for this is that some aspects of a person's epistemic situation cannot possibly be contained in the propositions that are conditionalized on. In particular, aspects of the person's epistemic situation that are not believed by the person cannot appropriately be included in the propositions conditionalized on. Epistemic conditional probability expresses rational degree of belief, given that the person believes the propositions conditionalized on. Because of the requirement that a person believe the information conditionalized on, aspects of the person's epistemic situation that the person does not believe to be true cannot be included in the information conditionalized on. In contrast to this, the relevant set of circumstances does not need to be known or even believed by the person. In the theory presented above, probability is conditional on the circumstances actually occurring, not upon the circumstances being known or believed to have occurred. Thus the set of circumstances can include aspects of the person's epistemic situation relevant to the proposition that are not believed by the person. For example, a person may be appeared to in a way that she is not conscious of; nonetheless, how she is appeared to may be relevant to some current belief of hers. Or she might be appeared to in a certain manner, but not form any beliefs about how she is appeared to. Upon theories of epistemic probability, in situations such as these no proposition describing how she is appeared to is conditionalized on in order to determine rational degrees of belief. This is simply because

the person does not believe she is appeared to in that manner. However, upon the theory of probability presented above, how the person is appeared to is relevant to rational belief because it is a relevant aspect of the person's epistemic situation. It is not required that
the person believe that she is appeared to in that way; what matters
is that how she is appeared to is a part of her epistemic situation.

   Consider the following example in which an epistemic agent
lacks certain beliefs about the epistemic situation. The agent is appeared to treely, and we are interested in the probability that a tree
is present conditional on the agent not being appeared to treely:

$P_{\text{appeared to treely}}$(a tree is present / not appeared to treely).

This probability depends upon what a person with a properly functioning mind would believe if he were appeared to treely, but fully
believed that he was not appeared to treely. I believe in some situations it would be reasonable for the person to believe rather strongly
that a tree is not present, because he fully believes that he is not
experiencing a tree. If we do not realize probability to the epistemic
situation and instead conditionalize on a proposition describing the
experience, we are interested in the following probability:

P(a tree is present / appeared to treely and not appeared to
treely).

This is problematic. It is undefined upon both the logical and personal theories of probability and thus those theories cannot account
for situations such as this. If we interpret probability as based upon
a properly functioning mind but not relativized to the epistemic situation, this may be defined. This interpretation of conditional probability assumes it is possible for a person with a properly functioning
mind to fully believe both that he is and is not appeared to treely.
If this is possible, then it is unclear what is rational to believe in
this situation. Certainly it is not clear that it is rational to strongly
disbelieve that a tree exists; thus this result is different from that of
the theory relativized to an epistemic situation. Attempting to capture all aspects of the epistemic situation in a proposition that is
conditionalized on does not give intuitively correct results in situations such as these.

   One might object that it is impossible for a person to both be
appeared to treely and fully believe that he is not being appeared

to treely. It might be thought that our beliefs about our experiences are incorrigible. More specifically, it might be claimed that a properly functioning cognizer's beliefs about his or her experiences are incorrigible. If so, the above problem would not arise for theories that do not relativize probability to an epistemic situation.

The response to this objection is to deny that beliefs about one's experience are incorrigible, even for a person with a properly functioning mind. Consider the following variation of J. L. Austin's example in which a person looks at a magenta colored object and yet believes it is vermilion. Perhaps the person was not paying attention to his visual field, but due to no defect in his mind he believes that the object is vermilion instead of magenta. We might wonder what the probability of a person making this mistake is. According to the theory based on proper functioning, we are interested in the following:

$P_{\text{object appears magenta}}$(object appears vermillion).

Since a person with a properly functioning mind could be mistaken about the color of the object, and even about how the object appears to him, this probability could be greater than 0.

Now suppose we look at this from the perspective of a traditional theory which does not conditionalize on the epistemic situation. According to these theories, we should conditionalize on a proposition describing the experience.[14] We would then be interested in the folowing probability:

P(object appears vermillion / object appears magenta)

This probability is equal to 0. According to the logical and subjective theories, the above probability is equal to:

$$\frac{P(\text{object appears vermilion \& object appears magenta})}{P(\text{object appears magenta})}$$

But an object cannot appear two different colors at once; thus P(object appears vermilion & object appears magenta) is equal to 0. From this it follows that the above conditional probability is equal to 0 on the logical and subjective interpretations. If we adopt the counterfactual definition of conditional probability presented above, but not relativized to an epistemic situation, then the above probability is still 0. If a person with a properly functioning mind fully believed the object appeared magenta, he would believe to degree zero that it appeared vermilion. Thus the above probability is 0 upon any theory that attempts to avoid relativizing probability to an epistemic situation by conditionalizing on propositions describing experience. It appears that a view of probability relativized to an epistemic situation accounts for these situations much more satisfactorily than alternative theories do.

Let us now consider other aspects of the conception of probability presented above. Like the logical theory, and unlike personal probability, the theory presented is an objective theory of probability. Even though probability is highly sensitive to what circumstances a person is in, it does not depend upon what particular person is in those circumstances.[15] Unlike the theory based upon proper functioning, subjective theories allow for the possibility that two different rational persons could be in the same circumstances, have exactly the same evidence, and yet assign wildly different probabilities to all contingent propositions. This is a problem for subjectivism because not all coherent probability assignments are rational. The rationality of a belief is not dependent upon the particular person holding that belief.

One difference between the logical theory of probability and personal probability is that personal probability is a normative theory and the logical theory can be thought of as a factual theory of probability. Personal probability is a normative theory because it does not simply tell us what people's degrees of belief are; it tells us what they should be. This separates personal probability from other theories of subjective probability which merely report a person's actual degrees of belief. The logical theory views probability as a logical relation; that part of the theory makes no normative claims about rational degrees of belief. It is a factual theory that defines partial entailment in terms of a logical relation. However, the logical theory is usually supplemented with a normative claim that rational degrees of belief should be equal to logical probabilities. The theory presented in this paper is also a normative theory. It makes claims about what our degrees of belief should be in order to be rational and it excludes many degrees of belief as being irrational. It does not merely report what people do believe, but it defines probability in terms of what they would believe if their minds were functioning properly.

Another major difference between the theory presented above and the traditional theories is that neither personal probability nor the logical theory makes reference to an agent in determining whether a belief or set of beliefs is rational. According to personal probability, beliefs are rational if they satisfy the probability calculus; no reference to an epistemic agent is needed. Of course the degrees of beliefs are beliefs of an agent, but whether they are rational or not has nothing to do with the agent; rationality is based upon coherence.[16] Similar considerations are true of logical theories. Probability on the logical theory is a logical relation and degrees of partial entailment are independent of any epistemic agent. Neither personal probability nor the logical theory requires reference to an epistemic agent in determining rational degrees of belief.

In contrast to the logical and personal theories of probability, the theory presented here provides an intimate connection between rational degrees of belief and an epistemic agent. Whether or not it is rational to believe certain propositions to certain degrees does not only depend upon the propositions and their relations to each other, but it also depends upon what a person with a properly functioning mind would believe. Rationality is not analyzed as being independent of an epistemic agent in a set of circumstances. One consequence of this is that probability is also relative to a certain species. From a theistic perspective it is plausible to believe that there are rational creatures other than humans and that their minds are designed to function quite differently from the way ours function. For example, it could be the case that all mathematical truths are self-evident to nondefective members of a different species. Perhaps this is true of angels. If this is so, the degree to which a properly functioning cognizer would believe mathematical propositions would depend upon what type of person it was. Certainly not all mathematical propositions are self-evident to properly functioning human cognizers, but they may be self-evident to properly functioning angels. Thus a mathematical proposition might have a very low probability relative to humans, but have a very high probability relative to some other species. It may also be the case that some conditional probabilities are defined for some species and undefined for other species. It may be impossible for humans to believe some propositions, but for angels it may be a simple matter to believe them. If so, certain conditional probabilities will be defined for angels that are undefined for humans. What it is rational for a person to believe depends upon the way his cognitive faculties were designed to function, and this may differ among species. Since probability is dependent upon what a properly functioning cognizer would believe, probability is species relative.

ASSESSMENT OF THE THEORY

I propose that the view of probability presented above is an improvement over traditional interpretations of epistemic probability. A theistic view of probability avoids many of the problems that face subjective and logical theories; further it does not appear to have any significant problems specific to it. However, in judging the adequacy of a certain interpretation of probability, we must make use of some criteria by which we can determine the advantages and disadvantages of it. W. C. Salmon has presented three criteria which he claims must be satisfied by any acceptable interpretation of probability.[17] In what follows we will investigate whether the theory of probability presented in this article satisfies Salmon's three criteria.

Salmon's first criterion is that of *admissibility*. This requires that probabilities satisfy the probability calculus. If an interpretation of probability does not satisfy the probability calculus, it is inadmissible and hence an unacceptable interpretation of probability. Both the personal and logical theories are admissible interpretations of probability because both guarantee that probabilities satisfy the probability calculus.

In contrast to the personal and logical theories, the theistic interpretation of probability does not guarantee that epistemic probabilities satisfy the probability calculus. Just representing probabilities by intervals instead of real numbers violates the calculus, since the probability calculus requires that probability be a real number. However there are more serious ways in which this interpretation violates the probability calculus. The probability calculus requires that every necessary proposition receive a probability of 1. Thus if the theory of probability presented here is to be admissible, it must require that a person with a properly functioning mind believe two things: (1) every necessary truth to degree 1; and (2) every logical consequence of a proposition at least as strongly as the original proposition. Perhaps this is a legitimate requirement for properly functioning cognizers of some other species, but it seems implausible to require that a properly functioning human believe every necessary truth to degree 1. There may be creatures who were designed to be logically omniscient and believe every necessary truth to degree 1, but that seems to be too strong a requirement for humans who are not logically omniscient. In defense of the criterion of admissibility many philosophers claim they are interested in ideal rationality. The relevance of this is not clear since this response concedes that humans are not logically omniscient and that it is unreasonable to require logical omniscience of a rational human. It is a mistake to require that human epistemic probabilities satisfy the probability calculus; therefore it does not count against the theory based upon proper functioning that it does not require rational degrees of belief to satisfy the calculus. The criterion of admissibility is not a legitimate criterion for human epistemic probability, although it may be a legitimate requirement for statistical probability.

Salmon's second criterion is that of *ascertainability*. An interpretation of probability satisfies this criterion if it is possible to determine the probability of propositions. The intuition Salmon is expressing with this requirement is that an interpretation of probability is useless if we cannot ordinarily know what the probability of a proposition is. One might object to the theory of probability presented here by claiming that we cannot know when a mind is functioning properly and hence we cannot have knowledge of probabilities.

The response to this objection claims that it is possible for us to know when a person's mind is functioning properly. One reason we claim that people are mentally ill is that we believe their minds are not working properly. Thomas Reid, who incorporated the idea of a properly functioning mind into his epistemology, also thought it was possible for us to know when a mind was working properly. According to Reid, disagreements about first principles, which are the dictates of common sense, are due to defects or prejudices in our minds (pp. 565–75). Fortunately we are able to recognize these defects and errors:

> Thus I have endeavoured to shew, that, although first principles are not capable of direct proof, yet differences, that may happen with regard to them among men of candour, are not without remedy; that

> Nature has not left us destitute of means by which we may discover errors of this kind; and that there are ways of reasoning, with regard to first principles, by which those that are truly such may be distinguished from vulgar errors or prejudices. (p. 575)

Of course, one can be a skeptic about probability just as as one can be a skeptic about anything else. However here, as elsewhere, we need not refute the skeptic's arguments in order to be within our rights in claiming knowledge of probabilities.

Salmon's third criterion for judging interpretations of probability is that of *applicability*. An interpretation of probability satisfies this criterion if it is useful in making rational decisions and in determining what to believe. An acceptable interpretation of probability should account for Bishop Butler's saying that "Probability is the very guide of life."[18] For example, personal probability is an unacceptable interpretation of probability because its subjectivity undermines any justification for using probability to make rational decisions or predictions. In order for the interpretation of probability based upon proper functioning to be acceptable it must be a useful guide to gaining knowledge and making decisions.

One might argue that we have no reason to think that a properly functioning mind can provide the basis for rational decisions. To illustrate, consider our goal to believe true propositions and not false ones. This objection questions our justification for thinking that a person with a properly functioning mind will believe true propositions more often than false ones or that such a person will make rational decisions more often than irrational ones. Perhaps our minds have been designed by a malicious Cartesian demon, and hence when functioning properly we will generally have false beliefs. A properly functioning mind could easily be a source of false beliefs.

Although this objection may be a serious problem for some theories which interpret probability in terms of a mind functioning properly, it clearly does not provide a reason for rejecting the theistic view of probability presented above. According to traditional theism, human cognitive faculties were designed in such a way that they would usually lead to true beliefs and not false ones. Reid expresses this by claiming that "the faculties which God has given us are not in their nature fallacious" (p. 565). More recently this idea has been stated by Plantinga:

In setting out to create human beings in his image, then, God set out to create them in such a way that they could reflect his capacity to grasp concepts and hold beliefs. Furthermore, he proposed to create them in such a way that they can reflect his ability to hold *true* beliefs. He therefore created us with cognitive faculties designed to enable us to achieve true beliefs with respect to a wide variety of propositions.[19]

This response to the objection claims that God wants humans to have true beliefs, and that he designed and created them in such a way that they would usually achieve this goal. Given this theistic perspective, it is reasonable to believe that a properly functioning mind would be a reliable foundation for decision making. It is this theistic framework that excludes the possibility of our minds being designed by a Cartesian demon and allows rational beliefs and decisions to be based upon what a person with a properly functioning mind would believe. Thus, this theistic view of probability satisfies the criterion of applicability. I believe it is the only interpretation of epistemic probability which satisfies both the criterion of ascertainability and of applicability.

One interesting result of the view of probability based on proper functioning is that it is relevant to probabilistic arguments presented for many philosophical positions. Since probability is a function of what a person with a properly functioning mind would believe, many claims about what a person with a properly functioning mind would believe can now be construed as implicit probability statements. For example, John Calvin thought that in the circumstances of observing the night sky, a properly functioning human would form beliefs about the magnificence of God. According to the theory presented above, Calvin's claim would imply that in those circumstances the epistemic probability of God existing is high. However, there is a big difference between claiming that in the circumstances of observing the night sky the probability of God existing is high, and claiming that the probability of God existing conditional on a proposition describing the night sky is high. Confusing these probabilities may account for the historical popularity of teleological arguments designed to show that the probability of God existing given our observation of order in the world is high. If the view of probability presented above is correct, the debate over the teleological argument is really a disagreement over what a properly functioning mind should believe.

In this paper we have investigated how a theist might view probability. Epistemological theories of probability interpret probability in terms of rational degree of belief, and we have seen that some doctrines of traditional theism are relevant to rationality. Therefore it is entirely natural for theists to have a view of probability that is significantly different from that found in other theories of epistemic probability. I hope this paper has demonstrated some of the advantages of looking at probability from a theistic perspective.[20]

NOTES

1. In addition to this subjective interpretation of probability, Bayesianism usually adds requirements about rational belief change.

2. Thomas Reid, *Essays on the Intellectual Powers of Man,* in *Philosophical Works,* with notes and supplementary dissertations by Sir William Hamilton (Hildesheim: Georg Olms Verlagsbuchhandlung, 1967), p. 695. All references to *Essays on the Intellectual Powers of Man* are to the edition of 1785, and will be denoted in the text by page numbers.

3. There are other theistic conceptions of rationality besides the one presented above. One might hold that rationality is connected with fulfilling intellectual obligations. Given this conception of rationality, a theist might have a unique perspective because of beliefs about the ontological status of those obligations and rules.

4. Alvin Plantinga, "Epistemic Justification," *Noûs* 20, no. 1 (March 1986), 15. and "Positive Epistemic Status and Proper Function" in *Topics in Philosophy,* vol. 2: *Epistemology,* ed. James Tomberlin (Northridge: California State University, 1988).

5. It is important to be clear about two fundamentally different possible interpretations of probability involving properly functioning minds. According to the position adopted in this paper, a properly functioning mind can produce degrees of belief as well as complete belief. Upon an alternative theory degrees of belief would be a measure of the degree to which a mind is functioning properly. These ways of viewing degrees of belief are not the same, and are fundamentally different. Upon one view a mind can be functioning properly without any improper functioning and yet produce degrees of belief. On the other view, when a mind is functioning properly with no amount of improper functioning, only instances of complete belief will be produced.

6. When I define $P_C(A)$ in terms of what a person with a properly functioning mind could believe, I do not mean that $P_C(A)$ is defined in terms

of what it is logically possible for a person with a properly functioning mind to believe. Instead, $P_C(A)$ is defined in terms of counterfactual situations in which a person with a properly functioning mind is in circumstances C. If one were to adopt the possible worlds analysis of counterfactuals, probability would be defined in terms of the closest possible worlds in which there is a person with a properly functioning mind in circumstances C.

7. Recently it has become popular to use sets of probability functions instead of intervals to represents vague degrees of belief. One disadvantage of this method is that it seems to assume that the agent has a probability function that is a member of the set. This seems to deny the intuition that one's degrees of belief may actually be vague.

8. Upon this account some propositions are possibly true, but cannot be conditionalized on. Some philosophers consider this a reason to reject such theories of conditional probability. See Bas C. Van Frassen, "Belief and the Will," *The Journal of Philosophy,* 81, no. 5 (May 1964), 235–56. However, probability is relativized to a set of circumstances according to this theory, and hence it is possible to have probability relativized to partial belief in such propositions.

9. An alternative method is to follow Ramsey in defining conditional probability in terms of conditional credence, for which a Dutch book justification can be given.

10. We are interested in P_C(at least one person believes $B\,/\,B$ is true).

11. In some situations it may be the case that for some properly functioning cognizers the rational degree of belief in proposition B is $<x,y>$, and for another group of properly functioning cognizers the rational degree of belief in B will be $<y+\varepsilon,z>$. The probability of B in those circumstances will be $<x,z>$, since that is the interval that includes the degrees of belief in B of all properly functioning cognizers. This does not imply that $y + .5\varepsilon$ is a rational degree of belief for anyone. It may be that no properly functioning cognizer can believe B to that degree in those circumstances. Our analysis of $P_C(B) = <x,y>$ does not claim that every real number or interval contained in $<x,y>$ is a rational degree of belief in proposition B in circumstances C; it only claims that all rational degrees of belief are contained in that interval. It may be that certain values or intervals in that larger interval are not rational degrees of belief in B in circumstances C.

12. For a contrary opinion, see Philip Quinn, "In Search of the Foundations of Theism," *Faith and Philosophy* 2, no. 4, (October 1985), 468–86.

13. A similar problem arises if the agent were to believe proposition R:

> R: All beliefs believed on the basis of a belief that I am appeared to treely are unjustified.

14. One might object that this case can be handled by Jeffrey's probability kinematics. But Jeffrey's proposal deals with a situation involving uncertain evidence, and this is a situation involving mistaken evidence.

15. An exception to this is when the circumstances include the identity of the epistemic agent.

16. Other requirements such as change of belief by conditionalization and diachronic coherence may be added, but that does not affect this basic point.

17. Wesley C. Salmon, *The Foundations of Scientific Inference* (Pittsburgh: University of Pittsburgh Press, 1966).

18. Salmon, p. 64.

19. Plantinga, "Epistemic Justification," p. 15.

20. I would like to thank Chris Menzel, Jerry Neu, Del Ratzsch, Nicholas Wolterstorff, and especially Alvin Plantinga for helpful comments on an earlier version of this paper.

Reasons, Redemption, and Realism: The Axiological Roots of Rationality in Science and Religion

Stephen Wykstra

> "Now, what I want is, Facts. Teach these boys and girls nothing but Facts. Facts alone are wanted in life. Plant nothing else, and root out everything else. You can only form the minds of reasoning animals upon Facts; nothing else will ever be of any service to them. This is the principle on which I bring up my own children, and this is the principle on which I bring up these children. Stick to Facts, Sir!"
>
> Thomas Gradgrind, Sir. A man of realities. A man of facts and calculations. . . . With a rule and a pair of scales, and the multiplication table always in his pocket, Sir, ready to weigh and measure any parcel of human nature, and tell you exactly what it comes to.
>
> "You are to be in all things regulated and governed . . . by fact. We hope to have, before long, a board of fact, composed by commissioners of fact, who will force the people to be a people of fact, and of nothing but fact. You must discard the word Fancy altogether. You have nothing to do with it."
>
> Charles Dickens
Hard Times

Dickens created Thomas Gradgrind in 1854. Twenty years earlier, across the Atlantic, the City College of New York appointed one Charles Pettit M'Ilvaine to teach a course on "The Evidences of Christianity." (The lectures went through half a dozen editions in the next decades; M'Ilvaine became bishop of the Episcopal Church of Ohio.) In lecture twelve, M'Ilvaine summarizes his method in a way that would do Gradgrind proud:

> the process by which we have arrived at the truth of Christianity is precisely similar to that by which the astronomer arrives at the most certain truths of the celestial bodies; or the chymist determines the most fundamental doctrines of his important science. The grand characteristic of the philosophy that Bacon illustrated, and Newton so nobly applied, and to which all science is so deeply indebted, is that it discards speculation; places no dependence upon theory; demands fact for everything, and in everything submits implicitly to the decision of fact, no matter how incomprehensible, or how opposed by all the speculations in the world. This is called *inductive* philosophy, in distinction from that of theory and conjecture.[1]

This inductive method, M'Ilvaine continues, follows "the great principle of all Newton's Principia, on which he set the ladder that raised him to the stars." It "collects its facts either by personal observation or testimony worthy of reliance," and "from these it makes its careful inductions, and determines the laws of science, with a degree of plain, unpresuming authority, to which every enlightened mind feels it ought to bow." And this same method, M'Ilvaine then urges, should be applied to Christianity:

> Let all conjectural hypotheses be set aside. Let the infidel and the Christian sit together in the chairs of Bacon and Newton, and with that stern rejection of mere theory, and lowly deference to fact, let the New Testament be brought to the bar. . . . The argument for the divine authority of the gospel is all composed of statements of undeniable facts, and of direct inferences legitimately drawn from them.[2]

So M'Ilvaine wants us, in Gradgrindian terms, "to be in all things regulated and governed by fact." And in so exhorting us, M'Ilvaine appeals to an image of science — an image that had, for all of his century and most of ours, enormous authority. I shall call it "the standard image" of science.

Why should we Christians believe the things we do? We believe that there is a Being, invisible and intangible, who made this world of rock and grass and moon and stars — and us. That this Maker of all chose a small Middle Eastern tribe, into whom he pounded the idea that he cares passionately about justice, and holiness, and us. That each of us has an eternal destiny that depends on our relationship with this Holy One of Israel; that this Holy One has come most fully to and for us in the person of Jesus of Nazareth. That this Jesus died by crucifixion in Jerusalem, but was raised to life; and that this made possible our reconciliation with God, opening to us a new life in his Spirit. These are big claims, fabulously big claims; they are not, on reflection, *easy* to believe. Why, then, should we — should anyone — believe them?

The answer is not simple. Believing what we should is, I take it, in large part a matter of believing with due regard for what we have good reason or grounds to believe. But Christian theism is itself not one but many claims; the reasons bearing on this Christian theistic complex are thus also complex: like a large tent, it is held to (and off) the ground by a network of poles and lines and stakes. Explicating this network is the large task of Christian apologetics — a task I shall not undertake here. My concern is instead meta-apologetic. I want to explore the *nature* of some of this supporting network. What is it for something to be a "good reason" for believing? What should (and should not) count as a "good reason" for believing; and *why* should (or shouldn't) it so count? These are the questions that I want to answer — or, at least, want answers to.

Another question I want answered is this: Should what counts as "good reason" be the same in religious as in scientific matters? One answer (call it the "standard answer") is "Yes." Western intelligentsia have, for centuries, taken science as the exemplar of rationality. They have thus held an "evidentialist" thesis that religious claims need the same sort of good reasons as do scientific claims about the world.[3] Underlying this "standard answer" has been some version of what I've called "the standard image" of science. Science is rational because its claims consist of observable facts and theories carefully inferred from them.

This standard answer has (from Pascal to Plantinga) had challengers. But until recently, the challengers have tended to assume the same image of science as their opponents. Agreeing that scientific claims are rationally founded on objective inference from observable facts, they have challenged only the thesis that all claims must be founded in this way. Religious truth, they have insisted, is properly a matter of faith (or revelation, or passion, or "subjectivity") not of scientific inference. During the sixties, of course, the standard image of science was itself challenged by Kuhn, Feyerabend, and others. Anti-evidentialists could now urge that subjective commitment is at the core of science as much as of religion.

But this is a pox on both houses that does justice to neither. Scientists *believe* their best theories about the world; but the Kuhnian rationale for paradigms, if one accepts it, is self-defeating, and can never justify such belief.[4] Kuhn's view is deeply skeptical about *truth* in science. Moreover, Christian commitment involves believing the truth-claims of Christianity. Is a Kuhnian skepticism toward the best claims of current *science* likely to encourage this? In the *Dialogues,* Hume gives just this move to Philo, who pretends to hold (as Cleanthes caustically puts it) "that if certainty or evidence be expelled from every other subject of enquiry, it will all retire to these theological doctrines, and there acquire a superior force and authority."[5]

So these are our questions:

(1) What is it for something to be a "good reason" for believing?
(2) What should (and should not) count as a "good reason" for believing; and *why* should (or shouldn't) it so count?
(3) Should what counts as "good reason" be the same in religious matters as in scientific matters?

I shall sketch an axiological way of thinking about these questions. "Axiology" is an old-fashioned word for value-theory: on the way of thinking I shall develop, the norms governing what counts as good reasons are rooted in our values or aims. This is so both in science and in religion: so far forth, there is something fundamentally common to rationality in science and religion. But though the "norms of good reason-hood" are rooted in values in the same way, the values are not the same values. Because of this, these norms appropriately differ for scientific and religious claims: what we demand for religious claims, in the way of good reasons, should differ from what we demand for scientific claims. Religious rationality and scientific rationality, while belonging to a common genus, are yet different species.

Sections 1 and 2 sketch (for science and religion respectively) a first approximation to the axiological account. Since my aim is to underscore how our values underlie and shape the norms of rationality appropriate to scientific and religious claims, I speak of these claims as belonging to different "modes of discourse," each with its own axiological *raison d'être*. But this first approximation, reminiscent of Wittgensteinian notions, also generates a key problem addressed by section 3. For religion and science do not merely provide useful linguistic constructions; they make claims about reality which either should or should not be *believed*. In section 3, I suggest how we can, while preserving the deeply human value-root of scientific and religious discourse, see that discourse as rightly eventuating in belief about how things really are. I also discuss how being Christian should affect our thinking about these things.

1. GOOD REASONS IN SCIENCE: THE STRATA OF SCIENTIFIC RATIONALITY

In this section I shall explore what counts as "good reason" within science. This question belongs to the branch of philosophy called "theory of scientific rationality" (or TSR, for short). To answer it we must attend to real science, which TSR doesn't always do. Pursuits like Carnapian inductive logic may have value, but many have doubted how much light they shed on real science. Such doubt drove much of the new wave of philosophy of science that has been swelling (and has perhaps crested and crashed) since the early 1960s. It gave rise to the conviction that TSR must be grounded on study of real science, especially the history of science.[6] For TSR aims to articulate the norms by which theories are accepted, debated, revised, and replaced in the actual life of science—and to do so in a way that illuminates why those theories have the claim on us they have.

We have seen how, in the last century, thinkers like M'Ilvaine modeled Christian apologetics on an image of scientific rationality. But we should now note that M'Ilvaine's image is some distance from images having currency today. In the passages quoted above, M'Ilvaine says that science, from carefully collected facts, "makes its careful inductions, and determines the laws of science, with a degree of plain, unpresuming authority, to which every enlightened mind feels it ought to bow." And in these "careful inductions," one "discards speculation; places no dependence upon theory; demands fact for everything, and in everything submits implicitly to the decision of fact."

This is not merely pre-Kuhnian. Inductive method, as M'Ilvaine sees it, is "opposed to that of theory and conjecture"—opposed, that is, to the use of *hypotheses* in science. In this opposition, M'Ilvaine is embracing what might be called the Reidian image of science. For it is above all due to Thomas Reid that antipathy to "hypotheses" became, by the late eighteenth century, the coin of the methodological realm.[7] To take just a few of Reid's polemics:

> The experience of all ages . . . shows how prone ingenious men have been to invent hypotheses to explain the phenomena of nature; how fond, by a kind of anticipation, to discover her secrets. Instead of a slow and gradual ascent by a just and copious induction, they would shorten the work, and by a flight of genius, get to the top at once.[8]

Or:

> [Scientific] discoveries have always been made by patient observation, by accurate experiments, or by conclusions drawn by strict reasoning from observations and experiments. Such discoveries have always tended to refute, but not to confirm, the theories and hypotheses which ingenious men have invented. [This] . . . ought to have taught man, long ago, to treat with contempt hypotheses in every branch of philosophy, and to despair of ever advancing knowledge in that way.[9]

So for Reid, the mistake lies not merely in accepting hypotheses too quickly, but in having any truck with them at all. Reid sees this as the moral of a historical story—the story of the birth of science. Since we no longer tell the story in the same way, a little history of history will put Reid in perspective. It will also provide a historical peg on which to hang my main theses about scientific rationality.

After the Enlightenment, secularists would portray the new science as emerging from a warfare against the authoritarianism of Aristotle and/or the Church. Reid also saw warfare, but against a different enemy. For him, Newton triumphed over the followers of Descartes, or, more generally, the adherents of "the mechanical philosophy." These mechanists (like Newton later) wanted to explain orbiting planets, falling apples, magnets, and much else. But to do so they developed theories about invisible vortices of subtle aether corpuscles. And these corpuscles, they thought, could interact in only one way: by impact, or "contact-action." The laws of motion, prior to Newton, were always laws of impact. Impact laws were special because, as mechanists saw it, contact-action is a uniquely *intelligible* causal interaction. It is *transparent to intellect* that a piece of matter will change its motion when another bumps into it. For this follows from the very essence of matter: it is an essential property of matter that it takes up space, or is impenetrable. (I here ignore differences between Cartesians and Gassendists.) So if we really want to *explain* why a magnet draws a nail, or why the earth draws an apple, we must show how these apparently mysterious phenomena result from underlying contact-action mechanisms: such mechanisms, though invisible to our senses, are perfectly intelligible and non-mysterious to our intellects.[10]

Enter, now, Newton with his new law of universal gravitation. This law, as mechanists saw it, could not be explained by any contact-action mechanism. To admit the law thus meant admitting that one bit of matter could affect another across empty space: it meant admitting action-at-a-distance as a *fundamental* force in nature. But such a force, the corpuscularians charged, is as mysterious as the phenomena it tries to explain. It is an unintelligible interaction — being opaque to the intellect. Newton's proposal, they said, reintroduces "occult qualities" into nature: accepting it would set science back fifty years.[11]

Reid must be seen in the context of these charges against Newton. For Reid was a partisan of Newton, and with other Newtonians, he took the best defense to be a good offense. The mechanists' hypotheses about aether vortices, he said, are vain constructions of imagination. And the problem is not just that the mechanists failed to test their hypotheses sufficiently; it is that hypotheses of their sort can *never* be factually established. As Reid saw it, science began only when, scrupulously following Newton's dictum that "hypotheses have no place in experimental philosophy," we confined ourselves to the sorts of propositions that can be "inductively demonstrated" from the facts.

Using Reid's image as a foil, I want to sketch a different view of scientific rationality. It is not Kuhnian, though it draws on the past decades of history and philosophy of science. Its central claims are that scientists regularly face options at three different levels (a theoretical level, a deeper methodological level, and a deepest axiological level), and that theory of rationality must illuminate change at each of these levels. I have developed this "levels schema" of scientific rationality elsewhere; here I must be brief, so as to move to parallels in theory of religious rationality.[12]

1.1 Theoretical Level of Scientific Rationality

At the first level, scientists evaluate claims that are broadly "factual"—claims that are, that is to say, about the world. Such claims are of various kinds, ranging from reports of meter readings to hypotheses about quarks and leptons. In evaluating such claims, scientists come to "cognitive stances" toward them. Cognitive stances, too, are of various kinds, ranging from regarding a hypothesis as worthy of further inquiry, to confidence that it will be a permanent part of scientific knowledge. Two preliminary tasks of TSR are to taxonomize the types of claims and stances that occur in the life of science. Since my purpose here is not to give such taxonomies, I shall speak of "accepting" (or "rejecting") some "theory"—or of making "theory choices."

We presume that scientists, in making theory choices, have a sense that some considerations are legitimately taken into account and others not. We presume that their theory choices rest on method, not madness: this is part of what makes science science. Scientists sometimes deride philosophers for speaking this way. Theories, they say, cannot be produced by rules, else it wouldn't take scientists to produce good theories—even philosophers could do it. But the norms at issue here are not for coming up with theories but for assessing them. And if theories are assessed with regard to reasons, something rulelike must be involved. For to appeal to reasons is to say that not just anything goes: some things do not count as good reasons; others do. That it gives me a headache is not, in science, a good reason for rejecting a theory; its boosting my popularity is not a good reason for accepting it. Reasons imply norms governing what counts as a good reason and what doesn't.

A central task of TSR, then, is to articulate the norms implicit in the processes by which scientists make rational theory choices. Such an account would enable us to explain why a scientist S chose some theory *T,* in terms of his employment of a set or cluster of criteria *C.* We can, following Sellars, see the explanation as representing a kind of practical inference:[13]

P1) *S* was resolved to judge theories by criteria *C.*
P2) *S* judged that theory *T* meets (doesn't meet) *C.*
C) So *S* accepted (rejected) *T.*

Such an explanation concerns scientific change at the "theoretical level."

Now for Reidians, criteria *C* comprised the stringent norms of "the inductive philosophy." This inductivism wasn't just a *professed* method to which they gave lip service. It was (though not consistently) practiced as well as preached. In the mid-eighteenth century, as Laudan shows, plausible theories were rejected *tout court,* not on empirical grounds, but because they referred to unobservable entities, failing inductivist norms.[14]

Today, no one endorses these norms. Why not? What's wrong with them?

For one thing, Reidian norms don't secure the theories Reid himself wants secured. These norms only allow one to extrapolate, taking a property or functional connection observed in a sample and projecting it to the entire population. It thus is unable to secure a theory like heliocentrism, which goes far beyond generalization about the wandering specks of light in the sky. But Newton's theory itself rested on heliocentrism (by argument from Keplerian and Galilean laws). So inductivism cannot even secure Newton's theory.

Behind this is a more general point. Reidian norms give only a science of the world's observable surface. Some scientists have, to be sure, tried to content themselves with this; some philosophers have even gloried in it. The Manifesto of the early Vienna Circle (then "the Ernest Mach Society"), signed by Carnap, Hahn, and Neurath, declared: "In science there are no depths; there is surface everywhere . . . ; everything is accessible to man." Statements apparently about deep things (atoms, electrons, and the like) derive their meaning "through reduction to the simplest statements about the empirical given."[15] Restricting science this way has its attractions: by giving up depth, one seems to get more certainty. But for most scientists, the price is too high. We desire theories that get beneath the world's observable surface, that explain the data we see in terms of underlying entities and processes we don't see. But this means that we have to enter the game Reid and M'Ilvaine deplore: the game of evaluating hypotheses. Here, of course, inductive norms are all but useless: you don't get to photons by generalizing from meter readings. So this puts us in need of a richer set of norms. But how much richer? And at what price?

We'll need norms of simplicity, for one thing. Reid rejected the appeal to simplicity: we are, he writes "led into error by the love of simplicity which disposes us to reduce things to few principles, and to conceive a greater simplicity in nature than there really is." The operations of nature, he continues, must be learned from "facts and observations": "if we conclude that it operates in such a manner, only because to our understanding that appears . . . simplest, we shall always go wrong."[16] To us it is quite evident that simplicity is crucial to evaluating theories; but this is partly because we want theories dealing with unobservables. (The role of simplicity in induction over observables has, to be sure, also become more evident.) Yet this has a price. It has proven very hard to articulate what simplicity consists in. Worse, no one seems to be able to give good reasons for thinking that simpler theories are (ceteris paribus) more likely to be true.[17]

If, despite this, we allow considerations of simplicity to be among our criteria C, why not allow other norms? Many scientists, we noted, rejected Newton's theory because it introduced a force not explicable by contact-action mechanisms. These scientists included some of the best minds of the age—from Huygens and Leibniz in the 1690s to the Bernoullis in the mid-1700s. So for them, criteria C included a norm that theoretical laws be in principle explicable by contact-action mechanisms. Why not allow this norm? What makes simplicity okay, but not this?

Let's back off and review. Science does not fit the Reidian mold: we have learned (we want to say) that Reidian norms are inadequate. That is one lesson; but it points to a deeper one. Scientific rationality cannot be identified with—and is not exhausted by—the norms at the first level of scientific change. For those norms themselves change; and their change represents (we want to say) something we've learned. If this is so, there must be a rationality to change not just in theories but in methodological norms. So of this too, TSR must give an account. And that account must do two things. First, it must illuminate what gives our current norms their normativity: why we ought to use them, accepting theories sanctioned by them. But second, it must explain past methodological commitments, not rendering all past scientists irrational for employing norms different than ours.

1.2 The Methodological Level of Scientific Rationality

To understand change in methodological norms, I believe we need to exploit an idea pioneered by Hans Reichenbach (and developed by Feigl, Sellars, and Salmon) in an effort to make one small step past Hume on the problem of induction.[18] Reichenbach focused on the straight rule, the most basic of inductive norms for drawing conclusions about a population based on an observed sample of it. The straight rule says this: if, in an observed sample of a population, a given percentage of members have some property P, you should (making a "straight" extrapolation) conclude that in the wider population, the same percentage of members have this property. In the simplest case, the percentage is 100 percent: because all observed copper has been conductive, we infer that all copper is conductive. Various conditions must be attached to how samples are taken. But the Humean problem of induction is why, even under the best conditions, we should employ this rule.

As Reichenbach saw it, Hume demonstrated conclusively that we cannot justify the rule. We cannot, that is, show that this norm leads to conclusions that are true, probably true, more probably true than not, or anything else in the neighborhood. But though we cannot justify the rule, argued Reichenbach, we can *vindicate* it. "Vindicating" a rule means showing that it is reasonable to use it because this gives us our best shot at achieving our goals. To show this, we need not prove that using the norm *will* achieve our ends. It would instead suffice if one shows only that *if* any means will work, this one will (and, perhaps, that one cannot show this of any other means).

Reichenbach's strategy is thus goal-theoretic; before looking at some details, suppose we generalize it into a form of explanation for any methodological commitment. At the *methodological level* of scientific change, our explanations will look something like this:

P1) *S* was resolved that science aim to achieve values *V*.

P2) *S* judged that employing criteria *C* would optimally promote *V*.

C) So *S* adopted criteria *C*.

We must now ask what sorts of things will be included among values *V*. Here we face an important option. We might insist that the only proper values for science are to increase our true beliefs about the world and to eliminate false beliefs. These are, as William James noted, two *distinct* values: much can depend on which of them is given more weight.[19] I shall refer to these (and only these) two values as "*alethic*" values. Some thinkers—among them Reid—appear to think that norms of theory-choice, to be rational, must be vin- dicated relative to *only* these two values. I will refer to this as a "*strictly alethic*" view of the norms of scientific theory-choice.

The strictly alethic conception, I want to argue, is too narrow. There are two sorts of reasons pressuring us to broaden it. The first is philosophical: we have been unable to give strictly alethic vindi- cations of indisputably central scientific norms. Consider two ex- amples. The first is Reichenbach's case for using the straight rule. The straight rule, as he saw it, licenses conclusions about "ultimate limiting frequencies." The conclusions, that is, do not concern just the proportion of events having a certain property in a series of events; they concern, more exactly, the *limit* reached by this proportion, for any further prolongation of the series.[20] But we have, Reichen- bach argued, no access to this limit other than through the straight rule (or some rival to it). We thus have no hope of showing that the straight rule *is* leading us to the truth concerning this limit. Why then should we use it? Here we need to notice two steps in Reichen- bach's case. The first is to argue that *if* there is a true conclusion regarding this limit, then if any rule will help us converge on it, re- peated applications of the straight rule will do so. But since we don't know the antecedent, we are taking a cognitive risk in using *any* rule here. Why then use any rule here? Why not just avoid the game altogether? Here Reichenbach takes a second step: what justifies our taking the risk is a *practical value*. The conclusions licensed by the straight rule, he argues, "sustain predictions." And, he says, we "*need* to make predictions"; we need to "for the purpose of action."[21]

Reichenbach's point, I believe, is that we are not purely contemplative beings, aiming just to gaze upon an increasing stock of certain truths. We are practical beings: we live in a world that has dangerous surprises, and from which our well-being must be wrested. Because of this, we need (and value) propositions that do certain *jobs* for us, enabling us to make predictions and to manipulate or control our environment. It is this that justifies our taking the risk of employing the straight rule. Because the value is not just one of valuing true propositions (or avoiding false ones), I shall call it a "nonalethic value." And the view that such nonalethic values are an essential part of the values V in which scientific norms are grounded, I shall call an "*extra-alethic conception*" of such norms.

Later, I shall consider how non-alethic and alethic values can be combined in our axiological account. But first, I turn to a second example: the shifts in the thought of Carl Hempel on such norms as simplicity. In 1960 Hempel regarded the norms of scientific theory-choice as justifiable relative to the goal of attaining a certain type of "body of information" about the world. This seems to reflect a strictly alethic view: a body of "information" means, I take it, a body of true propositions. ("Entirely different norms would be appropriate," he adds, "if our goal were instead to have an "emotionally reassuring or esthetically satisfying worldview."[22]) But has anyone really justified norms of simplicity relative to this alethic end? In the mid-sixties, we find Hempel reviewing the difficulties in past efforts to do so: "the problems . . . " he concludes, "are not as yet satisfactorily solved."[23] Finally, in 1981, we find Hempel, pessimistic about ever solving the difficulties, proposing an extra-alethic conception: such norms as simplicity, he says, may best be seen not as means to an independent goal, but "as *themselves* specifying the goals of science." That is, we judge theories by (among other things) their simplicity, not because we deem simpler theories more likely (*ceteris paribus*) to be true, but because the simplicity of a theory is (among other things) something we value for its own sake—it is, in Copernicus's phrase, "pleasing to the mind." Since the simplicity of a theory is now something (though not the only thing) we value *intrinsically,* he says, it "becomes a truism" that norms of simplicity should be among our criteria for judging theories.[24]

These two examples illustrate the philosophical pressure to move away from a strictly alethic conception of methodological norms. In section 3 I shall discuss how such a move can be reconciled with realism—with taking these norms to provide reasons for *believing* the claims they sanction. But here let us note that in both examples the pressure stems from what we might call "the veil of cognition" problem. One of the primary problems in modern epistemology concerns the "veil of perception": how can we justify thinking our perceptual faculties give true beliefs about the external world, given that we have no access to it other than through these faculties? So also for many norms of scientific cognition. Apart from reliance on something like the straight rule, we have no cognitive access to limit frequencies. Apart from norms of simplicity, we have no access to truths about electrons and the like. How then can we show that use of either norm gives us truth about these matters? We are thus driven to include non-alethic values among those vindicating such norms. Science aims to secure theories that do certain *jobs* for us—theories by which to predict and control our environment for the purposes of action (Reichenbach), and to find, in the "blooming buzzing confusion" around us, patterns whose simplicity is in itself "pleasing to the mind" (Hempel). In using the norms we do, we aim at far more (but not less) than just "obtaining the facts."

There are also, I noted, historical pressures for the same move to an extra-alethic conception. It is sometimes suggested that while the norms of theory-choice must be evaluated relative to the aims of science, these aims were themselves decided once and for all with the "founding intentions" of modern science.[25] If the past three decades of history of science have shown anything, it is that this is false. For even if we confine attention to the three-century span constituting the history of "modern science" (a dubious historiographical invention), the aims of science themselves have undergone deep and controversial changes. We have two examples in hand. The conflict between inductivists and hypotheticalists is a conflict between those valuing theories with high certainty and those valuing theories with depth. History has decided in favor of including the depth pole, but one can cite equally eminent scientists (and sometimes the same scientist at different times) on both sides of this value-divide. Similarly, the conflict between mechanists and Newtonians is a conflict between those valuing theories positing "intellectually transparent" mechanisms and those content with theories that posit lawlike generalizations that are themselves brute facts. We now favor the latter; but, historically, there are capable scientists on both sides. Only an antihistorical Procrusteanism sees all scientists agreeing on the values of science. Historically, the aims of scientific discourse are not only extra-alethic, but themselves in process.

But this points us to a deeper level of scientific rationality. If the values underlying scientific norms were strictly alethic, or if, though extra-alethic, they were agreed upon by all scientists, we might see the methodological level as the bottom line of scientific rationality. But these values were not laid down, once and for all, by the founders of modern science. Even within the three-century span of modern science, they have undergone deep and controversial changes. We must thus ask what it means to be rational at a third axiological level of scientific change—the level of change in the values or aims of science.

1.3 Axiological Level of Scientific Rationality

Mechanists like Huygens, we saw, rejected Newton's gravitational law because it failed to meet a contact-action norm; Huygens was committed to this norm because he valued theories that render the phenomena ultimately intelligible. But not all scientists—even among Huygens's contemporaries—shared this value-aspiration. There were axiological options.

Euler rejected the gravitational theory of LeSage because it failed to meet a narrowly inductivist norm; he was committed to this norm because he valued theories having near-apodictic certainty. But not all scientists—even among Euler's contemporaries—shared this value-aspiration. There were axiological options.[26]

When scientists face options in cognitive values, is there any rationality to how the options get settled? One way to approach this is, again, by framing it historiographically: can we envision any sort of internal explanation, any sort of explanation-by-reasons, that might be given of why scientists placed—or changed—their value commitments as they did? I believe we can. The reasons scientists give for value commitments suggests that a commitment (*qua* scientist) to certain values can itself be regarded as governed by certain widely shared meta-values, commitment to which determines what the agent is disposed to regard as appropriate or proper cognitive values. This is, I want to suggest, typically a function of at least two meta-values: first, of having a set of cognitive values as "high" as possible; and second, of having a value set which is "achievable." We thus have an *axiological level* of scientific rationality:[27]

P1) S was resolved that science aim to achieve the set of values
       that are jointly most high and achievable.
P2) S judged that set of values V constitutes such a set.
C)   So S resolved that science aim to achieve values V.

As an example of the meta-value of "height," consider the sort
of case advanced by Robert Boyle for the corpuscular (or "mechanical") philosophy, which guided (arguably as no small result of his
defense of it) much important scientific work well into the eighteenth century. In defending the mechanical philosophy, Boyle did
not only (or even primarily) give evidence for its truth. He argued
rather, and at some length, that while the sort of explanations to
which it aspires may be difficult to obtain, they are of a sort that
is exceptionally *satisfying* to the mind. Intellectually, they are *good
things* (as in the expression "good things are not easy"). For this
reason, they are things we should set our sights on; for as our parents tell us, we should (other things being equal) "aim high." I thus
refer to this meta-value as the "height" of a proposed value.[27]
     It is important to note that, as Boyle saw it, the "height" of
the mechanists' explanatory ambitions is something about which
rational discourse is possible. In part, such discourse is a matter of
making the values explicit and seeing that people do in fact "recognize" their height. Thus, we find Boyle arguing that even the Aristotelian natural philosophers "acquiesce in the explications made
by these (corpuscular principles), when they can be had, and seek
not any further."[28] Furthermore, Boyle thought that the intellectually satisfying character of corpuscular explanations rested on ("super-
vened on," as Hare would put it) their having certain features. Boyle
specifies five such features of the principles of the corpuscular program: their "intelligibleness," their being "few," "primary," "simple,"
and "comprehensive." Because such height-making features can be
identified and discussed, Boyle took rational discussion to be possible about the "height" of rival values.
     A second meta-value is "achievability." Good things need not
be easy, but their realization must not be impossible either. Of course,
a set of values need not be *completely* realizable; rather, it must be
reasonable to think that sustained commitment will lead to progressively fuller (if always partial) realization of them. This meta-
value is also illustrated by Boyle's arguments. According to Boyle,
the Aristotelians' main objection to his approach was that however

nice when we can get them, corpuscularian explanations are for the most part not obtainable. Boyle thus writes: "they [the Aristotelians] imagine, that the applications of them [corpuscular principles] can be made out but to few things."[29] Their main reason for thinking this was conceptual: the ontology of mechanical philosophy seemed too austere to explain the teeming diversity of nature. Against this, Boyle gave analogical arguments that this admitted austerity was no reason to think that the same phenomena were beyond the scope of mechanistic explanations. In undercutting the fear that the mechanical philosophy dooms one to increasing frustration and failure, Boyle is addressing whether its values are achievable.

Clearly, there is a tension between these two meta-values: trivially achievable values are likely to be wanting in height; while very high cognitive goals are likely to be of more dubious achievability. Much change in the values of science, I believe, occurs in this tension. Of course, one way to test "achievability" is to *try* to achieve one's ambitions. Testing a set of intellectual aspirations often requires commitment to them.

There is more to each of these levels than can be explored in a small paper. Let me now simply put the three levels together into a "levels schema." Note how the conclusions of higher levels are premises of lower ones:

Rationality at the Axiological Level

P1) S was resolved that science aim to achieve the set of values that are jointly most high and achievable.
P2) S judged that set of values V constitutes such a set.
C1) So S resolved that science aim to achieve values V.

Rationality at the Methodological Level

P3) S was resolved that science aim to achieve values V.
P4) S judged that employing criteria C would best promote V.
C2) So S was resolved to judge theories by criteria C.

Rationality at the Theoretical Level

P5) S was resolved to judge theories by criteria C.
P6) S judged that theory T meets (doesn't meet) C.
C3) So S accepted (rejected) T.

So Reichenbach's value-theoretic approach to induction, enriched by historical perspectives opened in the past decades, gives us a very different image of science from that which M'Ilvaine inherited from Reid. No longer does the history of science appear as a series of undeniable inductions from the facts by "self-evident" and immutable norms. For even the most common-sensical of our inductive norms are rooted in our valuings—our valuing of having a discourse that makes the world predictable and manipulable. And the history of science, by its remarkable extensions of common sense, represents our probing of nature with an evolving series of values and of devising and revising our inferential policies for achieving those values. On this image, science progresses not just in our "discovering facts," but in our discovering, through a praxis demanding both commitment and humility, what sort of discourse about nature we should value and what inferential practices are optimal means for achieving theories embodying those values. The history of science, on this image, is the axiological as well as the methodological laboratory of science.

To be sure, the Reid-M'Ilvaine picture is not all wrong. For something about that praxis—to be discussed in section 3—does give us confidence that science gives us a grip on "the facts," on the truth about what is. Nevertheless, science does not aim solely at "knowing the facts." It springs from a deeply human passion to make (or find) the world intelligible; and the facts do not dictate the forms that make them intelligible. Because such passion is at the heart of scientific rationality, the Reidian image is a betrayal of it. Gradgrind's unfortunate students might make good technicians, but they would never have produced modern science.

2. REDEMPTION AND THEORY OF RELIGIOUS RATIONALITY

Suppose philosophers of religion were to undertake something for religion akin to what philosophers of science call theory of scientific rationality (TSR, we've called it). Let's call the enterprise "theory of religious rationality" (or TRR). What would it be like?

Its aim would not be to "make" religious belief rational (philosophers of science do not "make" scientific beliefs rational), but to exhibit the rationality (and irrationalities) already in religious be-

lieving. To this end, it would attend to actual religious life, as TSR
has learned to attend to actual science. And it would have similar
tasks. As preliminary tasks, it would taxonomize the types of cognitive options encountered in the religious life, and the range of cognitive stances taken toward them. Its central task would then be to
articulate the norms governing these various stances, and to illuminate their normativity. Why should they—or the claims they sanction—have any claim on us? Why honor them with a title like "norms
of religious *rationality*"?

"Religious rationality"? In many quarters—religious as well as
secular—the very term will raise eyebrows. There is, in the history
of Christian thought, a long-standing debate between those like M'Ilvaine, who think the Gospel has a claim on us only because there
are facts which rationally establish its truth, and those (like Kierke-
gaard) who see Christian belief as requiring something deeper than—
even antithetical to—rationality. The debate has often degenerated
into name-calling, with one side sneeringly dismissed as "rational-
ists," and the other (equally sneeringly) as "fideists." When non-
Christian thinkers enter the debate, the polarization increases. For
the life of religious believing itself seems oddly dividing—it has, as
Paul puts it (2 Cor. 2:15–16), the fragrance of life to some, and the
stench of death to others. For all these reasons, "religious rationality" (implying that norms of rationality inform the life of religious
believing) is a far more controversial term than "scientific rationality." This, too, theory of religious rationality must illuminate, giving it a task that TSR seems not to face.

Toward these tasks of TRR, I shall propose the levels schema.
Here a caveat is needed. For the most part, the enterprise of theory
of religious rationality is still terra incognita. Philosophy of religion
has puzzled far more over the ontological argument or divine im-
passibility than over real religion in the life of real people. My proposal is thus highly programmatic, intended not as a theory so much
as a framework for one.

The proposal is guided by two cues. The first is the heart of
the levels schema: even for scientific discourse, norms are cognitive
policies grounded in our *valuings*. These valuings have an existential context: things happen that we don't anticipate; entirely predictable things need controlling; and not everything we want grows on
trees. Much thus hangs on how well we can predict, control, and

contrive; so we value a discourse that does these jobs. This has shaped our concept of scientific intelligibility, of what it is "to explain." To make events intelligible is (by the lights of *current* science: it has not always been so) to find simple nomological generalizations under which we can subsume particular events. Such laws are (by no accident) what we most need for the purposes of prediction and control. Scientific discourse, we might put it, aims to make the world *predictively* intelligible.

The second cue is that in religion — real religion of real people — we find quite different cognitive values at work. Consider Christian beliefs that our world was created by God; that we are made in the image of God; that we are fallen creatures; that God was in Jesus, reconciling the world to himself. Such beliefs must, to be sure, fit the facts of our experience and in *some* sense explain them. But in doing so, they do not much help us make precise predictions, control our environment, or build better airplanes. What then is their point? To see this, we must look at their existential context. And a large part of it is this: we find our lives messed up. We find ourselves in tangles which are deathlike, being deeply destructive of something for which we yearn but can scarcely name. In this context, we find ourselves valuing a discourse that does certain things: that makes sense of our yearning, diagnoses our conditions, and opens *redemptive* possibilities — of healing, reconciliation, transformation, flourishing. These redemptive values are especially pervasive in Judeo-Christian discourse, from the choruses of Psalm 107 to the Good News of one who came "that you might have life, and have it more abundantly" (John 10:10). A primary aim of such discourse, I suggest, is to make our lives *redemptively* intelligible.

Suppose, now, that evidential norms are rooted in cognitive values as the levels schema outlines. Since religious discourse aims at redemptive intelligibility, claims within this discourse need to be assessed by norms appropriate to *this* value. Norms of scientific rationality may then be quite out of place. Sometimes, when our lives cry out for redemptive change, what is important is not precise predictions, but the disclosure of unanticipated new meanings where old ones have been shattered. Demanding that religious discourse here provide precise predictions would be obtuse. Sometimes we find our lives in pits where what we most need to be delivered from is our way of taking things in our own hands. Religious discourse may here need to undercut the technological presumption that we know what it is that we ought to bring about. If we approach the claims of a theistic complex like Christianity—claims having to do with Creation, Covenant, Sin, Judgment, Grace, Incarnation, and the like—as if they must embody the values of scientific theorizing, we will not assess them by appropriate criteria; indeed, we will probably not even understand them. Their point is not to help us predict, control, and contrive the world.

But these negative points are not enough. If there are good reasons for some religious claims, there must be *some* sort of norms governing what count as reasons for them. What are they like?

2.1 Religious Rationality at the Substantive Level

I shall focus upon theistic religion. In theistic religious life, as in science, we take "cognitive stances" toward claims or propositions. And as in science, these claims are often *specifying* claims. Theists are not interested merely in a vague claim that God exists, just as scientists are not interested in a vague claim that atoms exist. Such claims, in religion as in science, become important by additional "specifying claims" that provide some detail.

But specifying claims for God differ from those for protons and the like. First: protons are specified largely in terms of lawlike regularities and dispositional properties; but God is a person, and persons are specified in terms of their actions, intentions, and character. Second: protons do not communicate; persons do. Theists take their beliefs to be not only *about* but also *from* God, arising from his communicative activity. For a variety of things—ranging from a person such as Jesus, an epistle like that of James, a rebuke from a sister in Christ, a job offer from Yale, or a persistent thought in prayer—the theist makes judgments about whether that thing is "from God." Norms of theistic rationality will thus have to help judge about what is (and is not) a "word" from God.

Moreover, theists see divine communications as of two types. The first we can call God's "revelation." Each of the great theistic religions—Judaism, Islam, and Christianity—has certain events, persons, and writings which they take as decisive loci of God's communicative activity. Taking these as revelation means taking them as having some authority binding on humans generally. Corporate reflection on revelation (giving the historic creeds of the church) does much to specify the theistic core claim.

But for Christian theism, revelation itself points to a second mode of specification. It calls one to a personal walk with Christ, in which one seeks to get in closer touch with God's intentions for one personally. Christians thus form beliefs that specify how God is active at this individual level. Such beliefs, while not having the corporate authority of God's revelation in Scripture and Christ, nevertheless play an extremely important role in the religious life. I shall call these "disclosure beliefs." In the religious life, then, theists face options among claims concerning both divine revelation and divine disclosure. Norms of theistic rationality will have to include norms for coming to cognitive stances toward both.

"Will have to," I said. But deists like Voltaire and Franklin, while believing in God, do not have to: they dismiss divine communication *tout court,* seeing it as vain human invention. As a kind of minimalist religion, deism is in some ways parallel to Reidian "minimalist" science. Both are a reaction against a confusing proliferation of options — deists, against the proliferating "revelations" claimed by enthusiasts; Reid, against the proliferating hypotheses of mechanists. Both eliminate confusion in one stroke: denying the admissibility of a whole *type* of claim, they restrict themselves to propositions that are demonstrable from the facts "by Reason." Christians are no more content with the deists' minimalist religion than scientists now are with Reidian minimalist science. But this puts them in need of a richer set of norms. How much richer? At what price?

2.2 Religious Rationality at the Methodological Level

Reid, we saw in section 1, believed (mistakenly) that the norms of strict induction could secure the Newtonian gravitational theory he so prized. Some theists have a similar illusion about Christian revelation. "The argument for the divine authority of the Gospel," M'Ilvaine wrote, "is all composed of statements of undeniable facts, and of direct inferences from them."[30] M'Ilvaine here has in mind the argument from miracles. His "undeniable facts" are the historical testimonies to the miracles of Jesus, especially his resurrection. From these, by common sense norms, we can infer the fact of Jesus' resurrection. And from the *miraculous* character of this we then infer that Jesus is from God. Miracles, as Locke put it, are "credentials of revelation," certifying Jesus as an "agent of revelation." This argument from miracles runs from Locke through Paley and M'Ilvaine to current evangelical apologists like Clark Pinnock, John Stott, and John Montgomery. By making miracles the strong point of their defense, these apologists think a minimalist (inductivist) methodology can yield a maximalist (revealed) religion.[31]

It is instructive to press hard on the strong point, pinpointing just where their case from miracles breaks down. A major problem lies in the *identification* of an event (say, a resurrection) as miraculous. The apologist, of course, needs a strong definition of miracle, if miracles are to be credentials of revelation. It will not do for him to define miracles as (say) events that inspire wonder: this, just because it makes every newborn baby a miracle, will not help establish any special divine messengers. The apologist needs a stronger definition — that miracles are acts of divine power which "transcend (or "violate") the laws of nature," say, or are "beyond the powers of created things." But once some such definition is adopted, the apologist must show that events like Jesus' healings or resurrection do indeed instantiate the definition. He must, that is, establish that his candidates are indeed "beyond the powers of created things," and so are special acts of God. And here, apologists like M'Ilvaine have a problem. For how can strictly inductive norms establish this?

They can't. To identify an event as transcending natural law, our apologist must rely on his best current accounts of nature, as gained by applying inductive norms to observed events. But since these norms are *inductive,* they have no closure principle making new data irrelevant. Hence, discovering an anomaly not fitting our best *current* theories seems to mean only this: that these theories do not yet correctly describe natural laws and powers. Instead of being beyond natural causes, the event may only betoken our inadequate understanding of how nature works. Indeed, science often progresses precisely when recalcitrant anomalies force us to revise our previous theories: to take all such anomalies as miracles would thus put science in the deep freeze. It would also give the apologist more "miracles" than he could handle. What the apologist then needs, and needs desperately, is some *criterion* for distinguishing his "miracles" from events showing only that our best current theories need revision. Despite valiant efforts, I do not think any such criterion has been found along inductive lines.[32]

Are apologists like M'Ilvaine wrong, then, in seeing miracles as relevant to claims regarding revelation? I don't think so. Such appeal to miracles is not just an artifact of philosophers: it occurs within the Christian religious life itself. Both Jesus and the apostles invoke Jesus' "works" as warrant for claims about Jesus. "Believe me," Jesus pleads, "for the works that I do" (John 10:38). Similarly Peter, at Pentecost, commends Jesus as "a man approved of God among you by miracles and wonders and signs, as ye yourselves also know . . ." (Acts 2:22). These indicate that miracles should have a place in any *Christian* theory of religious rationality. But what place? And by what norms?

For cues, let us look briefly at how miracle is presented within religious life. An interesting example is found in chapter 9 of the Gospel of John. The narrative presents Jesus healing a man born blind. He does so on the Sabbath. A group of Pharisees is divided, and the issue between them is whether Jesus is "from God." Some of them argue that he is not, because he violated the Sabbath. Others ask: "How can a man that is a sinner do such miracles?" To check whether this man had really recovered sight after being born blind, the Pharisees interrogate his parents. This persuades them that the event did occur. But the issue remains: what does the event mean? What does it say about Jesus? (This issue had arisen earlier, when Jesus had cast out demons: some Pharisees, John says, accepted the fact, but urged that it was by the power of Satan that Jesus did such things.) So for a second time, John tells us, the Pharisees call in the man: "How did Jesus open your eyes? Tell us the truth: this man is a sinner."

The man's response is twofold. Initially he seems to hedge: "Whether he is a sinner or not, I don't know; but one thing I do know: I was blind, and now I see." But the Pharisees press him: "We know that God spoke through Moses," they say, "but we don't know where this man is from." So the man gives them an argument:

> Now here is a remarkable thing: you don't know where he is from, yet he opened my eyes. We know that God does not listen to sinners; he listens to the Godly man who does his will. Since the world began it has not been heard of any man opening the eyes of one born blind. If this man were not from God, he could not do such a thing.[33]

This man, then, clearly takes the healing as a good reason for believing that Jesus is "from God." But what is it *about* this event that makes it a "good reason"? In part, of course, its uniqueness: such a thing, he says, "has not been heard of since the world began." This seems to be his reason for thinking such a thing wouldn't happen in the course of nature: it didn't take modern science to tell us that natural causes have limits. But modern science has taught us how hard it is to get these limits right, so this "uniqueness" doesn't get us far. A modern-day skeptic could press: "Why bring in God? We've often found nature doing unexpected things. This shows our theories need revision; we can't assign every new anomaly to God. By what *criterion* do we assign *this* to God?"

Does the story suggest any other features that make for miraculousness? Imagine something different happening to this man. Suppose he had been sitting blind by the road, and a frog had jumped into his mouth, whereupon he instantly grew two new heads (both blind). This too would be "unheard of from the beginning of the world." But would it be a miracle? Would he have thought the frog is "from God"? How is John's story different?

Two things stand out. The first concerns the man's initial answer. "One thing I know: I was blind and now I see." This is not just an unheard-of inexplicability (like growing two heads). It is utterly redemptive. It brings the man from darkness to light. It also brings him from isolation to community. Both begging and blindness, in first-century Israel, made one "unclean." John thus notes that parents were called in because the neighbors aren't even sure the man claiming new sight was that old blind beggar, so little had they noticed him. Even after the healing, John says, the Pharisees dismiss the man as "born in sin." Jesus, in contrast, seeks him out for follow-up instruction. In all these details, John's point seems to be that this event opens a door to new life for this man.[34]

Secondly, the man was changed not by a frog but by a person, Jesus, who addressed this man. Jesus, even as he spat on the ground to make clay, explains the man's blindness: "not that this man sinned, or his parents, but that the works of God might be made manifest in him." Then, declaring himself the light of the world and the healing a work of God, Jesus sends the man to Siloam to wash off the clay. There is thus a special *context* for the event: the man is addressed by a person making life-orienting claims.

This story thus suggests that three features are involved in taking the event as a miracle. The first is whether the event, by its uniqueness, seems to transcend natural causes—whether it seems inexplicable (under the conditions that actually obtained) in terms of our current understanding of natural law. The second is whether the event has a redemptive character: whether it in some way brings life out of death, opening a way to flourish. The third is whether it is done by a person making life-orienting claims—claims that, if one accepts them, would deeply affect how one lives. Each feature needs further explication, but waiving that task here, suppose we consider the proposal that if an event has these three features, one should conclude it is a miracle. Is this an appropriate norm?

To see what can be said for it, I think we must consider the existential context of this man. What would go on in this heart? Perhaps something like this:

> I have been in darkness since I was born—unclean, untouchable, a life of squalor before me. Now this Jesus has given me my sight. I can see; I can begin my life.
>
> But I scarcely know how to begin. I have been spat upon for years. The Pharisees still despise me as unclean. They say I was born in sin; that there is no meaning to my life. Some of them say my vision came by Satan's power. I'm still just another beggar; the only change is that I see those I beg from. Crawl back to the gutter, they say. Well, what else can I do? Sometimes I still feel consumed by bitterness and despair. How shall I live? What can I live for?
>
> But this Jesus also spoke to me. He said that I was healed by God's power; that I am a child of God, precious in His sight; that God is calling me for a purpose, and is offering me new life, empowered by His Spirit. And when he looked me up later, he claimed to be the Son of Man. He's asking something from me. He's asking everything from me.
>
> Who is telling the truth? Perhaps I should believe no one: what is truth? But no one has spoken to me as this Jesus did. To see is a beginning, but lots of beggars can see; I need a way to continue. The Pharisees offer none. To whom else shall I go?

If this man takes the event as miraculous, it will not just be because he cannot explain it naturally. It will be because the event occurs in connection with a person, Jesus, whom he sees as embodying something. For to take the event as a miracle is to orient his life toward what Jesus embodies, and this, he judges, gives him his best shot at finding his way—a way that makes sense of, and opens prospects of fulfilling, those longings that, as St. Paul puts it, "groan within us too deep for words" (Rom. 8:26). Because he needs redemption, he opts for a norm that gives him his best shot at getting (as recovering addicts say) in touch "with a Power greater than himself." This value informs his taking the event to be a miracle; it grounds the norm implicit in his taking. If this value is foreign to him, if he has his life together, then there is little point to calling the healing a miracle, to saying "God did this." Doing so certainly will not much help him in predicting and controlling the world.

The proposed norm, I am suggesting, is not justifiable relative to the strictly alethic aim of increasing true beliefs and decreasing false ones. But neither could Reichenbach justify the straight rule relative to so strictly alethic an aim. The straight rule, he thought, gets its grip only relative to a further nonalethic value—a value that arises from our need for what opens prospects of prediction. So also here. A norm like the proposed one, for judging "miraculousness," gets its grip by serving a nonalethic value—a value arising from our need for what opens prospects not for prediction but for redemption. In both cases there is risk. But as Reichenbach writes:

> We may compare our situation to that of a man who wants to fish in an unexplored part of the ocean. There is no one to tell him whether or not there are fish in this place. Shall he cast his net? Well, if he wants to fish in that place I should advise him to cast his net, to take the chance at least. It is preferable to try even in uncertainty than not to try and be certain of getting nothing.[35]

But science and religion use different nets. They are after different fish.

2.3 Religious Rationality at the Axiological Level

Norms of religious rationality, I have suggested, are rooted in the values which give religious discourse its point. But what about these values? Are there options here? Do such values undergo change? If so, can there be any rationality (or irrationality) in how they change, or in how the options get settled?

Of course there are options; of course they change. There are significant changes in how "redemption" is understood within the Christian tradition (just as there are in ideals of explanation within the history of science). The values change even more radically as we compare different religions — Christianity with Buddhism, for example. But value options also occur for us as individuals, perhaps most poignantly when the values concern redemptive transformation. For here we face alternate ways of weighing up what our lives are, and what is possible for them.

Does it make sense to speak of "rationality" at this level? I want to suggest that here too the meta-values of height and achievability come into play. Briefly consider one of the most famous conversions in history: that of Augustine, as he recounts it in Book 8 of his *Confessions*. On one hand, Augustine is pulled by a longing — a longing to have his life completely surrendered to God. I cannot here examine Augustine's conception of such a life; but it is clear that he has come to see it as having great *height*: even fully to *seek* it, he says, "must be preferred to the discovered treasures and kingdoms of men or to all the pleasures of the body."[36]

Yet it is not yet *his* value. He is ruthless about why: he finds himself "fettered in the bondage of his desire for sex." He describes this as an addict would: as holding him in chains. But *how* they hold him is significant. The vanities enslaving him were, Augustine says, like mistresses, and now they were:

> pulling me by the garment of my flesh and softly murmuring in my ear: "Are you getting rid of us?" and "From this moment shall we never be with you again for all eternity?" and "From this moment will you never for all eternity be allowed to do this or that?" My God, what was it that they suggested in these words "this" or "that" which I have just written? I pray you in your mercy to keep such things from the soul of your servant. . . . Violence of habit spoke the words: "Do you think you can live without them?"[37]

Augustine here agonizes about whether a God-surrendered life, however high a value, is really *achievable* for him. That this is his underlying question becomes even clearer when Continence, showing him a multitude of good examples, answers it:

> "Can you not do what these men and women have done? Or do you think that their ability is in themselves and not in the Lord their God?

It was the Lord God who gave me to them. Why do you try and stand
by yourself, and so not stand at all? Let Him support you. Do not
be afraid. He will not draw away and let you fall. Put yourself fear-
lessly in His hands. He will receive you and make you well."[38]

In religious life as in scientific, there are deep options in the values
to which we commit ourselves. And in both, the rationality by which
such options get settled involves an interplay between considerations
of height and achievability. In a person living out an addiction to
alcohol, one voice may say: "Perhaps some day I shall quit; but
perhaps this is all life is." But another voice may reply: "No, I am
not *meant* to be this. Something different is possible. If I die this
way, I shall never have lived." The first voice may counter: "Come
on, you've tried. Quit torturing yourself with a mirage." Augustine,
struggling for the redemption of his sexuality, may not have arrived
at exactly the right redemptive ideal. But his struggle to find it il-
lustrates the interplay of these two types of considerations.

2.4 So What?

Many who reject the demand for evidence for religious belief
are, it seems to me, right in rejecting the demand for *scientific* evidence. Their mistake is to see scientific evidence, as defined by the
inferential policies of science, as the only sort of evidence. By eschew-
ing this mistake, we open prospects for appropriate evidence. I say
"open prospects," because I don't mean that in having cleared scientific norms out of the way, we can justify any religious claim with
a simple eudaemonistic "believing it made my life better." The norms
of religious testing will have to be, in their own way, as exacting
as the norms to which we put scientific theories, for they are to be
norms of belief. But they will be norms rooted in different values.
And they will, perhaps, turn out to have been implicit in authentic
religious praxis all along.

The axiological conception of religious evidence also suggests
why, if there is an inferential case for Christian theism, one might
not be able to show this to others in the same way as one can for
scientific theories. For apprehending that evidence as evidence, being in the grip of the criteria by virtue of which it counts as evidence, may depend upon one's having entered into the axiology of

redemption. St. Thomas thought that the believings of faith, while requiring an evidential basis, were also "at the influence of the will" and its "loving desire" for God.[39] An axiological conception suggests how this could be so: for the valuations of the heart underlie our commitment to the norms determining what counts as evidence, which then guide our assent to specific claims. It is not, then, that faith is at the influence of the will only insofar as it is not guided by evidence, as if faith takes over only where reasons leave off. The valuations of faith are embedded in the very appeal to reasons, giving them their shape.

"The heart has reasons," said Pascal, "of which reason does not know." These reasons, we might say, are the heart's reasons for its valuings. And on the axiological conception, such reasons of the heart, even when unrecognized by reason, underlie reason's reasonings, no less in science than in religion.

3. VALUES AND TRUTH IN SCIENCE AND RELIGION: THREE STEPS TO REALISM

The axiological picture, as so far sketched, may suggest a non-realist view of religious discourse. For by it, our norms of theory-appraisal are means, not merely for increasing true beliefs and reducing false ones, but for achieving non-alethic values — for obtaining "modes of discourse" that "do certain jobs for us." This may, to some, suggest a nonrealist stance toward religious claims, regarding them as more or less useful constructions, rather than as more or less true (or false) accounts of how things are. I do not intend to suggest this. So here, I shall try to reconcile my account with realism. This will bring me to some concluding reflections about doing theory of rationality as a Christian.

To begin, let's try to clarify the problem. Adolf Grünbaum, replying to objections against determinism, considers a person who says that "his house could not have burned down because this fact would make him unhappy." This person, we may imagine, refuses to believe a report that his house has burned down, on the grounds that so believing would make him unhappy. We would, Grünbaum says, "show concern for the sanity" of such a person, for the fact that the truth of a proposition would make us happy (or unhappy) provides no grounds for believing (or disbelieving) it.[40] Now on the axiological account, "norms of religious rationality" are means for attaining beliefs that make our lives "redemptively intelligible." But isn't this just a fancy way of saying that these norms are means to some kind of happiness? Is not one who determines her beliefs by such norms, then, like the person Grünbaum describes? Let's call this (as it takes a cue from Grünbaum) *the Grünbaumian indictment* against "religious rationality" as I have glossed it.

Of course, the Grünbaumian indictment equally applies to scientific rationality if similarly glossed. Recall Hempel's shift. In 1965, he saw scientific norms as appropriate means to the goal of attaining a certain kind of "body of information about the world." (Entirely different norms would be appropriate, he said, if our goal were instead to have an "emotionally reassuring or esthetically satisfying worldview.") But by 1981, he proposes that standards like simplicity may "*themselves* specify the goals of science." Now this may, as he says, justify "in a near-trivial way" the use of such norms. But it also undercuts his earlier contrast between scientific norms and those that would be appropriate were our goal to attain a "worldview that is esthetically pleasing or emotionally comforting." This makes science itself prey to the Grünbaumian indictment. For once a theory's simplicity is seen not as a means to truth, but as an intrinsic value, how can it help justify *believing* the theory? Just such considerations have led many philosophers to epistemic antirealism about science. Reichenbach, Popper, Lakatos, Laudan, and Van Frassen (to name a few) all urge that scientific claims be not believed but only "accepted"—where "accepting" involves no belief as to truth or probable truth. Such antirealism is still not the mainstream in philosophy of science, but it is a powerful undercurrent—and many have gone under.

On such accounts, then, scientific belief is in the same plight as my account seems to put religious belief: both seem vulnerable to the Grünbaumian indictment. But I do not mean to resort to mere *tu quoque*—as if one helps religious belief by making scientific belief equally suspect. Rather I mean this. For both science and religion, the problem of realism has a common source: the irreducible role of non-alethic values in theory choice. So perhaps there is a common solution for both. I don't have the solution, but I may have some pieces of it. Let me put them on the table.

3.1 Step One

The Grünbaumian indictment is an argument from analogy. Consider someone who believes his house couldn't have burned down because this fact would make him unhappy: we would, says Grünbaum, think such a person irrational. But anyone who holds religious beliefs by using norms rooted in values like "redemption" is relevantly like this person. So such a person, we must by analogy conclude, is also irrational.

The first step in countering the argument is to find a disanalogy between the two cases. In the burning house case, the person forms his belief *solely* by whether it promotes the nonalethic value of being happy. Suppose, then, we have the axiological account propose that in religious (and scientific) rationality, non-alethic values operate *in tandem* with alethic values. There is, indeed, a simple way to think of this. Suppose we say that in both science and religion, we are, to be sure, after true beliefs, beliefs that correspond with reality. But we can't form true beliefs about everything: there would be too many truths for us; we'd be too busy believing. So we must make selections: about *what* things (if real) is it especially *important* for us to have true beliefs, and to avoid false ones. Non-alethic values are crucial because they are needed for this selection. They specify the *kind* of reality that we are interested in getting in touch with (if it is there). The core claim of the axiological account, then, is that nonalethic values shape cognitive norms because these norms must be geared to putting us in cognitive touch with "valued realities." The axiological account thus takes the ancient idea that our methods of inquiry must be appropriate to their subject matter, but gives it this new twist: since, prior to inquiry, one doesn't know whether this subject matter exists, it must be to what we would *value* knowing (if it exists) that our norms are apt means of inquiry.

But this first step does not get us entirely out of the Grünbaumian woods. We must distinguish two sorts of cases. In the first, nonalethic values, by specifying what kind of reality interests us, tell us what sort of hypotheses to *consider*; but once we have a hypothesis of this sort, we would evaluate it by strictly alethic norms. Here nonalethic values function in the context of discovery, not of justification. In the second sort of case, nonalethic values inform not just what sort of hypotheses we look for, but also (once a can-

didate is found) how we decide whether to accept it. It is this second
more debatable role that my axiological account gives nonalethic
values. The scientist, on my account, values true propositions describing *simple* nomic regularities (because these give intelligibility).
This value leads him, not only to *search* for simple hypotheses, but
also, given two hypotheses in other respects equal, to *accept* the
simpler of the two. But how can his *valuing* of simplicity (with no
belief that simpler hypotheses are more likely to be true) entitle him
to give this *evidential* weight to it? The same question can be pressed
about using considerations of redemptiveness to identify miracles.
We're not out of the woods.

3.2 Step Two

We must also attend to a *diachronic* dimension of theory evaluation. A theory is a historically evolving entity. We can think of it
as comprising a "core claim," and further "specifying claims" giving
this core more specificity. Copernicus's "heliocentrism" thus consists
of a core claim that the sun is (near) the center of our planetary
system, plus further specifying claims concerning the number of
planets, the size of their orbits, and so forth. Such "specifying claims"
are revised over time, giving different "versions" of heliocentrism,
as proposed by Copernicus, Galileo, Kepler, Newton, and so on.
It is such "theory-versions" (as I shall call them), not bare core claims,
that do explanatory and predictive work. Hence it is theory-versions
that scientists assess using norms of simplicity, empirical fit, and
the like. Now over the past few decades a number of philosophers
have argued that to evaluate a theory-version we must also look at
certain *diachronic* features of the series leading up to it — at whether
this series is (to use Lakatos's technical terms) "progressive" or "de-
generating."[41] Evaluating a theory-version at time *t*, in other words,
requires not just a snapshot showing its features at *t*, but a video
showing various characteristics of its family history.

Without descending into details, let us ask how such diachronic
assessment might help meet the Grünbaumian indictment. Core
claims get developed through a succession of theory-versions, which
typically must accommodate an empirical base increasing in scope
and precision; each newly proposed theory-version will be evaluated
by the accepted methodological norms. Now for a theory like helio-

centrism, these norms of course led to significant changes in specifying claims: say, one theory-version moves the sun slightly off-center;
it is replaced by a better theory-version that puts the planets on elliptical orbits; this is replaced by a yet better theory-version that adds
some new planets; the next theory-version adds gravitational per-
turbations in the elliptical orbits, and so on. But we should notice
two things. First, we can imagine the successive theory-versions differing in content far more than they in fact did. We can imagine
a Kepler finding that by the accepted norms, one got a better theory-
version by putting Venus on a square orbit; and a Galileo finding,
ten years later, that it was even better to reverse the order of planets
and put them on triangular orbits; and so on. Secondly, we can imagine that such radical shifts in content might never settle down or
stabilize. In fact, of course, the content-changes of heliocentrism
were relatively minor and quickly stabilizing.

This need not have been so; for other theories, it has not been
so. The versions of phlogiston theory, as Lavoisier put it, were "a
veritable Proteus, changing form at every instant":

> Now this principle has weight, and again it is weightless; Now it is
> free fire, and again it is fire combined with the element earth; Now
> it penetrates right through the pores of vessels, and again it finds bodies
> impenetrable.[42]

Similarly, the vortex theory of gravity, despite a century's work by
the best minds of Europe, never stabilized as heliocentric theory did
through the work of a handful of researchers. Aether theories of
light, despite the labor of top physicists in the nineteenth century,
never stabilized around any specifications of the properties or work-
ings of the aether. Successive versions of these core theories have
fluctuated as wildly in their content as a compass needle over a bed
of lodestone.[43]

What is the relevance of diachronic content-relations of successive theory-versions? Here I want to distinguish two things. First,
we might take such content-relations as telling us something about
the core idea which these versions seek to adumbrate. This, I take
it, is why Lavoisier noted the protean character of phlogiston theory; it is also what concerns Lakatos in his methodology of research
programs.

But there is also a second and deeper bearing. Consider again heliocentric theorizing. Copernicus, as I understand it, reinstated not only the core idea of heliocentrism, but also a strong commitment to simplicity as a norm for astronomical theorizing. This norm, I have proposed, reflects a *valuing*— a valuing of truths simple enough to make apparent oddities intelligible. Now suppose, having just adopted this norm, one hits on a hypothesis *H* which outshines all its rivals with respect to it and one's other norms. In this initial state, we might allow, one is only warranted in taking some relatively weak stance toward *H*— of "preferring" it, let us say, without much conviction about its truth. For that one *values* simplicity may not at this point do much to justify *believing* a hypothesis excelling its rivals in simplicity. But now suppose several decades have gone by, and one has (under pressure of further data) gone through a series of theory-versions under the auspices of one's norms. Might not this put one in a new position? If the series displays wild fluctuations, one might not only be much less confident (than in the initial state) about the core idea, but also somewhat less confident about one's methodological norms. If, on the other hand, one hits on a core idea which, in successive specifications, settles into convergence, one might be more confident (than initially) not only about the core idea, but also about these norms. One would have more reason to think that they are well-placed, allowing one to identify those core conceptions which progressively unfold an independent reality.

So my suggestion is this. Initially, a normlike simplicity is rooted in our valuing: it embodies a kind of vision, or ideal, of the sort of truth we are interested in learning about, if perchance it is there. At this initial point, the norm warrants only something quite weak in the way of "preferring." But once we have used the norm for some time, we will generate (from various core ideas) sequences of theory-versions which flesh out various core ideas. The diachronic content-relations of these give us a kind of feedback on our norms, increasing (or decreasing) our confidence that they put us on track to reality. Since we have no independent access to reality, we cannot wait for proof that the norms lead to truth before putting them to use. The proof—all we have—is in the putting.

Can a similar tack be taken for religious belief? Are there, in the religious life, types of convergence which, if they obtain, might serve a similar function? I shall again focus on theism, with its core belief in a personal God. Earlier I noted that this core gets specified partly through what theists take to be God's communication, of which we can distinguish "revelation" and "disclosure." Suppose we focus on the latter.

By what norms do Christians evaluate disclosure-claims? There is considerable diversity here; I shall return to this later. But there is also significant agreement, for what Christians agree to be God's revelation in Scripture itself gives guidance on this. The Bible does not just teach us some moral rules and leave us to apply them; it teaches us to seek God's presence daily. Thus Jesus promised his Holy Spirit "to remind of what he has said" and "to guide you into all truth" (John 14:26). Where "two or three gather in my name," he said, "there will I be also" (Matt. 18:20). Paul teaches "make your requests known to God" (Phil. 4:6); James says "If any of you lacks wisdom, let him ask God, who gives to all men generously and without reproaching, and it will be given to him" (James 1:5). And Scripture teaches that Scripture itself is "profitable for teaching, for reproof, for correction, and for training in righteousness" (2 Tim. 3:16).

This being so, Christians do have some common understanding of how God discloses himself to us as individuals. A few examples lie ready at hand.[44] Plantinga notes, for example, that "upon reading the Bible, one may be impressed by a deep sense that God is speaking to him." Alston speaks of how he might, "after asking God to reveal his will for me in a certain situation," have a "strong sense" that "what He wanted me to do was to give priority to work on philosophical theology."

These examples suggest that Christians identify God's disclosures in part by norms specifying the sort of *contexts* by which God characteristically discloses himself: in prayer; or through meditation on Scripture; or in fellowship with brothers and sisters in Christ; or through the preaching of the Word. We might call these "*prima facie accrediting contexts.*" They are (normally) not a matter of hearing voices, but of coming to some sense of how things stand on specifics in one's life. That this comes in the context of seeking God's face in Scripture, prayer, or fellowship is a *prima facie* reason for taking it as God's disclosure. Such context-norms are not, I should add, the only norms operative in such takings. Christians also sometimes speak of a phenomenological quality that characterizes some disclosures: Augustine thus says his mother spoke of "a kind of tone or savor, impossible to define in words, by which she could tell the difference between Your revelations to her and the dreams that came to her own spirit."[45] In addition, of course, Christians take there to be a system of defeaters that come into play in "testing the spirits." So context-norms should be thought of as part of a larger cluster of norms; this cluster character of religious norms has, of course, an analogue in science.

Against this backdrop, let us return to our main question. As in science, there is clearly a veil problem with such norms: we cannot evaluate their reliability directly, since we have no access, apart from them, to what God wants to say to us. So our question is whether, in using them, we have prospects for finding (or failing to find) convergences akin to those found in science, and what such convergences (or lack of them) might signify.

There are two obvious things to be said here. First: by using context- (and other) norms to seek God's will on a given matter, it is clearly *in principle* possible for a believer, over time, to find that contents of the putative disclosures either stabilize or wildly fluctuate. Moreover, both sorts of patterns are noted, and given weight, by religious believers. Anyone who talks with Christians about these things will find many who attest to very striking convergences in the contents of what they took as God's disclosures to them. But one will also find persons who, using what they took to be proper norms, found wild fluctuations in what they took God to be "speaking" to them on a given matter. This latter often leads them to modify—and sometimes to abandon—the ways in which they identify God's disclosures. The former, on the other hand, typically increases confidence that God is disclosing himself.

Second: there are clearly puzzling divergences *among* Christians in what they take God to be saying on certain matters. Christians who claim to rely upon prayer, meditation on Scripture, and the like can and do come to radically opposed conclusions about matters of considerable importance. They have disagreed about whether God wants us to reduce our nuclear arsenal or build a strong America; about slavery, celibacy, birth control, abortion, homosexuality, the Contras, and many other things. Immense human need is at issue in these things: if God does disclose his will, why is there not more diachronic convergence regarding them between various Christians? Does this not undermine the idea that such norms give access to God?

I can't answer this problem here; fortunately, I don't need to. That it *is* a problem doesn't hurt my case; it helps it. For my purpose is not apologetic but meta-apologetic. My aim has not been to show that Christians have reliable norms of religious rationality, but to explore the status of such norms. My present claim is that such norms, put into practice, can yield or fail to yield diachronic convergence which provides a kind of feedback on the norms, whether positive or negative. That there seem to be some serious problems of negative feedback thus helps my case. Of course, the Christian will not regard these problems as unanswerable. Scientists too, after all, are sometimes led (often heatedly) to conflicting conclusions by what they take to be the norms of science. Sometimes this is due to misapplication of the norms; sometimes it means the norms need revision. It has not yet led to wholesale abandonment of scientific project. Neither need it for the theistic project.

3.3 Step Three

It might be objected that although diachronic divergence gives reason to think a norm is *not* giving access to reality, convergence should not give any confidence that the norms succeed in giving such access. At the level of theories, it might be urged, it is a commonplace that since empirical data radically undermine a theory, a theory's making correct predictions does not entitle one to infer its truth. When we turn to the level of methodological norms, one might grant that if a set of norms does put us on track to reality, the norms would yield theories showing diachronic convergence. But when such convergence obtains, it does not follow that the norms are putting us on track. To think it does is not only to commit the fallacy of affirming the consequent; it also replays, at the level of method, the argument we have rejected at the level of theory.[46]

The first thing to say here is that it is not just underdetermination which causes the problem in going from data to theory. Even simple physical-object claims are, after all, radically underdetermined by observation: a physical object claim like "a bird flew overhead" has an immense number of observational implications. Nevertheless, we usually have no problem in going from a single observation to such belief. To be sure, our "going from" is not in this case by *inference*. We are hard-wired, so to speak, to form physical-object beliefs when our cognitive equipment is triggered by certain sensory input. And in going from a single observation to a vastly top-heavy physical-object belief, we are *trusting* this hard-wiring, this complex of dispositions that are part of our nature.[47]

Of course, tables are things that we can see; they are unlike God and electrons. But there is, I suggest, a level at which the norms governing our judgments about these things too must rest upon trust. When triggered by certain sorts of *cognitive input,* we find ourselves more confident that our norms are giving access to the way things are. We can to some extent articulate why this is so; but we shouldn't expect or demand this articulation to be an argument that rends the veil of cognition. In the realm of cognition by inference, as in the realm of perception, we ultimately find ourselves relying on dispositions that are part of our nature. Our task, in doing theory of rationality, is to articulate the norms implicit in these dispositions, to clarify their relations, and—sometimes—to improve and refine them. But it is not to justify them from a God's-eye perspective. Theory of rationality must be creaturely.

One last suggestion. I have suggested diachronic convergence as one cognitive input that increases confidence in our norms. I do not think it is the whole story. Ian Hacking has argued that in science, "practical ability breeds conviction."[48] For microscopic entities, he argues, realist convictions rightly come about "because of a large number of inter-locking low-level generalizations that enable us to control and create phenomena in the microscope. In short, we learn to move around in the microsopic world."[49] Similarly for subatomic particles, Hacking argues, "engineering, not theorizing, is the best proof of scientific realism about entities."[50] We come to belief in electrons when, by means of our specifications about their properties and powers, we can build experimental machines that *do* things for us. Philosophers of science, he says, have systematically neglected the field of experiment; they have thus ignored the real source of realism.

I think Hacking is on to something. But his phrase "breeds conviction" is telling. He gives persuasive accounts of how realism is generated as experimenters build particle accelerators, or refine microscopes. The details of his accounts carry us toward realism much as the actual experiments did for the scientists who did them. But here it is not exactly by *argument* that he does so. It is the successful experimental doings themselves (vicariously or firsthand) that produce conviction; and it does not so much argue us to realism as—in his phrase—"breed conviction" of it. Here too, perhaps we must trust our "hard-wiring."

Hacking's account also suggests another parallel for theory of religious rationality. Philosophers of religion also quite systematically ignore experiment—experiment in the religious life. And they thereby ignore how religious belief actually comes into play in "doing" things—in, say, changing lives, in breaking the bondage of sin. It is when we act on what Christian claims specify about God, when we risk being a fool if they are wrong, that we find things happening. At a deeper level, it is by using putative disclosures to *do things* that we test the norms for identifying God's disclosures, eventually coming to deep conviction about the beliefs they sanction. Jesus said:

> "If you *continue* in my word, you are my disciples, and you *will* know the truth. . . ."

This truth he speaks of may not make precise predictions; its value, he seems to say, lies in something different:

> ". . . and the truth will set you free."[51]

NOTES

The ideas in this paper have been gestating for many years, and I am indebted to many people for helping me begin putting them in writing. Above all, I thank Del Ratzsch for his generous and brotherly assistance.

I have also benefited from comments by colleagues at Calvin and at the Free University of Amsterdam, and by three former students, Trevor Rubingh, Houston Smit, and Brian Vander Wel. A 1987 Summer Institute in Philosophy of Religion, sponsored by the National Endowment for the Humanities, was a valuable opportunity to develop my ideas, receiving helpful suggestions from William Alston. And I thank Basil Mitchell and John Lucas for the opportunity to present an early version of this paper in their seminar at Oxford University.

Finally, I thank my undergraduate teacher D. Ivan Dykstra, who first gave me a glimpse of how value commitments underlie our various cognitive enterprises.

1. Charles M'Ilvaine, *The Evidences of Christianity,* 6th ed. (Philadelphia: Smith, English, and Co., 1861), p. 375.

2. Ibid., pp. 376–77.

3. For a different version of evidentialism, see my "Toward a Sensible Evidentialism: On the Notion of 'Needing Evidence,'" in W. Rowe and W. Wainwright, eds., *Philosophy of Religion: Selected Readings,* 2nd ed. (San Diego: Harcourt Brace Jovanovich, 1988), pp. 426–37.

4. Kuhn's defence of scientific belief (or "dogma") is that by dogmatically believing that their paradigm is true, scientists can better do the devoted drone-work that eventually, quite unwittingly, will uncover the shocking anomalies that lead that paradigm to be jilted for another. This clearly could not be *their* rationale for belief, nor does Kuhn intend it to be. See Thomas Kuhn, "The Function of Dogma in Scientific Research," in A. C. Crombie, ed., *Scientific Change* (New York: Basic Books, 1963), pp. 347–69.

5. David Hume, *Dialogues Concerning Natural Religion* (Indianapolis: Bobbs-Merrill, 1947), p. 132.

6. Precisely *how* theory of scientific rationality should be grounded in historical study of science is still under discussion. I discuss this in my "Toward a Historical Meta-Method for Assessing Normative Methodologies: Rationability, Serendipity, and the Robinson Crusoe Fallacy," in P. Asquith and R. Giere, eds., *PSA 1980,* vol. 1 (Philosophy of Science Association, 1980), pp. 211–22, and in "Curried Lakatos, or, How Not to Spice Up the Norm-Ladenness Thesis," in P. Asquith and T. Nickles, eds., *PSA 1982,* vol. 1 (Philosophy of Science Association, 1982), pp. 29–39. See also Larry Laudan's "Some Problems Facing Intuitionistic Meta-Methodologies," *Synthese* 67 (1986), 115–29.

7. On Reid's influence, I rely heavily on Larry Laudan's "Thomas Reid and the Newtonian Turn of British Methodological Thought," reprinted in Laudan's *Science and Hypothesis* (Dordrecht: Reidel, 1981), pp. 86–110.

8. *Essay on the Intellectual Powers of Man,* in *Works of Thomas Reid, D.D.,* ed. Hamilton, 6th ed. (Edinburgh, 1864), I: 235. Hereafter, page numbers are to *Works.*

9. Ibid., p. 472.

10. For a useful introduction to the mechanical philosophy, see Richard S. Westfall, *The Construction of Modern Science* (Cambridge: Cambridge University Press, 1977).

11. A useful introduction to Newtonian natural philosophy is Ernan McMullin's *Newton on Matter and Activity* (Notre Dame, Ind.: University of Notre Dame Press, 1978). Remaining indispensable is Alexandre Koyré's *Newtonian Studies* (Cambridge, Mass.: Harvard University Press, 1965).

12. I developed the levels schema in chap. 5 of my 1978 University of Pittsburgh Ph.D. dissertation: *The Interdependence of History of Science and Philosophy of Science: Toward a Meta-theory of Scientific Rationality* (Ann Arbor: University of Michigan Microfilms, 1978). Similar to my levels schema is the "hierarchical view" that Larry Laudan takes as his foil in his *Science and Values* (Berkeley: University of California Press, 1984), chap. 2.

13. A practical inference scheme was first used in this connection by Wilfrid Sellars in his "Induction as Vindication," *Philosophy of Science* 31 (1964), pp. 197–231.

14. See pp. 112–27 of Laudan's "The Epistemology of Light: Some Methodological Issues in the Subtle Fluids Debate," reprinted in Laudan, *Science and Hypothesis,* pp. 111–40.

15. Cited by John Watkins in *Science and Scepticism* (Princeton: Princeton University Press, 1984), p. 137.

16. Reid, pp. 470–71.

17. The difficulties are nicely summarized by Carl Hempel in his *Philosophy of Natural Science* (Englewood Cliffs, N.J.: Prentice-Hall, 1966), pp. 40–45.

18. See Hans Reichenbach, *Experience and Prediction* (Chicago: University of Chicago: 1938), pp. 339–372. Reichenbach's core idea has been developed by Wesley Salmon in various essays, e.g., his "Vindication of Induction," in H. Feigl and G. Maxwell, eds., *Current Issues in the Philosophy of Science* (New York: Holt, Rinehart, and Winston: 1961), pp. 245–56.

19. See section 7 of James's oft-reprinted "The Will to Believe."

20. Reichenbach, pp. 340–41.

21. Reichenbach, p. 346 and passim.

22. Carl Hempel, "Science and Human Values," in *Aspects of Scientific Explanation* (New York: Macmillan, 1965), p. 93. The essay first appeared in R. E. Spiller, ed., *Social Control in a Free Society* (Philadelphia: University of Pennsylvania Press, 1960), pp. 39–64.

23. Hempel, *Philosophy of Natural Science,* pp. 40–45.

24. Carl Hempel, "Turns in the Evolution of the Problem of Induction," *Synthese* 46 (1981), p. 404.

25. Gary Gutting, "Conceptual Structures and Scientific Change," *Studies in History and Philosophy of Science* 4 (1973), 227–30. For good recent discussions on change in the aims of science, see Laudan's *Science and Values,* and Ernan McMullin's "The Shaping of Scientific Rationality," in *Construction and Constraint* (Notre Dame, Ind.: University of Notre Dame Press, 1988), pp. 1–47, as well as chaps. 4 and 5 of Watkins's *Science and Scepticism.*

26. On Huygens see Koyré, Appendix A; on LeSage, Laudan's "Epistemology of Light. . . ."

27. I proposed "height" and "achievability" as constraints on scientific values in my 1978 dissertation, pp. 126–45. I there note (p. 130) that I hit on "achievability" as a constraint on scientific aims after hearing Larry Laudan criticize Christian morality on such grounds. (Laudan had claimed that the Christian ideal of sexual purity is irrational because it is utterly unachievable, leading only to neurotic frustration and guilt.) In *Science and Values,* Laudan states (p. 26, n. 3) that no advocates of the heirarchical view have proposed ways by which scientists rationally mediate disagreement about the aims of science. This is false, since just this was the point of my dissertation's discussion of achievability. But Laudan's book (pp. 50–53) does usefully distinguish various ways of applying an achievability criterion.

28. Robert Boyle "The Excellency and Grounds of the Corpuscular or Mechanical Philosophy" in Marie Boas Hall, ed., *Robert Boyle on Natural Philosophy* (Bloomington: Indiana University Press, 1965), pp. 190 and passim.

29. Ibid., p. 191.

30. M'Ilvaine, p. 377.

31. For Locke's views see both his *Reasonableness of Christianity* and his *Essay Concerning Human Understanding,* Book 4, chaps. 23 and 24. I discuss more recent versions in "The Problem of Miracle in the Apologetic from History," *Journal of the American Scientific Affiliation* 30 (December 1978), pp. 154–63.

32. The most tenacious attempt to give criteria for miraculousness along broadly inductive lines is that of Richard Swinburne in chap. 3 of his *The Concept of Miracle* (New York: St. Martin's Press, 1970). I do not believe Swinburne's attempt succeeds, but space prohibits discussion of the matter here.

33. John 9:30–33 (Revised Standard Version).

34. On the significance of Jesus' ministry to the "unclean" see Ben Meyer, *The Aims of Jesus* (London: SCM Press, 1979), chaps. 7 and 8; also illuminating is Marcus Borg's *Jesus: A New Vision* (San Francisco: Harper and Row, 1987), chapters 5 and 8.

35. Reichenbach, pp. 362–63. It is to be noted that for Reichenbach (p. 353) the straight rule sanctions not "beliefs" but "blind posits."

36. *The Confessions of St. Augustine,* trans. Rex Warner (New York: Mentor, 1963), p. 173.

37. Ibid., p. 180.

38. Ibid., p. 181.

39. On Aquinas see Kenneth Konyndyk's "Faith and Evidentialism," in R. Audi and W. Wainwright, eds., *Rationality, Religious Belief, and Moral Commitment* (Ithaca, N.Y.: Cornell University Press, 1986), pp. 85–86.

40. Adolf Grünbaum, "Free Will and the Laws of Human Behavior" in H. Feigl, W. Sellars, and K. Lehrer, eds., *New Readings in Philosophical Analysis* (New York: Appleton-Century-Crofts, 1972), p. 608.

41. See Imre Lakatos, "Falsification and the Methodology of Scientific Research Programmes," in I. Lakatos and A. Musgrave, eds., *Criticism and the Growth of Knowledge* (New York: Cambridge University Press, 1970), pp. 91–196.

42. From Lavoisier's "Reflections on Phlogiston" of 1785, quoted by Charles Gillispie, *The Edge of Objectivity* (Princeton: Princeton University Press, 1960), p. 230.

43. These are, at any rate, my impressions of the matter. I hope to unpack and support them in a forthcoming book.

44. Plantinga quoted from "Reason and Belief in God," in A. Plantinga and N. Wolterstorff, eds., *Faith and Rationality* (Notre Dame, Ind.: University of Notre Dame Press, 1983), p. 80. Alston, from "Christian Experience and Christian Belief," in *Faith and Rationality,* p. 107.

45. Augustine, p. 103.

46. For a trenchant deployment of this charge against convergent realists, see Larry Laudan, "A Confutation of Convergent Realism" in J. Leplin, ed., *Scientific Realism* (Berkeley: University of California Press, 1984), pp. 242–43.

47. I am here taking the sort of Reidian view deployed by Nicholas Wolterstorff in "Can Belief in God be Rational If It Has No Foundations" in *Faith and Rationality,* pp. 135–86.

48. Ian Hacking, *Representing and Intervening* (New York: Cambridge University Press, 1983) p. 191.

49. Ibid., p. 209.

50. Ibid., p. 274.

51. John 8:31–32.

PART II

Metaphysics and Theism

What If the Impossible Had Been Actual?

LINDA ZAGZEBSKI

1. COUNTERPOSSIBLES: THE STANDARD VIEW

What would have happened if $2 + 2$ had equalled 5? If I were to go backwards in time and change my lecture last week? If it had both rained and not rained here at this moment? I am assuming that each of these states of affairs is impossible, and impossible in as strong a sense as you like. None of them could have obtained no matter what. And likewise, each of the following propositions is necessarily false:

(1) $2 + 2 = 5$.
(2) I go backwards in time and change my lecture last week.
(3) It is both raining and not raining here at this moment.

But even if it is assumed that some state of affairs could never have obtained, can anything interesting be said about what would have been the case if it had? This is the question I wish to investigate in this paper.

According to the standard semantics of counterfactual conditionals, one of the peculiar features of a necessarily false proposition is the fact that it counterfactually implies every proposition whatever. For example, since proposition (3) is necessarily false, both Lewis and Stalnaker hold that the following propositions are both true:

(4) If it were both raining and not raining here at this moment, then I would be the Pope.

165

(5) If it were both raining and not raining here at this moment, then I would not be the Pope.

Since a necessarily false proposition is one whose truth is impossible, I shall call such propositions "impossible propositions." So, according to the standard view, for any such impossible proposition, pi, $pi > q$ and $pi > \neg q$ are both true for any q.[1] Let us call a 'would' counterfactual with an impossible antecedent a "counterpossible."[2]

My reaction to the standard view of (4) and (5) is not very strong. If every counterfactual conditional with an explicitly contradictory antecedent turns out to be true, I might find that acceptable. Much more worrisome, though, is the status of counterpossibles with antecedents which are more interesting because not explicitly contradictory. Consider (2) for a moment. If it is necessarily false, then on the standard view, both of the following are true:

(6) If I were to go backwards in time and change my lecture last week, then I would reach the same moment of time twice.

(7) If I were to go backwards in time and change my lecture last week, then I would not reach the same moment of time twice.

I am inclined to think that (6) is true, and true in a non-trivial way, and that (7) is false.

Those philosophers interested in the nature of God often maintain that God exists necessarily and is essentially good. If so, the propositions

(8) God does not exist

and

(9) God is not good

are necessarily false. But again, on the standard view this means that all of the following four propositions are true:

(10) If God did not exist, matter would not exist.
(11) If God did not exist, matter would exist anyway.

(12) If God were not good, there would be more evil in the world than there is.

(13) If God were not good, there would be less evil in the world than there is.

But I am strongly inclined to say that (10) and (12) are true and (11) and (13) are false. If so, there ought to be a way of showing this in the logic of counterfactual conditionals.

There have, of course, been attempts to justify the standard view that every counterpossible is true. The strongest justification I know of is by way of the following inference:

(i) Every impossible proposition pi entails any proposition q.

(ii) If a proposition p entails some proposition q, then $p > q$.

(iii) Every impossible proposition pi is such that $pi > q$.

Proposition (i) is obviously true if entailment is understood as strict implication, in which case it is one of the so-called Paradoxes of Strict Implication hotly debated during the fifties.[3] In the standard modal systems to say p strictly implies q is to say that it is impossible for p to be true and q false. But of course, if it is impossible for p to be true, it is impossible for p to be true and q false, no matter what q is.

But even if entailment is understood more narrowly than strict implication, there is still reason for thinking (i) is true. On any account we shall regard q as entailed by p if it can be derived from p by impeccable principles of deductive inference. But the following principles seem intuitively unassailable:

A) A conjunction entails each of its conjuncts.

B) Any proposition p entails $p \vee q$, no matter what q is.

C) The propositions $p \vee q$ and $\neg p$ entail q.

D) If p entails q and q entails r, then p entails r.

C. I. Lewis[4] and, much earlier, the author of *Quaestriones Exactissimae in Universam Aristotelis Logicam*, formerly attributed to Duns Scotus,[5] showed that using just these four principles any proposition is formally deducible from a contradiction by a derivation that has become familiar:

(1) $p \,\&\, \neg p$ Assumption

(2) p 1, principle A

(3) $p \lor q$ 2, principle B
(4) $\neg p$ 1, principle A
(5) q 3, 4 principle C

So by principle D:

(iv) A contradiction $p \,\&\, \neg p$ entails any proposition q.

If it is assumed that

(v) Every impossible proposition pi entails an explicit contradiction, $p \,\&\, \neg p$,

it follows that

(i) Every impossible proposition pi entails any proposition q.

There are those who deny the validity of the above deduction and are willing to pay the price of a radical departure from ordinary logic.[6] My aim, though, is to see if reasonable truth conditions for counterpossibles can be provided in a way that is less drastic.

So (i) is true as long as either entailment is understood as strict implication or if every necessarily false proposition is self-contradictory and principles A to D are valid principles of deductive inference. This means, of course, that the truth of such a proposition $pi \rightarrow q$ is trivial.

Let us turn now to (ii), a principle proposed by David Lewis and treated by John Pollock as an axiom of the logic of counterfactuals.[7] On this principle any counterfactual in which the antecedent logically implies the consequent is true. Pollock says the principle is "clear" and, to my knowledge, does not defend it. Lewis does not defend it either but says instead: "Further, it seems that a counterfactual in which the antecedent logically implies the consequent ought always to be true; and *one sort of impossible antecedent,* a self-contradictory one, logically implies any consequent" (emphasis mine).[8] Here he merely asserts (ii) and uses it to support (iii). But it is interesting that the support for (iii) just quoted would not apply to those cases, if any, in which the antecedent is impossible but not self-contradictory. Lewis himself thinks there are necessarily false sentences from which we cannot derive a contradiction. For example, he suggests that it is a necessary truth known *a priori* that there are talking donkeys in some possible world, but to deny that there are talking donkeys in some possible world is not self-contradictory.[9] We will return to these cases presently.

I know of no extended discussion of (ii), though it has been mentioned by other philosophers in connection with (iii).[10] If entailment is understood as strict implication, then I believe the examples I gave at the beginning of this paper show it to be false. In a much more restricted sense of entailment it is probably true, but in that sense I would no doubt deny (i). However, rather than go through the different notions of entailment which might be relevant here, I prefer to simply point out that the argument of (i) (ii) (iii) is inconclusive, and will turn to a different approach in the next two sections.

Aside from that argument, what other justification is there for the standard view (iii)? Lewis gives two other reasons. One is motivated by the desire to preserve the *reductio ad absurdum,* a common and valuable form of argument. If we want to show that a certain supposition is absurd, we sometimes argue that if it were true, then something ridiculous would follow. If p were true, q would be true; q is impossible; hence, p is impossible as well. This form of reasoning requires the truth of counterpossibles.

But the reductio procedure does not require that for every q, if p is impossible, $p > (q \,\&\, \neg\, q)$. It is enough that there be some impossibility which would be true if p were true. It is not necessary that *every* contradiction of the form $q \,\&\, \neg\, q$ be such that it would be true if some impossible proposition pi were true. So the need to preserve the reductio form of argument does not require that every counterpossible be true.

Finally Lewis justifies (iii) as follows: "There is at least some intuitive justification for the decision to make a 'would' counterfactual with an impossible antecedent come out vacuously true. Confronted by an antecedent that is not really an entertainable supposition, one may react by saying, with a shrug: If that were so, anything you like would be true!"[11]

I agree that we often say something like this, but the justification for it is not perfectly plain. Perhaps our reasoning is as follows: The supposition that this impossible proposition is true is so absurd that any other proposition might just as well be supposed true. In other words, the supposition that any arbitrary proposition q is true is no worse than the supposition that pi is true.

On the other hand, we can just as well find intuitive support for the contrary position. If some state of affairs φ could not have obtained no matter what, we might say there is literally nothing that would have been the case if φ had obtained. There simply is no "what if" in such a case. But this suggests that no counterfactual conditional with an impossible antecedent would be true. By the Law of Excluded Middle they would all be false.

Lewis considers just this option to his view (iii). He considers as an alternative that a counterfactual conditional is true only if there is at least one possible world in which the antecedent is true.[12] This means that all counterpossibles would end up false. But he rejects this possibility because of the desirability of defining 'might' counterfactuals in terms of 'would' counterfactuals.

"q might be true if p were true," symbolized as "q M p" (Pollock's notation) is defined as follows:

$$q \text{ M } p \equiv_{df} \neg (p > \neg q).^{13}$$

This means that since all 'would' counterpossibles are trivially true on Lewis's view, all 'might' counterpossibles are trivially false. That is, since $pi > \neg q$ is true for every pi and q, '$\neg (pi > \neg q)$' is false. So by the above definition, 'q might be true if pi were true' is false for every q and pi. But on the alternative account of 'would' counterpossibles in which they are all trivially false, the 'might' counterpossibles all come out trivially true by the same reasoning.

But the interdefinability of 'would' and 'might' counterfactuals leads to even stranger results than the ones we looked at at the beginning of this paper. Though it is true, on Lewis's view, that

> (4) If it were both raining and not raining here at this moment, then I would be the Pope,

it is nonetheless false that:

> (14) If it were both raining and not raining here at this moment, then I might be the Pope.

And though it is true that:

> (5) If it were both raining and not raining here at this moment, then I would not be the Pope,

it is false that:

> (15) If it were both raining and not raining here at this moment, then I might not be the Pope.

The pair of true (4) and false (14) and the pair of true (5) and false (15) seem to me to be exceedingly strange.

But just what does the interdefinability of 'would' and 'might' counterfactuals have to do with Lewis's defense of (iii)? He has given us two pairs of counterpossibles to consider. On his position, the 'would' counterpossibles are all true and the 'might' counterpossibles are all false. On the alternative view the 'would' counterpossibles are all false and the 'might' counterpossibles all true. Lewis says simply that the pair he prefers is "somewhat better intuitively" than the alternative pair. And, he says, the simple interdefinability of 'would' and 'might' seems plausible enough to destroy the appeal of a mixed pair of the Lewis 'would' and the alternative 'might'. Lewis continues, "There seems not to be much more to be said; perhaps ordinary usage is insufficiently fixed to force either choice, and technical convenience may favor one or the other pair depending on how we choose to formulate our truth conditions."[14]

But it seems to me there is more to be said. If the examples I have given are convincing, Lewis's alternative pair is no better than the one he prefers, and neither is a mix of the two. If it is a bad idea to have 'would' or 'might' counterpossibles all come out trivially true, it is also a bad idea to have them all come out trivially false. Some counterpossibles seem to be nontrivially true, and others nontrivially false. And for similar reasons, some might-counterpossibles seem to be nontrivially true and others nontrivially false. Ideally we should have truth conditions which reflect these intuitions. Furthermore, even though I am not committed to the interdefinability of 'would' and 'might' counterfactuals, it seems to me that if we can preserve it in the truth conditions, so much the better.

So far, then, the defense of the general thesis (iii) is less than persuasive. Furthermore, neither Lewis nor Stalnaker gains anything technically by (iii). It is not something they are forced into by their respective accounts of counterfactuals, and it makes their formulation of the truth conditions for counterfactuals rather inelegant. Lewis's version (p. 16) can be paraphrased as follows:

$p > q$ is true at a world w just in case *either* (i) p is false in every world accessible to w or (ii) some possible world accessible to w in which p is true and q is true is more similar to w than any possible world accessible to w in which p is true and q is not true. (emphasis mine)

Stalnaker simply invents a possible world which he calls the "absurd world" (called 'λ') in which all propositions are true in order to get (iii) to come out true. His defense of this move is brief: "The purpose of λ is to allow an interpretation of 'If A then B' in the case where A is impossible; for this situation one needs an impossible world."[15] Neither of them is forced to make all counterpossibles vacuously true. They are, however, able to get rid of them easily and there is, admittedly, the virtue of simplicity. But even then, it is no simpler to make them all true than to make them all false.

Counterpossibles are treated somewhat arbitrarily in the standard account of counterfactuals. This in itself would not be so bad if we didn't need to use these propositions in metaphysical arguments. In section 4, however, I will argue that their treatment can make a great deal of difference to metaphysics and, no doubt, to other areas of philosophy as well.

2. INTERESTING IMPOSSIBLE PROPOSITIONS

The standard semantics of modal and counterfactual logic allows no logically relevant distinctions among necessary falsehoods or among necessary truths. They have exactly the same logical entailments and counterfactual implications. On some views, such as those of John Pollock and David Lewis, they are even the same proposition. And the same can be said about necessary states of affairs. John Pollock, for example, says that logically equivalent states of affairs are the same state of affairs. He says:

Counterfactual conditionals tell us what would have been the case if something else had been the case. They are about "counterfactual situations" or states of affairs in a sense that requires that logically equivalent propositions describe the same situation.[16]

This means, of course, that if propositions (1) to (3) are necessary falsehoods, they are logically equivalent and on Pollock's account describe the same situation. And for the same reason the negations of (1) to (3) all describe the same situation. This strikes me as extremely implausible.

I am suggesting that it is not correct to say that if the impossible had been the case, then anything goes. We *can* say coherently and truly that certain things would have been the case had some impossible state of affairs obtained and that certain other things would not have been the case. The reason, I believe, is connected with the fact that it is a mistake to think of one necessary state of affairs as the same as any other, and for the same reason it is a mistake to think of one impossible situation as the same as any other. In particular, it is reasonable to think that some necessary states of affairs can enter into relations, including causal relations, with other states of affairs. Christians, in fact, are probably committed to this view. The necessary state of affairs of God's being good is no doubt causally related to the existence of a physical universe (though it is probably not causally sufficient). But it is surely not the case that the necessary state of affairs of its being the case that $2 + 2 = 4$ is causally related to the existence of a physical universe in that way. Furthermore, some philosophers, such as Thomas V. Morris, have suggested that God's existence is a necessary state of affairs which is causally related to other necessary states of affairs, such as the existence of numbers.[17] And even if it is thought that the claims made in these two examples are false, surely it is not because necessary states of affairs all have the same relations to other states of affairs.

This leads me to think that there are connections between impossible propositions which are independent of their status as logical impossibilities. Even if propositions have certain relations simply because one of them is a logical falsehood, there are still other connections between propositions which are independent of logical falsehood.

To see why it is natural to expect this to be the case, try the following thought experiment. Imagine for a moment that a large set of false propositions is numbered in lists as follows:

1.0	2.0	3.0	4.0
1.1	2.1	3.1	4.1
1.2	2.2	3.2	4.2
1.3 . . .	2.3 . . .	3.3 . . .	4.3 . . .

Suppose further that if proposition 1.1 had been true, proposition
1.2 might have been true, proposition 1.3 would have been true, but
all the propositions numbered 2 would have remained false. Suppose also that if 1.1 had been true, since 2.0 and 3.0 would still be
false, 3.1 would have been false. This seems to me to be a perfectly
coherent set of relations among some imagined set of false
propositions.

But suppose further that the propositions in lists 1 and 2 are
all necessary falsehoods, while those in list 3 are all contingent
falsehoods. Would this in any way destroy the coherence of the relations among this set of propositions as just described? It seems to
me that it would not. And if it would not, then it is not impossible
that there are counterfactual implications between propositions which
are independent of their individual necessity, contingency, or impossibility. In addition to the first three lists, there might be a fourth
list of propositions, each of which entails a contradiction. It might
then be the case that if any of these propositions were
true, every proposition would be true. If so, this would be a limiting
case.

Of course it might simply be denied that there are any propositions in lists 1 or 2. It might be held that all necessary falsehoods
are in list 4 since all entail contradictions. But what reason do we
have to think so?

I would like to propose an *a priori* argument that it is possible
that there is some proposition which is impossible, but not self-
contradictory. I will assume that to say a proposition is not self-
contradictory is to say that no proposition of the form '*p* & not
p' can be derived only from it and truths of logic in some adequate
formal system. I shall call such a proposition an Interesting Impossible Proposition (IIP).

(1) Assume that it is not possible that there is an IIP.
(2) Then there *are* no IIP's.
(3) So every impossible proposition is self-contradictory.
(4) The proposition 'There is a proposition which is false in
    all possible worlds but does not entail a contradiction' is
    not self-contradictory.
(5) Then the proposition 'There is an IIP' is not self-
    contradictory.

(6) So 'There is an IIP' is not impossible (3,5).
(7) So it is possible that there is an IIP.
(8) It is possible that there is an IIP and it is not possible that there is an IIP (1,7).
(9) Therefore, it is possible that there is an IIP (RAA).

The conclusion of this argument is curious because it means that if there are no IIP's, it is merely a matter of contingent fact. But we can go farther. If it is possible that there is an IIP, this is to say that there is an IIP relative to some world possible relative to the actual world. But in a modal system at least as strong as S4 the accessibility relation is transitive. So if there is an IIP relative to any world possible relative to the actual world, there is an IIP relative to the actual world, which is to say, if it is possible that there is an IIP, there is one. It is possible by the above argument; hence, there is one.

3. WHAT TO DO?

I have given an *a priori* argument that it is at least possible that there are impossible propositions from which no contradiction can be derived in an adequate formal system, and if the correct modal system is at least as strong as S4, there are in fact such propositions. I have also argued by examples that counterfactual conditionals with such interesting impossible propositions as antecedents are sometimes nontrivially true and sometimes nontrivially false. That is to say, there is some interesting impossible proposition pi and some proposition q for which $pi > q$ is true and $pi > \neg q$ is false. I have also offered the conjecture that some counterfactual implications between propositions hold independently of their modal status. Whatever the correct truth conditions for counterfactual conditionals may be, they should not be tied to the contingency or impossibility of the antecedent. How can this be expressed in the semantics of counterfactuals? In what follows I will give two suggestions, one adapted from Stalnaker and the other adapted from Lewis.

The basic idea behind Stalnaker's semantics is fairly simple. We say $A > B$ is true just in case if we add A to the stock of true propositions and modify them so as to make them consistent with

A, but make the modifications as small as possible, the resulting set of propositions includes *B.*

But we can retain this idea for counterfactual conditionals with IIP's as antecedents. Suppose we take the list of all true propositions, propositions true in the actual world, and add *A.* There are many things we can do with the resulting set of propositions. We can alter the truth value of individual propositions in the set in any number of ways, some of which constitute more serious changes in the set than others. One alternative is not to change anything. We can simply retain 'not *A*' in the set along with *A.* This ought to count as a major mutilation in the set. Or we could eliminate 'not *A,*' which in some cases would be to deny a necessary truth. But even then, this ought not be considered as great a mutilation as retaining 'not *A.*' The intuition I am relying on here is that it is a more serious change in the set of true propositions to alter them in a way which formally entails a contradiction than in a way which does not, even if the alternative also involves the denial of a necessary truth. Other adjustments in the truth value of propositions in the set would have to be made, and again, some alterations ought to be considered more serious than others. We ought to consider a change in the truth value of a necessary proposition, one true in all possible worlds, a greater change than any number of changes in contingent propositions. The relative degree of change for other changes could be handled as it is in standard counterfactual logic. Though each alternative set of propositions is maximal, in the case in which *A* is an impossible proposition, we need not think of them as descriptions of possible worlds.

We then say that if it takes a smaller change in the set of propositions true in the actual world to make *B* true than to make *B* false, then $A > B$ is true. If it takes a smaller change in the set to make *B* false than to make *B* true, then $A > \neg B$ is true. On this approach it would never turn out that both $A > B$ and $A > \neg B$ are true. If we do not assume that there is a unique case of minimal change, it may turn out that the changes required to make *B* true are equal to those needed to make *B* false. If so, then neither $A > B$ nor $A > \neg B$ is true. If we retain the definition of 'might' counterfactuals given on page 170, this procedure will also yield the truth value of such conditionals. And it will never turn out that 'If *A* were the case, *B* would be the case' is true, while 'If *A* were the case, *B* might be the case' is false, a result I found undesirable on the Lewis semantics.

The procedure just outlined is very close to the standard approach. Intuitively we think of degree of closeness to the actual world as measured by the degree of change from the actual world, though some degrees of change produce a description which, while intuitively consistent, do not describe possible worlds. As long as any maximal set of descriptions containing an impossible proposition represents a greater degree of change from the actual world than any maximal set of descriptions which does not contain an impossible proposition, the results of the procedure I have suggested for counterfactuals with possible antecedents ought to be exactly the same as those we get from the Lewis/Stalnaker approach.[18]

Suppose by way of illustration of the procedure I have outlined, we consider propositions (10) and (11). If we took a complete description of the actual world, substituted the proposition 'God does not exist' for 'God exists', and made minimal changes in the truth value of other propositions, what would be the result? If one of the necessary truths in the actual world is something like:

(16) Any contingent object in the world exists only because it was created by God,

since a change in the truth value of a necessary truth constitutes a greater change than the change in the truth value of any contingent truths, it follows that it is less drastic to change 'Matter exists' to 'Matter does not exist' than to deny (16). Therefore, (10) is true and (11) is false, as we would expect.

Similarly, if we substitute 'God is not good' for 'God is good', and if there is a necessary truth to the effect that a good being is motivated to produce good and nongood beings are not, this would have the consequence that the least drastic change in the resulting set of propositions would result in truths which entail that the world has a degree of good which is less than what it in fact has. And so (12) is true and (13) is false.

It seems to me that Lewis's formal model of counterfactuals can also be extended in a natural way to include counterpossibles. Lewis assigns to each world i a set $\$i$ of sets of possible worlds, called a *system of spheres* around i. For each such world i, $\$i$ is centered, nested, closed under unions, and closed under nonempty intersections. Any particular sphere around i is to contain just those worlds that resemble i to at least a certain degree. This degree is different for different spheres around i. The smaller a sphere, the more similar to *i* is a world which falls within it. On Lewis's model, each world in the system of spheres $i is accessible from *i*, which is to say, it is possible relative to *i*. Once he sets up his Ptolemaic astronomic system, he is able to give truth conditions for $A > B$ as follows:

> $A > B$ is true at *i* if and only if either there are no *A*-worlds in any sphere in the system of spheres $i, or there is a sphere in the system of spheres $i in which there are *A*-worlds and in which every *A*-world is a *B*-world.

We can modify the model by specifying that the set of worlds accessible from *i* is a sphere which is a subset of the system of spheres $i around *i*, so every accessible world is closer to *i* than is any inaccessible world. On the modified model we think of the "worlds" in which some IIP is true as farther removed from the actual world than any possible world. A "world" in which a contradiction is true would be farther away still.

We may retain the Lewis assignment of truth conditions for the modal operators $\Box$ and $\Diamond$. $\Box\varphi$ is true at a world *i* if and only if φ is true in every world accessible from *i*. $\Diamond\varphi$ is true if and only if φ is true in some world accessible from *i*. When *i* is the actual world, we say that "worlds" in which an IIP is true are not possible relative to the actual world.

Since for any *A,* there will always be some world in the modified $i in which *A* is true, we can eliminate the first disjunct of Lewis's truth conditions for counterfactuals above. The second disjunct alone is therefore sufficient to give the truth conditions for counterfactuals in this model, including counterpossibles.

As far as I can tell, this procedure also gives us the desired results for 'might' counterfactuals in the typical cases. It does not, however, say anything about the proper treatment of counterfactuals with antecedents which are self-contradictory. In particular, I do not know how to resolve the difficulty of a true (4) and a false (14), noted on page 170.

4. WHAT DIFFERENCE DOES IT MAKE?

Since counterpossibles have generally been considered uninteresting, it might be thought that even if the Lewis/Stalnaker treatment of them is a trifle eccentric, what harm can it do? In this section I would like to give some reason to think it could do quite a lot of harm. I will briefly give examples of cases in which the truth value of a counterpossible affects the outcome of a metaphysical argument or position. I believe there are many such examples, and there is nothing special about these few in particular.

The first example, from Aquinas (*De Veritate,* q. 1, art. 2), is mentioned by Alfred J. Freddoso.[19] Thomas argues that truth consists in a certain relation between world and intellect, so that if *per impossibile* there were no intellects but there were other things, there would be no truths. Aquinas is surely thinking of the truth of such a counterpossible as nontrivial, both because he would most assuredly deny the same counterpossible with consequent negated and because his claim rests on there being a special relationship between the existence of truths and the existence of God, a relationship which does not obtain between the existence of truths and $2 + 2 = 4$. So Aquinas's conceptual account of the nature of truth depends upon the fact that this counterpossible is true and true in a nontrivial way.

Another example can be found in van Frassen's discussion of Kant's First Analogy in *An Introduction to the Philosophy of Time and Space.* The First Analogy says that all change consists in alteration in the determinations of an enduring substance. Commenting on Kant's discussion, van Frassen says:

> Suppose, however, that all substances cease to be and other substances whose states are not simultaneous with any states of the former come into being. The way in which we have phrased this supposition suggests that the other substances exist after the former. But close scrutiny will show that this is not entailed: there is no ground for asserting *any* temporal relation between the states of the former and those of the latter, except nonsimultaneity. So there would be no way of ordering them all together into a single world history. Since we suppose that such an ordering is always possible, this supposition is absurd.[20]

A crucial step in this argument is the assertion of the counterpossible: *If all substances ceased to be and other substances came into being, there would be no way to order them all into a single world history.* Unlike the Aquinas example, this counterpossible is asserted without the assumption that the antecedent is impossible. Nonetheless, the counterpossible is neither denied nor reinterpreted in a trivial sense once it is concluded that the antecedent is impossible, and its nontrivial truth is necessary to get the desired conclusion.

A third example is theological. In "Perfection and Power"[21] Thomas V. Morris argues that though it is true that God couldn't have done evil since it is incompatible with his nature to want to, it is false that God couldn't have done evil even if he wanted to. This may be important if it is thought that perfect power requires that a being who has it not only can do anything he wants, but he *could* do anything he *wanted*. As Morris sees it, this point is important, since it calls attention to the fact that the lack of the possibility of God's doing evil resides in his firmness of will, not in any lack of power. Without the nontrivial truth of the counterpossible 'If God had wanted to do evil, he would have been able to', there does not seem to be any way to capture the difference between impossibility due to lack of power and impossibility due to lack of willing.

Another example arises in the account of God's omniscience. It seems to me that it is true that

(17) If God were not omniscient, he might not have believed that p (where p is some true contingent proposition)

and false that

(18) If God were not omniscient, he would still have believed p,

and it is important for one of my proposed solutions to the dilemma of divine foreknowledge and human free will that this be the case. If it is not the case, my solution cannot get going. But, of course, it cannot be the case on the standard semantics of counterfactuals.

5. CONCLUSION

The impossible is sometimes said to be the same as the unthinkable. David Lewis even suggests that the possibility operator '$\diamondsuit$' be read as: "It is entertainable that . . ." This is to suggest that we cannot even entertain the impossible, and so maybe the less said about it, the better. Of course, it is generally admitted that there are *propositions* expressing impossible states of affairs, though Lewis admits only one such, and so something has to be said about *them*. But whether they are thought to be one or many, it is usually agreed that they are indistinguishable from each other in their logical relations.

I have argued in this paper that the category of the impossible is much more interesting than this and that we have good reason to think that impossible propositions do not all have the same relationships to other propositions. In particular, I have argued that there are impossible propositions which are not self-contradictory. It seems to me that these propositions are not only entertainable but that we can say some interesting things about what would have been the case had certain ones obtained. I have suggested a way to extend the standard way analysis of counterfactuals to take into account that some counterpossibles are nontrivially true and some are nontrivially false. Finally, I have claimed by way of examples that the treatment of the truth conditions of these propositions can make a difference to metaphysical arguments.

My remarks in this paper have covered only a small part of the territory of the impossible. I suggest that the impossible is an ontological category of great interest, and may turn out to be important to an understanding of metaphysical problems.[22]

NOTES

1. I will follow John Pollock in using the symbol > for 'would'-counterfactual implication. So '$A > B$' is to be read as: 'If it were the case that A, then it would be the case that B.'

2. 'Even if' and 'might' counterfactuals have different truth conditions and need to be handled separately. I will have something to say about the 'might' counterfactuals later.

3. For a discussion of this issue see J. F. Bennett, "Meaning and Implication," *Mind* 63 (1954), 451–63; Peter Geach, "Entailment," *Aristotelian Society* Supplementary Volume XXXII (1958), 157–72; C. Lewy, "Entailment and Necessary Propositions," in *Philosophical Analysis,* ed. Max Black, (Ithaca: Cornell University Press, 1950), 195–210; "Entailment," *Aristotelian Society* Supplementary Volume XXXII (1958), 123–42; John Pollock, "The Paradoxes of Strict Implication," *Logique et Analyse* 9 (1966), 180–96, T. J. Smiley, "Entailment and Deducibility," *Proceedings of the Aristotelian Society* 59 (1958–59), 223–54; P. F. Strawson, "Necessary Propositions and Entailment-

statements," *Mind* 57 (1948), 184–200, and G. H. von Wright, "The Concept of Entailment," in *Logical Studies* (London: Routledge and Kegan Paul, 1957), 166–91.

4. C. I. Lewis and C. H. Langford, *Symbolic Logic* (New York: Century, 1932; 2nd ed., New York: Dover, 1959).

5. Quoted by William Kneale in "The Province of Logic," *Contemporary British Philosophy,* ed. H. D. Lewis (London, 1956), p. 239.

6. Nicholas Rescher and Robert Brandom deny the validity of the above deduction in *The Logic of Inconsistency* (Oxford: Basil Blackwell, 1980). They claim that it fails at step 4 and that we can allow the truth of a single contradiction without committing ourselves to logical anarchy. If so, of course, there is no reason to think that a contradiction counterfactually implies every proposition either. Furthermore, Anderson and Belnap, in "The Pure Calculus of Entailment," *Journal of Symbolic Logic* 27 (March 1962), 19–52, deny (i) on the grounds that the relationship of entailment between p and q requires a condition of relevance in the content of p and q.

7. Pollock, *The Foundations of Philosophical Semantics* (Princeton, N.J.: Princeton University Press, 1984), p. 128; also in "Four Kinds of Conditionals," *American Philosophical Quarterly* 12 (Jan. 1975), p. 55.

8. David Lewis, *Counterfactuals* (Cambridge, Mass.: Harvard University Press, 1973), p. 24.

9. Lewis, "On the Plurality of Worlds" (Oxford: Blackwell, 1986), p. 112.

10. In *A Theory of Counterfactuals* (Indianapolis: Hackett, 1986) pp. 253–54, Igal Kvart agrees with Lewis's principle (ii), but he rejects the idea that this is a good reason to take counterpossibles as true. Instead, he denies (i). On the other hand, Alfred J. Freddoso says in "Human Nature, Potency and the Incarnation" (*Faith and Philosophy* 3, no. 1, p. 44) he is inclined to the position that though a necessarily false proposition strictly implies every proposition, it does not counterfactually imply every proposition. He therefore accepts (i) on the broad interpretation of entailment, but rejects (ii). Neither Kvart nor Freddoso gives a justification for his rejection of (i) or (ii) apart from counterexamples to (iii) and the need to reject one or the other.

11. Lewis, *Counterfactuals,* p. 24.

12. Ibid., p. 25.

13. Stalnaker dissents from this definition in "A Defense of Conditional Excluded Middle" in *Ifs,* ed. William Harper, Robert Stalnaker, and Glenn Pearce (Dordrecht: Reidel, 1981), pp. 87–106.

14. *Counterfactuals,* pp. 25–26.

15. Stalnaker, "A Theory of Counterfactuals," *American Philosophical Quarterly* monograph series no. 2, *Studies in Logical Theory* (Oxford, 1928), p. 103.

16. *Foundations of Philosophical Semantics,* p. 141.

17. Morris, "Absolute Creation," *Anselmian Explorations* (Notre Dame, Ind.: University of Notre Dame Press, 1987), 161–78.

18. Lewis and Stalnaker differ slightly from each other. Stalnaker thinks

there will always be a world which is closer than any others, and hence, for any A and B, either $A > B$ or $A > -B$ is true. Lewis does not make the uniqueness assumption and so does not accept the Law of Conditional Excluded Middle.

19. See note 10 above.

20. B. C. van Frassen, *An Introduction to the Philosophy of Time and Space* (New York: Random House, 1970), p. 48.

21. *Anselmian Explorations,* pp. 70–75.

22. This paper was written during the fall 1987 while I was a senior fellow at the Center for Philosophy of Religion at the University of Notre Dame. I am grateful to the Center for its support and to the Notre Dame Philosophy Department for inviting me to present the paper at a philosophy colloquium. I am indebted to several people for help in its preparation: Aron Edidin, Howard Wettstein, Philip Quinn, Robert Audi, and especially Michael Kremer.

Nomo(theo)logical Necessity

Del Ratzsch

The logical status of physical natural law statements has been, to say the least, problematic. Just what *are* natural laws? And what sorts of statements express natural laws? The easily available categories of truth—such as necessary truth or contingent material generalization—have been widely perceived as unsatisfactory, and although enjoying sporadic popularity, the easily available categories of falsehood seem even worse. Laws and their expressions have a special sort of strength and character not easy to capture. Beyond that is a deeper ontological question. If statements of law have some special logical strength of character, what underlies that character? What is the ontological underpinning of law? In what follows, I will first review and explore some questions concerning the logical structure of law statements. There are, I think, five classes of candidates. Two—law statements as material or as categorical necessities—have been almost universally rejected traditionally, and I shall reject them as well. A third—lawhood as defined by particular roles in a deductive system—I shall reject fairly summarily as well. The remaining two—one employing universally quantified subjunctive conditionals and the other involving entailment of dispositional properties—both have a variety of technical difficulties, but they also have in common a feature which seems to me necessary to any adequate characterization of law. It is that common feature and its possible ontological implications which I find of interest and which I shall explore in the later part of the paper. Out of those ontological implications some suggestive theological implications will emerge, and I shall discuss those in the final section of the paper.

LAW STATEMENTS AS MATERIAL TRUTH FUNCTIONAL

Earlier in this century, various philosophers, impressed both with the promise of formal logic and with the prescriptions of positivists, endeavored to reduce everything in sight to forms that could be captured by the resources of first-order logic.[1] Attempts to capture the appropriate character of natural law statements in such terms were never successful. There was a variety of difficulties, but among the most serious was the inability of constructions from truth functional connectives to 'support' subjunctives.

For instance, it is generally admitted that if 'Iron expands when heated' states a law, then it follows that 'Were this bit of iron heated, then it would expand', and perhaps also that 'Were this object iron, it would expand if heated'. But ordinary material generalizations do not support those sorts of inferences. Consider Nelson Goodman's famous example: 'All the coins in my right pocket on VE day were silver'. We could not legitimately conclude from that that had this penny, *p,* been in my right pocket on VE day, it would have been silver. The generalization, in this case, does not support the relevant counterfactual.

Some of the material constructs proposed as giving the logical structure of law statements were more sophisticated than mere generalized material conditionals (for instance, Carnap's reduction sentences) but extensional truth functional logic simply did not have the required resources.

LAW STATEMENTS AS
(CATEGORICAL) NECESSARY TRUTHS

The view that law statements are necessary truths has not been a terribly popular one historically, although it would have the advantage that such statements would entail the relevant subjunctives. But few, until recently, have explicitly endorsed it. And taken baldly, it does seem counterintuitive. For instance, it would hardly *seem* a threat to the fundamental principles of coherence had our ordinary physical objects attracted each other proportionally to the inverse of their distances to the 2.00001 power. And it *seems* unlikely that first-order logic would collapse were the speed of light not a limiting constant. And so forth.

It may be, however, that the initial apparent implausibility of laws holding necessarily comes from an implicit tendency to think of necessities in terms of simple, immediate first-order entailments involving *categorical* predicates (or properties). For instance, we take as paradigm cases of necessary propositions such things as 'All bachelors are unmarried', '2 + 2 = 4', and so forth. The properties involved in the relevant states of affairs are categorical in the sense of being unconditional or nondispositional. And to think of laws as having that sort of character is, indeed, seriously counterintuitive. There is, however, a different sort of necessary statement that some have recently proposed as giving the structure of statements of law, and which appears much more plausible. We will look at that view shortly.

LAW STATEMENTS AS DEFINED BY DEDUCTIVE ROLES

A number of commentators have been attracted to the idea that whether or not some statement expresses a law depends (at least partially) upon whether or not it plays an appropriate sort of role in an appropriate sort of deductive system. Although the details of the roles and systems may differ, this general view can be found in writings ranging from those of Ernest Nagel to those of David Lewis.[2] Of course, it is well known that any deductive system can be axiomatized in any number of different ways. While some roles and characteristics (being true, being a proposition within the system, entailing or being entailed by specifiable propositions within the system, and so forth) do not change under varying axiomatizations, others (being an axiom, for instance) do. Thus, some propositions which fulfill one role in one axiomatization may fill some entirely different role in another. The roles frequently cited as defining lawhood — axiomhood, for instance — are among those roles which are changeable. But as an unrepentant realist, it seems to me that some things simply are laws and other things simply aren't, and that, consequently, *variable* status with respect to a deductive system cannot tell the whole story of what is or is not a proper statement of law. Things get even slipperier in views according to which a law statement is something which plays a specified role in whatever system gives us the "best combination of strength and simplicity," since that depends (presumably) on what we take "best" to come to, which depends on various of our epistemic values. It might be argued that if we are dealing with logical equivalences, the claim that some from among those equivalences really *are* laws, and others of the equivalences really *aren't* is incoherent. But logical equivalence does not constitute identity of propositions, and that logical equivalence to a law statement is an indicator of lawlikeness is, at a minimum, unclear.

I believe, then, that we can correctly reject the ideas that statements of natural law are either material statements, categorical necessities, or arbitrary components in particular deductive systems. After a short detour, we will turn to the remaining two options.

THREE GRADES OF SUBJUNCTIVE INVOLVEMENT

It is widely recognized that there are intimate connections between subjunctives and laws. On the most general level, as noted earlier, it is widely agreed that laws support subjunctives. That is usually taken to mean that statements of law (whatever they may be) *entail* subjunctives. One could simply stop at that point, claiming that laws are not themselves fundamentally subjunctive in character, although there is a connection in that subjunctives logically flow from them. Second, one could hold that statements of law contain *components* the proper *analysis* of which involves subjunctives. Or, third, one could simply identify law statements with certain types of subjunctives—universally quantified subjunctives, for instance.

We have already briefly examined one view on the first level — laws as categorical necessities. We now will examine a view from each of the remaining two levels. My own view is that there is indeed something fundamentally subjunctive about law statements and that, consequently, whatever the correct analysis of the structure of law statements turns out to be, it will lie somewhere on either the second or third level.

Let us begin with a view of the second sort—that law statements involve components the proper analysis of which (I believe) involves subjunctives.

LAWS AS DISPOSITIONAL NECESSITIES

Recent views according to which law statements are necessary are much more subtle than older ones. On these views — e.g. "causal powers" views — law statements express necessary connections between properties (or the having of properties), but not all the properties involved are categorical — in fact, the 'consequent' properties in such statements are, on these views, *dispositional* properties.[3] Thus, the logical structure of the law governing iron's expandability under heat is something like

(1) 'Being iron' entails 'expansiveness under heating'.

(Or that 'being crystal entails being fragile' might be a law.) The law, then, involves that dispositional property being essential to the nature of iron. Since, of course, dispositions can be thwarted, overridden and whatnot, a law statement, although necessary, would not have the wooden rigidity we normally associate with necessities.

Although this view has a number of attractions (some of which will emerge later), it is still seriously incomplete as an analysis until we know what sort of animal a dispositional property is. The attractiveness which this very fuzziness may permit may dissipate along with the fuzziness when we try to sharpen the picture up a bit.

There seem to be two broad categories of views concerning dispositional properties: that they are ultimately reducible to logically or materially connected underlying categorical properties, and that they are not so reducible. Both views have had some recent popularity, so we will briefly consider each in turn.

The idea that dispositional properties are reducible to categorical properties in some logical or material relationship has something of a history.[4] I take it that this alleged reducibility was what underlay Carnap's attempts at constructing reduction sentences from purely categorical and material resources. In any case, the founding intuition seems to be that a dispositional property (*fragility,* for instance) involves some sort of stable connection between, say, being hit in some specified way and being shattered. What is of interest is the exact nature of the connection, exactly what the connection is a connection between, and how that connection is to be captured and expressed formally. If we are restricted to the standard logical connectives, we must evidently choose between property entailment or some contingent material connections. But neither seems adequate.

If dispositions were construed as property entailments, and if law statements were property entailments of dispositions, then law statements would be of the following form:

(2) That x is A entails (that x is B entails that x is C).

It seems seriously implausible to claim that dispositions simply are entailments, but this proposal has other serious difficulties as well. To begin with, instances of the consequent of (2), i.e.,

(3) that x is B entails that x is C

will, if true, by themselves entail instances of (2) — at least if we hold the quite plausible views that modal propositions if true are necessarily true and that necessarily true propositions are entailed by any proposition whatever. Thus, the law — (2) — would follow trivially from the disposition alone, meaning that the antecedent of (2),

(4) that x is A

played no significant role whatever. But surely in the case of the statement concerning iron ((1) above), it isn't just irrelevant that it is *iron* under discussion.

In order to try to accommodate the role that the antecedent intuitively plays in such cases, it might be required (as some in fact do require) that the antecedent property be an *essential* property or even a *kind* property. That, however, will not change the fact that the antecedent plays no significant role. In fact, statements of the form (2) will still be true, no matter what essential or kind property the antecedent involves.

Worse yet, if something like (3) is correct, if properties B and C are related necessarily, and if that represents a disposition, then absolutely every object will have that disposition, since everything will be necessarily such that if it is B it is also C. But any property possessed by absolutely everything is often going to be seriously explanatorily tenuous.

If the antecedent is to play any significant role at all, then the antecedent must be within the scope of the same modality (if any) as the rest of the formula. That means on the present view that we must retreat at a minimum to perhaps something like

(5) That x is A entails (that $B * C$)

where the "*" represents some materially constructible connective.

That doesn't look too promising either. For one thing, depending upon what the proposals for '*' are, (5) may simply reduce to a variety of categorical entailment. For another, reducing dispositions to some material connection between categorical properties does not seem very plausible. Dispositions simply seem stronger than anything constructible from merely material resources. That, I take it, is why positivist-style reduction sentences never worked.

Thus, if the special character of law is buried in a disposition and then dispositions are interpreted as property entailments, the results are formally much too strong, and if the dispositions are interpreted purely materially, the dispositions are much too weak and the overall result may simply be a variety of categorical necessity.

It looks, then, as though if laws can be construed as expressing necessary connections between kind properties and dispositions, the dispositions cannot be reducible to some pair of categorical properties connected in ways expressible by the usual complement of logical connectives and operators.

There is, however, a different view of the nature of dispositions which has a respectable pedigree, and that is that the constituent properties of dispositions are linked subjunctively.[5] A proper analysis of, for example, the disposition *fragility* might perhaps be as follows:

(6) x is fragile: were x hit in manner m, x would shatter

Subjunctives, of course, represent a type of connection and a degree of strength not available with the more standard connectives, and their strength lies between that of necessity and that of mere material implication or equivalence. Subjunctives will also, of course, support subjunctives trivially. All of that is presumably in their favor. On this view of dispositions, then, a law statement will have the structure: (taking some grammatical license):

(7) 'being F' entails 'being such that were it A then it would be B'

(or possibly (8) 'being F' is logically equivalent to 'being such that were it A it would be B').

For example,

(9) 'being crystal' entails 'being such that (were it struck in manner m, it would shatter)'.

That may be seen as initially promising, but we're perhaps not out of the woods yet. If (9) is true, it will follow that (using ">" for the subjunctive)

(10) necessarily (x) $(Cx \supset (Mx > Sx))$

which in turn entails

(11) necessarily $(x)((Cx \wedge Mx) \supset Sx)$.

The acceptability of (11) seems to me not entirely obvious. Does the striking of a specified sort of crystal in a specified way *entail* the shattering of the crystal? The underlying problem here is that necessity swamps subjunctivity (e.g; $\Box(P > Q) \equiv \Box(P \supset Q)$). It is not clear to me how different from categorical necessity views the present view really turns out to be, and if they are inadequate, so may the present view be.

One could, of course, claim that dispositions are not subjunctive, but are either fundamentally unanalyzable or involve primitive and irreducible connections between properties.[6] However, I do not know how such a claim might be worked out and so will not consider it further.

In any case, although I find myself a bit uneasy about the general idea that law statements are necessities, this view of laws as entailments of dispositions seems to me still to be a live possibility. Lacking an analysis of dispositions, it is still incomplete, but such an analysis will, I suspect, be fundamentally subjunctive. That alleged fact will have some consequences, and we will come back to this view a bit later.

LAW STATEMENTS AS QUANTIFIED SUBJUNCTIVES

If law statements are required to support subjunctives, then there must be some close relationship between them, and some philosophers have been attracted to the position that statements of law simply *are* universally quantified subjunctives.[7] Thus, the law concerning iron's expansion if heated might be

(12) any iron were it heated would expand

i.e.,   (13) (x) $((Ix \wedge Hx) > Ex)$

or perhaps (14) (x) $(Ix \supset (Hx > Ex))$.

That sort of view has several initially attractive features. First of all, (13), for example, would support counterfactuals trivially—being one itself. Second, law statements, on this view, would not be necessities but would be stronger than material constructs. Traditionally, at least, that has been thought to be the logical space within which law statements are to be placed.

There are, however, some technical difficulties with this sort of view. I'm not entirely sure whether or not they are insurmountable. But in order to see what some of them are, we must detour into some analyses of subjunctives. Surprises and surprising morals lie there, and many of them apply to the previous view as well (assuming, as I do, that the proper analysis of dispositions is fundamentally subjunctive).

SUBJUNCTIVES AND POSSIBLE WORLDS

Serious attempts to analyze (or at least provide truth conditions for) subjunctives in terms of possible worlds began in the late sixties.[8] (By that point it had become abundantly clear that no construct out of the connectives of standard first-order logics would do.) The (simplified) basic idea is as follows. A given possible world, it is claimed, may bear closer similarity to some worlds than it does to others. And surely that is the case. We can imagine possible worlds only very slightly different from the actual world, as well as worlds wildly and bizarrely different from this world. Given the relative differences in similarity among worlds, we can rank other worlds in terms of their degree of similarity to this world (or to some other specified 'base' world), or, in other words, construct a similarity ordering among worlds. The proposed characterization in world terms for subjunctives was this: a conditional

(15) were A the case, then B would be too

is true in a world w if in the world most similar to w in the relevant respects and in which A is true, B is true as well—i.e., if the nearest A-world to w on the relevant similarity ordering is also a B-world.

The major proposals for world-analyses of subjunctives which followed the initial proposal differed in various ways, but were, for all that, basically variants of original theme. For instance, (among other differences) some analyses rejected the idea that there could be a uniquely closest A-world (in the above case) either because the ordering might only be partial (there might be ties in the similarity ranking) or because there was no A-world such that it was true of it that it was a closest A-world—for any A-world there was always a closer (although the sequence of A-worlds could be bracketed in the same way that a function which approaches a limit can be, and so forth).[9] But in these cases as well, the key was relative position on a similarity ordering, an ordering which was founded upon similarity in certain respects to the base world. The squabbles were not over the fundamental intuition but over the technicalities of the logical fine-structure of the ordering and whatever consequences that might have for the truth conditions for subjunctives.

So worlds can be ranked by relative similarity and the truth conditions for subjunctives can be given in terms of the truth value of the conditional's consequent in a specified world, worlds, or sequence of worlds, in the ordering (either complete or partial) in which the conditional's antecedent was true.

Exactly how all this is supposed to go was not, perhaps, quite clear. For instance, was a world like this one except with one extra tadpole more or less similar to this world than was one like this one except with one less butterfly, in cases where what was at issue was what would happen were I to heat a piece of iron?

Moreover, exactly how the orderings work is not entirely settled either. One intuition is that there is exactly one similarity array (for any base world), the location of any world in that array determined by some (perhaps primitive) global index of similarity *überhaupt* for that world. Thus, although world *a* may be more similar to *b* than is *c* in some particular *respects,* and although *c* may be more similar to *b* than is *a* in some other *respects,* the similarity ordering relevant to the truth or falsehood will represent some index of *overall* similarity, not directly tied to any particular set of respects. Another intuition is that similarity orderings are generated according to specific respects of similarity—some worlds are more similar than others in some respects, less similar than others in other respects. Thus, *different* orderings would be generated according to different respects of similarity—generated by, in effect, holding constant some features of the base world while making changes necessary to make true the antecedent of whatever subjunctive was in question.

Those differing intuitions result in different ways of viewing what is sometimes called the "pragmatic ambiguity" of subjunctives. Consider the following counterfactual:

(16) Had Caesar been in command in Korea he would have used the Bomb.

Is (16) true or false? Obviously true, some might say. He was exactly that sort. Obviously false, others might say, because what is true is

(17) Had Caesar been in command in Korea he would have used catapults.

The dissonance between the asserters of (16) and those of (17) pretty clearly involves some background matters — Caesar's actual favoritism toward catapults versus his actual propensity to use the best firepower available. The problem here, on the "respects" view, is over which respect to hold constant in generating the relevant similarity ordering which will determine which world is nearest, a different world being nearest on the different orderings. On the "*überhaupt*" view, the dispute is over which of Caesar's propensities to build (tacitly) into the antecedent, a different world being nearest for the two different antecedents. (We will here pointedly ignore compromise positions such as: Had Caesar been in command in Korea he would have launched the Bomb by catapult.)

For present purposes we do not need to settle on either the "respects" or the "*überhaupt*" intuition, since all the points of present relevance hold for both. First, the two will be extensionally equivalent. The *überhaupt* ordering and the specific orderings generated by reference to various respects are related in such a way that for any worlds a and b, respect of similarity R, and proposition A, if a is the nearest A-world to b on an ordering generated by reference to respect R, then a is the nearest $A\&R$-world to b on the similarity-*überhaupt* ordering. In fact, this bare *überhaupt* ordering is also (I suspect) one determinant in the generating of the orderings according to respects, being part of the matrix out of which they grow. (The above does not, however, entail that the entire orderings will coincide. But even if they do not, that will not affect the extensional equivalence.) Thus, any subjunctive will be assigned the same truth value, at a given world, whether we take the constants as part of the expanded antecedent (*überhaupt*) or as generative of a specific similarity ordering (respects).

Second, the similarity arrays will be rigid on either view. By that I mean that on either view it will be either necessarily true or necessarily false that

(18) *given* an ordering, the nearest world to the base world in which (say) *A* is true will (will not) be a world in which *B* is true.

That is not, of course, to say that the subjective itself will be modal but that once the ordering is laid down, however that is done, then the truth or falsehood of the subjunctive *follows* from that ordering by necessity. From any fully specified ordering generated by (*inter alia*) holding some respect *R* as a constant, the truth value of $A > B$ *follows*. And from the correlate *überhaupt* ordering, exactly the same truth value *follows* for $(A \wedge R) > B$. That entailment of truth value (or the necessity of the whole "corresponding conditional"—a conditional with a specification of ordering as antecedent and the subjunctive as consequent) is, again, what I mean by the rigidity of the orderings, and we have such an entailment on either view. In what follows I will adopt the "respects" locution for convenience.

QUANTIFIED SUBJUNCTIVES: SOME SEMANTICS

Returning now to the matter of the structure of law statements, consider as a candidate the simple universally quantified subjunctive.

(19) $(x)(Ax > Bx)$.

How do we analyze (19) in world terms?[10]

(19) does not point us to any particular world. It tells us that, with respect to each actual object in the world, in the nearest world where it is *A*, it is also *B*. There is, of course, no reason whatever to think that the nearest world where object *a* is *A* is the same world as the nearest one in which object *b* is *A*, and so forth. Otherwise, the nearest world in which anything was *A* would have to be a world in which everything (in this world) was *A*. Thus, it points us to an enormous number of worlds. But one problem with (19) as a law

analysis is that it doesn't for all that point us to enough worlds. When we espouse, say, some law of gravity, we do not mean it as having (loosely) application only to the things that in fact exist. We also take as an implication of the law that had there been one more rock in the world (which rock in fact doesn't exist) that it would have fallen if released above the ground and so forth. But, of course, since the above quantifier ranges only over existing objects, we never get directed to worlds other than worlds in which objects existing in this world are dropped.

In fact, for all I know, it may be some sort of biological law that had there been any unicorns, they would have had more than some number n of optic fibers for each square millimeter of retina. And that might be a perfectly respectable law, despite the lament-able absence of unicorns in this world. Here again, something of the form $(x)(Ux > Nx)$ won't do. It isn't just that Spot (and other things in this world) would have had that feature had *he* been a unicorn, but that *had there been* any unicorns at all (whether or not any of them would bear any connection to things in this world), *they* would have had that optic characteristic.

But that form too

(20) had there been any unicorns all of them would have had that optic characteristic

fails rather decidedly. It seems to direct us to the nearest world in which there are any unicorns at all, and then tells us to see whether or not all the unicorns in that world are so optically equipped. But even if they are, there seems no reason to think that to be decisive. For one thing, we are checking only one world (the closest unicorn-containing world). Why should we think that if it happens (perhaps *accidentally*) to be true that all (one?) unicorns in that world are as described, that that (single) unicorn in that world having a char-acteristic makes it a law in this world that unicornicity is accom-panied by that characteristic? Perhaps in the nearest world in which there are unicorns, it is object a that gets to be the unicorn, and a is F. But suppose that in the nearest world in which object b gets to be a unicorn, b isn't F at all. Why ought a's greater nearness in unicornicity make *any* other accidental characteristic a has in his unicorn mode a lawful characteristic of unicorns? And that is ex-actly what happens in this situation.

Perhaps a better way of approaching the question would be in terms of quantification over individual essences—a view which some maintain is the only way to talk sensibly about things in worlds anyway.[11] Thus, the universally quantified form of the relevant statements might be

(21) (e) (were e co-instantiated with A, then e would be co-instantiated with B).

(Notice that if law statements are property entailments they are already implicitly quantified in just this way. If the specified entailment does hold, then anything having the first property in any world will also have the second.) Suppose we try (21) in world talk. Here again, it will frequently be the case that the nearest world in which essence e_1 is co-instantiated with A will be a different world from the nearest one in which essence e_2 is co-instantiated with A. We will thus, again, have to canvass a huge range of different worlds to see whether or not all the essences get co-instantiated with B as well. But at least here the quantifier will range over all the right items in all the relevant worlds—neither of which happens on some of the other methods.

But although I am not sure what to make of it, there is at least an oddity here, and it is perhaps a glimmer of the special nature of laws (as a consequence, I suspect, of orderings being based (*inter alia*) on laws).

It is perfectly possible that the nearest world, w_1, in which, say, e_1 is co-instantiated with A is also a world in which e_2 is co-instantiated with A, but which is not the nearest world in which e_2 is co-instantiated with A. That being the case, although e_1 is B in its nearest A world (provided the claim holds), and although e_2 is B in *its* nearest A-world, e_2 can exist in w_1 quite happily alongside e_1 (or its exemplification) being both A and not-B. So the connections between A and B need not be *necessary*, and need not even *hold* in *all* the *worlds* relevant to the determination of truth value for the original quantified conditional. Yet the fact that worlds are clustered about the base world along *all* the relevant orderings in the way they are (with the first appearance of an A-exemplification by any given essence being a B-exemplification as well) certainly indicates that the connection between A and B is not sheer accident.

SUBJUNCTIVES AND ONTOLOGY

The next point to be noted is that despite the rigidity of the orderings, despite the necessity of all fully specified corresponding conditionals, some orderings are privileged. For instance, consider the subjunctive

(22) were I to release this chalk, it would fall.

We can evaluate that with respect to innumerable different orderings (or, alternatively, we can fill out the antecedent in a variety of ways). Suppose we choose to hold constant all the relevant laws of nature, etc., etc. On the resultant rigid ordering, the corresponding conditional (not the subjunctive consequent) is necessary, and the above subjunctive presumably comes out true. But suppose we were to hold constant (among other things) the present position of the chalk. In other words, suppose we ordered worlds with respect to (again, among other things) their similarity to this one in terms of the present location of the chalk. The resultant ordering will again be rigid, and the corresponding conditional (not the subjunctive) again necessary. The subjunctive in this case would presumably be false. Thus, we have two different, inconsistent, equally rigid orderings and two distinct but necessarily true corresponding conditionals. But it is perfectly evident that only one of those corresponding conditionals is 'activated' in some sense. One of the orderings makes a difference, and one doesn't—despite the rigidity of both. One of them (or at most one) somehow represents the 'real' ordering of worlds. In fact, we likely know which one it is. If I release the chalk we'll see it fall, despite the rigidity of the ordering and the necessity of the corresponding conditional associated with the ranking built around similarity to the actual present location of the chalk, five feet off the ground.

So obviously, again, some orderings are privileged. What that amounts to is that there is some real ordering of worlds, there are some subjunctives whose generative similarity respects are in some sense normative or binding. Others aren't.[12]

What is it that determines which orderings, which things held constant, get the world's attention? It certainly does not seem to be a matter of necessity. What it seems to be, at least in part, is a matter of law—whether physical, or whatever. What makes a world in which I release the chalk and it maintains its position five feet off the ground more distant (other things equal) than a world in which it falls is that the former world is different in respects which have real importance — among them that it has different laws, even though the chalk has the same location as it now does in this world (where I haven't in fact released it).[13]

It thus looks as though, if we are going to analyze subjunctives (whether simple or buried in dispositions) in terms of world similarities, laws are going to have to be prior in some sense. In fact, that priority is even suggested in the common phrase that "laws support subjunctives," instead of vice versa.

It is even reasonably clear in that light why law statements support subjunctives. Suppose that there is a lawful connection between A-type events and B-type events. If that law is a part of the collection of constants, then nearby A-worlds in most relevant orderings will be ones in which the law — i.e., the connections between A's and B's — holds. Since the nearest A-world is obviously an A-world, and since the law presumably holds in that A-world, then B will have the relevant status in that A-world as well. Thus, on the relevant ordering, the nearest A-world will be (say) a B-world as well, and the claim that 'were A the case, B would be too' will indeed be true in the base world — i.e., the law will support that subjunctive. But again, the law comes first ontologically and is responsible for the truth of the subjunctive. Thus, any attempt to *reduce* law statements to ordinary universally quantified subjunctives does not appear promising. Such attempts will be seriously circular.

(Of course, nearness apparently isn't based just on laws. For instance, it seems perfectly possible that some world with some difference in law so minute that it affects only the configuration of one snowflake per century might be more similar overall to this world than is one which shares all the same laws, but in which some allegedly random quantum event early on resulted in birds being the highest life form on earth as, e.g., S. J. Gould thinks is a possibility.)

The same point applies to the dispositional property view. If dispositional properties are in some basic sense tied to subjunctives, or have subjunctive analyses, what is the ontological underpinning of those subjunctives? What connects the relevant categorical properties in the requisite way? Why do fragile things *shatter* when *hit*? Why does iron *expand* when *heated*? The usual explanations of those facts involve micro-reductions to some underlying causal affairs. For instance, heat iron and the iron molecules tear around a bit more vigorously, rush at each other a bit more vigorously, and just naturally push or repel each other farther away, hence expansion. But surely more vigorous pushing does not *logically* entail expansion. What is the connection? We could pursue the micro-reduction down a few more levels, but the same type of question will eventually emerge and have to be addressed: what is the connection between the properties in question? We could, of course, in the above case simply say that iron molecules are (essentially) the sorts of things that rebound when pushed, i.e., that they have a reboundative virtue (or worse, a repulsive virtue). But not only does that not seem to get us very far, but that seems to turn the kind property *iron* into something itself implicitly dispositional, and we seem to have compounded the very problem we're trying to deal with. Alternatively, we could say that (at whatever ultimate level of micro-reduction we stop) the properties in question are simply linked in the requisite lawful manner. But that, too, seems to represent little progress, since the starting point for all this was the question of what laws and law statements are. Thus, it looks as though causal powers views, whatever their merits, are seriously incomplete. On any plausible rendering, they require appeal to dispositional properties, and the only plausible analyses of dispositions involve subjunctives, and the only plausible analyses of subjunctives involve presuppositions about laws. We seem to be led into the same sort of circularity that more straightforwardly subjunctive views lead into.

ONTOLOGY AGAIN

It thus seems to me that the question of what undergirds the subjunctives that lie near (or at) the heart of various views is ultimately inescapable regardless of which of the last two views we accept. But it might, again, be proposed that something explicitly or implicitly subjunctive gave the logical structure of law statements, but that those subjunctives were somehow primitive and did not in turn depend upon prior law in the generation of similarity orderings among worlds and that the proposal is thus not ultimately circular.

First, making out exactly what the claim involves and how it is to work might be difficult. (Goodman, I take it, despaired of essentially this project.)[14] What might the orderings rest upon? Any position without a good answer to that question makes there being any lawful regularities at all almost incredible. Suppose we put it in world terms again. For instance, for a universally quantified subjunctive to be true, there must be an ordering upon which, e.g., every object which shows up in any world in the ordering as an A, must also be a B in the *first* world in which it shows up as an A, although it can do anything else it pleases elsewhere. Having that turn out to be the case not only with every essence of the relevant sort which is exemplified in this world, but also with objects which don't show up in this world as well, seems incredible enough. Having it happen with respect to numerous laws which have various interconnections with each other seems even more incredible. And having that turn out to be the case in a way which doesn't depend upon prior law, plan, or some such other thing is very nearly beyond belief. Without any reasonable backing such subjunctives begin to look like interworld correlates of monumental accidental generalizations, should there even turn out to be any true ones.

Construing law statements as *ordinary* universally quantified subjunctives, although having some virtues, won't help us answer the questions at hand. Nor will construing them as entailments among dispositions. (I have developed in some detail elsewhere a number of more technical considerations and difficulties having to do with what inferences do or do not hold for quantified subjunctives.)[15]

A POSSIBLE FOUNDATION

Standard subjunctives, then, whether universally quantified, buried in dispositions or natures or not, do not seem promising candidates as the source of the peculiar logical character of laws. One of the reasons, again, is that subjunctives normally themselves depend partially upon natural laws for the firmness of character they have. Despite that, I still find the basic idea that laws are fundamentally subjunctive and that the character of the relevant subjunctives is in some sense prior to generalizations of properties of objects quite attractive on alternate days. Is there any way to give laws priority over properties, maintain the subjunctive character of law statements (and not merely their 'support' of subjunctives) and avoid any sort of pernicious circularity?

I think that the answer may be yes, and that the key is to be found in the fact that there is one kind of subjunctive which does not depend wholly upon prior natural law, thus offering a possible escape from the regress—what Plantinga has called 'counterfactuals of freedom'.[16] Counterfactuals (subjunctives) of freedom are subjunctives having to do with freely chosen actions of agents, e.g.,

> (23) were Jones to be offered the chance to buy a stolen horse he would resist.

If we do have freedom of a substantive sort, then the truth of such subjunctives is not purely a matter of either necessity, natural law, or chance, but it is a matter of free choice, character, and so forth. And the more stable and firm and reliable the character of the agent in question, the more general such subjunctives will be. Thus, for an absolutely reliable character, there would be counterfactuals of freedom of a universally quantifiable sort. Such subjunctives—even for an agent with absolutely reliable character—would nonetheless still not be law-based subjunctives, nor would they be purely arbitrary. They would be agent-based or character-based subjunctives.

But (to slip back into the world talk) what would be the determinant of what is held constant in the generating of the relevant ordering for such subjunctives? Can there be any ground of the required sort which lies between lawful or logical determination, on the one hand, and caprice, on the other? Philosophical anthropologists (and who isn't?) have long fought over the status of human actions. It was once widely argued that there was nothing between the poles of rigid determinism and random chance—neither one, of course, conducive to or compatible with human freedom. What was needed, clearly enough, was some way of locating human actions between those two poles (and notice, incidentally, how those poles of determinism and chance at least parallel the old legal dilemma between necessity and accidental generalization). One proposed answer was the notion of agent causation, that genuine persons could cause events although not in turn caused to do so, and not as a consequence of purely random antecedents. Persons could *initiate* causal chains (thus not be mere cogs in previously developing chains, or bound by causal chains) for *reasons* (thus not randomly) which were themselves not causally determined.

So the notions of character and agent causation might provide a source of some of the major constants around which subjunctives pivot, but a source not in turn based upon antecedent laws — the feature of regular subjunctives which would make the attempt to reduce law statements to some construct of such subjunctives circular.

Thus, we could have a stable, 'real', ordering which would support subjunctive predictions, expectations, Goodmanian projections, and so forth, and which would not involve a circularity, if we had the right sort of agent, whose choices and character were normative for reality — i.e., whose constant character would determine the constants which are determinant for which orderings are 'real' — some of those being universally quantified subjunctives (or counterfactuals) of freedom — and which consequently would determine which "ordinary" subjunctives are true.

Attributing the choice of constants to an agent would also remove the otherwise radical implausibility of an ordering of worlds in which, for a variety of pairs of different features, the *first* time *any* object exemplifies the first of a pair of features in the ordering, it also exemplifies the second in that world, even though the relationship might not hold at other worlds. That's a nifty sort of pattern. An agent might well find it attractive. If laws indeed involve universally quantified subjunctives in some way, then human agents who are scientists certainly might find what cashes out as that pattern in world talk attractive — hence their talk about the beauty of physics, their wonder that the world falls into elegant mathematical patterns, and so forth. Agents typically find that sort of thing absorbing.

And if we take this sort of view of natural law — law as involving constructs of universally quantified subjunctives of freedom — then what is or isn't natural law will be independent of the role its statement plays in any of our deductive systems, our best systems of explanation, and so forth. Law will be something objectively 'out there' whether we get it right or not — exactly the right result, it seems to me.

So the notion of agent causation (falling between determinism by prior law, and caprice) as a source of the constants (including these subjunctives of freedom) that determine which orderings are binding on the world and which aren't, which in turn determines which universally quantified ordinary subjunctives are true and which aren't, which dispositions are exemplified and so forth, looks initially as though it gives us quite a number of the features we need. What is required is an agent with a thoroughly stable character who freely governs the relevant parts of reality. Surely a reasonable request.

The cat, of course, has long since left the bag. This view in some form or other is what many Christians have been espousing for years—that natural laws are expressions of a faithful God's free governance of the world.[17] On this view, all activity other than creaturely free choices is God's activity, and all subjunctives other than those of (individual or group) freedom turn out to be stipulations of how God either does act or would act in given circumstances. What makes an AB world nearer than a $A\bar{B}$ world? That in the relevant circumstances (A) God would freely perform an action which would bring about (or constitute) actuality's following a B track rather than a $\bar{B}$ track. Were I to drop this chalk, God would bring it about that it fell.

This sort of view, it seems to me, has quite a number of attractions. It locates laws in what many have seen as the right general logical location, between categorical necessity and accident. It also avoids subjectivism, relativism, and circularity. It can also be adjusted to handle quite nicely the intuition shared by many that God could have decreed at least slightly different laws even had he created the same objects he in fact did (an intuition usual causal powers views do not wish to accommodate and apparently cannot in any case unless the entailment claim is dropped).

On the other hand, it might tend toward the occasionalist end of the spectrum, since all natural events turn out to be activities of God's governance. Some may see that as objectionable—surely God doesn't get directly involved with, say, the movements of my arm. But many Christians have long believed that God is at every moment upholding his creation in such a way that without that immediate upholding the creation would cease to exist. The present type of occasionalistic view is not far removed from that, and if that doctrine of God's upholding the creation is right, then God's involvement at least with the existence of the arm that I move is already quite immediate.

Further, this view would make God's providence more immediate as well and would fit with a conception of miracles as being
fundamentally of a piece with all the rest of God's activity in a way
that many other views would not. That, too, some might see as an
attraction.

And, finally, there have been philosophers who have argued
that our concepts of *cause, power,* and so forth have grown out of
our own experiences as agents who cause things, who have various
powers. If those concepts are indeed fundamentally agent-concepts,
then in attributing them to other sorts of objects we may be anthro-
pomorphizing nature (or agentomorphizing it), whereas a more occasionalistic agent-based view may have some inherent conceptual
advantages.

Some advocates of causal powers views have seemed to feel that
putting all the causal weight onto a dispositional property of an object escapes the hazards of occasionalism. Perhaps that is the case,
but if what I have said about dispositions is right, that distance from
occasionalism may be illusory. *Something* has to account for the connection between the properties tied together in a disposition, and
if it isn't simple entailment, if sheer accident won't do, if law simply
begs the question, then what is it? If it is in fact an activity of God's
freedom, then God is involved in the breaking of struck glass, the
expansion of heated iron—and the raising of my arm when I will
it appropriately. Of course, it may be that the proper analysis of
a subjunctive is neither categorical nor subjunctive, but no one has
provided any clues as to what it might then be (although there are
extensional equivalents in the literature).

There remains one substantial incompleteness. The present
view requires both thoroughly reliable, uniform character and nearly
limitless freedom and choice within the same divine agent. But exactly what is the relationship among character, choice, and freedom?
Does character determine choice? If so, are such choices free (since
not determined by any sort of law or mechanism either external or
internal) or not (since, albeit by one's own character, still determined)?
Are free choices merely freely in accord with character? Is character
reducible to collections of free choices or sets of subjunctives of
freedom? I do not claim to know the answers to all those questions,
but it does seem to me clear that in any agent, creaturely or divine,
things do go together in such a way that reliability of character is
not destructive of freedom—a person's being of good moral charac-

ter is hardly warrant for denying that person morally significant freedom.

With any view of the sort I'm suggesting, there will be, of course, two further hitches for some. One, accepting this view requires belief in God, and two, it requires acceptance of the idea of agent causation. But those are, I think, relatively minor hitches. All of us have had direct experience with the latter, and most of us, I suspect, have had experiences with the former, denials notwithstanding.

Various people used to argue (and some still do) that laws always require lawgivers, arguing from that claim and the existence of natural law to a Lawgiver. That was widely perceived as laughable philosophical confusion — at best a bad joke. A joke it may have turned out to involve, but not necessarily either a bad one or one on whom it was originally thought.

NOTES

I am indebted to my colleagues in the Calvin College Philosophy Department, especially Ken Konyndyk, for more discussions of this paper than some of them thought strictly necessary. I am also indebted to several contributors to *Faith and Philosophy* 4, no. 4, especially Chris Menzel and Nick Wolterstorff, as well as to the general editor, William Alston. I am most ferociously indebted, however, to Alvin Plantinga.

1. See, e.g., Frederick Suppe, *The Structure of Scientific Theories* (Urbana: University of Illinois Press, 1977), and Harold Brown, *Perception, Theory and Commitment* (Chicago: University of Chicago Press, 1977).

2. Ernest Nagel, *The Structure of Science* (New York: Harcourt, Brace and World, 1961), p. 68, and David Lewis, *Counterfactuals* (Cambridge, Mass., Harvard University Press, 1973), p. 73.

3. R. Harre and E. Madden, *Casual Powers* (Oxford: Blackwell, 1975).

4. Carnap's well-known views here are discussed in, e.g., Carl Hempel, *Aspects of Scientific Explanation* (New York: Free Press, 1965), p. 109. For a more recent attempt, see F. Wilson, "Dispositions: Defined or Reduced," in the *Australasian Journal of Philosophy* 47 (1969), 184–204.

5. See, e.g., Elizabeth Prior, Robert Pargetter, and Frank Jackson "Three Theses about Dispositions," in *American Philosophical Quarterly* 19, no. 3 (July 1982), 251–57. These three have published other works on this issue as well.

6. For general discussion, see E. J. Lowe, "Laws, Dispositions and Sortal Logic" in *American Philosophical Quarterly* 19, no. 1 (January 1982), 41–50, and also his "Sortal Terms and Natural Law" in the same journal, 17 no. 4 (October 1980), 253–60. Also of interest is Elliot Sober, "Dispositions and

Subjunctive Conditionals, or, Dormative Virtues Are No Laughing Matter," *Philosophical Review* 91, no. 4 (October 1982), 591–96.

7. For instance, Robert Stalnaker, "A Theory of Conditionals," reprinted in Ernest Sossa, ed., *Causation and Conditionals* (London: Oxford University Press, 1975), p. 177.

8. Stalnaker, pp. 165–79.

9. For instance, David Lewis, *Counterfactuals*.

10. Quantified subjunctives have been explored in only a very few places, for example: John Pollock, *Subjunctive Reasoning* (Dordrecht: Reidel, 1976): Peter van Inwagen, "Laws and Counterfactuals," *Noûs* 13 (1979), 439–53, and a few remarks of David Lewis in *Counterfactuals*. I know of no discussions of quantified subjunctives in world terms except my "Quantified Subjunctives, Modality and Natural Law," in David Austin, ed., *Philosophical Analysis: A Defense by Example* (Dordrecht: Reidel, 1987).

11. Alvin Plantinga, "World and Essence," *Philosophical Review,* 1970.

12. See Also Alvin Plantinga, *The Nature of Necessity* (Oxford: Oxford University Press, 1974), chap. 9.

13. Ibid., chap. 9.

14. Nelson Goodman, *Fact, Fiction and Forecast* (Cambridge, Mass.: Harvard University Press, 1955).

15. See my "Quantified Subjunctives" (above, note 10).

16. Plantinga's original discussion of the concept (although not the terminology) is in *The Nature of Necessity,* chap. 9

17. Francis Oakley discusses some historical views in this region in chap. 3 of *Omnipotence, Covenant and Order* (Ithaca, N.Y.: Cornell University Press, 1984).

Theism, Platonism, and the Metaphysics of Mathematics

CHRISTOPHER MENZEL

1. THE DILEMMA OF THE THEISTIC PLATONIST

Theists generally hold that God is the creator of all there is distinct from himself. Traditionally, the scope of God's creative activity has extended across two disjoint realms: the physical, whose chief exemplars are ordinary middle-size objects, and the mental or spiritual, encompassing such things as angels and souls. Now, many theists are also Platonists, or "metaphysical realists." That is, in addition to the physical and mental realms, some theists also acknowledge the existence of a realm of *abstract* objects, like numbers, sets, properties, and propositions. For such theists, the traditional understanding of creation presents a philosophical and theological dilemma. On the Platonist conception, most, if not all, abstract objects are thought to exist necessarily. One can either locate these entities outside the scope of God's creative activity or not. If the former, then it seems the believer must compromise his view of God: rather than the sovereign creator and lord of all things visible and invisible, God turns out to be just one more entity among many in a vast constellation of necessary beings existing independently of his creative power. If the latter, the believer is faced with the problem of what it could possibly mean for God to *create* an object that is both necessary and abstract.

Though not utterly incompatible with a robust theism, the first horn of the dilemma seems undesirable for the theistic Platonist. God remains the greatest possible being, since, presumably, it is not

208

possible for any being to exert any influence over abstract entities; but the Platonist must put severe, indeed embarrassing, qualifications on the scope of God's creative activity and on his status as the source of all existence. This leaves the Platonist with the second horn, viz., making sense of the idea of creation with respect to necessary, abstract objects. In another place Tom Morris and I have argued that sense can indeed be made of this idea.[1]

An early obstacle to avoid is the (roughly) deistic model of the creation. On this model, God's creation of an object is conceived of as a distinct, isolable, temporally located event of (at most) finite duration, and after its occurrence the object continues to exist of its own ontological momentum. This model is no doubt incompatible with the thesis at hand, since there could be no time at which God could have brought a necessary, hence eternal, being into existence. But there is just no *a priori* reason whatever to rule out the possibility of eternal creatures. Hence, a more subtle model is needed.

A model that is both philosophically and theologically sounder on this point is that of continuous creation. In its most fundamental sense, to create something is to cause it to be, to play a direct causal role in its existing.[2] It is this broader conception of creation that is incorporated in the model in question. On that model, God is always playing a direct causal role in the existence of his creatures; his creative activity is essential to a creature's existence at *all* times throughout its temporal career, irrespective of whether or not there happens to be a specific time at which he *begins* to cause it to exist.[3] This then provides us with a framework in which it can be coherently claimed that God creates absolutely all objects, necessary or not: one simply holds that, necessarily, for any object *a* (other than God himself) and time *t,* God plays a direct causal role in *a*'s existing at *t*.[4]

With that obstacle removed, the next step is to give some account of the sort of causal relation there could be between God and the abstract objects we want to claim he creates. Here Morris and I essentially just reclothe the venerable doctrine of divine ideas in contemporary garb. We call the refurbished doctrine "theistic activism." Very briefly, the idea is this. We take properties, relations, and propositions (PRPs, for short) to be the contents of a certain kind of divine intellective activity in which God, by his nature, is essentially engaged. To grasp a PRP, then, whether by abstracting from perceptual experience, or perhaps by "combining" PRPs already grasped, is to grasp a product of the divine intellect, a divine idea. This divine activity is thus causally efficacious: PRPs, as abstract products of God's "mental life," exist at any given moment *because* God is thinking them;[5] which is just to say that he creates them.

2. ACTIVISM, NUMBERS, AND SETS

With regard to PRPs then, the activist model provides a coherent, substantive (if programmatic) account of the sort of activity in which God is engaged that gives rise to abstract objects. On the face of it, though, a substantial, indeed perhaps the most important, portion of the abstract universe is not obviously accounted for, viz., the abstract ontology of mathematics. In particular, how do numbers and sets fit into the picture? Traditionally, these entities are not thought of as PRPs of any kind, and hence they find no clear place in the story thus far.

I want to argue that a place can be found, though the search is going to lead us into some fairly deep waters. Let's begin with numbers. A natural view of the numbers, as I will argue below, is that they are properties. For the past century, however, the dominant view of the numbers has been that they are abstract *particulars* of one kind or another. The philosophical roots of this view go back to Frege, in particular, to one of his most distinctive doctrines: that there is an inviolable ontological divide between the denotations (*Bedeutungen*) of predicates, or concepts (*Begriffe*), and the denotations of singular terms, or objects (*Gegenstände*). Taking 'property' to be a loose synonym for 'concept', this doctrine entails that no property can be denoted by a singular term. Since in mathematics the numbers *are* in fact denoted by singular terms, e.g., most saliently, the numerals, it follows that the numbers are not properties but objects, or, loosely once again, particulars.

Now, while few would dispute the inviolability of the distinction between properties and particulars, there are well-known and notorious difficulties with the idea that this is simultaneously a distinction between the semantic values of predicates and the semantic values of singular terms.[6] We needn't rehearse these in detail here. For present purposes let's just note first that our ordinary usage itself doesn't easily square with Frege's doctrine. For there exist a prodigious number of singular terms in natural language that, to all appearances, refer straightforwardly to properties: abstract singular terms ('wisdom', 'redness'), infinitives ('to dance', 'to raise chickens'), gerunds ('being faster than Willie Gault', 'running for president'), and so on. Now, there are several non-Fregean semantic theories in which this fact of natural language is preserved, i.e., theories that are type-free in the sense that difference in ontological type (property, particular, etc.) is not reflected in a difference of semantic type (referent of predicate, referent of singular term, etc.) that prevents singular terms from referring to properties.[7] Hence, we can consistently maintain, *pace* Frege, that at least some properties are the semantic values of both predicates and singular terms. There are thus good reasons for rejecting Frege's semantic doctrine, and hence no cogent reasons for rejecting the idea that numbers are properties *a priori* on Fregean grounds.

There are two plausible accounts that identify the numbers with properties, both of which trace their origins back to the beginnings of contemporary mathematical logic. The first extends back to Frege himself. Frege clearly saw that statements of number typically involve the predication of a numerical property of some kind. For Frege, what is involved is the predication of such a property to a *concept.* Thus, for example, the statement 'There are four moons of Jupiter' is the predication of the property **having four instances** (which is expressed by the quantifier 'There are four') of the concept **moons of Jupiter.** Frege's concept/object doctrine however prevented him from taking this property itself to be the number four, assigning that function rather to its extension.[8] As we've just seen, though, one needn't follow Frege here. In the absence of this doctrine, one is free to make the identification in question, and hence, in general, to take the number n to be the property of having n instances.[9]

Cantor suggested a different though related view in his (often entirely opaque) discussions of the nature of number. Cantor's insight was that the notion of number is understood most clearly in terms of a special relation between *sets*: we associate the same number with two sets just in case they are "equivalent," i.e., just in case a one-to-one correspondence can be established between the members of the sets. In assigning the same number to two sets then, we are isolating a common property the two sets share; such properties (roughly) Cantor identifies as the cardinal numbers. In his words, the cardinal number of a given set M is

> the general concept under which fall all and only those sets which are equivalent to the given set.[10]

More precisely, the number n is a property common to all and only n-membered sets, or more simply, the property of having n members.[11] Russell presents essentially the same account in *The Principles of Mathematics,* though he ultimately rejects it (unnecessarily, as it happens) because of problems he finds with its nonextensional character.[12]

There are thus at least two ways of understanding the numbers to be properties, both of which are natural and appealing. The first, quasi-Fregean account has a semantical bent, focussing in particular on the predicative nature of statements of number, while the Cantorian account emphasizes the intuitive connection between number and relative size in the more general, abstract form of one-to-one correspondence between sets. Both, however, provide us with good reasons for thinking that numbers are properties of some kind. If so, we have found room for numbers within our theistic framework as it stands.

Now, of course, if we adopt the Cantorian view of number, then it obviously remains to explain just how *sets* fit into our picture. We could avoid this question by choosing instead the quasi-Fregean picture, since it makes no appeal to sets. We will not so choose, however, for two reasons. First, for reasons I will not go into here, I think the Cantorian view is the superior of the two accounts. Second, perhaps more importantly, we want to be able to give our picture the broadest possible scope, and hence we want it to encompass all manner of abstract flora and fauna whose existence Platonism might endorse.

So what then are we to say about sets? Are they, too, assimilable into our framework as it stands? Formally, yes. Both George Bealer and Michael Jubien, for instance, have developed theories in which sets are identified with certain "setlike" properties; roughly, a set $\{a,b, \ldots\}$ is taken to be the property **being identical with a or being identical with b or. . . .**[13] Given sufficiently powerful property theoretic axioms, one can then show that analogues of the usual axioms of Zermelo-Fraenkel (ZF) set theory hold for these setlike properties, and hence that one loses none of ZF's mathematical power.

But this is not an altogether happy move. For instance, as Cocchiarella has noted, intuitively, sets are just not the same sort of thing as properties. Sets are generally thought of as being wholly constituted by their members; a set, "has its being in the objects which belong to it."[14] This conception is deeply at odds with the view of PRPs that underlies metaphysical realism, which "are in no sense to be thought of as having their being in the objects which are their instances."[15] Since however it is this very idea of sets as having their being in their members that motivates the axioms of ZF, and since this is an inappropriate conception of properties, there seems to be no adequate motivation for a ZF-style property theory.

So there is at least ground for suspicion of the thesis that sets are just a species of property. It would be desirable, then, if our account could respect the intuitive distinction between the two sorts of entity. In particular, we should like to trace the origin of sets to a different, and more appropriate, sort of divine activity than that to which we've traced the origin of PRPs. But what sort? Here we have a fairly rich (though often unduly obscure) line of thought to draw upon from the philosophy of set theory. A common idea one often encounters in expositions of the notion of set is that sets are "built up" or "constructed" in some way out of previously given objects.[16] Though generally taken to be no more than a helpful metaphor in explaining the contemporary iterative conception of set, a number of thinkers seem to have endorsed the idea at a somewhat more literal level. Specifically, their writings suggest that sets are the upshots of a certain sort of constructive *mental* activity.

Adumbrations of this idea can be seen in the very origins of set theory. Cantor himself held that the existence of a set was a matter of *thinking* of a plurality as a unity.[17] His distinguished mentor Dedekind is plausibly taken to be embracing a similar line when he writes that

> [i]t very frequently happens that different things . . . can be considered from a common point of view, can be associated in the mind, and we say they form a *system S.* . . . Such a system (an aggregate, a manifold, a totality) as an object of our thought is likewise a thing.[18]

Comparable thoughts are expressed by Hausdorff, Fraenkel, and more recently by Schoenfield, Rucker, and Wang.[19] Of these it is Wang who seems to develop the idea most extensively. He writes:

> It is a basic feature of reality that there are many things. When a multitude of given objects can be collected together, we arrive at a set. For example, there are two tables in this room. We are ready to view them as given both separately and as a unity, and justify this by pointing to them or looking at them or thinking about them either one after the other or simultaneously. Somehow the viewing of certain objects together suggests a loose link which ties the objects together in our intuition.[20]

I interpret this passage in the following way. Wang here is keying on a basic feature of our cognitive capacities: the ability to selectively direct our attention to certain objects and collect or gather them together mentally, to view them in such a way as to "tie them together in our intuition"; in Cantorian terms, to think of them as a unity. Wang stresses the particular manifestation of this capacity in *perception,* one of a number of related human perceptual capacities emphasized especially by the early Gestalt psychologists.[21] It is best illustrated for our purposes by a simple example. Consider the following array:

$$\bullet \quad \bullet \quad \bullet$$

$$\bullet \quad \bullet \quad \bullet$$

$$\bullet \quad \bullet \quad \bullet$$

Think of the dots as being numbered left to right from 1 to 9, beginning at the upper left-hand corner. While focusing on the middle dot, 5, it is possible to vary at will which dots in the array stand out in one's visual field (with perhaps the exception of 5 itself), e.g., [1,5,9], [2,4,5,6,8], or even [1,5,8,9]. The dots thus picked out, I take Wang to be saying, are to be understood as the elements of a small "set" existing in the mind of the perceiver.

The account obviously won't do as it stands. The axiom of extensionality, for instance, seems not to hold on this picture: if you and I direct our attention to the same dots, then each of us has his own "set," despite the fact that they have the same members. More importantly, human cognitive limitations put a severe restriction on the number and size of sets there can be. Wang is well aware of this, and hence builds an account of the nature of sets based on an *idealized* notion of collecting. Irrespective of the success of Wang's efforts, such an idealization, I believe, can be of use to us here in developing a model of divine activity that works sets into our activist framework.

The idea is simple enough: we take sets to be the products of a collecting activity on God's part which we model on our own perceptual collecting capacities. Consider first of all the things that are not sets in this sense. While the number of these "first-order" objects that we can apprehend at any given time is extremely limited, presumably God suffers from no such limitations; all of them fall under his purview. Furthermore, we can suppose that his awareness is not composed of more or less discrete experiential episodes, the way ours is, and hence that he is capable of generating not just one collection of first-order objects at a time, but all *possible* collections of them simultaneously.[22] We suppose next that, once generated, the "second-order" products of this collecting activity on first-order objects are themselves candidates for "membership" in further collectings, and hence that God can produce also all possible "third-order" collections that can be generated out of all the objects of the first two orders. The same, of course, ought to hold for these latter collections and for the collections generated from them, and so on, for all finite orders. Finally, in a speculative application of the doctrine of divine infinitude, we postulate that there are no determinate bounds on God's collecting activity and hence that it extends unbounded through the Cantorian infinite.[23]

Identifying sets with the products of God's collecting activity, then, and supposing that God in fact does all the collecting it is possible for him to do, what we have is a full set theoretic cumulative hierarchy as rich as in any Platonic vision. In this way we locate not just the Platonist's PRPs, but the entire ontology of sets as well firmly within the mind of God.

3. A VOLATILE ONTOLOGY

Alas, but as is so often wont to be the case in matters such as this, things are more complicated than they appear. The lessons of the last hundred years are clear that caution is to be enjoined in constructing an ontology that includes sets and PRPs. Too easily the abstract scientist, eager to exploit the philosophical power of a Platonic ontology, finds himself engaged unwittingly in a metaphysical alchemy in which the rich ore of Platonism is transmuted into the worthless dross of inconsistency. Our account thus far is a laboratory ripe for such a transmutation. There are several paradoxes that, on natural assumptions, are generated in the account as it stands.

The first is essentially identical to a paradox originally discovered by Russell and reported in §500 of the *Principles*.[24] In the cumulative or "iterative" picture of sets we've developed here, all the things that are not sets form the basic stuff on top of which the cumulative hierarchy is constructed. Now, the chief intuition behind the iterative picture, one implicit in our theistic model above, is that any available objects can be collected into a set; the "available" objects at any stage form the basis of new sets in the next stage. Thus, since propositions are not sets, all the propositions there are are among the atoms of the cumulative hierarchy; and since all the atoms are available for collecting (God, after all, apprehends them all "prior" to his collecting), there is a set S of all propositions. I take it as a basic logical principle that for any entities x and y and any Property **P**,

(*) if $x \neq y$, then $[\lambda \, \mathbf{P} x] \neq [\lambda \, \mathbf{P} y]$,[25]

i.e., that if x is not identical with y, then the proposition $[\lambda \, \mathbf{P} x]$ that x is **P** is not identical with the proposition $[\lambda \, \mathbf{P} y]$ that y is **P**.[26] Consider then any property you please; the property **SET** of being a set, say. Then by (*), there is a one-to-one correspondence between Pow (S) (the power set of S) and the set $T = \{[\lambda \, \mathbf{SET}(s)] : s \in \text{Pow}(S)\}$. But $T \subseteq S$, since T is a set of propositions, hence Pow$(S) \leq S$,[27] contradicting Cantor's theorem.

A strictly analogous paradox arises for properties (and, in general, relations as well). This is true in particular if one holds that every object a has an *essence,* i.e., the property **being a,** or perhaps **being identical with a.**[28] For the same reasons we gave in the case of propositions, properties (and relations) are also among the atoms of the cumulative hierarchy, and hence there is a set M of all properties. Essences being what they are, we have, for any x and y, that

(**) if $x \neq y$, then $E_x \neq E_y$,

where E_z is the essence of z. Consider then Pow(M). By (**) there is a one-to-one correspondence between Pow(M) and the set $E = \{E_z : z \in \text{Pow}(M)\}$. But $E \subseteq M$, since E is a set of properties, hence Pow(M) $\leq M$, contradicting Cantor once again.[29]

There are three quick replies to these related paradoxes to consider. The first is to question the fine-grainedness principles (*) and (**). Certainly there are views of PRPs on which this would be appropriate. Possible worlds theorists in the tradition of Montague, for example, define PRPs such that they are identical if necessarily coextensional, a "coarse-grained" view incompatible with the fine-grained view we are advocating here. Similarly, views that might be broadly classified as "Aristotelian" hold that properties and relations exist first and foremost "in" the objects that have them, not separate from them, and are "abstracted" somehow by the mind. Such views rarely find any need for PRPs any more fine-grained than are needed to distinguish one state of an object, or one connection between several objects, from another. Whatever the appeal of these alternatives, the problem is that they are out of keeping with our activist model. If we are pushing the idea that PRPs are literally the products of God's conceiving activity, then it would seem that properties which intuitively differ in content, i.e., which are such that grasping one does not entail simultaneously grasping the other, could not be the products of exactly the same intellective activity and hence must be distinct. This is especially pronounced in the cases of singular propositions and essences that "involve" distinct individuals, such as those with which we are concerned in (*) and (**); it is just not plausible that, for example, singular propositions "about" distinct individuals could nonetheless be the products of the same activity. To abandon these principles in the context of our present framework, then, would be unpalatable.

The second reply is simply to deny the power set axiom. After all, one might argue, many set theorists find the axiom dubious; so why suppose it is true in general, and in the arguments at hand in particular?

The power set axiom has indeed been called into question by mathematical logicians and philosophers of mathematics over the years. The root cause of this disaffection, however, has always been the radically nonconstructive character of the axiom—mathematicians are not in general able to specify any sort of general property or procedure that will enable them to pick out every arbitrary subset of a given set. In this sense, it is the Platonic axiom *par excellence,* declaring sets to exist even though humans lack the capacity to grasp or "construct" them.

It should be clear that any sort of objection on these grounds, as with the previous objection, is just out of place here. For obviously we are far from supposing that set existence has anything whatever to do with human cognitive capacities. Quite the contrary; on our model, the puzzle would rather be how the power set axiom could *not* be true. For supposing that God has collected some set *s,* since each of its members falls under his purview just as the elements of some small finite collection of our own construction fall under ours, how could he not be capable of generating all possible collections that can be formed from members of *s* as well? So this response to the paradoxes is ineffective.[30]

The third reply is that, since there are at least as many propositions (and properties) as there are sets, it is evident that there is no set *S* of all propositions any more than there is a set of all sets; there are just "too many" of them. Hence the argument above breaks down. The same goes for properties, so the second paradox fares no better.

Briefly, the problem with this reply is that how many of a given sort of thing there are in and of itself has nothing whatever to do with whether or not there is a set of those things.[31] The reason there is no set of all sets is not that there are "too many" of them, but rather that there is no "top" to the cumulative hierarchy, no definite point at which no further sets can be constructed. On our model as it stands, however, as nonsets, the propositions and properties there are exist "prior" (in a conceptual sense) to the construction of all the sets. Hence, they are all equally available for membership. But if so, there seems no reason for denying the existence of the sets *S* and *M* in the paradoxes.[32] So an appeal to how many PRPs there are won't turn back the arguments.

4. A RUSSELL-TYPE SOLUTION

Though always discomfiting, the discovery of paradox needn't necessarily spell disaster. As in the case of set theory, it may rather be an occasion for insight and clarification. Russell's original paradox of naive set theory was grounded in a mistaken conception of the structure of sets that was uncovered with the development of the iterative picture. Perhaps, in the same way, the paradoxes here have taken root in a similar misconception about PRPs. There are two avenues to explore.

The final paragraph in the last section uncovers a crucial assumption at work in the paradoxes: that all PRPs are conceptually prior to the construction of the sets; or again, that all the PRPs there are are among the atoms of the hierarchy. The Russellian will challenge this. He will argue that one cannot so cavalierly divide the world into an ordered hierarchy of sets on the one hand and a logically unstructured domain of nonsets on the other. For although they are not sets, the nonsets too fall into a natural hierarchy of logical *types*. More specifically, in the simple theory of types, concrete and abstract particulars, or "individuals", are the entities of the lowest type, usually designated 'i'. Then, recursively, where $t_1, \ldots, t_n$ are types, let $(t_1, \ldots, t_n)$ be the type of n-place relation that takes entities of these n types as its arguments. So, for example, a property of individuals would be of type (i); a 2-place relation between individuals and properties of individuals would be of type $(i,(i))$; and so on. The type of any entity is thus, in an easily definable sense, higher than the type of any of its possible arguments.[33] By dividing entities whose types are the same height into disjoint levels we arrive at a hierarchy of properties and relations analogous to, but rather more complicated than, the (finite) levels of the cumulative hierarchy.

To wed this conception with our current model we propose that *both* sets and PRPs are built up *together* in the divine intellect so that we have God both constructing new sets *and* conceiving new PRPs in every level of the resulting hierarchy. Thus, at the most basic level are individuals; at the next level God constructs all sets of individuals and conceives all properties and relations that take individuals as arguments; at the next level he constructs all sets of entities of the first two levels and conceives all properties and relations that take entities of the previous (and perhaps both previous) level(s) as arguments, and so on. Thus, since there are new PRPs at every level, it is evident that there will be no level at which there occurs, e.g., the set of *all* properties, and hence it seems the para-

doxes above can be explained in much the same way as Russell's
original paradox.[34]

Easier said than done. Serious impediments stand in the way
of implementing these ideas. First of all, there are several well-known
objections to type theory that are no less cogent here than in other
contexts. For example, on a typed conception of PRPs, there can
be no universal properties, such as the property of being self-identical,
since no properties have all entities in their "range of significance."[35]
The closest approximation to them are properties true of everything
of a given type. But, thinking in terms of our model, even if many
PRPs *are* typed, there seems no reason why God shouldn't also be
able to conceive properties whose extensions, and hence whose ranges
of significance, include all entities whatsoever.

Along these same lines, type theory also prevents any property
from falling within its own range of significance, and in particular
it rules out the possibility of self-exemplification. Thus, for example, there can be no such thing as the property of being a property,
or of being abstract, but only anemic, typed images of these more
robust properties at each level, true only of the properties or abstract entities of the previous level.

Standard problems aside, much more serious problems remain.
In many simple type theories, including our brief account above,
propositions are omitted altogether. Those that make room for them[36]
lump them all together in a single type (quite rightly, in the context
of simple type theory). This clearly won't do on the current proposal since the entities of any given type are all at the same level
and hence form a set at the next level, thus allowing in sufficient
air to revive our first paradox.

A related difficulty is that this proposal is still vulnerable to
a modified version of the second paradox as well. Consider any relation that holds between individuals u and sets s of properties of individuals, e.g., the relation I that holds between u and s just in case
u exemplifies some member of s. Let A be the set of all properties
of individuals. For each $s \in \mathrm{Pow}(A)$, we have the property $[\lambda x\ Ixs]$
of bearing I to s. By a generalization of the fine-grainedness schemas
(*) and (**) (cf. note 29), for all $s,s' \in \mathrm{Pow}(A)$ we have that

(***) if $s \neq s'$, then $[\lambda x\ Ixs] \neq [\lambda x\ Ixs']$.

Consider now the set $I = \{[\lambda x\ Ixs] : s \in \mathrm{Pow}(A)\}$. By (***) there is
a one-to-one correspondence between $\mathrm{Pow}(A)$ and I. But $I \subseteq A$, since

I is a set of properties of individuals. Hence, Pow(*A*) ≤ *A*, contradicting Cantor's theorem.

A little reflection reveals a feature common to both paradoxes that seems to lie at the heart of the difficulty. First, we need an intuitive fix on the idea of (the existence of) one entity *presupposing the availability of* another. The idea we're after is simple: for God to create (i.e., construct or conceive) certain entities, he must have "already" created certain others; the former, that is to say, presuppose the availability of the latter. For sets this is clear. Say that an entity *e* is a *constituent* of a set *s* just in case it is a member of the transitive closure of *s*.[37] Then we can say that a set *s* presupposes the availability of some entity *e* just in case *e* is a constitutent of *s*. For PRPs we need to say a little more. As suggested above, there seems a clear sense in which PRPs, like sets, can be said to have constituents. Thus, a setlike "singleton" property such as [λ*x x* = Kripke] contains Kripke as a constituent. But not just Kripke; for the identity relation too is a part of the property's makeup, or "internal structure"; it is, one might say, a structured composite of those two entities. (We will develop this idea in somewhat more detail shortly.) Combining the two notions of constituency (one for sets, one for PRPs), we can generalize the concept of presupposition to both sets and PRPs: one entity *e* preupposes the availability of another *e** just in case *e** is a constituent of *e*.

Now, even though the properties [λ*x* I*xs*) are properties of individuals, if we look at their internal structure, we see that many of these properties presuppose the availability of entities which themselves presuppose the availability of those very properties, to wit, those properties **P** = (λ*x* I*xs*] such that **P** ∈ *s*. (Analogously for those propositions *p* = [λ SET(*s*)] such that *p* ∈ *s*.) Call such properties *self-presupposing*; this notion, independent of the power set axiom, is sufficient for generating Russell-type paradoxes.[38] Conjoined with power set, the possibility of self-presupposing properties can be held responsible for the sort of unrestrained proliferation of PRPs of (in general) any type that fuels the Cantor-style paradoxes as well.

The source of all our paradoxes, then, in broader terms, lies in a failure so far adequately to capture the dependence of complex PRPs on their internal constituents. What we want, then, is a model that is appropriately sensitive to internal structure, but which at the same time does not run afoul of any of the standard problems of type theory.

5. A CONSTRUCTIVE SOLUTION

Let's review. Our excursion into type theory was prompted by doubts over the idea that PRPs are conceptually prior to the construction of sets. Type theory suggested an alternative: PRPs themselves form a hierarchy analogous to the cumulative hierarchy of sets such that a PRP's place in the hierarchy depends on the kind of arguments it can sensibly take. The idea then was to join the two sorts of hierarchy into one. However, even overlooking the standard problems of type theory, we found that the resulting activist model (sketch) was still subject to paradox. Our analysis of these paradoxes led us to see that our problems stemmed from the fact that our models were insensitive to the dependence of PRPs on their internal constituents.

How, then, do we capture this dependence? Here we can draw on some recent ideas in logic and metaphysics. Logically complex PRPs are naturally thought of as being "built up" from simpler entities by the application of a variety of logical operations. For example, any two PRPs can be seen as the primary constituents of a further PRP, their conjunction, which is the result of a *conjoining* operation. Thus, in particular, the *conjunction* of two properties **P** and **Q** can be thought of as the relation $[\lambda xy \, Px \wedge Qy]$ that a bears to b just in case Pa and Qb. A further operation, *reflection,* can be understood to act so as to transform this relation into the property $[\lambda x \, Px \wedge Qx]$ of having **P** and **Q**. Related operations can be taken to yield complements (e.g., $[\lambda x \, \neg Px]$), generalizations (e.g., $[\lambda \exists x \, (Px)]$), and PRPs that are directly "about" other objects such as our setlike property $[\lambda x \, x = \text{Kripke}]$, or the "singular" proposition $[\lambda \, \textbf{PHL}(\text{Kaplan})]$ that Kaplan is a philosopher.[39]

On this view, then, the constituents of a complex PRP are simply those entities that are needed to construct the PRP by means of the logical operations, just as the constituents of a set are those entities that are needed to construct the set. It is in this sense that a complex PRP is dependent on its constituents. This then suggests that, analogous to sets on the iterative conception, PRPs are best viewed as internally "well-founded," or at least noncircular, in the sense that a PRP cannot be one of its own constituents.[40]

This picture of PRPs is especially amenable to activism. For as with set construction, the activist can take the logical operations that yield complex PRPs to be quite literally activities of the divine intellect. This leads us to a further, more adequate model of the creation of abstract entities. At the logically most basic level of creation we find concrete objects and logically simple properties and relations (whatever those may be). The next level consists of (*i*) all the objects of the previous level (this will make the levels cumulative), (*ii*) all sets that can be formed from those objects, and (*iii*) all new PRPs that can be formed by applying the logical operations to those objects. The third level is formed in the same manner from the second. Similarly for all succeeding finite levels. As in our initial models, there seems no reason to think this activity cannot continue into the transfinite. Accordingly, we postulate a "limit" level that contains all the objects created in the finite levels, which itself forms the basis of new, infinite levels. And so it continues on through the Cantorian transfinite.

Now, how do things stand with respect to our paradoxes? As we should hope, they cannot arise on the current model. Consider the first paradox. Since there are new propositions formed at every level of hierarchy, there cannot be a set of all propositions any more than there can be a set of all non-self-membered sets. Similarly for the second paradox: since essences (as depicted above) contain the objects that exemplify them in their internal structure and hence do not appear to be simple, they too occur arbitrarily high up in the hierarchy and hence also are never collected into a set. What about the two new paradoxes above? The first of these is just a type-theoretic variant on the original paradoxes and so poses no additional difficulty. And although the concept of self-presupposition can be reconstructed in our type-free framework, the corresponding paradox still cannot arise, since there can be no set of all non-self-presupposing properties as the paradox requires.[41] We seem at last to have found our way out of this dense thicket of Cantorian and Russellian paradoxes.

But our task is still not quite complete. Recall that one of our first orders of business was to work (cardinal) numbers into the activist framework. We opted for the Cantorian-inspired view that the numbers are properties shared by equinumerous sets. But just where do they fit into our somewhat more developed picture? Intuitively, numbers seem to be logically simple; they do not appear to be, for example, conjunctions or generalizations of other PRPs. Hence, they seem to belong down at the bottom of our hierarchy. It follows that there is a set C of all numbers at the next level, according to our model. But this supposition, of course, assuming the truth of the axioms of ZF, leads to paradox in a number of ways. For example, one can use the axiom of replacement on C to prove that there is a set of all von Neumann cardinals. I've argued elsewhere[42] that, on certain conceptions of the abstract universe that might allow "overly large" sets, it is appropriate to restrict this axiom to sufficiently "small" sets, and such a restriction would not permit its use here. This would still not redeem the situation, though. On our model, I think we must hold that for every set there exists a definite property which is its cardinal number. For it seems quite impossible that God should construct a set without also conceiving its cardinality, the property it shares with any other set that can be put into one-to-one correspondence with it. Hence, the set C of all numbers must itself have a cardinality $k,$ and so $k \in C$. But it is easy to show (with only unexceptionable uses of replacement) that k is strictly greater than every member of C,[43] and hence that $k > k$. Once more we have to confront paradox.

Happily, there is a simple and intuitive solution to this paradox. How many numbers must we say there are? Given our understanding of the numbers as properties of sets, and our reasoning in the previous paragraph, if we divide up the universe of sets according to size, then there must be as many numbers as there are divisions. Numbers are thus in a certain sense dependent on sets in a way that other sorts of properties are not. This suggests a natural way of fitting numbers into our hierarchy in such a way as to avoid paradox: a given number is not introduced into the hierarchy until a set is constructed whose cardinality is that number. The number is then introduced at the next level; God, we might say, doesn't conceive the number until he "has to." Since there are larger and larger sets at every new stage in our hierarchy, there will be no point after which new numbers are no longer introduced, and thus there can be no set of them. Hence, our numerical paradox above cannot get started.

Since our model is informal, the only rigorous way of demonstrating that it is indeed paradox-free is to formalize the picture of the abstract universe it yields and then to prove the consistency of the resulting theory. This can be done. The universe of the activist model can be formalized in a first-order theory that includes all of ZFC and a rich logic of PRPs that embodies all the fine-grainedness principles above; and this theory is provably consistent relative to ZF.

6. LOOSE ENDS

Many difficult and important issues remain, of course. Perhaps the most pressing are those having to do with modality. For instance, a natural question facing activism is whether God could have created more, fewer, or other PRPs than the ones he in fact created. Morris and I argued in "Absolute Creation" that there is a relatively straightforward answer to this question, but the hierarchical picture developed here suggests that the question is somewhat more subtle. In particular, does it not seem possible that God could have continued his collecting activity and generated a set that contains all the objects in the actual universe? Couldn't he then have generated new PRPs that would have contained that set as a constituent? If so, then it seems there could at least have been more PRPs than those that exist in fact. A second issue is engendered by the fact that the constructive nature of complex PRPs seems to entail the doctrine known as *existentialism,* i.e., the doctrine that PRPs are ontologically dependent on their constituents.

An adequate treatment of these issues will require a clear account of modal propositions and their truth conditions. This in turn raises the question of how modal propositions, and modal PRPs generally, are to be worked into the activist universe. Important issues all, deserving much further exploration; for the time being we will rest content with the ones we've managed to address thus far.[44]

NOTES

1. "Absolute Creation," *American Philosophical Quarterly* 23 (1986), 353–62; reprinted in Thomas V. Morris, *Anselmian Explorations* (Notre Dame, Ind.: University of Notre Dame Press, 1987).
2. "Direct" as opposed to merely causing the thing to exist by bringing about some other series of events that are causally sufficient for its existence. We take the notion of causation here to be primitive; in particular, we cannot analyze it counterfactually (cf. note 5).

3. This doctrine is strongly suggested by St. Paul (Col. 1:16) and the writer of the Hebrews (1:3), and is at least implicit in St. Thomas (e.g., *Summa Theologica* I, q. 45, art. 3). Its most overt expression in the modern period is found in Descartes (*Principles of Philosophy,* 1, XXI). The doctrine has been defended most recently by J. Kvanvig and H. McCann in their paper "Divine Conservation and the Persistence of the World," in Thomas V. Morris, ed., *Divine and Human Action* (Ithaca: Cornell University Press, 1988).

4. Note that it is compatible with this view that other persons *collaborate* with God in acts of creation. Our view only stipulates explicitly that God necessarily plays a direct causal role in the existence of every object at every time; other persons might also play such roles with respect to some objects.

5. Note that we can't analyze the causal relation here counterfactually as simply the claim that if God hadn't thought abstract objects, they wouldn't have existed, since (on the existing semantics for counterfactuals) it is equally true that if abstract objects hadn't existed, God wouldn't have. Despite this *logical* symmetry between God and abstract objects, we claim that there is a causal asymmetry.

6. Not least of these is Frege's own well-known puzzle of the concept **horse.** See "On Concept and Object," in *Translations from the Philosophical Writings of Gottlob Frege,* translated and edited by P. Geach and M. Black (Oxford: Basil Blackwell, 1952), 42–55.

7. Cf., e.g., G. Chierchia, "Topics in the Syntax and Semantics of Infinitives and Gerunds," Ph.D. dissertation, Dept. of Linguistics, University of Massachusetts (1984); R. Turner, "A Theory of Properties," *Journal of Symbolic Logic* 55 (1987), 455–72; G. Bealer, *Quality and Concept* (Oxford: Oxford University Press, 1982).

8. G. Frege, *Foundations of Arithmetic,* trans. J. L. Austin (Evanston, Ill.: Northwestern University Press, 1980). See also T. Burge, "Frege on the Extensions of Concepts, from 1884 to 1903," *The Philosophical Review* 93 (1984), 3–34.

9. This of course can be understood noncircularly in the usual Fregean/ Russellian way. This is essentially the analysis of number developed in Bealer, *Quality and Concept,* chap. 6.

10. Quoted in M. Hallett, *Cantorian Set Theory and the Limitation of Size* (Oxford: Oxford University Press, 1984), 122. Hallett, I should note, disputes the idea that Cantor held that cardinal numbers are concepts or properties.

11. For a recent development and defense of this position, see P. Maddy, "Sets and Numbers," *Noûs* 15 (1981), 495–511.

12. B. Russell, *The Principles of Mathematics* (New York: W. W. Norton, 1937), 112ff.

13. See Bealer, *Quality and Concept,* chap. 5, and M. Jubien, "Models of Property Theory," unpublished ms.

14. N. Cocchiarella, "Review of Bealer, *Quality and Concept,*" *Journal of Symbolic Logic* 51 (1983).

15. Ibid.

16. Cf., e.g., G. Boolos, "The Iterative Conception of Set," *Journal of Philosophy* 68 (1971), 215–31.

17. G. Cantor, *Gesammelte Abhandlungen* (Berlin: Springer, 1932), 204.

18. R. Dedekind, *Essays in the Theory of Numbers,* trans. W. W. Beman (New York: Dover, 1963), 45.

19. F. Hausdorff, *Grundzuge der Mengenlehre* (Leipzig: von Veit, 1914); A. Fraenkel, *Abstract Set Theory* (Amsterdam: North-Holland, 1961); J. Schoenfield, *Mathematical Logic* (Reading, Pa.: Addison-Wesley, 1967); R. Rucker, *Infinity and the Mind* (Boston: Birkhauser, 1982); H. Wang, *From Mathematics to Philosophy* (London: Routledge & Kegan Paul, 1974).

20. *From Mathematics to Philosophy,* 182.

21. Cf., e.g., W. Köhler, *Gestalt Psychology* (New York: New American Library, 1947).

22. That is, possible in the sense of all the collections he can form from all the nonsets there happen to be; I don't want to suggest that there could be sets containing "merely possible" objects, of which I think there are none.

23. Let me register my awareness that this is no trivial postulate and that it deserves much further discussion for which there is simply no room here.

24. A very similar paradox arises in connection with the notion of a possible world. See M. Loux, ed., *The Possible and the Actual* (Ithaca: Cornell University Press, 1979), 52–53; P. Grim, "There Is No Set of All Truths," *Analysis* 44 (1984), 206–8; S. Bringsjord, "Are There Set-theoretic Possible Worlds?" *Analysis* 45 (1985), 64; C. Menzel, "On Set Theoretic Possible Worlds," *Analysis* 46 (1986), 68–72; and P. Grim, "On Sets and Worlds: A Reply to Menzel," *Analysis* 46 (1986), 186–91.

25. This is what can be called a "fine-grainedness" principle that is natural to those conceptions of PRPs that tend to individuate them on psychological grounds, e.g., that properties are identical if it is not possible to conceive of the one without conceiving of the other. Cf., e.g., R. Chisholm, *The First Person* (Minneapolis: University of Minnesota Press, 1981), chap. 1; A. Plantinga, *The Nature of Necessity* (Oxford: Oxford University Press, 1974). For more formal developments cf. Bealer, *Quality and Concept,* and C. Menzel, "A Complete Type-free 'Second-order' Logic and Its Philosophical Foundations," Report No. CSLI-86-40, Center for the Study of Language and Information, Stanford University, 1986. Please note that I will be abusing metalanguage/object language and use/mention distinctions mercilessly throughout this paper.

26. Notational remark: $[\lambda x_1 \ldots x_n \varphi]$ is an n-place relation that holds among entities $a_1, \ldots, a_n$ just in case $\varphi_{a_1 \ldots a_n}^{x_1 \ldots x_n}$. Where $n = 0$, this is just the proposition that φ.

27. Where $A \leq B$ means, in essence, that A is in one-to-one correspondence with a subset of B.

28. Cf., e.g., Plantinga, *Nature of Necessity,* chap. 5.

29. Both of these arguments are essentially just special cases of an argu-

ment schema that is generally applicable to all n-place relations, $n \geq 0$ (where 0-place relations are propositions). Let A be the set of all n-place relations, for some given n. Then for any $(n + 1)$-place relation $\mathbf{R}$, where x^i_{n+1} is the sequence $x_1 \ldots x_{i-1} x_{i+1} \ldots x_{n+1}$, we have the fine-grainedness principle that, for any x and y,

$(**_n)$ if $x \neq y$, then $[\lambda x^i_{n+1} \mathbf{R} x_1 \ldots x \ldots x_{n+1}] \neq [\lambda x^i_{n+1} \mathbf{R} x_1 \ldots y \ldots x_{n+1}]$,

where the complex terms here signify the n-place relations that result from "plugging" x and y respectively into the ith argument place of $\mathbf{R}$. Assuming that any object can be so plugged into our relation $\mathbf{R}$, it follows from $(**_n)$ that there is a one-to-one correspondence between $\text{Pow}(A)$ and the set $B =$

$\{[\lambda x^i_{n+1} \mathbf{R} x_1 \ldots z \ldots x_{n+1}] : z \in \text{Pow}(A)\} \subseteq A$, and hence that $\text{Pow}(A) \leq A$.

30. As we'll see below, we can even give the objector the power set axiom, since there are other paradoxes that still arise in the current picture. But I prefer to meet the objector head on here to defend the legitimacy and appropriateness of power set in our activist framework.

31. I have argued this at length in "On the Iterative Explanation of the Paradoxes," *Philosophical Studies* 49 (1986), 37–61.

32. Of course, the paradoxes above aside, in such a picture the axiom of replacement would have to be restricted in some way, else replacing on, e.g., the set $\{[\lambda \, \mathbf{SET}(x)] : x$ is a set$\}$ would yield the set of all sets. See "On the Iterative Explanation."

33. Specifically, let the order $\text{ord}(i)$ of the basic type i be 0; and if t is the type $(t_1, \ldots, t_n)$, let $\text{ord}\,(t) = \max(\text{ord}(t_1), \ldots, \text{ord}\,(t_n)) + 1$; then we can say that one type t is higher than another t' just in case $\text{ord}(t) > \text{ord}(t')$.

34. Note that to pull this off in any sort of formal detail one would have to assign types to sets as well. Since sets on the cumulative picture would be able to contain entities of all finite types, we would also have to move to a transfinite type theory. However, as we'll see, the issue is moot.

35. To use Russell's term; see his "Mathematical Logic as Based on the Theory of Types," in J. van Heijenoort, ed., *From Frege to Gödel* (Cambridge, Mass.: Harvard University Press, 1967), 161.

36. E.g., the theory in E. Zalta, *Abstract Objects* (Dordrecht: D. Reidel, 1983), chap. 5.

37. I.e., just in case it is a member of s, or a member of a member of s, or a member of a member of a member of s or. . . .

38. More generally, for any $n + 1$-place relation $\mathbf{R}$ whose i^{th} argument place ranges over sets of n-place relations among individuals, and whose other argument places (if any) range over individuals, we define the condition of being *self-presupposing with respect to* $\mathbf{R}$ ($\text{SP}_{\mathbf{R}}$) such that, for any n-place relation $\mathbf{P}$ among individuals, $\text{SP}_{\mathbf{R}}(\mathbf{P})$ iff for some set s, $\mathbf{P} = [\lambda x^i_{n+1} \mathbf{R} x_1 \ldots s \ldots x_{n+1}]$ and $\mathbf{P} \in s$, where x^i_{n+1} is as in note 29. Consider now the set $s^* = \{\mathbf{P} : \neg\text{SP}_{\mathbf{R}}(\mathbf{P})\}$ (which exists by the axiom of separation), and let $\mathbf{P}^* = [\lambda x^i_{n+1}$

$Rx_1 \ldots s^* \ldots x_{n+1}]$. Question: $SP_R(P^*)$? I leave it to the reader to show that $SP_R(P^*) \equiv \neg SP_R(P^*)$. (Fine-grainedness is needed from left to right.) A similar paradox that doesn't rely on power set is found in Grim, "On Sets and Worlds."

39. These are ideas with syntactic roots in W. V. Quine, "Variables Explained Away," reprinted in his *Selected Logic Papers* (New York: Random House, 1966), and P. Bernays, "Über eine natürliche Erweiterung des Relationenskalkuls," in A. Heyting, ed., *Constructivity in Mathematics* (Amsterdam: North-Holland, 1959), 1–14, and have close algebraic ties to L. Henkin, D. Monk, and A. Tarski, *Cylindrical Algebras* (Amsterdam: North Holland, 1971). For fuller development within the context of metaphysical realism, cf. Bealer, *Quality and Concept*; Zalta, *Abstract Objects,* and Menzel, "Type-free 'Second-order' Logic." Several categories of logical operations have been omitted here to simplify exposition.

40. This claim is severely called into question in J. Barwise and J. Etchemendy, *The Liar: An Essay on Truth and Circularity* (Oxford: Oxford University Press, 1987). A full defense of the claim would have to deal at length with their challenge.

41. In type-free terms, for any $n + 1$-place relation **R**, we define the condition TSP_R such that $TSP_R(y)$ iff for some $z, y = [\lambda x_{n+1}^i Rx_1 \ldots z \ldots x_{n+1}]$ and $y \in z$. It is easy to see that, on the present model, nothing — in particular, no n-place relation — satisfies this condition. For any n-place relation of the form $[\lambda x_{n+1}^i Rx_1 \ldots s \ldots x_{n+1}]$, where s is a set, contains s as an internal constituent, and hence on our current model can only have been constructed after the construction of s. Thus, there is no set $s^* = \{y : \neg TSP_R(y)\}$ (since this would be the universal set) and so no property $y^* = [\lambda x_{n+1}^i Rx_1 \ldots s^* \ldots x_{n+1}]$.

42. In "On the Iterative Explanation of the Paradoxes."

43. One can, for example, use the theorem (which requires only replacement on ω) that there are arbitrarily large fixed points in the mapping $\aleph$ of (von Neumann) ordinals onto (von Neumann) cardinals. This entails that for any $n \in C$ there is an $m > n$ such that $|\{j \in C : j < m\}| = m$. But $\{j \in C : j < m\} \subseteq C$, hence $|C| = k \geq m > n$.

44. I am indebted to Jon Kvanvig, Hugh McCann, Tom Morris, Rick Otte, Al Plantinga, Del Ratzsch, and Nick Wolterstorff for encouragement, discussion, and critical comments.

Philosophy of Mind and the Christian

CHARLES TALIAFERRO

What are persons? Are we thoroughly physical beings or do we contain some nonphysical part, something we may call a soul, spirit, or mind? What is our sensory experience of color, sound, taste, smell and tactile feelings of heat and cold, pleasure and pain? How are these related to our bodily states, our neurochemical processes, the state of our brain and bodily organs? For example, is your feeling pain the very same thing as some material state or is it the case that while material states bring about painful feelings, these feelings are not themselves material? What is it to have certain beliefs, motives, desires, dreams, and appetites? Do each (or any) of these items have a spatial location? Is there an unconscious and, if so, how is it related to the conscious? Do we sometimes act freely and, if we do, how is this free agency related to the laws of nature? What is it that makes you the same person over time? Can persons survive bodily death, the cessation of brain processes and the disintegration of our bodily frame?

These questions make up the better part of what is typically classified as the philosophy of mind. Given their breadth, the title 'philosophy of mind' may not be the happiest one available as 'mind' tends to suggest the narrowly intellectual or cerebral side of personal life. Furthermore, it is evident that this opening salvo of questions involves far more than theories about persons, for some of them involve issues in the philosophy of matter and the physical world. After all, we cannot intelligently inquire into the relationship of our feelings and we ourselves *in toto* to physical events and processes unless we have some competent grasp of the nature and character of physical reality. For now let's leave to one side quibbles over what to christen this motley bundle of questions and take up the more general projects of weighing alternative answers to the fundamental question of what is a person and consider whether the Christian philosopher is entitled to address the relevant issues in a distinctive fashion. Is there a particular method which those of us who are Christians may use with intellectual impunity in answering these questions that differs from our non-Christian colleages?

METHODS AND WHAT IS AT STAKE

It is certainly plausible to think the answer to this last question is 'no'. The Christian philosopher is on thin intellectual ice if she abandons the methods practiced by many, perhaps most, non-Christian philosophers. One should strive for self-consistency and coherence. One should adhere to such canons of good reasoning as don't explain the obscure in terms of the even more obscure; don't flaunt evident, well-confirmed scientific theories (at least not without very good reasons!); don't make arbitrary *ad hoc* assumptions to save your theory which is only very weakly supported by evidence in the first place, and so on. One could, then, answer our question about methodology with the same answer and confidence as we might well respond to the question about whether there is a peculiarly Christian method for making chairs and tables. Build chairs and tables that are sturdy, functional, and aesthetically pleasing; presumably there is no distinctively Christian technique in doing so.

But in taking this tack we do well to be clear that how we answer the above set of questions will in some measure determine whether we are Christian philosophers in the first place, for to be a Christian in anything remotely like the classical understanding of Christianity is to possess a philosophy of mind, a philosophy of the divine mind or person, God, and created minds or persons.

Consider the following set of central convictions which many or most Christians share. I list them in somewhat rough form without attention to precise analytical fine points or pretense at being exhaustive. Each of these has implications for the philosophy of mind.

1. God is all powerful.
2. God is all-knowing.

3. God is an all-good, purposive agent.
4. God loves.
5. God is responsible for the existence of the cosmos, its origin and continuation.
6. God is a necessarily existing being, whereas the created cosmos exists contingently.
7. God is everywhere present in the cosmos.
8. God is spirit or incorporeal.
9. God is triune; one in substance, three in persons.
10. The second person of the Divine Godhead became incarnate as a human being in the life of Jesus Christ.
11. Human beings are in the image of God.
12. They (or we) think, feel, and have sensory experiences of the world.
13. We have bodies.
14. The material world was created as a good reality. (In Genesis God is said to see the cosmos as good.)
15. We are agents who are morally accountable for at least some of our acts of commission and omission.
16. We are capable of having some experience of God. (Christians speak about the indwelling of the Holy Spirit and a union with God.)
17. Bodily death is not the ultimate extinguishing of personal life, for at least some created persons will enjoy life with God after bodily death.
18. Jesus Christ was crucified, dead and buried and afterward was resurrected and ascended into heaven.
19. There is a heaven and hell.
20. There are angels and demons, incorporeal, personal agents.

Each of these has some bearing on the philosophy of mind. There are theories of the person which are incompatible with some of these convictions and some theories of the person which cohere and even lend positive support for these convictions. Before turning to examine these theories and then backing up my claim, I note that not all those who are rightly called Christians adopt each item on our list. Some modern Christians reject number 20, but seem to be content with 1 through 19. The list of religious beliefs relevant to philosophy of mind could also be extended to less central items, but there is no need to do so to make some headway in exploring the nature and relevance of philosophy of mind for the Christian.[1] To do such exploring and assess the prospect of a distinctively Christian philosophical methodology, it will prove useful to demarcate the dominant theories of mind in the current literature.

I focus here upon the principal theories about the status of ourselves as persons and our experiences in relationship to the physical world. I shall therefore concentrate on what I take to be the most central preoccupation of the philosophy of mind. Each of these theories addresses the foundational issue about whether the mental world of experience, feeling, emotion, and thought is distinct from the physical world of bodies, material events, and processes.

> *Eliminative Materialism*: Strictly speaking what we call psychological undergoings or mental activity such as thinking, sensing, perceiving, and the like do not exist distinct from physical, material undergoings and activities. Such so-called mental entities can be eliminated from a comprehensive, exhaustive account of ourselves and the world. What we call pain is really certain neural activity. Just as many of us have come to abandon talk of witches and demon possession, psychological talk can be eliminated (at least in principle) from our description of ourselves and the world, being replaced by straightforward talk of physical objects and processes.

> *Identity Theory*: There are mental or psychological undergoings and activities but these are the very same things as certain physical undergoings and activities. I do experience pains and have beliefs, but these are themselves material events. Some identity theorists have argued that psychological terms like pain mean the same thing as physical terms, though it is more common for them to maintain that psychological and physical terms have different meanings but both turn out to refer to the very same thing. Thus, talk about pain and talk about electrical brain activity are different descriptions of the same thing (a material process). Another popular form of the identity theory is the claim that the mental is composed of nothing more than physical objects and processes. My be-

ing in pain is composed entirely of physical objects undergoing material processes.

Functionalism: Psychological or mental events are identifiable in terms of certain causal roles. The most popular forms of functionalism are materialistic, the thesis being that to be in pain (and other psychological states) is to be understood in terms of being brought about by certain material events such as skin tissue damage and to result in certain other material states, such as avoidance of recurring damage. Materialistic functionalists charge that what fills these causal roles, what is caused by skin damage and causes damage-avoidance behavior, turns out to be material states and events. Functionalists criticize the notion that we are immediately apprised of the character of our internal mental states as something nonphysical. It is possible in principle to accept functionalism and not be a materialist by maintaining that what occupies the designated causal roles turns out to be immaterial. As none of the major proponents of functionalism take this route, I treat the theory here as exclusively materialistic. It could be classified as a version of the identity theory above, but I list it separately owing to its distinctive prominence as a kind of neo-identity theory.

Property Dualism: Psychological properties and undergoings are not identical with physical properties and undergoings. Thus, being in pain is not the same property as being in a certain physical state, even if every case of being in pain is accompanied by or brought about by physical states. Most property dualists believe that the person herself is physical albeit she possesses some nonphysical properties.

Substance Dualism: Not only are psychological properties distinct from physical properties (as maintained by the property dualist), but you and I are ourselves nonphysical. I am a nonphysical individual who is in causal interaction with this body. Some dualists have believed that the causal interplay between persons and bodies is only one directional, viz., your body affects you but you do not exercise causal power over the body, or you affect the body but your body does not exercise causal power over you. Most substance dualists reject these one-directional accounts and embrace the thesis that persons and bodies interact. In the treatment of substance dualism below, I employ the term 'person' rather than 'soul' or 'mind' to designate the self as a nonphysical reality.

Idealism: This could also be titled 'eliminative mentalism' or 'identity mentalism'. The idealist may argue either that there are no material events whatever but only mental events (eliminativism) or that there are material events but material events turn out to be the same thing as mental events, experience, and sensations (identity mentalism).[2]

In subsequent treatment of these theories let's assume a fairly loose, provisional understanding of what are physical events and objects. In fact, the task of analyzing in precise terms the nature of physical things is not easy. But for present purposes let's think of physical things as objects like tables, mountains, human bodies, stars. Alternatively, we can think of physical items as those things which are either posited by contemporary physics or things like them (atomic and subatomic reality). Both accounts are inexact but sufficient for us to proceed. I have argued in detail elsewhere that all the extant accounts of what is a physical object face philosophical problems.[3] Our procedure here need not be seen as begging the question against the idealist, for the idealist can accept such an understanding of the physical along with the proviso that these items turn out to be patterns of experience.

It should be clear how some of these theories of mind bear upon the Christian convictions cited earlier. If we adopt eliminative materialism, it appears that we have undermined central beliefs about ourselves, beliefs which are pivotal in the Christian schema (12, 15, 16, and 17, for starters). And if we extend eliminative materialism to cover not merely our terrestrial life but to range over all of reality, it becomes problematic how we can consistently subscribe to any of the beliefs on our list about God's personal reality. What sense could it make to claim that God created the cosmos, knows and loves creatures, and so on, if all psychological items like knowledge, emotion, and creative agency turn out to be eliminable in a comprehensive account of all that exists?

It seems to me that any recognizably Christian worldview will have to preserve some sense in which the mental world of intentions, emotions, and feeling are not eliminable or to be explained away. Christianity is surely compatible with a range of particular theories about created persons. For example, the truth of Christianity does not entail the truth of a specific theory of the unconscious or the biological character of human appetites (fascinating areas of philosophy of mind which I will have to leave to one side here). But Christianity is not so flexible that it can survive a wholesale elimination or even substantial denigration of the psychological. As Alvin Plantinga points out in his "Advice to Christian Philosophers," the God of Christian theism is personal: "God is the premier person, the first and chief exemplar of personhood."[4] As such, Christian philosophers are committed to believing that at least some psychological explanations are *bona fide* accounts of events in the world and not to be subsumed under more fundamental material laws of nature.

So, how the Christian philosopher answers our chief question about the status of persons will in some measure determine whether she is indeed a Christian. If one believes God is a person and distinct from the physical world, one cannot believe that all persons are physical. If one has some reason to believe God exists and is a nonphysical person, then one has some reason to reject the thesis that all persons whatever are physical and thus to reject comprehensive versions of eliminative materialism, the identity theory, functionalism, and property dualism. But is the Christian rightly advised to adopt a different philosophical method than the non-Christian? Plantinga suggests that the Christian is entitled to draw upon her religious convictions in thinking about the character of human experience and who we are. His remarks serve to bring to light some respect in which the Christian may occupy a different starting point or find herself working within a different framework than the non-Christian. I think Plantinga has raised a viable, promising option. But precisely what would this method involve? At the outset let us be clear about some of the problems which may be involved with using one's philosophy of God to justify one's philosophy of human persons. Doesn't it appear that any reasons we have to believe in the existence of God will be weaker than reasons we have to accept one philosophy of mind rather than another? Some of the arguments for the existence of God, notably the design argument, rest upon *a prior,* independently justified conviction about human persons.[5] Moreover, it appears that the philosophy of human persons must be logically prior to the philosophy of God, for our referring to God as a person derives its meaning and sense from our understanding and reference to humans. These worries may well lead us to advise Christian philosophers to first bracket their theistic beliefs and develop a coherent, plausible philosophy of mind. Only when that is done can we hope to go on to do solid philosophy of God.

In what follows I propose to meet some of these worries and indicate ways in which a defensible, comprehensive methodology can be fashioned along the lines Plantinga suggests. I draw attention to a significant way in which evidence for theism is not entirely dependent upon nor derived from philosophy of mind and thus can offer us independent reasons for accepting a particular theory of the person. I also draw attention to formal features of theism which can counter some arguments for physicalism, most notably the physicalists' simplicity argument. Rather than being concerned in an abstract way with discussing the framework within which to do philosophy of mind from a respectable Christian outlook, I aim at providing good reasons for a specific theory of the person which both draws upon and lends support to classical Christian theism. I accept substance dualism with respect to created persons like you and me and our bodies as well as an analogous dualism between God and the world. The remainder of the paper is divided among four sections: (1) an overview of the relationship between the two types of dualism. I contend that substance dualism is not subject to some popular religious objections. In (2) I discuss arguments that can be marshaled for accepting substance dualism; in (3) I reply to two major objections to dualism about persons, and in (4) I conclude with reflections on the methods of Christian philosophy.

1. DUALISM

The position of substance dualism is not popular with either contemporary philosophical psychologists or many theologians. In fact the contemporary attitude of some philosophers and theologians toward dualism is ably summarized by Daniel Dennett: "Dualism is not a serious view to contend with, but rather a cliff over which to push one's opponents."[6] But dualism is not without its defenders today and it has clearly been the dominant understanding of persons in the history of the Christian religion.[7] Because of dualism's current bad press, it is important at the outset to clarify the version of dualism I defend, distinguishing it from the ill-formed theories which are so often criticized.

To begin with, consider some of the reasons why Christian theologians have rejected a dualist understanding of the person. I think the reasons are chiefly three: (*a*) Theories of dualism have often been associated with the thesis that persons are naturally immortal. That is, we are such that our continuation after the disintegration of our bodies is something natural or an outcome of our intrinsic nature, whereas biblical teaching and religious experience testifies that if we do survive death it is owing to the miraculous intervention of God. Dualism obscures our reliance upon God to bring about what I noted as 17 above. (*b*) Related to (*a*) is the criticism that the truth of dualism does not cohere with the central emphasis on the Christian teaching of the bodily death and resurrection of Christ. If we are not our bodies, why would Christ have become incarnate, have lived among us in bodily form, have been crucified and then have risen bodily from the tomb (numbers 10 and 18)? (*c*) Finally, the idea that we are fundamentally nonphysical tends to denigrate the body morally and emotionally, conceiving of it as a second-class citizen. This is unacceptable, for the body is integral to personhood and this is underscored in Scripture (especially in the Old Testament) and the tradition of creation-centered spirituality. So, theologians charge that dualism is unable to do justice to what I have listed as 13 and 14 above.[8]

The substantive dualism I shall be setting forth is not subject to these objections. I maintain that persons are nonphysical but causally embodied. The body is integral to personhood but not essential for it. Thus, it is possible that you or I may continue to live after the demise or ceasing to be of our bodies. This is not due to our own power, so to speak, but due to the merciful agency of God (contra (*a*)). The dualism I defend is by no means body-denigrating or dismissive of our embodiment. Dualism (as I shall use the term here) offers an account of what it means to have a body. Thus, I understand this to be my body by virtue of my being in certain causal relations like the following: if this body is injured, I feel pain; I think with this physical brain; I see, hear, smell, taste, and feel with these organs and nerve endings; my action and speech in this world are in and through this body, and so on. In offering an account of what it means to be embodied, dualism does not at all offer any grounds for thinking the body is unimportant or to be loathed. Persons are distinct from their bodies and they are embodied in a fashion such that in this life we are to treat person and body as a single unit in moral, practical, political, religious, and aesthetic contexts. (If Dennett were suddenly to appear behind me and push me over a cliff, I would plummet downward, body and all.) I see no reason why dualism cannot give the fullest measure of weight to the importance of our own bodily integrity and Christ's incarnation, life, death, resurrection, and ascension (contra (b) and (c)).

The current resistance to dualism by Christian theologians is curious, as dualism seems especially well suited to bolster the credibility of believing persons are capable of surviving death and accepting the coherence of traditional treatments of the incarnation. I consider both points briefly, employing what may be termed the principle of identity (a principle I use in arguing for dualism in the next section): If I am identical with my body, then whatever happens to my body, happens to me and *vice versa*. This follows from the principle of identity which we may formulate as for any A and B, if A is B, then whatever is true of A is true of B. This is sometimes called indiscernibility of identicals.[9]

Many Christians do not simply believe that we will survive bodily death (number 17), but that immediately upon death we will be with God and enjoy some form of afterlife before any kind of ultimate resurrection of the body. These Christians may believe in and anticipate an apocalyptic historical bodily resurrection in which they are reunited with their earthly bodies, but they also believe that prior to this parousia they will either have some other body or exist in a disembodied fashion with God. Think of Dante's portrayal of this intermittent stage in his *Divine Comedy* in which persons in hell, purgatory, and paradise have some bodily reality. If the identity theory is correct, then whatever is true of me is true of my body. But if it is true of my body that it is scattered about the earth, then I am scattered about the earth. How can I exist disembodied, if I am a body? How can I receive a new body, if I am identical with some other body and it is buried or burnt or on the ocean floor? If dualism is correct, then body switching or existing disembodied is not conceptually absurd—at least there is no obvious reason to think so. If I am not this body, then there are things which may be true of me (I may be in experiential union with God), which is not true of the body (it having ceased to be *in nihilium* in thermonuclear heat, say).[10]

Consider the classical understanding of the incarnation. The Second Person of the Trinity predated the particles that constituted the physical body of Jesus Christ, first-century Nazarene. If the identity theory is correct, then this supposition is absurd. How can something predate or exist prior to when it exists? If Christ is (or was) those molecules, then Christ could not have existed prior to those molecules. Dualism allows that while the Second Person of the Trinity became incarnate, coming to be infleshed or embodied, strictly speaking the person himself is not identical with that body. This need not suggest any kind of docetism (the heresy that denies Christ's humanity). Christ was truly embodied, perceiving the world through those eyes, touching people with those hands, feeling pain because of those wounds, and so on. The dualist and idealist seem better placed to allow for a classic understanding of the incarnation than those who embrace the other alternatives.[11] So, I conclude that dualism with respect to created persons has some desirable features from the standpoint of classical Christian teachings. Moreover it seems to provide a respect in which God and created persons are analogous. Neither God nor you are wholly material. By characterizing the God-world relationship as dualistic we bring out this parallel character.

2. MINDS AND BODIES

I now turn to consider some of the arguments for and against the various theories of mind. In doing so it will be important to return to the general topic of philosophical method.

Every philosopher must begin somewhere. It is perfectly respectable to begin with what appears to be our ordinary experience until we have reason to reject it. (How would it be to begin with what does not seem to us to be the case?)[12] I propose at the outset that ordinary experience does give us some reason to be skeptical of eliminative materialism and the identity theory (and thus functionalism as well). In short, I think we have some reason to accept the view that the psychological and physical are distinct, which amounts to the claim that we have some reason to accept either the property dualist or substance dualist theories. Why?

Because we at least appear to have subjective experiences of pain, pleasure, sensory undergoings of color, heat, odor, and so on. Furthermore it seems that attending to these states is very different from attending to the physical states which may or may not accompany them. I can certainly conceive of the movement of the brain and nervous system which give rise to pain without any notion of the pain itself and I can think of some given pain experience without thereby entertaining any idea of the accompanying material movements. Now, the fact that I can think of some property without thinking of another does not establish that the two are not intimately related, nor that the same object does not (or cannot) possess both properties. I can think of Champe having the property of being a father without thinking of his having the property of being a bank robber. Sadly, he may possess both properties. But if there is reason to believe one can conceive of some property, be it the property of being a father or being in pain, without conceiving of another, being a bank robber or being in a certain material state, then one has reason to believe the properties are not identical. So, my claim at the outset is that such appeal to ordinary experience gives us some presumptive reason in the direction of property dualism. This is not contested by many materialists; many antidualists concede that dualism is the commonsense view. Some even charge that nondualist theories are suspect unless they are able to account for why so many are tempted to be a dualist in the first place.[13]

Having proposed that there is presumptive reason for accepting at least a dualism (or nonidentity) of psychological and physical properties, let me add that I think there is presumptive reason to reject idealism or eliminative mentalism. It does appear that I can conceive of straightforward physical properties like being a mountain or being a water molecule without conceiving of any psychological properties. Of course, as we shall see below, additional arguments can be mustered to overturn this initial case for a dualist outlook, but I maintain that ordinary experience places the burden of proof on those opposing dualism (of properties, at least).

Let us now examine the different theories of mind to consider what positive reasons may be offered on their behalf. Much of what follows will have to summarize rather briefly lines of reasoning and objections I have dealt with in far greater detail in *Consciousness and the Mind of God* and elsewhere.[14]

Have eliminative materialists given us compelling reasons for overturning our commonsense or presumptive stance favoring dualism? I think the two strongest reasons offered rest upon the desirability of achieving a unified account of the sciences in particular and of reality in general. Dualist accounts of persons amount to a bifurcation of nature and leave us with the daunting project of finding laws that bridge radically different kinds of entities.

No doubt there are respects in which the simplicity of a hypothesis can give it greater credibility than a more complex one. "There are some cats" is a simpler and more plausible hypothesis than "There are 123,678,295 cats." But surely the appeal to simplicity alone, what may be called the simplicity argument, cannot outweigh the apparent evidence of there being mental states like pain and so on.[15] Moreover, if simplicity alone is considered sufficiently weighty so as to overturn the presumptive case for dualism, the idealist can employ the simplicity argument in favor of her antimaterialist schema. After all, if we do demand a uniform understanding of reality, why not think of it as fundamentally mental? More on the simplicity argument below.

As for the laws of nature, eliminativists and other opponents of dualism charge that mental processes cannot enter into well-formulated laws of nature because of their intrinsic vagueness and indeterminacy. For example, what is the difference between someone having a belief that there is a rabbit behind the tree and believing there are parts of a rabbit behind the tree and believing there is a stage in a rabbit's life behind the tree?

Several replies are in order. First, one may simply deny that laws of nature can be strictly formulated. Many now deny that there are strict, deterministic laws that do govern all aspects of our psychophysical world. Causal indeterminism has a respectable place in contemporary physics. As such, it is not clear that all events or processes can be fit into precisely formulated covering laws. Second, we may charge that while we are unclear about the precise character of mental events (perhaps I have no way of knowing which rabbit belief Jones is entertaining), it does not follow that Jones's beliefs lack determinate features, features which in principle could be introduced in laws of nature, whether the laws be probabilistic or deterministic. Third, it is plausible to believe that our grasp of physical objects is no more (and can be no more) precise or free of vagueness than our grasp of psychological states, because it is on the basis of our psychological states that we form any notion of physical objects to begin with. More on this below.

Let me consider more substantive reasons for embracing the dualist stance, reasons that count against the materialist identity theory and functionalism.

There is no evident contradiction in claiming that someone is in a psychological state but not in the physical state posited by identity theorists and functionalists. I know of no inconsistency or incoherence involved in imagining that I have certain skin tissue damage *et al.* but do not have the accompanying painful feelings. This imagined state of affairs would be inconsistent or incoherent if mental terms have the same meaning as physical terms. More radical still, it appears that I can conceive of my being in certain psychological states and even existing *tout court* without having this particular body or any body whatever. It is evident that my body cannot be conceived of existing in this disembodied state. If it is true that I have certain properties (the property of being able to exist disembodied) which my body and any body whatever fails to have, then it follows that I am not my body or any body whatever. Recall the principle of identity at work here, if *A* is *B,* anything true of *A* is true of *B.*[16]

Not everything we think is possible is possible. For example, at the outset it may seem that there could be a barber who shaves all and only those who do not shave themselves. After further reflection we find out that there cannot be such a barber. But the fact that some state of affairs seems to be possible and seems to be possible after careful reflection on the involved properties does give us respectable grounds for assuming it to be possible. We are warranted in believing it to be possible in the absence of any contrary evidence. Critics of this argument against the identity theory and functionalism systematically underestimate the force of thought experiments about possible states of affairs. Thus, Margaret Wilson has claimed that "The fact that we can conceive that p does not entail that p is even possible: all that follows (at best) is that we have not yet noticed any contradiction in p."[17] And Sydney Shoemaker has charged that the purported conceivability of the mental in the absence of the physical gives reason to believe that we have not noticed an *a priori* entailment from mental predicates to physical predicates.[18] This weighing of conceivable states of affairs seems to me to be too modest. Such a move fails to do justice to the positive epistemic import of it seeming to someone that a certain state of affairs is possible. Surely the fact that I think I can conceive of there being a restaurant counter one mile long gives me good reason to believe that such a counter is possible. Clearly my thought experiment about restaurants entitles me to conclude something more substantive than the thesis that I have not (or not yet!) noticed anything contradictory about such a counter or that I have not detected any formal entailment relations rendering my thought experiment absurd. If so, we have reason to be skeptical of Wilson's and Shoemaker's characterization of conceiving possible states of affairs.

I believe that the thought experiment about possible forms of material and personal life gives us reason for accepting the substantive dualist point of view. Along with the different versions of the identity theory and functionalism, property dualism seems to fall prey to the thought experiment, for while it preserves what I take to be the correct thesis that physical and psychological properties are distinct, it still retains the thesis that persons themselves are physical, material entities. But if our argument above is plausible and if I have properties no physical object can have, it follows that I am not a physical object. Physical objects cannot enjoy disembodied existence nor can they be destroyed and gain new bodies. Whether or not I actually ever will be disembodied or gain some Danteish postmortem body, it is plausible to believe that such extraordinary happenings are metaphysically possible.

Can these reasons for accepting substance dualism be strengthened? I believe it is here that the Christian philosophers' convictions about God as a nonphysical person in causal interaction with the material cosmos may play an independent, positive role in the dualists' court. Perhaps we cannot even attain this conception of God without having secured some understanding of what it is to be a human person. Let us assume this is correct. It is by no means essential that we need to know substance dualism of person and body is correct or even plausible to get our concept of God off the ground. All we need in order to derive our notion of God is a rough understanding of personhood which is not thoroughly material, even if it turns out that all persons we seem to encounter are material. This conceptual derivation of the notion of God does not entail strict evidential derivation. That is, while our very grasp of the notion of God may derive from some notion of human persons, it does not follow that all our evidence (or justification) for believing there is such a being must be entirely derived from our philosophy of human minds. Once secured (however provisionally), our understanding of God can be extended and enjoy its role in theistic metaphysical arguments such as the arguments from design, contingency, religious experience, simplicity, miracles, history, and even the ontological argument. In my judgment there are plausible versions of each of these arguments which lend positive epistemic support to theism.[19] But I contend that if any of these arguments do lend support for theism and the evidence employed in one or more of them does not presuppose the truth of substance dualism, then the resultant conclusion can have an independent role in our thinking of human persons. If we have positive reason for thinking there is a nonphysical person in causal interplay with the cosmos we have positive reason for rejecting the thesis that all persons are accounted for by eliminative materialism, the identity theory, functionalism, and property dualism. Alternatively, imagine one's belief in God is properly basic, in Plantinga's sense, and therefore justified. If so, the Christian philosopher is justified in reaching the same negative judgment about thoroughgoing versions of materialism. Further reason would have to be given to conclude that if God is nonphysical, so are you and I, but what this approach to the philosophy of God and humans secures is a reason for rejecting materialism as true in all cases. Materialism is not necessarily true, nor is a dualism of the person and the physical conceptually absurd. In this fashion, I think there is credence to a Plantinganian notion that the Christian philosopher may have some distinctive resources in arguing for a philosophy of mind.

Theists also seem to me to be in a position to offer a ready reply to the materialists' simplicity argument. The materialists' account of cosmic laws seems in no wise superior as far as simplicity is concerned. In the theistic worldview, laws of nature are envisioned as themselves the manifestation of the intentional agency of God. The reality of such laws are in no wise abrogated, laws that may be formulated without any explicit notion of volition or agency. But they are accounted for by personal agency, a singular ultimate reality.[20] By appealing to her own account of the unified character of causal explanations, the theist need not presuppose the truth of substance dualism, just as the materialist need not presuppose the truth of the identity theory or eliminative materialism. But by spelling out an alternative, broadbased metaphysics, the theist at least blocks any pretense that simplicity is gained only on materialist ground. More on this below.

Could the thought experiment of disembodied personal life used in our argument for dualism be mistaken? Perhaps. I do not attribute infallible conceptual powers to you and me on these matters. The pattern of reasoning for substance dualism is akin to theistic arguments for the God-world distinction, viz., we can conceive of the world not existing at all or ceasing to be *in nihilum* and conclude the world is contingent. God *qua* necessarily existing, perfect being cannot cease to be or not have existed (belief number 6 I listed earlier.)[21] Perhaps both God-world and person-body thought experiments are incoherent, though I judge that in the absence of reasons to think they are incoherent; the fact that both seem to be possible is reason to think they are indeed possible states of affairs.

Let us consider briefly two objections to dualism we have not yet covered which, if plausible, threaten the presumptive dualist argument developed here. Some philosophers have maintained that were it not for these objections, substance dualism would be the preferred, most reasonable philosophy of mind.[22]

3. CAUSAL INTERACTION AND INDIVIDUATION

Objection one. Dualism posits an inordinate ontological rift between persons and bodies. The objection is akin to the one cited earlier in support of eliminative materialism but different in one respect. In order for objects to be causally interrelated they must share substantive properties. The abstract object Justice cannot cause a molecule to stir. It is unreasonable to suppose that events so radically distinct as a nonphysical person or soul-like substance can causally influence something solidly material and spatial like a human body. If successful, this objection undermines the theistic-dualist treatment of the simplicity argument discussed above, for while the theist achieves simplicity by construing laws of nature as a manifestation of divine agency, she is still straddled with positing a causal interplay between radically distinctive realms, the nonphysical and the physical.

Objection two. Dualism leads to intractable problems about individuation. After all, how are we to distinguish nonphysical persons? Imagine there are two such persons who have the same memories, beliefs, desires, dreams, and the like. Being nonphysical, they cannot be individuated physically and, being mentally indistinguishable, they cannot be individuated psychologically. What is it in virtue of which there are two persons and not more or less?

Neither objection has any force. In my judgment the materialist is unable to establish any nonquestion begging evidence for the assumption that the physical and nonphysical cannot causally interact. Why couldn't they interact? The absurdity behind the example of Justice is owing to its being an impersonal *abstracta,* certainly a nonagent, whereas the dualists construe the person not as an abstract object, but an individual agent. I also note that there is even less reason now than earlier this century to deny a dualist account of person-body interaction owing to developments in quantum theory. Reasons have been advanced to believe that atomic and subatomic life are not deterministically fixed, the interplay of particles being such that more than one outcome, motion, or event is possible. The physical world does not admit of a closed, fully deterministic analysis. What is the problem with supposing a person *qua* nonphysical individual engages in activity such that one of the physically possible outcomes occurs as opposed to others?[23]

As for the problem of individuation, I do not think the dualist is in any worse position than the physicalist. What is it in virtue of which material objects differ? Imagine two objects with the same shape, size, weight, color, and so on. The two cannot be said to differ because of distinguishable general properties. So, what is it that grounds their difference? It is unilluminating to claim they differ because of occupying different places or regions of space, because this simply invites the question of what is it in virtue of which places or spatial regions differ? Perhaps material objects are distinct in virtue of their having certain spatial relations such as being several feet apart? There are many problems with this thesis, but I note only one here. Spatial relations do not account for the numerical difference of objects. Rather, it is in virtue of material objects being distinct that they (ever) bear spatial relations to one another. Edwin Allaire correctly observed: "Relations—I'll stick with spatial ones— presuppose numerical difference; they do not account for it. The thisness and the thatness of things is presupposed in saying the one is to the left of the other."[24] Obviously the spatial relation of being several feet apart does not have occult properties making the objects of the relata distinct. This proposal is no more helpful than the other.

My conclusion is that both dualists and nondualists face difficulties in accounting for the individuation of objects. As such, this difficulty does not give us reasons to reject dualism and embrace materialism.[25]

4. CONCLUDING REFLECTIONS

Given the limitations of space, I can hope to have done little better than work out in a very sketchy form some of the reasons to accept dualism and outline the strategy which I believe the Christian philosopher is entitled to employ. I have had to focus upon the most central issue in the philosophy of mind and leave to one side many of the fascinating questions in the field I noted at the outset of this chapter. The Christian method I have articulated here about our metaphysical status as persons is one that involves taking into account a wide range of what can constitute the Christian's well-earned (or at least justified) religious beliefs. It should not be puzzling that Christianity has proved to be so clearly related to the philosophy of mind, for it has been a fundamental dictum of much Christian theology from the beginning that our awareness of God is closely related to the awareness of ourselves. At certain points in Christian tradition critical differences are emphasized between ourselves and God—God being perfect, eternal, without origin, necessarily existing, and so on, whereas we are imperfect, temporal, have origins, exist contingently, and so on. But any worldview recognizably Christian must preserve a fairly robust sense in which God and we are persons. We are in the image of God.

Earlier I queried whether there is a specifically Christian method for constructing chairs. I doubt it, but let's extend this matter of carpentry. Obviously the aim of producing a functional chair is served by some attention to the size and shape of those who will sit in it. A good chair for Daniel may not be good for a huge Goliath. In making the chair for Daniel, let us keep one eye on what we know he is like. In doing philosophy of mind, let us keep one eye on our other beliefs, or, to put the point more forcefully, keep an eye on the One in whom we believe.

NOTES

1. Other relevant beliefs include God is eternal or outside of time, bread and water become the body of Christ under certain conditions, the fellowship of those who follow Christ constitutes the Mystical Body of Christ, intercessory prayer is efficacious, there are postmortem realms of purgatory and limbo in addition to heaven and hell, there can occur cases of demon possession. Some theologians have employed the Christian understanding of sacraments in developing their theory of matter and mind. Most recent projects of this sort are championed by Arthur Peacocke and William Temple. Cf. Temple's classic *Nature, Man and God* (London: Macmillan, 1934) and Peacocke's *God and the New Biology* (New York: Harper & Row, 1986).

2. Given the restrictions governing the length of this essay, I have had to offer only the briefest sketch of the available options. By 'identity theory' I have sought to group together (but not conflate or identify) what philosophers sometimes distinguish as type, token, and compositional theories. My subsequent objection to the identity theory applies with equal force against each of these. There are numerous good anthologies in philosophy of mind replete with examples of most of the positions I explore here. Ned Block's two-volume set *Readings in Philosophy of Psychology* (Cambridge, Mass.: Harvard University Press, 1980) is the best to appear in recent years. Jerome Shaffer's "Recent Work on the Mind-Body Problem" is a good overview of some of the main debates in the literature and also includes a respectable bibliography, *Recent Work in Philosophy,* ed. K. G. Lucey and T. R. Machan (Totowa: Rowan & Allanheld, 1983). Unfortunately, contemporary anthologies neglect to give much attention to the renewed interest in idealism. For those interested, I commend John Foster's *The Case for Idealism* (London: Routledge & Kegan Paul, 1982) and T. L. S. Sprigge's *The Vindication of Absolute Idealism* (Edinburgh:

Edinburgh University Press, 1983). Our list of conceivable positions in the philosophy of mind is severely limited. There are many versions of idealism which could be delimited. So-called neutral monism could also be singled out, but this stance is not a prominent one today.

3. I do this in *Consciousness and the Mind of God,* chap. 2, a book-length manuscript in preparation. In Foster's book (cited above) there is a critique of some modern conceptions of the physical world. See also Howard Robinson's *Matter and Sense* (Cambridge: Cambridge University Press, 1982), especially "Matter: Turning and Tables" and the contribution by Karl Popper in *The Self and Its Brain* by Popper and John Eccles (New York: Springer International, 1977).

4. Alvin Plantinga, "Advice to Christian Philosophers," *Faith and Philosophy* 1, no. 3 (July 1984), 265. Reprinted in this volume. For contrary views on whether the Christian God is a person, see "The Personal God and a God Who Is a Person" by Adrian Thatcher, *Religious Studies* 21, no. 1 (March 1985) and "Is God a Person?" by Gary Legenhausen, *Religious Studies* 22, nos. 3 and 4 (1986).

5. The close relationship between dualism of mind and body and God-world dualism is evident in theistic critics who charge that the inadequacy of the first reveals the inadequacy of the second. Cf. Jonathan Barnes, *The Ontological Argument* (Edinburgh: Macmillan, 1972), especially p. 84; Thomas McPherson's *The Argument from Design* (Edinburgh: Macmillan, 1972); T. R. Miles's *Religious Experience* (Edinburgh: Macmillan, 1972), and J. C. A. Gaskin, *The Quest for Eternity* (New York: Penguin Books, 1984), especially p. 173. See Kenney's close linkage between philosophy of mind and the reasonability of theism in his *Religion and Reason* (Oxford: Basil Blackwell, 1987). "The conclusion of the argument from design can only be made intelligible if there is some independent account given of the coherence of a transcendent mind," p. 84.

6. Dennett, "Current Issues in the Philosophy of Mind," *Recent Work in Philosophy,* p. 157.

7. I count Thomism as a form of dualism, though contemporary Thomists may diverge as to whether they subscribe to property or substantive dualism. Note T. L. S. Sprigge's judgment: "Cartesianism provides a particularly persuasive metaphysical underpinning for Christianity," *Theories of Existence* (Middlesex: Penguin Books, 1986), p. 14.

8. Adrian Thatcher has set forth some religious reasons for rejecting dualism in "Christian Theism and the Concept of a Person" in *Persons and Personality,* edited by A. Peacocke and G. Gillett (Oxford: Basil Blackwell, 1987). Grace Jantzen mounts a sustained attack on substance dualism as well as God-world dualism while seeking to preserve a substantive Christian world view. See her *God's World, God's Body* (Philadelphia: Westminster Press, 1984). I critically assess her stance in "The Incorporeality of God," *Modern Theology* 3, no. 2 (January 1987), 179–88.

9. Cf. Roderick Chisholm, *Person and Object* (La Salle, Ill.: Open Court, 1976). In developing the argument for dualism employing this princi-

ple it is critical to avoid confusing *de re* and *de dicto* reference. When we use the identity statement '*A* is *B*' in a *de dicto* fashion it may not seem correct that whatever is true of *A* is true of *B*. For example, while Albert is the tallest boxer, Albert could exist without being the tallest boxer (he could have been a pacifist and avoided the sport altogether), whereas the tallest boxer could not exist without being the tallest boxer. But if we use our terms 'Albert' and 'tallest boxer' to rigidly pick out in a *de re* fashion the individual, *him,* then the principle of identity is preserved. In fact, Albert could exist without being the tallest boxer and it is likewise true with respect to the individual who is the tallest boxer that he could exist without being the tallest boxer (he could have been a pacifist and avoided the sport altogether). Cf. my "Nagel's Vista or Taking Subjectivity Seriously," *Southern Journal of Philosophy* 26, no. 3 (September 1989), 393–401 and the earlier "A Modal Argument for Dualism," *Southern Journal of Philosophy* 24, no. 1 (Spring 1986), 95–108.

10. For a range of theories of the afterlife, see John Hick's *Death and Eternal Life* (New York: Harper & Row, 1976). Some nondualist, Christian accounts of the afterlife involve commitment to the thesis that an object (like a human body) can cease to be and later come back into existence, a thesis many find implausible. But see Bruce Reichenbach's *Is Man the Phoenix?* (Grand Rapids, Mich.: Eerdmans, 1978) and George Mavrodes' "The Life Everlasting and the Bodily Criterion of Identity," *Noûs* 11, no. 1 (1977), 27–39. I argue that neo-identity or physical composition theories of the person cannot make body switching intelligible and hence cannot allow for a schema of the afterlife in which persons receive fresh, glorified bodies in "Pollock's Body Switching," *Philosophical Quarterly* 36, no. 3 (October 1985), 57–61.

11. Cf. Tom Morris, *The Logic of God Incarnate* (Ithaca: Cornell University Press, 1986).

12. Cf. Chisholm, *Person and Object.* See also Richard Swinburne's treatment of methodology in *The Evolution of the Soul* (Oxford: Oxford University Press, 1986).

13. Many opponents of Cartesian dualism admit that the position they attack is either the commonsense or at least commonly held theory of the person, the metaphysics of the ordinary person of the street. Cf. Thomas Hobbes, *The English Works of Thomas Hobbes of Malmesbury* (London: John Bohn, 1839), IV: 62; Daniel Dennett, *Content and Consciousness* (London: Routledge & Kegan Paul, 1969), pp. 3–5; David Lewis, "An Argument for the Identity Theory," *Journal of Philosophy* 63 (1966), 25; Thomas Nagel, "Physicalism," *Philosophical Review* 74 (1965), 340; Brian O'Shaughnessy, *The Will,* 2 vols. (Cambridge: Cambridge University Press, 1980), I: 29; Richard Rorty, *Philosophy and the Mirror of Nature* (Oxford: Basil Blackwell, 1980), p. 17; J. J. C. Smart, "Materialism," *Journal of Philosophy* 60 (1963), 661; Derek Parfit, *Reasons and Persons* (Oxford: Oxford University Press, 1984), pp. ix–x, 219, and Lynne R. Baker, *Saving Belief* (Princeton, N.J.: Princeton University Press, 1987), p. 48. Donald Davidson, Wilfred Sellars, and William Lycan insist that we must explain why it seems the mental is distinct from the physical, why people are tempted to embrace Cartesian dualism; cf. Davidson's "Men-

tal Events" in *Experience and Theory,* ed. Foster and Swanson (Amherst: University of Massachusetts Press, 1970) and William Lycan's *Consciousness* (Cambridge, Mass.: MIT Press, 1987), p. 42. Some of the strategies employed to discount this *prima facie* evidence seem to me entirely inadequate. In *Brainstorms* and elsewhere, Dennett cites cases in which subjects mistakenly identify their own motives or report being in pain and yet not feeling it (Cambridge, Mass.: MIT Press, 1978). These cases are purported to exhibit the theory-laden character of mental states. Paul and Patricia Churchland and Stephen Stitch cite such cases to show that explanations in terms of beliefs and desires are not just theoretical, but they are bad (ultimately eliminable) explanations of our action and internal states. But these cases only give us some reason to doubt we have infallible, incorrigible access to our mental states. They do nothing to prompt us to aver what I take to be the evident fact that we are immediately apprised of our mental states, the phenomenal feel of pain and desire. The Dennett-Churchland-Stitch strategy here seems as implausible as the skeptic's strategy that concludes all our sensory experience is mistaken on the grounds that on occasion we have hallucinations. The fact (if it is a fact) that we may be mistaken about which beliefs we act upon gives us no reason to think we are mistaken in thinking we have any beliefs at all and that in the vast majority of cases our beliefs do enter into explaining behavior, why we do this rather than that.

14. *Consciousness and the Mind of God* is a book-length manuscript in preparation. Cf. my defense of dualism cited earlier as well as my "The Argument from Transposed Modalities," *Metaphilosophy,* forthcoming, and "Dualism and the Problem of Individuation," *Religious Studies* 22 (1986), 263–76. Apart from Swinburne's *The Evolution of the Soul,* cited above, *The Elusive Mind* and its sequels by H. D. Lewis represent the most sustained case for dualism in the recent literature (London: Allen and Unwin, 1969). Alvin Plantinga develops a succinct argument for dualism in *The Nature of Necessity* (Oxford: Clarendon Press, 1974).

15. For a detailed discussion of the role of simplicity in assessing hypotheses, see Richard Swinburne's *The Existence of God* (Oxford: Clarendon, 1979).

16. Cf. A. J. Ayer: "One can imagine oneself waking to find oneself deprived of any bodily feeling or any perception of one's own body; one can imagine oneself seeming to wander round the world like a ghost, intangible to others and only occasionally visible . . . a spectator of a world in which one does not participate," *Central Questions of Philosophy* (London: Weidenfield & Nicolson, 1973), p. 124. In the course of arguing that the case for dualism I have advanced here does not beg the question, I recount and assess nondualist positions that concede disembodiment is possible, "A Modal Argument for Dualism." Work by D. M. Armstrong, David Lewis, John Pollock, and Richard Boyd is critically evaluated.

17. Margaret Wilson, *Descartes* (Boston: Routledge & Kegan Paul, 1982) p. 191.

18. Sydney Shoemaker, "On An Argument for Dualism," in *Knowledge*

and *Mind: Philosophical Essays,* ed. Carl Ginet and Shoemaker (New York: Oxford University Press, 1983), p. 248.

19. Cf. Swinburne's *The Existence of God* for a recent treatment of the central theistic arguments. A less technical, sympathetic overview of the arguments is provided by William Wainwright in *Philosophy of Religion* (Belmont: Wadsworth, 1988). In *Consciousness and the Mind of God* I critically discuss the central theistic arguments. The strategy of employing the theistic arguments of natural theology to establish the coherence of theism is explored by Gaskin. "In the absence of any certainty that a belief is incoherent, any evidence that it is true will also be evidence that it makes sense," *The Quest for Eternity,* p. 173.

20. For a good overview of theistic treatments of natural laws see Francis Oakley's *Omnipotence, Covenant and Order* (Ithaca: Cornell University Press, 1984), chap. 3. See, too, Ratzsch's "Nomo (theo) logical Necessity," *Faith and Philosophy,* vol. 4 (October 1987), pp. 383–492, and Alfred Freddoso's "The Necessity of Nature," *Midwest Studies in Philosophy,* vol. X (Minneapolis: University of Minneosta Press, 1986), pp. 215–42. In *Does God Have a Nature?* Plantinga writes that: "The very causal laws on which we rely in any activity are no more than the record of God's regular, constant and habitual dealings with the stuff of the universe he has created" (Milwaukee: Marquette University Press, 1980), p. 3.

21. Such thought experiments come into play in the course of the cosmological and ontological arguments.

22. Among others, this seems to be Peter Carruthers' position. In the final analysis he dismisses the problem of causal interaction, but concludes (I believe wrongly) that the problem of individuation overturns the dualist position, *Introducing Persons* (Albany: State University of New York Press, 1986), chaps. 2 and 3.

23. I see no compelling reason whatever to accept Jerry Fodor's claim: "Whatever has causal powers is *ipso facto* material," *Psychosemantics* (Cambridge, Mass.: MIT Press, 1988), p. x. Compare Roger Faber's *Clockwork Garden* (Amherst: University of Massachusetts Press, 1986).

24. Edwin Allaire, "Bare Particulars" in *Universals and Particulars,* ed. Michael Loux (Notre Dame: University of Notre Dame Press, 1976), p. 300.

25. I have addressed the problem of individuation in detail in my "Dualism and the Problem of Individuation."

Intellect, Will, and
the Principle of Alternate Possibilities

Eleonore Stump

INTRODUCTION

We ordinarily suppose that the ability to do otherwise is necessary for freedom. We do not attribute free will to our computers because we know that they are constrained by their programmers to do exactly what they do, and we blame people such as Franz Stangl, the commandant of Treblinka, just because we do not believe their claims that they had no option but to do what they did. These intuitions are thought to be captured in what has been called the principle of alternate possibilities, sometimes formulated in this way:

> (PAP) A person is morally responsible for what he has done only if he could have done otherwise.[1]

In recent literature, a strong case has been made that this formulation of our intuitions is mistaken and that the principle of alternate possibilities does not hold. The argument against PAP rests on putative counterexamples to it, generally called 'Frankfurt-type' or 'Frankfurt-style' examples because of Harry Frankfurt's influential presentation of such cases.[2] A typical Frankfurt-style conterexample to PAP involves an agent, S, a mechanism of coercion, M (hypnosis, manipulation of brain pathways, etc.), and a series of actions, A_1A_n, which S is in the process of deciding among. In the example, S decides on some one of these actions, A_m, and decides in a way which prompts our intuitions to suppose both that his decision is freely made and that he bears responsibility for the action. But, the example continues, if in the process of deciding S had inclined to any action other than A_m, mechanism M would have operated and brought it about that S formed a volition to do A_m. It is consequently not possible for S to do otherwise than A_m, the example implies, and yet in actual fact S is responsible for what he does. PAP is thus false.

As an instance of a Frankfurt-style example, consider the following variation on an incident from Dostoevsky's *The Possessed*. Peter Verkhovensky wants a convict named Fedya to kill the Lebyatkin family, and he offers Fedya a large sum of money to do the murders. But Verkhovensky also has a back-up plan. Verkhovensky recognizes that the bribe may not be enough to make Fedya want to do the murders, and he watches for any sign that Fedya might reject his offer. (Or, we might suppose, he has the technology to monitor Fedya's neural pathways, and he looks for the firing of the first neurons in the neural pathway whose completed firing is necessary for rejection of the bribe.) If he detects in Fedya any movement toward a disinclination to accept the bribe (or if he detects the firing of the first neurons in the pathway necessary for rejection), Verkhovensky will have Fedya anesthetized and surgically fitted with a device that stimulates just those neural pathways necessary to bring about in Fedya an effective desire to murder the Lebyatkins. Because the anesthetizing and surgery put Verkhovensky to more trouble, he prefers to try bribery first; but if it looks as though there is any chance the bribery won't succeed, he will certainly put his alternate plan into effect. As things turn out, however, the alternate plan is unnecessary. Fedya is a hardened criminal and desperate for cash besides; he grasps eagerly at Verkhovensky's offer and commits the murders with relish. It goes counter to the intuitions of most people to suppose that Fedya is not responsible for the murders. Underlying such intuitions is the thought that there is no reason to excuse Fedya in any way just because Verkhovensky had a plan for coercing him which he might have put into effect but in fact did not. It seems that considerations of moral blame or praise should be based on some intrinsic characteristic of Fedya's and not on considerations of what Verkhovensky or anyone else does in some other possible world. Furthermore, Fedya in the example is entirely ready, even eager, to commit the murders, and counterfactual claims about how Fedya might have been made murderous if he hadn't been willing to kill hardly seem to undermine the blameworthiness of the attitude he actually has. But if Fedya is responsible for murdering the Lebyatkins in such circumstances, then we have an apparent violation of PAP, since it was not open to Fedya not to murder the Lebyatkins.

This example also sheds some light on how PAP is to be interpreted. In the first place, PAP is clearly meant to apply to internal actions, such as willing to murder, as well as to external or bodily actions. We can hold a person responsible for what he wills even if he doesn't act on those volitions. A committed Fascist living in occupied France during the last war who willed the death by torture of Jewish men, women, and children but was prevented from acting on his will by his boss, a staunch member of the resistance, would nonetheless be morally blameworthy, and so morally responsible, for what he willed. In the case of Fedya, most of us would find him morally reprehensible for willing to murder an innocent family even if sudden paralysis, say, prevented him from translating his desires into action.[3] And yet in this example it is not open to Fedya not to will to murder the Lebyatkins because Verkhovensky's neurological device would stimulate those neural pathways in Fedya which would produce in him a volition to murder.

Secondly, when we say that it is not open to Fedya to do otherwise, it is clear that we do not mean that it is not possible that Fedya do otherwise. There is a possible world in which Fedya exists and Verkhovensky does not, for example; for that matter, there is a possible world in which Fedya never becomes a criminal and never has any criminal desires. So to say that it is not open to Fedya not to desire to murder the Lebyatkins is not to claim that there is no possible world in which Fedya exists and doesn't kill the Lebyatkins but rather to imply that Fedya's murdering the Lebyatkins is unavoidable for Fedya after a certain time. (And in general in this paper by 'at t it is open to S to do A', I will mean that it isn't the case at t that not doing A is unavoidable for S.) Analyses of unavoidability are, of course, controversial, but for present purposes perhaps this will do:

> (U) An action A is unavoidable for an agent S just in case for any state of affairs x such that S has the power to bring about x, it is necessarily the case that, given the laws of nature and the history of the world, if S brings about x, then S does A.[4]

For the sake of clarity, then, we might recast PAP in this way:

(PAP′)   A person is morally responsible for an internal or ex-
         ternal action of his only if that action was not unavoid-
         able for him (where unavoidability is to be understood
         in the sense given in (U) above).

In subsequent references to PAP in this paper, the principle should be taken in the sense of (PAP′).

Frankfurt is a compatibilist, and attacks on PAP based on Frankfurt-style examples are generally supposed to give aid to compatibilists, who want to deny that causal determination of an agent's actions is incompatible with the agent's acting freely and being responsible for his actions. But not all incompatibilists can give unqualified adherence to PAP. In particular, Christian philosophers and theologians have traditionally maintained an incompatibilist or libertarian interpretation of free will, and yet there are Christian doctrines which seem to violate PAP. For example, the good angels (those who did not fall with Satan) and the redeemed in heaven are said to have free will and to be morally responsible for what they do, but it is not open to them to do evil.[5] So for any set of alternative actions $A_1–A_n$ which a good angel or a redeemed person can imagine doing, if only one action A_m in that set is good, then it is not open to the agent in question to do otherwise. Furthermore, God himself is said to have free will and yet to be impeccable, so that the considerations affecting good angels and redeemed persons in heaven apply to God as well. If we also hold, as is traditional, that God has his attributes essentially, then if only one of the alternative actions God can envisage is good, only that action is possible for him.[6] But it would strike many Christians as odd to say that God is not morally responsible, say, for keeping his promises because it was not open to him, or even possible for him, to do otherwise. One (but, of course, not all) of the reasons generally given for worshipping and praising God is his goodness. If moral responsibility is tied to the ability to do otherwise, however, then it would appear that an essentially impeccable God lacks moral responsibility for at least many of the good actions attributed to him and so shouldn't be praised for moral goodness in connection with them either—a religiously absurd conclusion, which would rule out as confused or mistaken sentiments such as "Praise the Lord, for the Lord is good"

(Psalm 135:3). So it seems that PAP is inconsistent with certain traditional Christian views.

It would, of course, take a great deal more work to make a strong argument for the claim that PAP is incompatible with such traditional Christian doctrines; the considerations just adduced are no more than suggestions for how such an argument might go. In this paper, however, it is not my concern to develop or examine such an argument but only to ask what would follow if a sound argument to this effect could be given. In particular, I want to ask two questions. (1) Can we consistently maintain an incompatibilist account of free will, of the sort crucial for formulating an acceptable Christian response to the argument from evil, for example, and still reject PAP? (2) What are the intuitions underlying the common commitment of very many of us to PAP; can those intuitions be accommodated in some other way if PAP is rejected? In considering these questions, I will rely on Harry Frankfurt's hierarchical theory of free will, John Martin Fischer's list of conditions for incompatibilist free will, and Thomas Aquinas's specifically Christian account of the nature of the will and the relation between intellect and will. I will first say something briefly about these positions; then I will argue that, while in most ordinary circumstances PAP applies, on Aquinas's understanding of the will we can reject PAP and still meet not only Fischer's incompatibilist conditions for free will but also Frankfurt's conditions, which are in one respect more stringent. On the account I will defend, Fedya in the example above, the redeemed in heaven, and an essentially impeccable God, all of whom cannot do otherwise (at least at some time or with regard to some actions), nonetheless have free will, both in an incompatibilist sense and in Frankfurt's sense. I will conclude with some considerations designed to show that the intuitions which make many of us feel strongly committed to PAP can be maintained on Aquinas's theory of the will, even when PAP itself is rejected.

FRANKFURT'S HIERARCHICAL THEORY OF THE WILL

Frankfurt considers wanting or desiring to be the genus of acts of willing, or volitions, and he considers a volition to be an effective desire, one that moves an agent all the way to action if unimpeded.[7] According to Frankfurt, agents can have first-order desires, desires to do something, and also second-order desires, desires to have certain first-order desires. Frankfurt uses the term 'second-order desire' ambiguously, and it will be helpful here to make a revision of Frankfurt's account by sorting out that ambiguity. On this revision, when an agent wants to make a certain first-order desire his volition, then he has a second-order desire; and when this second-order desire is effective, that is, when he succeeds in making that first-order desire his volition, then he has a second-order volition.[8] To be a person is to care about one's will, that is, to have second-order desires and volitions. An agent who has no second-order desires or volitions is "a wanton," in Frankfurt's view; such an individual may be human but is not a person.

This notion of a person is the basis for Frankfurt's account of freedom of will. We can take the fundamental notion of freedom as the absence of obstacles to what one wants. Locutions involving the expression 'free from' specify which obstacles are absent, and locutions involving the expression 'free to' indicate the range of things available to the agent to do without obstacle. Freedom of action (as distinct from freedom of will with regard to an action) is the absence of obstacles to doing what one wants to do. Freedom of will is, analogously, the absence of obstacles to willing what one wants to will; an agent has free will, then, just in case he has the ability to will what he wants to will. Obstacles to an agent's willing what he wants to will can be external, as when a person wills to stay in a room only because by means of some neurological device a scientist has succeeded in producing in him the volition to stay in the room. They can also be internal, as when a person who wants to leave a room wills to stay in it after all because he cannot conquer his superstitious fear of a black cat asleep on the lintel over the door.

On the revised Frankfurt account, in order to have freedom of will an agent must meet the following conditions: (1) he has second-order desires, (2) he does not have first-order volitions which are discordant with those second-order desires, and (3) he has the first-order volitions he has *because of* his second-order volitions (that is, his second-order volitions have, directly or indirectly, produced his first-order volitions; and if his second-order volitions had been different, he would have had different first-order volitions).[9] On this account, the superstitious man who doesn't succeed in willing to leave the room doesn't have free will because, although he manifests a second-order desire (desiring to have the sort of will which would not be responsive to a fear of black cats), his first-order volition to stay in the room is discordant with that second-order desire; and so he fails to meet the second condition (and possibly also the third, depending on what other second-order volitions he has) of the revised Frankfurt conditions for freedom of will.

Frankfurt's account of freedom of will is thus a strong one, because it requires the absence of both internal and external obstacles to an agent's will if that agent's volitions are to be free. Ordinarily, when we ask whether a person acts with free will, what we are asking is in effect whether there is an external obstacle of this sort acting on his will, and the issue between compatibilists and libertarians can be understood at least in part as a dispute over whether the causal influences which certain compatibilists claim operate on a person constitute an external constraint on his will. If it were not for the clumsy locution, we might call Frankfurt's sense 'complete freedom of will' since it encompasses and exceeds the ordinary sense of free will as absence of external obstacles to willing what one wants.

It is important to add that Frankfurt distinguishes acting freely from acting with freedom of will. If a person has done what he wanted to do because he wanted to do it and the will by which he was moved when he did it was his own will, then he acted freely, whether or not he also acted with freedom of will. On Frankfurt's view, assessments of moral responsibility should depend primarily on whether or not an agent acted freely.

INCOMPATIBILIST FREE WILL

It will be helpful also to say something at the outset about conditions for an agent's having free will in an incompatibilist sense. In a recent paper[10] John Martin Fischer argues that on an incompatibilist understanding of freedom, for any agent S and action A, S's doing A is free just in case A meets the following three conditions:[11]

1. A is not causally determined
2. A is in an appropriate sense S's own act

3. *A* does not issue from a desire of intensity *i,* when (i) the desire's having intensity *i* would explain why *A* occurs, and (ii) any desire with intensity *i* is irresistible.

In the subsequent parts of this paper, I will rely on this understanding of incompatibilism, with the following glosses and revisions. (1) To say that *S*'s action *A* is not causally determined is to deny that *A* is the result of an unbroken causal sequence which originates in something other than *S*'s beliefs and desires and in virtue of which *A* is unavoidable for *S,* in the sense of 'unavoidable' laid out in (U) above. (2) Frankfurt's account of the will has been criticized for relying on unexamined assumptions about what counts as an agent's own desire or act of will.[12] Elsewhere,[13] as part of a revision of Frankfurt's account, I have argued that an agent's volition is his own only if his intellect[14] represents what is willed as the good to be pursued (at that time, under some description), and the agent forms the corresponding volition in consequence of that representation on the part of his intellect. We can add that an agent's action is his own only if it stems from his own volition;[15] and the notion of an agent's own act, employed in Fischer's condition (2), should be understood in this way.

It is worth noticing that Frankfurt's account of acting freely (as distinct from acting with freedom of will) is comprised under condition (2). To act freely, according to Frankfurt, is to do what one wants to do when one wants to do it and when the volition one acts on is one's own. For an agent to act freely, then, in Frankfurt's sense, is for the agent's action to be his own, that is, to stem from his own volition.[16] Frankfurt's conditions for acting freely, and consequently his conditions for being responsible for one's actions, are thus weaker than those an incompatibilist would espouse, since they do not include Fischer's condition (1).

Looked at in another way, all of Frankfurt's conditions for acting with freedom of will can be taken as an additional, stringent gloss on this second condition of Fischer's. To be free, an agent's action must be his own in the sense that it stems from his own volition, and an agent's volition is his own only if his intellect at the time of the volition represents the object of the volition as good under some description. But in cases of conflict, either among second-order desires or between second-order and first-order desires, when the agent acts against some second-order desire, there will always be some part of the agent's intellect which does not represent the object of the volition actually formed as the good to be pursued. And in such cases there is a certain sense in which the volition, and so the subsequent action also, is not the agent's own. Consequently, there is a sense in which it is true to say that for an agent to be fully or completely free, for Fischer's second condition to be met perfectly, all of Frankfurt's conditions for acting with freedom of will need to be met.

(3), Fischer's last condition, seems to me, at best, too broad. The addition of condition (3) is prompted by consideration of heroin addiction or kleptomania or something of that sort, where we feel inclined to attribute to the addicted agent or to the kleptomaniac diminished responsibility, because it seems that the agent is moved by irresistible desires which somehow compel him to do what he does, so that he doesn't do it freely. But consider the sort of case suggested by the biblical story of Naomi in Moab with her Moabite daughters-in-law, Ruth and Orpah.

When Naomi's sons die, she anticipates a difficult life for herself and her daughters-in-law. For herself, she can think of nothing better than to return home; but in a spirit of altruism towards Ruth and Orpah, she urges them to return to their families in Moab, who will be much better able to provide for them than she will. After an initial tearful protest, Orpah follows the course that is clearly in her self-interest; she leaves Naomi and goes home. Ruth, on the other hand, is unshakable in her determination not to leave Naomi; and when Naomi repeatedly urges her to do so, Ruth answers her with these well-known lines:

> Entreat me not to leave you or to return from following after you, for where you go, I will go, and where you dwell, I will dwell. Your people shall be my people, and your God my God. Where you die will I die, and there I be buried. The Lord do so to me and more also if anything but death part me and you.

And Naomi, seeing that Ruth is steadfast in her determination to go with her, gives up trying to dissuade her.

We often say of someone that doing a certain action would be inconceivable for her, and we can add to the biblical story here by simply stipulating that, for Ruth, leaving Naomi was unthinkable, that Naomi gave up trying to persuade her just because she saw that what she was urging on Ruth was something which Ruth found inconceivable to do. By saying that Ruth's leaving Naomi was inconceivable to her, I don't mean to suggest that Ruth literally could not conceive the possibility of leaving Naomi. It is clear that she could. She has Orpah's example in front of her and Naomi's urging behind her. Nor do I mean that she has no temptation to leave Naomi, or that she does not contemplate leaving Naomi as a real option. Sometimes we don't know what is inconceivable for us, and we discover it as we perceive the depth of our resistance against yielding to someone else's persuasion or giving in to the temptation of following someone else's example in a course of action we detest. In an example Frankfurt cites from Trollope,[17] a certain British aristocrat doesn't discover that giving in to the temptation he feels to snoop and spy is inconceivable for him until he begins the process and meets with an unconquerable aversion to it in himself.

What exactly makes an action inconceivable for an agent is hard to spell out and may well vary from person to person;[18] but one way to explain Ruth's speech to Naomi is to suppose that, when all things are considered, her intellect can find no way of presenting the abandonment of Naomi as a good to be pursued. We might imagine Ruth explaining her plan to her Moabite family by saying something like this: "I'm sorry, but it's unthinkable for me to abandon her now. She was always good to me, and it would be heartlessly cruel to repay all her past kindnesses by deserting her just when she needs me most. I know all the prudential arguments in favor of leaving her, and I've thought and thought about them. But in the end it is plain to me that I just couldn't do such a thing, I *must* go with her." We can suppose that Ruth was initially torn between the desire to return to her own family and the desire, arising from love and compassion, or from a sense of duty, to go with Naomi. But on reflection, she can find no way to understand her desire to return home except as base, ignoble, and self-seeking. In short, she can find no way to resist the competing desire to go with Naomi. We can, then, speak of this desire as irresistible. It will, of course, not be irresistible in the way that an addict's desire for a drug may be irresistible. The addict's desire stems from an acquired bodily need and is manifested first in urgent physical craving; if it is irresistible, it is so because the addict finds himself powerless to resist this craving. Ruth's desire, on the other hand, originates at least in part in

her intellect and has very little if anything to do with physical craving; if it is irresistible, it is so because Ruth's intellect finds it impossible to come to any conclusion other than that going with Naomi
is the good to be pursued. Furthermore, if the addict's desire really
is irresistible, then if his second-order desire were to be the desire
not to take the drug, he would take it nonetheless. But given what
was said above about second-order desires as the expression of reasoning, if Ruth's second-order desires were different, she might very
well not go with Naomi. If her second-order desires were different,
it would be because her intellect did find some way to avoid the conclusion that going with Naomi was the good to be pursued; and
in that case, she would be able to resist the desire to go with Naomi,
so that that desire would not be irresistible for her then. The irresistibility of the desire in the addict's case is disconnected from his
intellect; in Ruth's case, it flows from her intellect and is dependent
on it.

Few of us would be inclined to suppose that attributions of
praise or blame ought to be withheld in this case because, on reflection, Ruth found it inconceivable to leave Naomi, or that, in deciding to go with Naomi, Ruth acts with diminished responsibility
because of the irresistibility of her desire. Nor does Ruth's freedom
seem diminished in the way that the freedom of a heroin addict or
kleptomaniac is, because she finds it impossible to resist her desire
to do what she does.[19] But the example of Ruth, as I've explained
it here, is apparently an instance covered by Fischer's condition (3).
Given condition (3), we would have to say that Ruth did not act
freely, and so condition (3) seems too broad.

What distinguishes the case of Ruth from the case of the heroin
addict or kleptomaniac is that we assume the addict or kleptomaniac
is moved to do what he does against his will, as it were. A reluctant
addict is divided against himself, and the desire for the drug is analogous to an external force coercing him to do what he doesn't want
to do. The paradoxical character of these claims is diminished by
Frankfurt's hierarchical conception of the will. An unwilling addict
has second-order desires not to take heroin, but his effective first-
order desires are discordant with those second-order desires and so
discordant with what the addict himself really wants.[20] In fact, if
the desire for the drug is really irresistible, then it will move the addict to action not only when his second-order desires are against

taking the drug but even when (if such a thing is possible) the addict's intellect at the time of taking the drug doesn't represent taking the drug, under any description, as the good to be pursued. (Irresistible desires of this sort are thus distinguished from desires involved in ordinary incontinence, which may move an agent to action against his second-order desires but which do so because at the time the agent's intellect represents the object of that desire, under some description, as the good to be pursued.) In such a case, the desire for taking the drug isn't the addict's own, in the sense of Fischer's condition (2) above. Ruth, on the other hand, is doing precisely what she herself wants to do in acting on the desire which is irresistible for her; there is no discord between her second-order desires and her first-order desire not to leave her mother-in-law, and her intellect clearly does represent going with Naomi as the good to be pursued.

In order not to rule out Ruth's sort of action as unfree, then, condition (3) needs at least to be narrowed to apply only to cases where the irresistible desire moving an agent is in conflict with his own second-order desires, such as the case of an unwilling heroin addict moved by an irresistible desire for the drug. On the other hand, cases of the kind involving heroin addiction seem to be ones in which the irresistible desire isn't really the agent's own. Unlike the case of desires involved in incontinence, irresistible desires of this sort move an agent to action not only against the agent's second-order desires but also (if such a thing is possible) against the representations of the agent's intellect. If this interpretation of the relevant kind of irresistible desire is correct, then condition (3) can simply be dropped, since the sort of irresistible desires it applies to (if in fact there are any of that sort) are all covered by Fischer's condition (2).

Finally, it is worth pointing out that although Frankfurt is a compatibilist, an agent could meet Frankfurt's conditions for freedom of the will and also meet Fischer's conditions (1) through (3) for incompatibilist free will, as I have glossed them. Frankfurt's conditions neither include nor exclude Fischer's condition (1), but Frankfurt's own explanation of his conditions[21] shows that he means his conditions to include Fischer's condition (2), and perhaps condition (3) also (though not necessarily in the sense in which I have glossed these latter two conditions). What Frankfurt's account of free will adds to Fischer's conditions for incompatibilist free will is the requirement that the agent care about what his will is, and in a way which doesn't produce psychological discord in him. It is thus clearly possible to be an incompatibilist and still adopt Frankfurt's conditions for free will.

AQUINAS ON THE RELATION OF INTELLECT TO WILL

No one can do justice to Aquinas's theory of the will in a few pages. It is rich, complicated, and controversial, and a thorough treatment of it would require a book-length study.[22] Furthermore, embedded as it is in medieval psychology, it naturally gives rise to questions about Aquinas's account of the soul and the function of the will in it, which cannot be examined here. In what follows, then, I will simply sketch the basic outlines of Aquinas's theory of the will in order to make us aware of a different conception of will from the one to which we are accustomed.

Contemporary philosophers tend to operate with a conception of the will founded on a picture of the will as the steering wheel of the mind, neutral in its own right but able to direct other parts of the person. Aquinas's conception of the will is quite different. He takes the will to be not a neutral steering capacity, but a bent or inclination. The will, he says, is a hunger, an appetite, for goodness (*ST* IaIIae, q.10 a.1 and Ia, q.82 a.1). The motivation for this conception of the will is theological. God, who is the ultimate good, has built into human persons the engine by which they can be drawn to him. He has implanted in them a hunger for the good, namely, the will, which (if all goes as it should) will move them with desire and leave them restless and hungry until they find rest and satisfaction in him.

On Aquinas's view, the will is free. It can't be coerced or compelled, and it can move itself (*ST* IaIIae q.6 a.4 ad 1, Ia q.82 a.1, q.83 a.1). Aquinas is sometimes taken for a theological compatibilist (that is, a compatibilist who believes that freedom of the will is compatible with theological determinism), and whether his view of the will's freedom, taken together with his view of divine grace and his general account of God's action in the world as primary cause, constitutes a compatibilist or an incompatibilist account of the will's freedom is a difficult and complicated question which can't be adjudicated in a few paragraphs in passing. But for present purposes, I think we can leave this question to one side. What is at issue here is not whether Aquinas himself is a compatibilist or an incompatibilist, but rather just Aquinas's understanding of the nature of the will and the way it functions. And it is certainly possible to consider Aquinas's understanding of the will without going on to ask what is entailed by combining that understanding with his account of God's grace and operation in the world.

The will is a blind mouth, on Aquinas's theory. It is a hunger for goodness, but by 'goodness' here, Aquinas means goodness in general and not this or that specific good thing; that is, the will wills what is good, where the phrase 'what is good' is used attributively and not referentially. And by itself the will makes no determinations of goodness. Apprehending or judging things with respect to goodness is the business of the intellect. The intellect presents to the will as good certain things under certain descriptions, and the will wills them because the will is an appetite for the good and they are apprehended as good. For this reason the intellect is said to move the will, not as an efficient cause moves but as a final cause does, because what is understood as good moves the will as an end (*ST* Ia q.82 a.4).[23]

The will does will some things by necessity. Because God has created it as a hunger for the good, the will by nature desires the good; and whatever is good to such an extent and in such a way that a person cannot help but see it as good, the will wills by natural necessity. One's own happiness is of this sort, and so a person necessarily wills happiness (*ST* Ia q.82 a.1). But even things which have a necessary connection to happiness aren't willed necessarily unless the willer is cognizant of their necessary connection to happiness (*ST* Ia q.82 a.2). Except for happiness and those things so obviously connected with happiness that their connection is overwhelming and indubitable, however, the will is not determined to one thing, because of its relation to the intellect.

What the intellect determines with respect to goodness is somewhat complicated because the intellect is itself moved by other things. To begin with, the will moves the intellect as an efficient cause, by willing it to attend to some things or to neglect others (cf. *ST* IaIIae q.17 a.1). Of course, the will does so only in case the intellect represents doing so at that time, under some description, as good. Every act of willing is preceded by some apprehension on the part of the intellect, though not every apprehension on the part of the intellect need be preceded by an act of the will (*ST* Ia q.82 a.4). Secondly, the passions—greed, wrath, fear, etc.—can influence the intellect, because in the grip of a passion, such as wrath, something will seem good to a person which wouldn't seem good to him if he were calm (*ST* IaIIae q.9 a.2). The intellect, however, isn't compelled by the passions in any way, but can resist them (cf. *ST* Ia q.81 a.3 and *ST* IaIIae q.10 a.3), for example, by being aware of the passion and correcting for its effects on judgment, as one does when one decides to leave a letter written in anger until the next morning rather than mailing it right away.

The way in which the will is moved is also complicated. A power of the soul, Aquinas says, can be in potentiality in two ways, either with regard to the exercise of its power, as when the sight is not actually seeing, or with regard to the determination of its act, as when the sight sees something white but can see something black (*ST* IaIIae q.9 a.1). The will is similarly moved in two ways. In one way, it is moved to the exercise of its act; that is, it is moved to will rather than not to will. In another way, it is moved to will this particular thing rather than some other. There is no object of the will which can move the will necessarily in the first way, because it is always in a person's power not to think of that object and consequently not to will it actually.[24] In the second way, if the will is presented by the intellect with an object which can be considered good under some descriptions and not good under others, then the will is not necessarily moved by that object either. So, for example, the further acquisition of money can be considered good under some descriptions, for instance, under the description *means of sending the children to school,* and not good under some other descriptions, e.g., *wages from an immoral and disgusting job.* For these reasons, the will cannot be constrained to move in a particular way by something outside the willer, because, with a salient exception, no matter what object is presented to the intellect, it is open to the intellect to consider it under some description which makes it seem not good. If, however, the will is presented with an object which is good no matter how it is looked at, which is overwhelmingly, obviously good, then the will cannot will the opposite of that object. It is open to the will not to will that object by willing that the intellect not think about it; but if the intellect does see it in all its goodness, then it is not open to the will not to will it. For reasons of this sort, Aquinas says, the will is moved necessarily not only by happiness but also by God's goodness, in the beatific vision in which God's goodness is clearly seen (*ST* IaIIae q.10 a.2; *ST* Ia q.82 a.1).

It is apparent, then, that on Aquinas's account the will is part of a complicated feedback system composed of the will, the intellect, and the passions and set in motion by God's creating the will as a hunger for the good. How this system might be thought to work can be seen by giving a simple example of an interaction between will and intellect. Suppose that Anna has just won some money in a contest and that she plans to use the money to buy a frilly pink canopy bed for her daughter, something she has been coveting but unable to afford. As she sits reading a magazine, she comes across an advertisement urging readers to give money to support children in third-world countries and showing a picture of a ragged, emaciated child. Anna no sooner glances at the ad than she turns the page. Why does she do so? The answer to the question will, of course, involve the will's issuing commands which result in Anna's turning the page; but underlying these commands is something like the will's directive to the intellect not to think about the ad and the needy children it describes. The will makes this directive in virtue of a hasty calculation on the part of the intellect that looking at the ad is not good. That calculation will include some vague or scarcely formed thoughts to this effect, that looking at the ad may stimulate compassion and a desire to help, that helping will involve giving away some or all of the prize money, and that giving away the prize money is not good. Informing or influencing this calculation will be Anna's coveting of the frilly pink canopy bed for her daughter, a passion in Aquinas's sense. Perhaps without the influence of that coveting Anna's calculations about the ad might have been different. Furthermore, that Anna's desire is so strong or is in a position to influence her calculations as it does is itself a result of earlier choices Anna has made. Had she chosen different friends or different reading, for example, she might have developed more altruism and less interest in furniture.

Even now, however, Anna's coveting doesn't compel her to calculate as she does, because it is open to her intellect to recognize the pull of her desire and correct the calculation accordingly. Anna might, for instance, take note of the fact that she has turned the page hastily, reflect on that fact, and conclude that she needs to consider the ad and its request more carefully. She doesn't do so, we might be inclined to say, because she doesn't want to, she doesn't want to risk being moved to give away any of her prize money. But, of course, on Aquinas's theory, if she doesn't want to do so, it is because of a representation by the intellect that at that time, under some description, doing so isn't good. (By talk of the intellect's representations here, it is important to reemphasize, I do not mean to suggest that all acts of will are preceded by explicit, conscious, or self-aware deliberations. The intellect's considerations may be only tacit or implicit, and not in any way conscious, and yet may still count as the reason for a person's willing what she does, if she would give those considerations as the reason for willing as she did, when she is asked to give an explanation.)[25] Any willing of Anna's, then, will be influenced in important ways (but not caused, constrained, or compelled) by previous choices Anna has made; and not only any choice, but even any consent, on Anna's part will involve an often complicated interaction of intellect and will. For that reason, although Aquinas's account of the will assigns a large role to intellect, Aquinas is not committed to seeing immoral actions simply as calculating mistakes. Cases difficult for accounts such as Aquinas's to analyze, cases of incontinence, for example, can also be handled by emphasizing the interaction of intellect and will. In cases where the intellect seems to be representing something as good and yet the will does not will it, the intellect is in fact being moved by opposite motives both to represent that thing as good and not so to represent it, so that the intellect is double-minded or fluctuates between the two representations (cf., e.g., *ST* IaIIae q.17 a.2).

APPLICATION OF AQUINAS'S THEORY OF THE WILL

In sketching this outline of Aquinas's theory, I don't for a moment suppose I have shown that Aquinas has a coherent, empirically adequate account of the will; it is clear that this brief summary leaves a host of questions unanswered. Aside from questions about whether these views of Aquinas can be reconciled with what he says elsewhere concerning God's action on the will, we might also ask about the large role assigned to the intellect in this theory or about some of the more perplexing features of the relation between intellect and will. On even this brief sketch, however, it is apparent that the part of Aquinas's account laid out here is perfectly consistent with Fischer's conditions for incompatibilist free will. And while it does not entail Frankfurt's conditions for freedom of the will, it is also not incompatible with them, if we take second-order desires and volitions, as I have argued elsewhere that we ought to do,[26] as resulting naturally from reasoning on the part of the willer's intellect. With Fischer's and Frankfurt's conditions on free will presupposed, what sort of answer does Aquinas's account of the will give to the questions with which this paper began? Can the necessary volitions of God, good angels, and the redeemed in heaven be said to be free? More generally, can we consistently maintain an incompatibilist account of free will and reject PAP? If PAP is rejected, can the intuitions which seem so strongly to support it be accommodated in some other way?

Consider first what Christian doctrine says about the redeemed in heaven. In heaven they are united with God in the beatific vision and they see the goodness of God plainly; in that state they are unable to sin. The reason for their inability to sin is explained by Aquinas's theory of the interaction between intellect and will. Since they see God's goodness plainly, their intellect is no longer in a position to suppose that apparent goods are real goods; by comparison with the overwhelming goodness of God the lack of true goodness in apparent goods is evident. The intellect consequently has no basis on which to represent these apparent goods as real goods, and as a result the will cannot desire them. The inability to sin on the part of the redeemed is thus not a result of an external constraint on the will, imposed from without by some benevolently despotic agent or caused extrinsically by some coercive force. It is a result of the redeemed person's own hunger for goodness; that is, it is a consequence of that person's beliefs and desires, in the interplay of will and intellect brought about by the vision of God's goodness.[27] A redeemed person is thus in a state analogous to that of Ruth in my example above. In my version of the biblical story of Ruth, Ruth cannot bring herself to leave Naomi, even in the face of Orpah's example and Naomi's arguments. The prudential reasons for doing so are clear to her, and she is even tempted to follow Orpah. But in the end it becomes clear to her that she can't bring herself to abandon Naomi — or as we might put it, what becomes clear to her is that her desire not to leave Naomi is irresistible. This irresistible desire of Ruth's is not wrought in her by Naomi or by any other external agent or force. It stems just from the fact that after all her reflection and all the temptation to do the prudent thing, Ruth finds abandoning Naomi unthinkable. And we can explain Ruth's state in this condition on Aquinas's account of the relation between intellect and will by saying that in the end for Ruth at that time there is no way in which, or no description under which, her intellect can represent abandoning Naomi as a good to be pursued, and therefore there is no way in which Ruth's will can form the volition to leave Naomi.

I argued above that the case of Ruth is not covered by Fischer's condition (3). Is that case, or the case of the redeemed in heaven, ruled out as unfree by either of Fischer's first two conditions or by Frankfurt's conditions? The answer seems to me clearly 'no'. An incompatibilist can plausibly claim that the causal chain responsible for Ruth's going with Naomi originates in Ruth's beliefs and desires.[28] And it is clear that Ruth, as well as the redeemed person in heaven, acts on volitions which are her own, in the sense of stemming from her intellect's representation of the object of the volition as the good to be pursued. In fact, in both cases, the willer may be said to have no discord between her second-order and her first-order desires and volitions. The intellect of Ruth, or of the redeemed person, represents the object of her will and her willing of it altogether as good, and so with respect to the volition at issue there will be no discord between her second-order and her first-order desires and volitions. Given Aquinas's account of the will, then, both Ruth and the redeemed person meet all of Fischer's and Frankfurt's conditions for freedom of will. But on the assumption in my example that Ruth's desire is irresistible and on Christian doctrine about the redeemed, PAP is violated with respect to each of them. For both Ruth and the redeemed person, doing what she does is unavoidable for her. In the case of the redeemed person, given the laws and the history of the world, there is no state of affairs she can bring about such that she does an evil action, because her intellect sees God's goodness so clearly that it cannot represent some object incompatible with that goodness as the good to be pursued. And something analogous is true of Ruth; because even in the face of temptation on reflection her intellect finds leaving Naomi, no matter how it is represented, unthinkably cruel and heartless and thus inconceivable for her to do, her will cannot form the volition to do so.[29]

The case of God's impeccability is an extension of the case involving Ruth and the redeemed in heaven. Because God's intellect always sees clearly and plainly what is really good, his intellect never presents apparent goods as real ones, and his will never wills what is not good. God's impeccability, on Aquinas's theory of the will, is thus a consequence of his omniscience; and if God is essentially omniscient, then it will be impossible for God ever to do what is not good. On the other hand, nothing in these conclusions rules out the claim that the causal chain responsible for any action on God's part always originates in God's beliefs and desires,[30] and that the volition on which God acts is appropriately his own. Furthermore, none of the usual reasons for attributing discord between a person's first-order and second-order desires (e.g., intemperance, indecision, etc.) can be applied to God. For these reasons, even with regard to those actions where it is not possible for God to do otherwise, God can always meet both the Fischer and the Frankfurt conditions for freedom of will.

It is worth noting here that attempts to demonstrate an incompatibility between God's omnipotence and his impeccability rely on a different understanding of the cause of divine impeccability, and they tend to assume unreflectively a more contemporary theory of the will.[31] They presuppose a notion of the will as neutral and as sovereign, not subject to anything; and so they see the impossibility of God's doing evil as a restriction, a limitation on his power. Consequently, they conclude that one cannot consistently maintain both omnipotence and impeccability. But, as we have seen, Aquinas would reject such a theory of the will. On his view, there is a sense in which the will is by nature subject to the intellect; and if the intellect has not miscalculated in some way, perhaps as a result of an interaction between intellect and will, the object of the will is invariably a real, rather than an apparent, good. If (as seems reasonable to suppose) intellectual power is a kind of power, then on Aquinas's theory of the will, omnipotence not only is compatible with impeccability but actually entails it, because God will be capable of doing what is not good only in case his intellect is capable of miscalculating and so is deficient in intellectual power.

FISCHER'S REASONS–RESPONSIVE MECHANISM

In a recent paper, "Responsiveness and Moral Responsibility,"[32] Fischer argues for a view which has some resemblance to Aquinas's. Fischer wants to give an outline of a theory of moral responsibility compatible with our basic moral intuitions about responsibility but also consistent with a rejection of PAP. He does so by using what he calls 'an actual-sequence model' of responsibility. In Frankfurt-style examples, Fischer says, "the kind of mechanism which operates is reasons-responsive, although the kind of mechanism that would operate in the alternative scenario is *not*."[33] On Fischer's theory of moral responsibility, "an agent is morally responsible for performing an action insofar as the mechanism that actually issues in the action is reasons-responsive. When an unresponsive mechanism actually operates, it is true that the agent is not free to do otherwise; but an agent who is unable to do otherwise may act from a responsive mechanism and can thus be held morally responsible for what he does."[34] By 'reasons-responsiveness' here Fischer has in mind what he calls 'weak reasons-responsiveness'. For an agent to act on a weak reasons-responsive mechanism, it must be the case that there is some possible world in which there is sufficient reason to do otherwise than the agent does, the agent's actual mechanism operates, and the agent does otherwise. For an agent to be responsible on Fischer's theory, the actual sequence mechanism on which he acts must be weakly reasons-responsive.[35]

Fischer's account of moral responsibility is thus like Aquinas's in emphasizing the role of reason, but it differs from Aquinas's in two respects. In the first place, Fischer doesn't provide a theory explaining the role of reason in ascriptions of responsibility, as Aquinas does. Fischer constructs his account by considering what is common to certain difficult cases where our intuitions are generally inclined to assign moral responsibility to an agent, and he concludes that the crucial common feature in such cases is the operation of a certain mechanism responsive to reasons. But his account does not provide a deeper explanation, as Aquinas's theory does, for why the presence or absence of a "reasons-responsive mechanism" should be crucial to ascriptions of responsibility. This point is, of course, no reason for rejecting Fischer's theory, since it is doubtless possible for Fischer or someone else to construct the missing explanation and add it to Fischer's present account; but it is nonetheless worth noting that, as things stand, Aquinas's theory is broader and deeper than that offered by Fischer.

Secondly, and more importantly, Fischer's way of introducing reason into his account differs from Aquinas's. Aquinas's theory requires that it be the agent's own intellect which represents the object of volition as the good to be pursued if an agent is to be morally responsible for what he does. For Fischer, however, for an agent, S, to be responsible for an action, A, it need be the case only that the following conditions be met:

1. there is some possible world w_1 in which there is sufficient reason for S to do otherwise than A
2. in w_1 S uses the mechanism S used in the actual world in doing A
3. in w_1 S does otherwise than A.

Unlike the role of reason in Aquinas's theory, these conditions of Fischer's are not sufficient for moral responsibility. Consider Raymond, the protagonist of the film *The Manchurian Candidate,* who was programmed by his captors to kill his boss. (Those who find ludicrous the powers the movie attributes to brainwashing can substitute the more fashionable, surgically implanted neurological device, which has the same effect.) Suppose that in some world w_1 Raymond has sufficient reason for not killing his boss; suppose that his boss is his best friend as well as his patron. But suppose also that in w_1 Raymond's captors, too, have sufficient reason for not having Raymond kill his boss, because in that world Raymond's boss is a spy working for Raymond's captors and useful to their organization. In that world Raymond is as much of a robot as he is in the actual world, and yet he does not kill his boss, because in that world Raymond's captors want his boss to live. In this case Raymond meets all of Fischer's conditions for weak reasons-responsiveness: there is some possible world in which there is sufficient reason for Raymond to do otherwise than kill his boss, and in that world Raymond uses the same mechanism he used in the actual world in killing his boss (namely, the mechanism involving brainwashing or a neurological device), but he doesn't kill his boss.[36] And yet, even though Fischer's conditions for weak reasons-responsiveness are met, Raymond clearly is not morally responsible for killing his boss in the actual world, in which he is controlled and programmed by his captors.

Fischer's account is thus flawed in a way that Aquinas's is not. Unlike Fischer's account of moral responsibility, Aquinas's theory of the will succeeds in ensuring that the action of the agent in question really is that agent's own. As Fischer's account is constructed, the weak reasons-responsive mechanism whose operation is supposed to guarantee the agent's moral responsibility for what he does could turn out to include the intellect of those who coerce and control the agent. It isn't enough to remedy Fischer's account to add the condition that the mechanism be the agent's own mechanism, because presumably the mechanism Raymond uses when he kills his boss as he is programmed to do is a mechanism which is somehow his; it is his brainwashed mind, or his neurologically altered brain.

To rule out this sort of case involving Raymond, what we need is an account of the sort Aquinas provides, which requires that the mechanism be the agent's own intellect and explains the crucial role of the intellect in volition, thereby denying moral responsibility to an agent whose intellect is programmed or whose will is coerced. On Aquinas's theory, Raymond wouldn't count as morally responsible if he killed his boss while programmed (or in some other way coerced) to do so, because the act Raymond did in such a case wouldn't be appropriately his own. It wouldn't stem from Raymond's own volition, because it wouldn't be Raymond's intellect representing the murder as the good to be pursued, and so Raymond's will would will the murder for some reason other than that Raymond's intellect represented it as the good to be pursued. Someone might suppose that Raymond's captors could introduce into Raymond's intellect the thought that murdering his boss is good and thereby program Raymond to murder, so that Aquinas's account suffers from the same deficiency as Fischer's: Raymond could meet all the conditions for freedom and still be the puppet of his captors. But this objection will not hold up under scrutiny. If Raymond's captors introduce a thought into his intellect, it is open to Raymond to reflect on that thought and either accept or reject it, so that the resulting judgment will be Raymond's, and there is no embarrassment for Aquinas's account in saying that Raymond is free. On the other hand, if Raymond's captors control all his thoughts, so that he can't exercise his own judgment at all, then it isn't Raymond's intellect which represents the murder as good. In fact, in this case it isn't altogether clear what it means to speak of *Raymond's* intellect, since all the intellectual functioning in Raymond is that of his captors. In this case, then, Raymond isn't free, but that is no problem for Aquinas's account since in this case Raymond's intellect and will aren't functioning as they need to do in order to count as free on Aquinas's account of the will.

CONCLUSION

Reflection on the differences between Aquinas's account and Fischer's is instructive for the basic question with which this paper began, whether incompatibilists can consistently reject PAP. If we take the root notion of freedom to be doing what one wants, the problem with Raymond's action in the film is that he isn't doing what *he* wants to do in murdering his boss; or if he is, he isn't willing what *he* wants to will in forming the volition to murder. It seems to me arguable that the reason we have strong intuitions supporting PAP is that in most ordinary circumstances there is virtually no chance that we are doing (or willing) what *we* really want to do (or will) unless it is possible for us to do (or will) otherwise. In most ordinary circumstances, if there is no alternate possibility open to us, it is because some external force or agent is constraining us to act as we do, so that what we do isn't what we ourselves really want to do. The theory that PAP is necessary for any acceptable theory of moral responsibility or of free will is consequently something like the Newtonian theory of the will: it holds for the most part, for most situations of the sort encountered in ordinary experience.

But what reflection on queer Frankfurt-style examples or esoteric theological doctrines shows us is that the association between the presence of an alternate possibility and the ability to do what we ourselves really want holds only for the most part. There are certain peculiar cases, cases such as that of Fedya or Ruth or the redeemed in heaven, where (for varying reasons) it isn't open to the agent to do otherwise than she does, and yet it is clear that the agent is doing what she herself really wants to do. How it can be that an agent does what she herself really wants to do when there is no alternate possibility open to her is explained on Aquinas's theory of the will and the Fischer and Frankfurt conditions for free will. Because the will is not a neutral capacity for choosing but a hunger for the good, which takes as good what the intellect represents as good (as a result of a complicated process of interaction between will and intellect), it is possible for a person to will freely and yet have no alternate possibility open to her. The reason for this is that in such a case (as, for example, in the case of Ruth or a redeemed person in heaven) her intellect finds any alternate possibility inconceivable, not possibly representable as good. Furthermore, as the case of Fedya shows, it is possible for a person to will freely when there is no alternate possibility open to him, because while an external force is available to close off alternate possibilities, that force doesn't actually operate. It is Fedya's own intellect which represents his action of murder as good, with the result that it is Fedya's own will which forms a volition for it. In this way, Aquinas's theory of the will, together with the Fischer and Frankfurt conditions on free will, explains why we can consistently maintain an incompatibilist theory of free will and yet reject PAP,[37] and it shows how the intuitions on which PAP is based can be supported while PAP itself is denied.[38]

NOTES

        1. Harry Frankfurt, "Alternate Possibilities and Moral Responsibility" *Journal of Philosophy* 66 (1969), 828.
        2. See, e.g., "Alternate Possibilities and Moral Responsibility." Frankfurt's case against PAP has been vigorously disputed by Peter Van Inwagen; see his "Ability and Responsibility," *Philosophical Review* 87 (1978), 201–24, reprinted in his book *An Essay on Free Will* (Oxford: Clarendon Press, 1983), pp. 161–82. Van Inwagen's strategy consists of tying responsibility to event particulars, where x and y are identical event particulars just in case they have the same causes. Then an agent is responsible for a particular event only in case he could have prevented that event particular. If successful, this strategy would be effective against certain common kinds of Frankfurt-style examples, including the one involving Fedya given below. It would not be effective, however, against the main cases considered in this paper (cases involving an impeccable deity, the redeemed in heaven, or agents who find inconceivable any

alternative to the action they take), because in those cases, even if Van Inwagen's understanding of event particulars is correct and his strategy is successful, an agent who is apparently responsible for a particular event could not have prevented that event. For an interesting argument that Van Inwagen's strategy is in fact not successful, see John Martin Fischer, "Responsibility and Control," *Journal of Philosophy* 79 (1982), 24–40.

    3. An exception to this claim would be cases in which an external agent had implanted this willingness in Fedya when, left to himself, Fedya would have repudiated such willingness.

    4. I have based this formulation of unavoidability on one discussed by Thomas Flint, "Compatibilism and the Argument from Unavoidability," *Journal of Philosophy* 84 (1987), 423–40. That definition of unavoidability is couched in terms of a relation between an agent and a proposition; for ease of exposition only, I have rephrased it to substitute actions for propositions. See also Peter Van Inwagen, *An Essay on Free Will*, p. 68. It should be pointed out that as it stands (U) is too still broad. Because we obviously do not want to say that Fedya murders the Lebyatkins in all possible worlds, we need some way of specifying a subset of possible worlds in order to explain our intuition that for Fedya murdering the Lebyatkins is inevitable, although it isn't necessary that Fedya commit the murders. But among the worlds picked out by (U) there will be some in which Fedya begins to incline not to commit the murders and Verkhovensky dies of a heart attack before he can implant or activate the mechanism causing Fedya to murder, or in which the implanted mechanism is inactivated by some sort of chance event, or in which Fedya dies before the murders can be carried out, and so on. Adding the needed conditions to make (U) precisely right is likely to prove a byzantine process, which would distract from the main focus of this paper; and so for my purposes here I will content myself with this imprecise formulation.

    5. See, for example, Anselm, *De libertate arbitrii*.

    6. In fact, since the laws of nature and the history of the world are either in God's control or irrelevant to considerations of God's ability to do evil, perhaps unavoidability collapses into impossibility in God's case.

    7. Frankfurt's classic paper on the subject is "Freedom of the Will and the Concept of a Person," *Journal of Philosophy* 68 (1971), 5–20; other papers by Frankfurt relevant to the same subject include "The Importance of What We Care About," *Synthese* 63 (1982), 257–72; "Alternate Possibilities and Moral Responsibility," *Journal of Philosophy* 66 (1969), 828–39; and "Identification and Wholeheartedness," in *Responsibility, Character, and the Emotions: New Essays in Moral Psychology*, ed. Ferdinand Schoeman (Cambridge: Cambridge University Press, 1987). I have discussed Frankfurt's theory of the will at length in "Sanctification, Hardening of the Heart, and Frankfurt's Concept of Free Will," *Journal of Philosophy* 85 (1988), 395–420; the presentation of Frankfurt's views here is largely taken from that paper.

    8. This revision is explained and argued for in "Sanctification, Hardening of the Heart, and Frankfurt's Concept of Free Will."

    9. I have changed Frankfurt's formulation of these conditions slightly

to take account of a distinction between second-order desires and second-order volitions which seems to me useful in this connection; see "Sanctification, Hardening of the Heart, and Frankfurt's Concept of Free Will," pp. 399–402.

10. John Martin Fischer, "Responsibility and Control," *Journal of Philosophy* 89 (1982), 24–40. For purposes of this paper, I have slightly altered Fischer's formulation, which is cast in terms of conditions for an action's being unfree.

11. These are clearly necessary conditions for incompatibilist free will, but there is considerable question about whether they are sufficient. Some people suppose that if an agent, S, does an action, A, with free will, there is a possible world like this one in every respect including S's beliefs and desires up to the time of the action, but in which S does the complement of A. If A is refusing an offer to cut up S's daughter into small pieces for the sake of nothing but a dollar, then on this view S does A freely only in case there is a possible world just like this one including S's holding all the same beliefs and desires, but in which S does not refuse the offer. This view seems to me to require too much for freedom of the will. In particular, it isn't clear to me that it is coherent to suppose a person could hold nothing but ordinary beliefs about the value of a dollar and the disvalue of the torture of a small child and yet consent to torture the child for no reason other than gaining a dollar. (In this respect, I am persuaded by an argument of Van Inwagen's; see note 19.) Furthermore, this condition seems to me to embody PAP and build it explicitly into the conditions for freedom of will. The arguments against PAP in this paper are thus also arguments against including such a fourth condition in the list of the Fischer conditions for incompatibilist free will.

12. See, e.g., Irving Thalberg, "Hierarchical Analyses of Unfree Action," *Canadian Journal of Philosophy* 8 (1978), 211–25, and Gary Watson, "Free Agency," *Journal of Philosophy* 72 (1975), 205–20.

13. "Sanctification, Hardening of the Heart, and Frankfurt's Concept of Free Will," pp. 407–411.

14. By 'intellect' here I mean something like the agent's computing faculty and not that part of his mind which is rational as distinct from irrational.

15. An incontinent desire, say, for another helping of lasagna when one means to diet, does not fail to count as the agent's own on this analysis, because a case can be made that at the time of the choice the dieter's intellect represents the second helping, under some description (e.g., necessary means of relaxation or well-earned reward), as the good to be pursued.

16. Frankfurt's analysis of what it is for an agent's volition to be his own is different from mine; see his "Identification and Wholeheartedness."

17. "Rationality and the Unthinkable," in Harry Frankfurt, *The Importance of What We Care About* (Cambridge: Cambridge University Press, 1988), pp. 177–90.

18. For an excellent discussion of an action's being inconceivable for a person, see Harry Frankfurt, "Rationality and the Unthinkable."

19. In a very interesting paper, "When Is the Will Free?" (*Philosophi-*

cal Perspectives, vol. 4: *Action Theory,* ed. James Tomberlin, (Atascadero, Ca.: Ridgeview Publishing Co., 1990)), Peter Van Inwagen argues a position in some respects the mirror image of that being defended here. On this view, we rarely have free will, because in cases like that of Ruth in my example as well as in most ordinary cases, it is impossible to conceive coherently of a world in which the agent holds the beliefs and desires that she does in the actual world and in which she yet does something different from what she does in the actual world. Van Inwagen's argument depends on a rule he calls 'Beta-prime': From

(i) p, and x now has no choice about p,

and

(ii) $(p \rightarrow q)$, and x now has no choice about $(p \rightarrow q)$,

deduce

(iii) q, and x now has no choice about q.

His first example of an argument employing Beta-prime includes a conditional he maintains is a necessary truth: If I regard A as indefensible, then I am not going to do A (where A is some action). From that conditional and Beta-prime, he deduces this: I am not going to do A and I now have no choice about whether I am not going to do A. And from this he draws the following further conclusion: "The general lesson is: if I regard a certain act as indefensible, then it follows not only that I *shall not* perform that act but that I *can't* perform it." Because a very tight connection between free will and the ability to do otherwise is a basic assumption for Van Inwagen in this paper, he takes this argument and others like it to show that we very rarely have free will. Now since the tight connection between free will and the ability to do otherwise is what this paper of mine is designed to call in question, it is possible for me to agree with Van Inwagen's arguments and yet not agree with his conclusion that we rarely have free will. But, in fact, I am not entirely persuaded by his arguments either. Even if we have no hesitation about accepting Beta-prime or the necessity of the relevant conditional, it isn't clear to me that Van Inwagen has established the sort of conclusion he wants, namely, that I can't perform A. Beta-prime and the conditional show that I *now* have no choice about whether I am not going to do A; but what we are entitled to deduce from this is only the claim that I can't *now* perform A, and not the broader claim that I can't perform A. One might suppose that Van Inwagen would license the inference from 'S can't now perform A' to 'S can't perform A' in virtue of his theory of event individuation (see note 2). But in discussing responsibility, Van Inwagen grants that a person may be responsible (and so, on his account of responsibility, able to do otherwise) even with respect to actions regarding which he is now unable to do otherwise. Van Inwagen holds that an agent will be responsible in this way if earlier it was in the agent's power whether or not to put himself in the position he is in now, where he is unable to do otherwise; and Van Inwagen accepts the common view that a person's earlier actions contribute to making him the sort of person he is now, with the sorts of beliefs and desires which rule out his now doing otherwise than he does. In that case, however, from the fact that a person's beliefs and desires at t_1 make it very unlikely or even impossible that he do other than he does at t_1, it doesn't follow that he has no choice at all with respect to the actions he performs at t_1, only that he has no choice t_1 simultaneously with the holding of those beliefs and desires; but that he holds those beliefs and desires may itself be the result of choices he has made earlier, and in having those choices he has a choice about the actions he does at t_1. (See also note 24.)

20. For an argument that what an agent really wants is what is expressed in his second-order desires, see "Sanctification, Hardening of the Heart, and Frankfurt's Concept of Free Will."

21. See, e.g., "Freedom of the Will and the Concept of a Person."

22. For a study of Aquinas on this subject, see Jeffrey Hause, *Aquinas on the Will* (Ph.D. dissertation, Cornell University, 1990).

23. My gloss on Fischer's condition (2) above is, of course, based on this part of Aquinas's account of the will's freedom.

24. For this sort of reason, I think Van Inwagen is wrong to suppose that our beliefs and desires leave us no choice with regard to action even at the time we have those beliefs and desires. Van Inwagen's examples are all cases in which the object of the volition (that is, the thing to be wanted or the state of affairs to be willed) obtrudes itself on the mind of the agent: the telephone rings, for example, and the agent has to decide whether or not to pick it up. In such cases, the beliefs and desires concerning the object of volition are very likely to be occurrent. But, as Aquinas points out, even in those cases in which an agent's beliefs and desires would make his willing something unavoidable for him, he may not will it because his intellect is not attending to the relevant object of volition, either because the object of volition hasn't been called to mind or because the will has directed the intellect not to reflect about that object of volition. Furthermore, unless the case is like that of Ruth, where the agent finds alternative courses of action inconceivable, Aquinas would say that even when the agent attends to the object of volition, the agent's beliefs and desires allow him to choose or to reject that object because the object can be seen under different descriptions, and so can be thought of as good or as not good. Where Aquinas would agree with Van Inwagen is in this, that if an agent sees an object of volition under a certain description as good, that is, if the agent has formed the beliefs and desires that warrant that object of volition as the good to be pursued, and if those beliefs and desires are occurrent, then it isn't at that time open to the agent to will otherwise. (For reasons for thinking that the agent can nonetheless will otherwise, see note 19.)

25. See Robert Audi, "Acting for Reasons," *Philosophical Review* 95 (1986), 511–46.

26. "Sanctification, Hardening of the Heart, and Frankfurt's Concept of Free Will," pp. 399–402.

27. Someone might suppose that if the sight of God could keep a person from moral evil, then the fall of Satan is inexplicable and so is the doctrine that a good God doesn't bring it about that everyone comes to heaven,

since he can do so readily by giving all persons a vision of his goodness. But on traditional Christian doctrine God keeps all his creatures from full sight of himself until they have had the opportunity to move either toward him or away from him. The reasons for his doing so, in my view, involve at least in part the difficulties of establishing a relationship of love and friendship between an omnipotent, omniscient, perfectly good person and persons limited in knowledge, power, and goodness. For some discussion of these issues, see my paper "Petitionary Prayer," *American Philosophical Quarterly* 16 (1979), 81–91.

28. I put this point in the way I do because the logic of the argument doesn't require, and it is not part of my purpose here to defend, the claim that incompatibilism is true and compatibilism is false. The central point at issue in this paper is only whether the assumption of incompatibilism is inconsistent with the rejection of PAP.

29. These cases have some similarity to cases discussed by Susan Wolf in her excellent paper "Asymmetrical Freedom," *Journal of Philosophy* 77 (1980), 151–66, reprinted in John Martin Fischer, *Moral Responsibility,* (Ithaca, N.Y.: Cornell University Press, 1986), pp. 225–40. She says of such cases that the character of the agent in question is determined but that nonetheless "it seems absurd to say that it [the agent's character] is not under his control. His character is determined on the basis of his reasons, and his reasons are determined by what reasons there are" (p. 232). Aquinas's account of intellect and will seems to me to provide the underlying explanation for the truth of this point, although there seems to me something highly misleading, in the context of this discussion, in speaking of a person's character as determined in such cases. In Wolf's sense of 'determined' an agent's character can be both determined and still under his own control, but the sense of 'determination' common in such discussions is usually characterized by opposing it to control on the part of the agent. While much of Wolf's paper seems to me correct and insightful, I don't agree with her analysis of incompatibilism as the view that an agent is free only if there is no causal determination of his *actions* or her general thesis that there is an asymmetry between morally praiseworthy acts and morally blameworthy acts. For helpful discussion showing that Wolf's asymmetry thesis is false, see John Martin Fischer and Mark Ravizza, "Responsibility and Inevitability," forthcoming; I am grateful to the authors for making the paper available to me in typescript.

30. Or the divine analogues to beliefs and desires, if God is simple.

31. See, for example, Nelson Pike, "Omnipotence and God's Ability to Sin," *American Philosophical Quarterly* 6 (1969), 208–16.

32. In *Responsibility, Character, and the Emotions,* ed. Ferdinand Schoeman (Cambridge: Cambridge University Press, 1987).

33. Ibid., p. 85.

34. Ibid., pp. 85–86.

35. Fischer also adds the qualification that the relevant mechanism must be temporally intrinsic, that is, that its description must not entail the occurrence of the action it is supposed to bring about. For the sake of brevity, I

am omitting consideration of this and other details of Fischer's account. (See also note 36.)

36. Fischer says that he is deliberately leaving vague the notion of 'same mechanism' (p. 95), but in practice he tends to take the relevant mechanism as a type or kind. So, for example, he suggests that the normal faculty of practical reasoning and a procedure involving direct stimulation of an agent's brain are mechanisms of the sort he has in mind (p. 85); he also speaks of mechanisms as a kind of process, a kind of physical process or a kind of manipulation (p. 97). These passages suggest that Fischer would accept brainwashing or the employment of a neurological device as the kind of mechanism he had in mind. One might suppose that my objection to his account could consequently be undermined simply by adopting a narrower understanding of mechanism. One might suppose, for example, that the mechanism on which Raymond operates in the actual world is the mechanism of being brainwashed to kill his boss. This mechanism is obviously not operative in the possible world in which Raymond does not kill his boss; and so on this understanding of mechanism, my counterexample fails. But Fischer explicitly rules out this understanding of mechanism, and for excellent reasons. On his account of responsibility, if the mechanism is described in such a way that the operation of the mechanism involved in an agent's action includes the occurrence of that action, it would always follow that the agent was not responsible for his action, since on Fischer's account an agent is responsible for an action only in case there is a possible world in which the agent acts on the same mechanism but does a different action. And in general, the problem for Fischer's account in making more precise the notion of 'same mechanism' will be to avoid this sort of dilemma, in which a fine-grained description of the mechanism inappropriately denies responsibility to agents who do seem responsible, and a more coarse-grained description of the mechanism invites counterexamples in which an agent who doesn't seem responsible meets Fischer's conditions for responsibility because the mechanism controlling the agent is in the hands of persons who are themselves acting on reasons-responsive mechanisms.

37. If this result is right, then arguments by incompatibilists against compatibilism need to be restructured. Such arguments often assume PAP, then argue that if determinism is true, no agent has the ability to do otherwise, and conclude that therefore determinism is incompatible with responsibility. But if PAP is not true, or holds only for the most part, then the strategy of such arguments will not be successful. In "Incompatibilism Without the Principle of Alternate Possibilities," *Australasian Journal of Philosophy* 64 (1986), 266–76, Robert Heinaman argues that attacks on PAP based on Frankfurt-style examples leave PAP unscathed because there are two senses of 'could have done otherwise': (1) was not deterministically caused, and (2) had an alternate route open. Agents in Frankfurt-style examples could not have done otherwise only in sense (2), but PAP was intended in sense (1); and therefore, the Frankfurt-style examples in no way undermine PAP. There is some insight in this point of Heinaman's. I don't think it saves PAP, because it isn't clear that there is a distinction of the sort Heinaman wants between two senses of 'could have

done otherwise'. But what is right about his point is that the issue between compatibilists and incompatibilists which PAP was supposed to help adjudicate is a controversy about the causal chain eventuating in an action—the actual-sequence chain of events, as Fischer calls it—rather than about the implications of counterfactual mechanisms for coercing actions.

    38. I am grateful to William Alston, Thomas Flint, John Martin Fischer, Carl Ginet, William Mann, Philip Quinn, William Rowe, and Peter Van Inwagen for comments on this paper, and I am indebted to Norman Kretzmann for many helpful questions and suggestions on earlier drafts.

PART III

Moral Theory and Theism

An Argument for
Divine Command Ethics

PHILIP L. QUINN

Theists who agree in taking the Old Testament both seriously and fairly literally share religious reasons for sympathy with a divine command conception of ethics. Both Exodus 20:1–17 and Deuteronomy 5:6–21, which recount the revelation of the Decalogue, picture God as instructing his Chosen People about what they are to do and not to do by commanding them. He reveals his will and does not merely transmit information, and so it is natural enough to suppose that the authority of the Decalogue depends in some way upon the fact that it expresses the divine will. And a long tradition of voluntarism in moral theology has evolved from this natural starting point.

But religious reasons and philosophical reasons do not always coincide and sometimes conflict. There is a distinguished tradition of philosophical criticism of theological voluntarism whose genealogy extends all the way back to Plato's *Euthyphro*. So when the recent philosophical project of rehabilitating divine command ethics got under way, the first item on the agenda was to evaluate the force of the objections to divine command ethics raised by its philosophical critics, to see whether they had refuted the divine command conception by showing it to be incoherent, false, or implausible. Much of my own earlier work in this area of philosophy was devoted to the task of providing clear and precise formulations of the basic ideas of the divine command conception and defending them against a variety of objections.[1] In order to conduct such a defense, one must consider each objection on its own merits and try to rebut the ob-

jections one by one. And since ingenious critics are apt to come up with new objections as fast as one can rebut the old ones, a defense is likely to be a protracted if not endless undertaking.

Besides, this sort of defense of a position against objections is often only a proper part of the case that has to be made if it is to be reasonable to accept the position. A successful defense against objections shows that good reasons for rejecting a position are absent; it does not follow from this alone that good reasons for accepting the position are present. Another possibility is that there are neither good reasons for rejecting nor good reasons for accepting the position and that the most reasonable thing to do is to withhold judgment on it. So it would be desirable to supplement a defense of the divine command position against objections with an argument in its favor that furnishes good reasons for accepting the position. It is this supplementary project that this paper is meant to advance.

I shall construct an argument whose conclusion is one of the central claims of theological voluntarism and whose main premise is one of the key tenets of a wide range of theistic belief systems. That premise is the doctrine of divine sovereignty. My view is that this argument, or something very much like it, does have the capability of giving many theists, and particularly a great many traditional Christians, good reasons for accepting a version of theological voluntarism. It will not, of course, be capable of furnishing good reasons for accepting its conclusion to everyone, to all rational persons, to all theists, or even to all Christians. But I doubt that any argument with a philosophically or theologically meaty conclusion has such a general capacity for providing good reasons, and so my argument will be none the worse for lacking such a capacity. The fact that its ability to provide good reasons is limited in scope does not imply that this ability is not genuine within its limits.

I qualify my position by claiming this capability for my argument or something very much like it because, in order to formulate my argument with precision, I have to adopt a particular interpretation of the doctrine of divine sovereignty. There are alternative interpretations of that doctrine, some stronger and others weaker than mine. So there will also be arguments that can be constructed which are parallel to mine, and some of them will prove more and others less than my argument does. What gives rise to this situation is perplexity about the extent of divine sovereignty. Is God sovereign over only contingent things? Is he also sovereign over some but not all necessities? Or is he sovereign over absolutely everything, including his own existence, so that he is self-caused? Depending on how one answers questions of this sort, one gets conceptions of divine sovereignty that vary in strength. Since I am not certain how best to interpret the doctrine of divine sovereignty, I follow the course of moderation and adopt for purposes of my argument an interpretation of intermediate strength. I leave it to those readers who favor stronger or weaker conceptions of divine sovereignty to construct the parallel arguments that incorporate such alternative conceptions. It seems to me that even the weakest of the plausible assumptions about divine sovereignty has the consequence that our obligations depend in part on divine fiat.

The paper is divided into four sections. In the first, I present my views about what it is that an argument for divine command ethics has to aim at establishing. In the second, I discuss the doctrine of divine sovereignty, introduce the technical machinery I need in order to express the interpretation of it I shall adopt for purposes of argument, and formulate the principle of sovereignty that will serve as the main premise of the argument. In the third, I state the argument in detail and comment on some of its features. And, in the fourth and final section, I consider and respond to what I take to be an important objection.

I. THE PROBLEM POSED

What is the domain of divine command theory in ethics? Though there is not perfect unanimity on this issue, most theorists seem convinced that divine commands bear, at least in the first instance, on the deontological status of action. In speaking of the deontological status of an action, I mean to refer to whether it has such properties as being morally permitted, being morally forbidden or prohibited, and being morally obligatory or required. The basic idea is that there is a correlation between the state of God's will, expressed by his commands, and the deontological status of actions. In addition, this correlation is not merely contingent or accidental; it is a matter of broadly logical or metaphysical necessity.

Thus, for example, a divine command theorist would typically endorse the thesis that there is a necessary coincidence of divine commands and moral obligations. This thesis may be expressed as follows:

(1) Necessarily, for all actions A, A is morally obligatory if and only if A is commanded by God.

In other words, being commanded by God is both logically necessary and logically sufficient for being morally obligatory. And a complete divine command theory would contain similar theses concerning moral permissions and prohibitions; prohibited actions will be those God commands not be performed, while permitted actions will be those God does not command not be performed.

But (1) and similar theses are symmetric. Though (1) tells us that being commanded by God is logically necessary and sufficient for being morally obligatory, it also says that being morally obligatory is logically necessary and sufficient for being commanded by God. Moreover, this logical symmetry insures counterfactual symmetry on standard accounts of the semantics of counterfactuals. Suppose, for instance, that truth-telling has been commanded by God and is obligatory. We ask: What if truth-telling had not been commanded by God? Given (1), the answer is this:

(2) If truth-telling were not commanded by God, it would not be obligatory.

But, as long as (1) is assumed, this too is the case:

(3) If truth-telling were not obligatory, it would not be commanded by God.

And so counterfactuals will not serve in this context to capture the idea that there is, according to divine command theory, an important asymmetry in some relation connecting obligations and divine commands. For the divine command theorist characteristically also wishes to assert both that truth-telling is obligatory because it is commanded by God and that it is not the case that truth-telling is commanded by God because it is obligatory.

One way to understand these assertions is in terms of an explanatory asymmetry. On this view, the fact that truth-telling is commanded by God explains the fact that truth-telling is obligatory and not vice versa. But it seems likely that this explanatory asymmetry will itself want an explanation at a deeper level. Presumably, if there is such a deeper explanation, it will have to be in terms of some metaphysical asymmetry. One possibility is that the property of being obligatory supervenes upon the property of being commanded by God and not vice versa. Another is that actions are in some manner caused to be obligatory by being commanded by God and not vice versa. For the moment let us refrain from choosing among the possibilities. The general point is that what is distinctive of divine command theories are claims like these:

(4) Truth-telling being obligatory is metaphysically dependent on truth-telling being commanded by God.

and

(5) It is not the case that truth-telling being commanded by God is metaphysically dependent on truth-telling being obligatory.

So I propose to make claims akin to these conclusions of the argument I maintain will provide many theists with good reasons for accepting theological voluntarism.

More precisely, my argument will conclude with claims about the deontological status of actions being asymmetrically metaphysically dependent on the will of God. For, as I see it, it is at the deepest level God's will, and not his commands, which merely express his will, that determines the deontological status of actions. So, for example, I shall argue that the obligatoriness of truth-telling is metaphysically dependent on the obligatoriness of truth-telling being willed by God but that the obligatoriness of truth-telling being willed by God is not metaphysically dependent on the obligatoriness of truth-telling. The question then, is this: Is there an interpretation of the doctrine of divine sovereignty that will underwrite such an argument?

The question having thus been posed, the next section takes the first step toward answering it by formulating a principle of divine sovereignty to serve as the first premise of such an argument.

2. A PRINCIPLE EXPOUNDED

What is it that the doctrine of divine sovereignty asserts? To start with a slogan, the claim is that nothing distinct from God is independent of God. But this needs clarification. What is it to be distinct from God? And what is it to be independent of God? In answering these questions, I shall appeal to an ontology of states of affairs.

I begin by rehearsing definitions, formulated by Roderick Chisholm, of two relational concepts.[2] These definitions make use of the concepts of *de re* necessity and obtaining as well as the intentional concepts of conceiving and accepting. The definitions are these:

> (6) The state of affairs p involves the state of affairs q = Df. p is necessarily such that, whoever conceived it, conceives q

and

> (7) The state of affairs p entails the state of affairs q = Df. p is necessarily such that (i) if it obtains then q obtains and (ii) whoever accepts it accepts q.

Using these two notions, we can specify fine-grained, intentional identity-conditions for states of affairs as follows:

> (8) The state of affairs p is identical with the state of affairs q = Df. p both involves and entails q, and q both involves and entails p.

Of special interest in the present context is the fact that we can also define the concept of one state of affairs being wholly distinct from another in the following way:

> (9) The state of affairs p is wholly distinct from the state of affairs q = Df. p neither involves nor entails q, and q neither involves nor entails p.

And then we are in a position to specify what it is for a state of affairs to be wholly distinct from God existing in this manner:

> (10) The state of affairs p is wholly distinct from the state of affairs of God existing = Df. (i) p does not involve God existing, (ii) p does not entail God existing, (iii) God existing does not involve p, and (iv) God existing does not entail p.

I shall interpret the doctrine of divine sovereignty as the claim that every obtaining state of affairs that is in this sense wholly distinct from God existing is metaphysically dependent on being willed by God.

Perhaps some examples of states of affairs that are and states of affairs that are not wholly distinct from God existing will help in clarifying the force of the proposed interpretation. Such states of affairs as 7 + 5 being equal to 12, the property of triangularity existing, theft being wrong, and the number two existing are wholly distinct from God existing. So on this interpretation of divine sovereignty some states of affairs that obtain necessarily are nonetheless metaphysically dependent on being willed by God. It gives partisans of absolute creation such as Thomas Morris and Christopher Menzel some of the extension of divine sovereignty over the realm of necessity called for by their theological activism.[3] But God being omniscient is not wholly distinct from God existing, for God being omniscient does entail God existing. And God existing or roses being red is not wholly distinct from God existing, since the former state of affairs involves the latter. Thus, on this interpretation, the doctrine does not make God sovereign over the entire domain of the necessary.

As I have said, my interpretation of the doctrine of divine sovereignty is meant to be moderate. There obviously are stronger versions of the doctrine. One might hold that every obtaining state of affairs whatsoever, including the state of affairs of God existing, is metaphysically dependent on being willed by God. Or it might be said that every obtaining state of affairs that is not identical with the state of affairs of God existing is metaphysically dependent on being willed by God. And there clearly are weaker versions too. It might be claimed that all and only contingently obtaining states of affairs are metaphysically dependent on being willed by God. Or one might even maintain that only some contingently obtaining states of affairs are metaphysically dependent on being willed by God, others being metaphysically dependent only on various secondary causes or on nothing at all. I know of no conclusive arguments in favor of my interpretation to the exclusion of all the alternatives to it. In adopting it for the purposes of argument, I follow the generally sound maxim that good things are apt to be found somewhere in the middle between extremes. But I am not indissolubly wedded to this interpretation. It would be useful to see a thorough comparative study of its merits and those of its rivals, but limitations of space preclude me from undertaking that project in this paper.

So instead I move on to a discussion of the notion of one state of affairs being metaphysically dependent on another. Because I assume that this notion is at bottom causal, I take as my undefined philosophical concept one state of affairs contributing to bringing about another. I start from the notion of causal contribution rather than from the idea of causal sufficiency in order not to rule out two possibilities. One is free human action; the other is objective indeterminacy in inanimate nature. On a libertarian view of free action, the state of affairs of Jones freely raising his arm being willed by God cannot bring about the state of affairs of Jones freely raising his arm. But presumably the divine will can contribute to bringing about the state of affairs of Jones freely raising his arm by, for example, conserving Jones in existence while he raises his arm. Similarly, on certain interpretations of contemporary microphysical theory, the state of affairs of uranium atom U spontaneously decaying being willed by God cannot bring about the state of affairs of U spontaneously decaying. But of course the divine will can contribute to bringing about the state of affairs of U spontaneously decaying by conserving U and its decay products, respectively, during different and successive segments of the decay process.

The notion of one state of affairs being metaphysically dependent on another may then be defined as follows:

(11) The state of affairs p is metaphysically dependent on the state of affairs q = Df. q contributes to bringing about p, and it is not the case that p contributes to bringing about q.

I do not assume that only contingently obtaining states of affairs can enter into the relationship of metaphysical dependency. And now we are in a position to spell out what is meant by a state of affairs being metaphysically dependent on being willed by God in this fashion:

(12) The state of affairs p is metaphysically dependent on being willed by God = Df. p being willed by God contributes to bringing about p, and it is not the case that p contributes to bringing about p being willed by God.

Finally, using the concepts defined by (10) and (12), we can formulate our principle of divine sovereignty in the following way:

(13) Necessarily, for all states of affairs p, if p obtains and p is wholly distinct from the state of affairs of God existing, then p is metaphysically dependent on being willed by God.

It is this principle that I take to provide the starting point for an argument which will underwrite theological voluntarism. And it is to the task of stating that argument that I next turn my attention.

3. THE ARGUMENT STATED

For ease of exposition, I shall state the argument in terms of the familiar example of truth-telling being obligatory. I shall then discuss the interesting question of whether (13) is a strong enough principle to underwrite parallel arguments for all cases in which deontological moral status is correctly attributed to actions.

The first premise of the argument is the appropriate instantiation of the general principle of divine sovereignty expressed by (13). It is this:

(14) If truth-telling being obligatory obtains and truth-telling being obligatory is wholly distinct from the state of affairs of God existing, then truth-telling being obligatory is metaphysically dependent on being willed by God.

It is safe enough to assume that

(15) Truth-telling being obligatory obtains.

I take it to be a deliverance of enlightened conscience that truth-telling is at least *prima facie* obligatory, and this is all that is needed to make it legitimate to assume (15), since I have not distinguished *prima facie* and all-things-considered obligations. Appeal to the definitions of technical concepts expressed by (6), (7), and (10) suffices to show that

(16) Truth-telling being obligatory is wholly distinct from the state of affairs of God existing.

And so by applying *modus ponens* to (14), (15), and (16) we can deduce the conclusion that

(17) Truth-telling being obligatory is metaphysically dependent on being willed by God.

Applying the definition expressed by (12) to (17) and using the rule of conjunction elimination, we may further conclude both that

(18) Truth-telling being obligatory being willed by God contributes to bringing about truth-telling being obligatory.

and that

(19) It is not the case that truth-telling being obligatory contributes to bringing about truth-telling being obligatory being willed by God.

And this completes the argument, for (18) and (19) together exhibit just the sort of asymmetrical metaphysical dependence between obligations and the divine will I had earlier claimed ought to be present in the conclusions of an argument to provide theists with good reasons for accepting theological voluntarism. Note the structural analogy between (4) and (5), on the one hand, and (18) and (19), on the other.

Clearly the principle of sovereignty expressed by (13) will license a very large number of arguments parallel to the one expressed by (14) through (19). Among the deontological states of affairs that can in this fashion be argued (soundly, in my opinion) to be metaphysically dependent on being willed by God are promise-keeping being obligatory, worshipping idols being forbidden, torturing children being forbidden, studying theology being permitted, and air travel being permitted. So it might seem that (13) is powerful enough to get us to the conclusion that all obtaining deontological states of affairs are metaphysically dependent on being willed by God. But this is not so, for the simple reason that not all obtaining deontological states of affairs are wholly distinct from the state of affairs of God existing. Consider the state of affairs of obeying God being obligatory. According to theism, it surely obtains. Yet it seems clearly not to be wholly distinct from the state of affairs of God existing, because it apparently both involves and entails God existing. Hence it seems plain that an argument parallel to the one expressed by (14) through (19) but about obedience to God rather than truth-telling being obligatory will be unsound. Thus, powerful though it is, (13) cannot, apparently, serve for theists to show that the entire realm of obligation is metaphysically dependent on the divine will.

Several ways of responding to this situation are open. One might dig in one's heels and insist that (13) is the correct principle of divine sovereignty. If one took this tack, one would be stuck with saying either that obeying God being obligatory is not, after all, metaphysically dependent on being willed by God, which strikes me as an odd concession for a thoroughgoing theological voluntarist to make, or that, although obeying God being obligatory is metaphysically dependent on being willed by God, this is not established by considerations of divine sovereignty. Alternatively, one might advocate a stronger principle of divine sovereignty. One that would suffice to dispose of the case at hand is this:

> (20) Necessarily, for all states of affairs p, if p obtains and p is not identical with the state of affairs of God existing, then p is metaphysically dependent on being willed by God.

Because the state of affairs of God existing neither involves nor entails the state of affairs of obeying God being obligatory, the latter state of affairs is not identical with the former. So if (20) were the correct principle of divine sovereignty, it would underwrite a sound argument analogous to the one expressed by (14) through (19). But if it were correct, it would also follow that such states of affairs as God being omniscient and God being omnipotent are metaphysically dependent on being willed by God. Despite what can be said on behalf of such claims by absolute creationists, I do not find them plausible, and for that reason I incline toward rejecting (20). My conclusion is that a thoroughgoing theological voluntarist had best continue to insist that obeying God being obligatory is metaphysically dependent on being willed by God but concede that this is not a consequence of the doctrine of divine sovereignty. And, of course, similar things should be said about such obtaining deontological states of affairs as disobeying God being forbidden.

So I hold that considerations of divine sovereignty can provide good reasons for accepting the view that many obtaining deontological states of affairs are metaphysically dependent on the will of God. But I disavow the view that such considerations provide good reasons for holding that all such states of affairs are so dependent.

Those who wish to subscribe to the view I disavow will have to endorse a principle of divine sovereignty stronger than any I am willing to adopt. Because I believe many theists, and in particular Christians, would on reflection endorse a principle of divine sovereignty
at least as strong as the one I am prepared to defend, I conclude
that the doctrine of divine sovereignty is capable of furnishing for
them good reasons for accepting the voluntaristic view that most
if not all of the deontological realm is metaphysically dependent on
God's will.

4. AN OBJECTION CONSIDERED

Limitations of space prevent me from responding to all the objections I anticipate critics might lodge against this argument. But
I shall consider one that is both historically influential and philosophically substantial. Examining this objection will also enable
me to cast additional light on the doctrine of divine sovereignty.

In his *A Review of the Principal Questions in Morals,* Richard
Price represents morality as necessary and immutable. He supposes
that some theists will find this objectionable. It may seem, he says,
that "this is setting up something distinct from God, which is independent of him, and equally eternal and necessary."[4] Price's reply
is to claim that if "we must give up the unalterable natures of right
and wrong, and make them dependent on the divine will; we must,
for the same reason, give up all necessary truth, and assert the
possibility of contradictions." It seems to me that we should read
Price as trying to confront the doctrine of divine sovereignty with
a dilemma. Either there are necessary truths, in which case there
are things distinct from God that are independent of him, or there
are not, in which case contradictions are possible. So either the doctrine of divine sovereignty is false or contradictions are possible. But
contradictions are not possible. Hence the doctrine of divine sovereignty is false.

It seems clear that a defender of divine sovereignty can reply
to this line of argument by conceding that there are necessary truths
while denying that it follows from this concession that there are things
distinct from God which are independent of him. For we may divide the necessarily obtaining states of affairs into those such as God

existing which are not distinct from God and those such as 2 + 2 being equal to 4 which are distinct from God. Principles of divine sovereignty such as (13) and (20) tell us that necessarily obtaining states of affairs of the latter sort are metaphysically dependent on the divine will and so are not independent of God. So all the necessary truths will either not be distinct from God or, if distinct, not be independent of him. And if some deontological states of affairs, such as torturing children being forbidden, that are distinct from God obtain necessarily, as I tend to think they do, then they too will be metaphysically dependent on the divine will. The corresponding moral truths, though eternal and necessary, will not be independent of God. Since such deontological states of affairs obtain in every possible world, they are willed by God in every possible world. But all this shows is that the divine will too is in some respects necessary and immutable.

Price goes on to observe that "something there certainly is which we must allow not to be dependent on the will of God." He cites as examples "this will itself; his own existence; his eternity and immensity; the difference between power and impotence, wisdom and folly, truth and falsehood, existence and non-existence." Defenders of even such strong conceptions of divine sovereignty as those expressed by (13) and (20) can accept this observation. Such states of affairs as God having a will, God existing, God being eternal, and God being immense are not wholly distinct from the state of affairs of God existing. So (13) does not imply that they are metaphysically dependent on being willed by God, and someone who accepts (13) can consistently maintain that they are not dependent on the will of God. Such a person can allow that such things as God's will, his existence, and his eternity and immensity are not dependent on the will of God. And because the state of affairs of God existing is self-identical, (20) does not imply that it is metaphysically dependent on being willed by God. So even someone who accepts (20) can consistently hold that there is something—namely, God's existence—that is not dependent on the will of God.

Price's discussion seems to presuppose that only contingent things can depend upon the divine will or, to put it another way, that if something distinct from God is eternal and necessary, it is bound to be independent of him. Strong principles of divine sovereignty, when coupled with ordinary views about which things are necessary, are inconsistent with this presupposition. As far as I can make out, there is no good reason to accept the presupposition, and it is rational enough for supporters of strong versions of the doctrine of divine sovereignty to reject it. I conclude, then, that Price's objection fails to show that strong versions of the doctrine of divine sovereignty are all false. Thus it also fails to show that arguments for theological voluntarism with respect to most if not all of the deontological component of ethics which have strong principles of divine sovereignty such as (13) or (20) among their premises are unsound.

NOTES

1. Philip L. Quinn, *Divine Commands and Moral Requirements* (Oxford: Clarendon Press, 1978), especially pp. 39–64, and Philip L. Quinn, "Divine Command Ethics: A Causal Theory," in *Divine Command Morality: Historical and Contemporary Readings,* ed. Janine Marie Idziak (New York and Toronto: Edwin Mellen Press, 1979), pp. 305–25.

2. Roderick M. Chisholm, *The First Person: An Essay on Reference and Intentionality* (Brighton: Harvester Press, 1981), p. 124.

3. Thomas V. Morris and Christopher Menzel, "Absolute Creation," *American Philosophical Quarterly* 23 (1986): 353–62.

4. Richard Price, *A Review of the Principal Questions in Morals,* chap. 5. All my quotes come from pp. 149–50 of vol. II of *British Moralists,* ed. L. A. Selby-Bigge (Indianapolis: Bobbs-Merrill, 1964).

Some Suggestions for Divine Command Theorists

I

The basic idea behind a divine command theory of ethics is that what I morally ought or ought not to do is determined by what God commands me to do or avoid. This, of course, gets spelled out in different ways by different theorists. In this paper I shall not try to establish a divine command theory in any form, or even argue directly for such a theory, but I shall make some suggestions as to the way in which the theory can be made as strong as possible. More specifically I shall (1) consider how the theory could be made invulnerable to two familiar objections and (2) consider what form the theory should take so as not to fall victim to a Euthyphro-like dilemma. This will involve determining what views of God and human morality we must take in order to enjoy these immunities.

The sort of divine command theory from which I begin is the one presented in Robert M. Adams's paper, "Divine Command Meta-ethics Modified Again."[1] This is not a view as to what words like 'right' and 'ought' *mean*. Nor is it a view as to what our *concepts* of moral obligation, rightness and wrongness, amount to. It is rather the claim that divine commands are constitutive of the moral status of actions. As Adams puts it, "ethical wrongness *is* (i.e., is identical with) the property of being contrary to the commands of a loving God."[2] Hence the view is immune to the objection that many persons don't mean 'is contrary to a command of God' by 'is morally wrong'; just as the view that water *is* H_2O is immune to the objection that many people do not mean 'H$_2$O' by 'water'. I intend my discussion to be applicable to any version of this "objective constitution" sort. It could just as well be an "ultimate *criterion* of moral obligation" view[3] or a view as to that on which moral obligation *supervenes*. I will understand 'constitutive' to range over all these variants. Thus I can state the basic idea in the following way.

1. Divine commands are constitutive of moral obligation.

There is, of course, a variety of terms that could be used to specify what divine commands are held to constitute. These include 'right', 'wrong', 'ought', 'obligation', and 'duty'. For reasons that will emerge in the course of the paper, I prefer to concentrate on '(morally) ought'. I have used the term 'moral *obligation*' in 1, because it makes possible a more succinct formulation, but whenever in the sequel I speak of moral obligation I do not, unless the reader is warned to the contrary, mean to be trading on any maximally distinctive features of the meaning of that term. I will rather be understanding '*S* has a moral obligation to do *A*' simply as an alternative formulation for '*S* morally ought to do *A*'. I shall often omit the qualifier 'morally' where the context makes it clear what is intended.

Should we think of each particular obligation of a particular agent in a particular situation as constituted by a separate divine command, or should we think of general divine commands, like the Ten Commandments, as constituting general obligations, from which particular obligations follow? No doubt, God does command particular people to do particular things in particular situations; but this is presumably the exception rather than the rule. Therefore in this paper I will have my eye on the idea that general divine commands are constitutive of general obligations or, if you like, of the truth or validity of general principles of obligation.

II

Now for my Euthyphro-like dilemma. The original dilemma in the *Euthyphro* had to do with whether an act is pious because it is loved by the gods or is loved by the gods because it is pious. The analogue that is most directly relevant to a divine command ethics is the following. Is it that:

    2. We ought to, e.g., love one another because God commands
       us to do so.

or is it that:

    3. God commands us to love one another because that is what
       we ought to do.

The divine command theorist apparently embraces the first horn
and rejects the second. Of course, the dilemma is often thought to
pose a fatal problem for theists generally and not just for divine command theorists. For it is commonly supposed that both horns are
unacceptable, and that, since the theist must choose one or the other,
this implies the unacceptability of theism. However I shall be contending that both horns, suitably interpreted, are quite acceptable,
and that if the divine command theorist follows my suggestions he
can grasp both horns as I interpret them.

    The two classic objections to divine command ethics (to the
acceptance of the first horn of the dilemma) that I shall be considering are the following.

    A. This makes divine commands, and hence, morality, arbi-
trary. Anything that God should decide to command would *thereby*
be obligatory. If God should command us to inflict pain on each
other gratuitously we would thereby be obliged to do so. More specifically, the theory renders divine commands arbitrary because it
blocks off any moral reason for them. God can't command us to
do *A* because that is what is morally right; for it doesn't become
morally right until He commands it.

    B. It leaves us without any adequate way of construing the
goodness of God. No doubt, it leaves us free to take God to be
metaphysically good, realizing the fullness of being and all that; but
it forecloses any conception of God as *morally* good, as exemplifying the sort of goodness that is cashed out in being loving, just, and
merciful. For since the standards of moral goodness are set by divine commands, to say that God is morally good is just to say that
He obeys His own commands. And even if it makes sense to think
of God as obeying commands that He has given Himself, that is
not at all what we have in mind in thinking of God as morally good.
We aren't just thinking that God practices what He preaches, whatever that may be.

These objections are intimately interrelated. If we could answer the second by showing how the theory leaves room for an acceptable account of divine goodness, we could answer the first. For if God is good in the right way, there will be nothing arbitrary about His commands. On the contrary His goodness will ensure that He issues those commands for the best. Hence I will initially concentrate on the second objection.

In the most general terms it is clear what the divine command theorist's strategy should be. He must fence in the area the moral status of which is constituted by divine commands so that the divine nature and activity fall outside that area. That will leave him free to construe divine moral goodness in some other way than conformity with God's own commands, so that this can be a basis for God's issuing commands to us in one way rather than another. The simplest way of doing this is to make 1. apply only to human (or, more generally, creaturely) obligation. Then something else can constitute divine obligation. This move should be attractive to one who supposes that what gives a divine command its morality-constituting force is solely God's metaphysical status in the scheme of things. God is our creator and sustainer, without Whose continual exercise of creative activity we would lapse into nothingness. If God's commands are morally binding on us solely because He stands in that relation to us, it follows that they are not morally binding on Himself; and so if there are any moral facts involving God they will have to be otherwise constituted. But, apart from objections to thinking of the moral authority of God exclusively in terms of power and status, this view would seem to presuppose that moral obligation is something quite different as applied to God and to human beings. For if it is the same, how could it be constituted so differently in the two cases? And if what it is for God to have an obligation is something quite different from what it is for a human being to have an obligation, how is divine obligation to be construed? I have no idea.[4]

Hence I shall take a more radical line and deny that obligations attach to God at all. 1. implies that divine moral goodness is a matter of obeying divine commands only if moral *obligation* attaches to God; for only in that case can divine moral goodness be a matter of God's satisfying moral obligations. If the kinds of moral status that are engendered by divine commands are attributable only to creatures, then no puzzles can arise over the constitution of divine morality by divine commands. If this move is to work we will have to develop an account of divine moral goodness that does not involve the satisfaction of moral obligations.

But our first task is to defend the claim that moral obligation does not attach to God. Stated more generally, the position is that terms in what we might call the (morally) 'ought' family—'ought', 'required', 'permitted', 'forbidden', 'duty', 'obligation'—do not apply to God, that it is impossible for God to have duties or obligations, that it cannot ever be true that God *ought* to do something or other. How can this view be supported?

The position has been argued for from the premise that God lacks "significant moral freedom." It is assumed that terms of the "morally ought" family apply to a being only if that being has a choice between doing or failing to do what it ought to do. But if God is *essentially* perfectly good, as I shall be assuming in this paper,[5] it is, in the strongest way, impossible for God to fail to do what is right. Therefore it can't be correct to speak of God's duties or of what He ought to do.[6] I am not happy with this line of argument. Although it seems clear that my being determined from the "outside" (e.g., by causal factors that were in place before I was born) prevents my having moral obligations, it is not equally clear that we get the same consequence from a determination that springs from my own nature. Of course in my case it might be argued that my nature in turn was determined to be what it is by factors that existed before I was born. But God's nature is not determined by anything other than Himself, much less anything that existed before He did. Hence it is not at all clear that if God acts from the necessity of His own nature that prevents Him from acting freely in a way that is required for moral obligation.

The support I do want to muster is like the previous one in appealing to the essential perfect goodness of God, but it exploits that point in a different and a more direct way, by focusing on the lack of divine opposition to acting for the best rather than the lack of freedom the previous argument infers from that. If God is essentially perfectly good, then it is metaphysically impossible that God should do anything that is less than supremely good; and this includes the moral good as well as other modes of goodness. If it is morally better to be loving than to be indifferent and morally better to love everyone than to be agapistically selective, it will be metaphysically impossible for God to display indifference or partiality. I shall now argue that the lack of any possibility of God's doing other than the best prevents the application of terms in the 'ought' family to God.

The intuitive idea here is that it can be said that agents ought to do something, or that they have duties or obligations, only where there is the possibility of an opposition to what these duties require. Obligations *bind* us, *constrain* us to act in ways we otherwise might not act. They *govern* or *regulate* our behavior, *inhibit* some of our tendencies and *reinforce* others. We can say that a person ought to do A only where there is, or could be, some resistance on her part to doing A. But how to support this intuition?

For one thing, we can point to the conditions under which it is appropriate to use these terms. To the extent that we think there is no possibility of S's failing to do A we don't tell him that he ought to do A, or speak of S's duty or obligation to do A. If an assistant professor in my department not infrequently failed to show up for his classes, it would be quite in order for me, as chairman of the department, to call him into my office and remind him of his obligation to meet his classes regularly. Even if he has so much as given signs of a strong temptation to play hooky, the sermon might have a point. But suppose that he has in fact unfailingly taught his classes and, furthermore, has conscientiously performed all his academic duties, even engaging in acts of supererogation. And, given that, suppose I were to remark to him, when passing in the hall one day, "You ought to meet your classes regularly." That remark would naturally evoke intense puzzlement. "What are you talking about? When haven't I met my classes?" The utter naturalness of that response does strongly suggest that the possibility of deviation is a necessary condition of the applicability of terms in the 'ought' family. The oddness of saying that God ought to love His creatures is just the above writ large. The absurdity is compounded by thinking of God saying to Himself, in stentorian Kantian tones, "Thou ought to exercise providence over Thy creation."

However, it may, quite reasonably, be contended that these considerations have to do only with the conditions of appropriateness for certain kinds of illocutionary acts and not at all with the truth conditions of ought judgments. Even if there would be no point in my *exhorting* or *enjoining* my colleague to meet his classes, the fact remains that it is his duty to do so, that he ought to do so, however little possibility there is of failure. Similarly, it may be claimed that although it is inappropriate for us to issue moral *injunctions* or *commands* to God, it is still *true* that God, like any rational agent, *ought* to love other rational agents and treat them with justice. This is just one example of the general point that it may be inappropriate to say something, or to say it with a certain illocutionary force that is, nevertheless, perfectly true. It is inappropriate and puzzling for me to say that I *know* that I feel sleepy, rather than just reporting that I feel sleepy, just because we all take it for granted that a normal person in a normal condition knows what his feelings are at a given moment. This inappropriateness has been taken, e.g., by Wittgenstein as a reason for denying that 'know' has any application in these cases.[7] But it seems clear to me that the inappropriateness of saying that I know I feel sleepy is simply due to the overwhelming obviousness of the fact that I know it if it is the case, and that this inappropriateness has no tendency to show that I don't or can't know such things. An analogous interpretation of the oddity of 'ought' judgments in the absence of presumption of the possibility of deviation, at least for the human cases, is strongly suggested by the following consideration. A natural way to mark out these cases is to say that they are cases in which there is no reason to think that the person is at all tempted to fail in her duties or obligations, to fail to do what she ought to do. But this presupposes that the person *has* duties and obligations, even though there is no point in reminding her of the fact.[8]

I am prepared to accept this objection to the inappropriateness argument and even to find the conclusion false as well, at least in its application to human beings. Utter dependability, of the sort of which we are capable, does not cancel obligations but merely insures their fulfillment. But, I claim, an essentially perfectly good God is another matter. However, we will have to find some other way of supporting that claim. The mere fact that it is out of order for anyone to tell God what He ought to do is not sufficient.

At this point I will turn to the most distinguished of my predecessors in holding this thesis, Immanuel Kant.[9] In the *Foundations
of the Metaphysics of Morals* he writes.

> if the will is not of itself in complete accord with reason (the actual
> case of men), then the actions which are recognized as objectively
> necessary are subjectively contingent, and the determination of such
> a will according to objective laws is constraint.
>
> The conception of an objective principle, so far as it constrains
> a will, is a command (of reason), and the formula of this command
> is called an *imperative.*
>
> All imperatives are expressed by an "ought" and thereby indi-
> cate the relation of an objective law of reason to a will which is not
> in its subjective constitution necessarily determined by this law. This
> relation is that of constraint. Imperatives say that it would be good
> to do or to refrain from doing something, but they say it to a will
> which does not always do something simply because it is presented
> as a good thing to do.
>
> A perfectly good will, therefore, would be equally subject to
> objective laws (of the good), but it could not be conceived as con-
> strained by them to act in accord with them, because, according to
> its own subjective constitution, it can be determined to act only though
> the conception of the good. Thus no imperatives hold for the divine
> will or, more generally, for a holy will. The "ought" is here out of
> place, for the volition of itself is necessarily in unison with the law.
> Therefore imperatives are only formulas expressing the relation of
> objective laws of volition in general to the subjective imperfection
> of the will of this or that rational being, e.g., the human will.[10]

It is clear that despite differences in terminology, and deeper
differences in the background ethical and metaphysical scheme, Kant
is espousing at least something very close to the thesis currently under discussion. "The 'ought' is here out of place, for the volition of
itself is necessarily in unison with the law." Just because God acts
for the good by the necessity of His nature ("only though the conception of the good"), He cannot "be conceived as constrained . . .
to act in accord with them" (objective laws of volition). But it is not
clear that Kant has anything significant to add by way of support.
Such support as is proffered is based on the claim that "All imperatives are expressed by an 'ought'." (Actually the argument needs the

converse of this, that every 'ought' judgment is, or perhaps has the force of, an imperative. Consider it done.) Without pausing to go into the question of what Kant means by 'imperative' let's just take the most obvious alternative, viz., that he means 'imperative'. In that case his argument could be spelled out as follows.

1. An ought judgment has the force of an imperative.
2. An imperative can be (properly, meaningfully, . . .) addressed only to one who does not necessarily conform to what it demands (enjoins, . . .).
3. God necessarily conforms to what would be commanded by moral imperatives (necessarily does what it is good to do).
4. Therefore moral imperatives cannot be addressed to God.
5. Therefore ought judgments have no application to God.

But this is just a version of the inappropriateness argument already considered and is subject to the same objection. Even if imperatives are not appropriately addressed to God, it still might be true that God ought to do so-and-so. This objection applies to the above argument by denying the first premise. It is a mistake to think that an ought judgment always or necessarily has the force of an imperative. One could make an ought judgment just to state a fact about someone's obligations.

What now? At this point I will confess that I do not have a knockdown argument for my thesis. In fact I doubt that there is a more fundamental and more obvious feature of moral obligation from which the feature in question, the possibility of deviation, can be derived. All I can hope to do is to indicate the way in which this feature is crucial to obligation. Since I am only concerned to recommend the thesis to the divine command theorist as his best hope of avoiding a horn of the Euthyphro dilemma, all I need do, in any case, is to exhibit the plausibility of the thesis.

Let's look at the matter in the following way. In suggesting that God is perfectly good, morally as well as otherwise, even though He is not subject to obligations, we are presupposing a fundamental distinction between value or goodness, including moral goodness, on the one hand, and the likes of duty, obligation, and ought, on the other. This not only involves the obvious point that the concept of the moral goodness of *agents* and *motives* is a different concept from the concept of an obligation to perform an action. It also includes the claim that the moral goodness of an action must be distinguished from its moral obligatoriness. The fact that it would be, morally, a good thing for me to do *A* must not be confused with the fact that I morally ought to do *A,* that it is morally *required* of me, that I am morally blameworthy in case I fail to do it. All that is needed to nail down this distinction is the phenomenon of supererogation, a widely though not universally accepted phenomenon. Let's say that it would morally be a good thing for me to see to it that the children of some remote Siberian village have an opportunity to take piano lessons. Nevertheless, so I claim, I have no obligations, moral or otherwise, to do so; I am not morally blameworthy for not doing it. (If you think I am morally blameworthy for not doing this, pick your favorite example of a morally good but not obligatory action.) Note that Kant, in the passage quoted above, is also presupposing such a distinction. He thinks of "objective laws of the good" as specifying what it would be (morally) good to do, and as such they are applicable even to a holy will. But these "laws" determine obligations only when addressed "to a will which does not always do something simply because it is presented as a good thing to do."

Given this distinction, it is clear that '*S* morally ought to do *A*' adds something to 'It would be a morally good thing for *S* to do *A*'. I am taking it as obvious that the latter is a necessary condition for the former. This being the case, there can be a distinction between them only if the former goes beyond the latter in some way. And what way is that? By posing this issue we can see the strength of our thesis. It provides an intuitively plausible way of specifying at least part of what there is to an obligation to do *A* other than its being a good thing to do *A*. Let's spell this out a bit, continuing to think of the distinction, among the things it would be good for me to do, between those I am obliged to do and those I am not.

One thing required for my having an obligation to do *A,* e.g., to support my family, is that there are general principles, laws, or rules that lay down conditions under which that action is required (and that those conditions are satisfied in my case). Call them "practical rules (principles)." Practical principles are in force, in a nondegenerate way, with respect to a given population of agents only if there is at least a possibility of their playing a governing or regulative function; and this is possible only where there is a possibility of agents in that population violating them. Given that possibility, behavior can be guided, monitored, controlled, corrected, criticized, praised, blamed, punished, or rewarded on the basis of the principles. There will be social mechanisms or inculcating and enforcing the rules, positive and negative sanctions that encourage compliance and discourage violation. Psychologically, the principles will be internalized in higher level control mechanisms that monitor behavior and behavioral tendencies and bring motivational forces to bear in the direction of compliance and away from violation. There can be something like the Freudian distinction of id, ego, and superego within each agent in the population. I take it that terms like 'ought', 'duty', and 'obligation' acquire a use only against this kind of background, and that their application presupposes that practical principles are playing, or at least can play, a regulative role, socially and/or psychologically. And this is at least an essential part of what is added when we move from saying that it would be a good thing for S to do A to saying that S *ought* to do A.

Instead of arguing, as I have just been doing, that a regulative role of practical principles is presupposed by *particular ought judgments,* I could, as Kant does, exploit the fact that practical principles themselves, and more specifically the subclass that can be called moral principles, are naturally expressed in terms of 'ought', and argue more directly for the inapplicability of *moral principles* to God.[11] Under what conditions does the principle that "one ought to take account of the needs of others" apply to an agent, as well as the evaluative principle that it is a good thing for one to take account of the needs of others. For reasons of the sort we have been giving, it seems that such a principle has force, relative to an agent or group of agents, only where it has, or can have, a role in governing, directing, and guiding the conduct of those agents. Where it is necessary that S will do A, what sense is there in supposing that the general principle "one ought to do A" has any application to S? Here there is no foothold for the 'ought'; there is nothing to make the ought principle true rather than or in addition to the evaluative statement plus the specification of what S will necessarily do. That is, the closest we can get to a moral law requiring God to love others is the conjunction of the evaluative statement that it is a good thing for God to love others, plus the statement that God necessarily does so.

Note that these very general considerations as to what it takes for ought statements to be applicable are not limited to the moral ought, but equally apply to, e.g., legal, institutional, and prudential oughts, obligations, etc. It is my legal duty to do A only if there is a law in force in my society that, applied to my case, lays on me a requirement to do A. And laws are in force only if there is at least a possibility that they will be disobeyed; otherwise they have no governing or constraining work to do, i.e., no work to do. I should also make it explicit that I am not purporting to deal in this essay with what makes the difference between moral and nonmoral obligations, duties, oughts, goodness, etc. I am simply assuming that there is such a difference and that we have a secure enough working grasp of it to make this discussion possible. Let me also underline the obvious point that I have not claimed to give a complete account of what it takes for practical principles, whether moral, legal, institutional, or whatever, to be in force *de jure* as well as *de facto,* so as to engender real obligations. The account of this will, of course, be different for, as an example, legal and moral obligations. It is the claim of the divine command theorist that moral obligations are engendered by and only by practical principles isued as divine commands. I am not concerned to determined what can be said for this claim. My concern with the divine command theory in this essay extends only to considering what it would take for the theory to answer certain objections. And so I am concerned with only part of what is required for ought statements to apply to *S,* the part that has to do with the possibility of deviation from what the ought statement requires.

What about 'right' and 'wrong'? Can we say that God acts *rightly* in loving His creatures even if we can't say that He is acting as He *ought*? A. C. Ewing, in the passage referred to in note 10, endorses that position. Nothing in this paper hangs on this, but I am inclined to think that as 'right' is most centrally used in moral contexts, it is tied to terms of the 'ought' family and borrows its distinctive force from them. In asking what is the right thing for me to do in this situation, I am, I think, typically asking what I ought to do in this situation. Ewing and others hold the view that 'right' in moral contexts means something like 'fitting' or 'appropriate' (in a certain way) and hence does not carry the force of 'required', 'bound', and 'culpable if not' that is distinctive of 'ought' and 'obligation'. I am disinclined to agree, but I can avoid the problem here.

This exhausts what I have to say in support of the view that a necessary condition of the truth of 'S ought to do A' is at least the metaphysical possibility that S does not do A. On this view, moral obligations attach to all human beings, even those so saintly as to totally lack any tendency, in the ordinary sense of that term, to do other than what it is morally good to do. And no moral obligations attach to God, assuming, as we are here, that God is essentially perfectly good. Thus divine commands can be constitutive of moral obligations for those beings who have them without its being the case that God's goodness consists in His obeying His own commands, or, indeed, consists in any relation whatsoever of God to His commands.

Eleonore Stump has urged, in conversation, that if God should break a promise He would be doing something He ought not to do, and that this implies that 'ought' does have application to God. My reply is that if God should do something that is forbidden by a valid and applicable moral principle (and the objection assumes that God's breaking a promise would have that status), this would show that it is possible for Him to act in contravention of moral principles. In that case He would not be essentially perfectly good, and so we would not have the reasons advanced in this paper for supposing that He has no moral obligations. That is, Stump's argument shows only that 'ought' would be applicable to God under certain counterfactual conditions (indeed counterpossible conditions if God is essentially perfectly good), not that 'ought' is applicable to Him as things are.

But God is represented in the Bible and elsewhere as making promises, e.g., to Noah and to Abraham, and as making covenants with Israel. But by the very concept of a promise or of a covenant it engenders obligations. It is contradictory to say "God promised Abraham to give him descendants as numerous as the dust of the earth, but God was not thereby obligated (even *prima facie*) to give Abraham that many descendants." It is equally self-contradictory to say "God entered into a covenant with Israel to establish them forever in the land of Canaan if they would keep His commandments, but God was not thereby obligated to establish them forever in the land of Canaan if they kept His commandments." So how can God fail to have obligations?

I think this argument does show that if God has no obligations it is not strictly true that He makes promises or covenants. Does my view then imply that all these reports are false? No. We can hold that the biblical writers were speaking loosely, analogically, or metaphorically in so describing the transactions, just as they were in speaking of God "stretching out His arm" and doing so-and-so. They were choosing the closest human analogue to what God was doing in order to give us a vivid idea of God's action. It would be more strictly accurate to say that God *expressed the intention* to make Abraham's descendants as numerous as the dust of the earth, and that He expressed the intention to establish Israel in the land of Canaan forever if they kept His commandments. Just as we can express intentions without obligating ourselves (provided we don't promise) so it is with God. The difference, of course, is that we can count on an expression of intention from God as we can on a promise from a human being, indeed can count on it much more, because of the utter stability and dependability of God's character and purposes.

III

If there is a conceptual distinction between *S*'s satisfying moral obligations and *S*'s actions being morally good, and if the former is not a conceptually necessary condition for the latter, as the phenomenon of supererogation shows, then there is no difficulty in applying the concept of moral goodness to an agent and his actions even if the concept of moral obligation has no application to that agent. In particular, we can think of God as perfectly good, morally as well as otherwise, even if that moral goodness does not consist in the perfect satisfaction of obligations. To put some flesh on this skeleton we might think of it in the following way. By virtue of practical principles that morally require certain things of us, *we* are morally obligated to act in certain ways; speaking summarily, as the occasion dictates, let us say that we are obligated to act justly, show mercy, and care for the needs of others. Now let's remember Kant's suggestion that an 'ought' statement says "that it would be good to do or to refrain from doing something, but they say it to a will which does not always do something simply because it is presented as a good thing to do." This presupposes that the "same thing" can be said to a will of the other sort, a holy will; i.e., the "same thing," the same type of behavior, can be said to such a will to be a good thing. Extricating ourselves from this Kantian dramaturgy, the morally good things that we are obligated to do can perfectly well have the status for God of morally good things to do, even though He is not *obliged* to do them.[12] Justice, mercy, and lovingness can be moral virtues for God as well as for humans, though in His case without the extra dimension added to our virtues by the fact that exhibiting them involves satisfying our obligations. Some of God's moral goodness can be supervenient on the same behavior or tendencies on which, in us, satisfaction of moral obligations as well as moral goodness is supervenient. It can be morally good, both for God and humans, to act with loving concern for others, but only we have the privilege of being morally obliged to act in this way.[13]

Since we can develop a satisfactory conception of the moral goodness of God without thinking of God as having moral obligations, we can also escape the arbitrariness objection to divine command ethics. So far from being arbitrary, God's commands to us are an expression of His perfect goodness. Since He is perfectly good by nature, it is impossible that God should command us to act in ways that are not for the best. What if God should command us to sacrifice everything for the acquisition of power? (We are assuming that this is not for the best.) Would it thereby be our moral obligation? Since, on our present assumptions, it is metaphysically impossible for God to command this, the answer to the question depends on how it is best to handle subjunctive conditionals with impossible antecedents. But whatever our logic of subjunctive conditionals, this is not a substantive difficulty just because there is no possibility of the truth of the antecedent.

To help nail down the point, let's consider another form of the arbitrariness objection, that on the divine command theory God could have no reason, or at least no moral reason, for issuing the commands He does issue. Now if it is ruled that the only thing that counts as a moral reason for issuing a command to S to do A is that S morally ought to do A, or has a moral duty or obligation to do A, then God cannot have a moral reason for His commands on a divine command ethics. Since S has a moral obligation to do A only in virtue of God's command to do A, this is not a fact, antecedent to the command, that God could take as a reason for issuing the command. But surely there can be other sorts of moral reasons for commands and injunctions, e.g., that an act would be repaying of a kindness or that it is a morally good thing to behave in a certain way. More generally the moral goodness of doing *A,* or anything on which that moral goodness supervenes, can be a moral reason for doing *A* or for requiring someone to do *A.* Thus if the moral goodness of acts is independent of their obligatoriness, God can have moral reasons for His commands.

IV

Thus the divine command theorist escapes the supposedly fatal consequences of the first horn of the Euthyphro dilemma. But perhaps the maneuvers by which this escape was negotiated result in impalement on the second horn. We evaded the first horn by taking God's moral goodness, including the moral goodness of divine actions, not to be constituted by conformity to moral obligations, and hence not to be constituted by conformity to divine commands, even on this ethical theory.[14] But doesn't that leave us exposed to the second horn? We are not confronted with that horn in the original form, "God commands us to love our neighbors because that is what we ought to do," but with a closely analogous form, "God commands us to love our neighbor because it is morally good that we should do so." And that possesses the sort of feature deemed repellent to theism just as much as the first form, viz., that it makes the goodness of states of affairs independent of the divine will, thereby subjecting God to valuational facts that are what they are independent of Him. It thereby contradicts the absolute sovereignty of God; it implies that there are realities other than Himself that do not owe their being to His creative activity. If it is true, independently of God's will, that loving communion is a supreme good, and that forgiveness is better than resentment, then God is subject to these truths. He must conform Himself to them and so is not absolutely sovereign.

One way of meeting this objection is to assimilate evaluative principles to logical truths. If evaluative principles are logically necessary, then God's "subjection" to these principles is just a special case of His "subjection" to logical truths, something that is acknowledged on almost all hands.

However I am going to suggest a more radical response. The

difficulty with this horn of the dilemma is generally stated as I just stated it, in terms of a Platonic conception of the objectivity of goodness and other normative and evaluative statuses. If it is an objective fact that X is good, this is because there are objectively true general principles that specify the conditions under which something is good (the features on which goodness supervenes) and S satisfies these conditions. To go back to the *Euthyphro*:

> Socrates: Remember that I did not ask you to give me two or three examples of piety, but to explain the general idea which makes all pious things to be pious. . . . Tell me what is the nature of this idea, and then I shall have a standard to which I may look, and by which I may measure actions, whether yours or those of anyone else, and then I shall be able to say that such and such an action is pious, such another impious. [6]

What is ultimate here is the truth of the general principle; any particular example of goodness has that status only because it conforms to the general "Idea."

I want to suggest, by contrast, that we can think of God Himself, the individual being, as the supreme standard of goodness. God plays the role in evaluation that is more usually assigned, by objectivists about value, to Platonic Ideas or principles. Lovingness is good (a good-making feature, that on which goodness supervenes) not because of the Platonic existence of a general principle, but because God, the supreme standard of goodness, is loving. Goodness supervenes on every feature of God, not because some general principles are true but just because they are features of God. Of course, we can have general principles, e.g., "lovingness is good." But this principle is not ultimate; it, or the general fact that makes it true, does not enjoy some Platonic ontological status; rather it is true just because the property it specifies as sufficient for goodness is a property of God.

We can distinguish (a) "Platonic" predicates, the criterion for the application of each of which is an "essence" or "Idea" that can be specified in purely general terms, and (b) "particularistic" predicates, the criterion for the application of each of which makes essential reference to one or more individuals. Geometrical terms like 'triangle' have traditionally been taken as paradigms of the former. There are rather different subclasses of the latter. It is plausible to suggest, e.g., that biological kind terms like 'dog' are applied not on the basis of a list of defining properties but on the basis of similarity to certain standard examples. Putnam has extended this idea to natural kind terms generally. Again, there are "family resemblance" terms like 'game' or 'religion', the application of which again seems to rely on standard paradigm cases. A subtype closer to our present concern is the much discussed 'meter'. Let's say that what makes a certain length a meter is its equality to a standard meter stick kept in Paris. What makes this table a meter in length is not its conformity to a Platonic essence but its conformity to a certain existing individual.[15] Similarly, on the present view, what ultimately makes an act of love a good thing is not its conformity to some general principle but its conformity to, or approximation to, God, Who is both the ultimate source of the existence of things and the supreme standard by reference to which they are to be assessed.

Note that on this view we are not debarred from saying what is supremely good about God. It is not that God is good *qua* bare particular or undifferentiated thisness. God is good by virtue of being loving, just, merciful, etc. Where this view differs from its alternative is in the answer to the question, "By virtue of what are these features of God good-making features?" The answer given by this view is: "By virtue of being features of God."

It may help to appreciate the difference of this view from the more usual valuational objectivism if we contrast the ways in which these views will understand God's (perfectly good) activity. On a Platonic view God will "consult" the objective principles of goodness, whether they are "located" in His intellect or in a more authentically Platonic realm, and see to it that His actions conform thereto. On my particularist view God will simply act as He is inclined to act, will simply act in accordance with His character, and that will necessarily be the best. No preliminary stage of checking the relevant principles is required.

My particularistic suggestion exhibits some instructive similarities and dissimilarities to a recent deployment by Eleonore Stump and Norman Kretzmann of the doctrine of divine simplicity in connection with the Euthyphro dilemma.[16] In terms of the contrast I have been drawing, they use the doctrine of simplicity to show that one can be both Platonistic and particularistic about value. They do not deny that God is perfectly good by virtue of conforming to perfect goodness, but they avoid subjecting God to an independent reality by maintaining, in accordance with the doctrine of simplicity, that God *is* perfect goodness. Thus the supreme standard of goodness is both perfect goodness, the Platonic Idea, and God Himself. As Kretzmann once put it to me in conversation, the really staggering fact is that the Idea of the Good is a person. Since I have difficulties with the doctrine of simplicity I have felt forced to choose between Platonism and particularism; but I agree with Stump and Kretzmann that God can be perfectly good in an eminently non-arbitrary sense without being subject to some independent standard.

I will briefly consider two objections to my valuational particularism. First, it may seem that it is infected with the arbitrariness we have been concerned to avoid. Isn't it arbitrary to take some particular individual, even the supreme individual, as the *standard* of goodness, regardless of whether this individual conforms to general principles of goodness or not? To put it another way, if we want to know what is good about a certain action or human being, or if we want to know why that action or human being is good, does it throw any light on the matter to pick out some other individual being and say that the first is good because it is like the second? That is not advancing the inquiry. But this objection amounts to no more than an expression of Platonist predilections. One may as well ask: "How can it be an answer to the question 'Why is this table a meter long?' to cite its coincidence with the standard meter stick?" There just are some properties that work that way. My suggestion is that goodness is one of those properties, and it is no objection to this suggestion to aver that it is not.

Here is another response to the objection. Whether we are Platonist or particularist there will be some stopping place in the search for explanation. An answer to the question "What is good about X?" will cite certain alleged good-making characteristics. We can then ask: "By virtue of what does good supervene on those characteristics?" The answer to that might involve citing the relation of those features to other alleged good-making characteristics. But sooner or later either a general principle or an individual paradigm is cited. Whichever it is, that is the end of the line. (We can, of course, ask why we should suppose that this principle is true or that this individual is a paradigm; but that is a different inquiry.) On both views something is taken as ultimate, behind which we cannot go,

in the sense of finding some *explanation* of the fact that it is constitutive of goodness, as contrasted with a defense of the claim that
it is constitutive of goodness. I would invite one who finds it arbitrary to invoke God as the supreme standard of goodness to explain
why this is more arbitrary than the invocation of a supreme general
principle. Perhaps the principle seems self-evidently true to him. But
it will not seem so to many others; and it seems self-evident to some
that God is the supreme standard. And just as my opponent will
explain the opposition to his claims of self-evidence by saying that
the opponents have not considered the matter sufficiently, in an im-
partial frame of mind or whatever, so the theistic particularist can
maintain that those who do not acknowledge God as the supreme
standard are insufficiently acquainted with God or have not sufficiently considered the matter.

Secondly, it may be objected that, on theistic particularism,
in order to have any knowledge of what is good we would have to
know quite a bit about God. But many people who know little or
nothing about God know quite a bit about what is good. The answer to this is that the view does not have the alleged epistemological implications. It does have some epistemological implications. It
implies that knowing about the nature of God puts us in an ideal
position to make evaluative judgments. But it does not imply that
explicit knowledge of God is the only sound basis for such judgments. The particularist is free to recognize that God has so constructed us and our environment that we are led to form sound value
judgments under various circumstances without tracing them back
to the ultimate standard. Analogously, we are so constructed and
so situated as to be able to form true and useful opinions about water
without getting so far as to discern its ultimate chemical or physical
constitution, without knowing what makes it water.

As a final note on particularism, I should like to point out its
connection with certain familiar themes, both Christian and otherwise. It is a truism of what we might call "evaluational development" (of which moral development is a species) that we more often
come to recognize and appreciate good-making properties through
acquaintance with specially striking exemplifications than through
being explicitly instructed in general principles. We acquire standards in art, music, and literature, through becoming intimately familiar with great works in those media; with that background we

are often able to make confident judgments on newly encountered works without being able to formulate general principles on which we are relying. Our effective internalization of moral standards is more often due to our interaction with suitable role models than to reflecting on general moral maxims. The specifically Christian version of this is that we come to learn the supreme value of love, forgiveness, and self-sacrifice by seeing these qualities exemplified in the life of Christ, rather than by an intellectual intuition of Platonic Forms. I do not mean to *identify* these points about our access to the good with the particularist theory as to what it is that makes certain things good. They are clearly distinguishable matters. But I do suggest that a full realization of how much we rely on paradigms in developing and shaping our capacities to recognize goodness will render us disposed to take seriously the suggestion that the supreme standard of goodness is an individual paradigm.

V

This completes my suggestions to the divine command theorist as to how she can avoid the allegedly fatal consequences of both horns of the Euthyphro-like dilemma we have been considering. It only remains to set out explicitly the relationship between the positions I have suggested to escape each of the two horns. That relationship derives from the distinction between value and obligation, more specifically the moral forms thereof. To blunt the first horn I have suggested that we take divine commands to be constitutive only of moral obligation, only of facts of the form 'S morally ought to do A', 'S morally ought not to do B', and 'S is morally permitted to do C', leaving value and goodness, moral and otherwise, to be otherwise constituted. When we combine this point with the view that God is not subject to obligations, moral or otherwise, we find that the theory does not saddle us with an inadequate conception of divine moral goodness and hence that it does not represent the basis of human moral obligation as arbitrary. To deal with the second horn, and to fill out the view with an account of goodness and value, we take it that the supreme standard of goodness, including moral goodness, is God Himself, that particular individual, rather than some general principle or Platonic Idea. A creaturely X has value to the extent that it imitates or approximates the divine nature in a way appropriate to its position in creation. This is the most general account of value (as contrasted with obligation) for any sort of value, including the moral goodness of persons, motives, and actions. My visiting a sick friend is a good thing to do because and only because it constitutes an imitation of the divine nature that is appropriate for me and my current situation. But that leaves untouched the question of whether I *ought* to do this, whether it is my *duty* or *obligation,* whether I am *required* or *bound* to do it, whether I would be *culpable, guilty, blameworthy, or reprehensible* for failing to do it. This, according to the view here developed, is a matter of whether God has commanded me to do it, or whether my doing it follows from something God has commanded.[17] The divine *nature,* apart from anything God has willed or done, is sufficient to determine what counts as good, including morally good. But we are *obliged, bound,* or *required* to do something only on the basis of a divine command.

This then is my suggestion as to how to recognize a fundamental role for divine commands in morality without being impaled on one or another horn of a Euthyphro-like dilemma. I have not shown, or even argued, that divine commands *are* constitutive of moral obligation; nor have I entered into the question of how they could be. I have merely aspired to develop a view of God, morality, and value that leaves open the possibility that they should play this role.[18]

NOTES

1. *Journal of Religious Ethics* 7, no. 1 (1979).
2. Ibid., p. 76.
3. So long as the "criterion" for the application of a term is not determined by the meaning of the term.
4. It would be even less productive to cite differences between the content of divine and human moral goodness. No doubt there are numerous and important differences. Divine virtues do not include obedience to God, temperance in eating, and refraining from coveting one's neighbor's wife. But as the last sentence in the text indicates, there is an overlap too. And even if there were no overlap in content it would still be possible that that by virtue of which X is morally good is the same for God and for humans.
5. I shall not argue for this. Indeed, it is no part of my aim in this paper to establish the positions I am recommending to the divine command

theorist. I aspire only to exhibit them as plausible, and to show how they strengthen the theory.

6. See Bruce R. Reichenbach, *Evil and a Good God* (New York: Fordham University Press, 1982), chap. 7; Thomas V. Morris, "Duty and Divine Goodness," *American Philosophical Quarterly* 21, no. 3 (July 1984).

7. *Philosophical Investigations,* trans. G. E. M. Anscombe (Oxford: Basil Blackwell, 1953), I: 246.

8. Of course, if we adopt a non-cognitive interpretation of ought judgments, according to which their meaning is exhausted by their role in prescribing, exhorting, enjoining, etc., and according to which they are not used in the making of truth claims, then we will hold that there can be no truths about what one ought to do, independently of the appropriateness of performing acts of enjoining and the like. The applicability of the terms, in that case, hangs solely on the appropriateness of speech acts like exhorting. But our entire discussion presupposes an objectivist account of morality. Otherwise the question to which the divine command theory is an answer, viz., "In what does a moral obligation to do *A* consist?" would not arise.

9. There are medieval precedents, and I am indebted to Rega Wood for calling them to my attention. See William of Ockham, *Quest. in II Sent.,* qqs. 15, 19; Duns Scotus, *Opus Oxon.,* IV, d. 46, q. 1, n. 1; Peter Lombard, *Sent.,* I, d. 43, c. unicum. A particularly clear formulation is found in Nathaniel Culverwell, *An Elegant and Learned Discourse of the Light of Nature,* ch. 6; reprinted in *Divine Command Morality: Historical and Contemporary Readings,* ed. Janine Marie Idziak (New York and Toronto: Edwin Mellen Press, 1979).

10. *Foundations of the Metaphysics of Morals,* trans. Lewis White Beck (New York: Liberal Arts Press, 1959), pp. 29–31. For some contemporary endorsements of this position see A. C. Ewing, *The Definition of Good* (London: Routledge & Kegan Paul, 1948), p. 123; and Geoffrey J. Warnock, *The Object of Morality* (London: Methuen, 1971), p. 14.

11. This applies most directly to principles *requiring* actions, but interdictions can be expressed in terms of 'ought not', and permissions in terms of 'not ought not'.

12. I am, of course, not suggesting that the content of human and divine morality are exactly the same! I am only pointing out that the absence of divine obligations does not prevent an overlap.

13. See Morris, "Duty and Divine Goodness," sections III and IV, for another affirmation of this point.

14. The same considerations will lead to taking divine goodness to be independent of all divine volition. For if God's being good is a matter of His carrying out what He wills (rather than commands), the arbitrariness objection applies in full force. And divine goodness again becomes trivialized as "God carries out His volitions, whatever they are."

15. To be sure, it is arbitrary what particular stick was chosen to serve as the standard, while I am not thinking that it is arbitrary whether God or someone else is "chosen" as the supreme standard of goodness. That is a way

in which the analogy is not perfect. The example was used because of the respect in which there is an analogy, viz., the role of the individual standard in truth conditions for applications of the term.

16. "Absolute Simplicity," *Faith and Philosophy* 2, no. 4 (Oct., 1985), pp. 375–76. For a more extended presentation of the same idea see Norman Kretzmann, "Abraham, Isaac, and Euthyphro: God and the Basis of Morality," in *Hamartia, The Concept of Error in the Western Tradition: Essays in Honor of John M. Crossett,* ed. D. V. Stump, E. Stump, J. A. Arieti, and L. Gerson (New York and Toronto: Edwin Mellen Press, 1983).

17. I don't mean to restrict this "following" to deductive implication. It also includes, e.g., being a reasonable application of some general command issued by God.

18. Earlier versions of this paper were presented at the Pacific Regional Meetings of the Society of Christian Philosophers, at Cornell University, and at meetings of the Society for Philosophy of Religion. I would like to thank participants in all those sessions for many useful suggestions. Special thanks go to Robert Adams, Jonathan Bennett, Norman Kretzmann, Louis Pojman, John Robertson, Richard Swinburne, Eleonore Stump, Stewart Thau, and Linda Zagzebski.

Egoistic Rationalism:
Aquinas's Basis for Christian Morality

SCOTT MACDONALD

Recent Christian philosophers interested in the foundations of Christian morality have been preoccupied with formulating a divine command metaethics (DCM) and defending it against the well-known, deep difficulties it faces.[1] This seems to me a puzzling preoccupation since there is nothing in Scripture or the Christian tradition that constrains a Christian to hold such a metaethics. Of course there is a great deal in the Christian tradition to justify the view that divine commands provide much of the *content* of Christian morality, but this by itself is no reason for thinking that when a Christian uses the word 'right' she means 'commanded by God (or a loving God)' or that the rightness of the acts commanded consists in their being commanded by God (or a loving God).

Not only does the Christian tradition not require a DCM, the greater part of the Christian *philosophical* tradition has actually eschewed it. For well over a thousand years Greek philosophy provided the framework for the philosophical understanding of the foundations of Christian morality, and the Greek ethical tradition, founded by Socrates, shows no sympathy for a DCM. It favors instead a sort of rationalist foundation for morality. Aquinas, for instance, maintains that divine commands (the moral precepts of divine law) are an expression of divine reason.

> [L]aw is a kind of rule and measure of acts . . . but the rule and measure of human acts is reason, which is the first principle of human acts. . . . Thus it follows that law is something having to do with reason. (*ST* IaIIae.90.1) Those morals (*mores*) which agree with

327

reason are called good and those which are discordant with reason
are called bad since human morals are called [good or bad] by their
relation to reason, which is the proper principle of human acts. (*ST*
IaIIae.100.1)

According to Aquinas, then, an act is not made morally right by
its having been commanded by God; it is morally right, and the law
which commands it is morally good, in virtue of its being in accordance with reason.

But with regard to the things that are commanded, the will must be
regulated by reason if it is to have the nature (*rationem*) of law. And
one should understand the claim that the will of a ruler has the force
of law as qualified in this way, otherwise the will of a ruler would
be wickedness (*iniquitas*) rather than law. (*ST* IaIIae.90.1.ad3)

In this paper I'm going to argue that the Greek ethical tradition as represented by Aquinas offers an alternative to a DCM worth
more careful attention from Christian philosophers. My argument
consists in three contentions. First, I'll argue that Aquinas's metaethics is plausible in its own right, and I'll support this contention
simply by sketching (in sections 1 through 3) the main outlines of
Aquinas's metaethics. This sketch will not amount to a complete
defense of Aquinas's metaethical views, but I hope that Christian
philosophers who agree with me about its plausibility will turn to
the details of such a defense.

My second main contention is that Aquinas's understanding
of Christian morality on the basis provided by his metaethics re-
solves certain difficulties often associated with rationalist varieties
of religious morality. From the theist's point of view the central objection to rationalist accounts of religious morality is that they seem
to provide no essential connection between God and morality. In
section 4 I'll look at the connection between the fundamentally naturalistic metaethical theory developed in sections 1 through 3, on the
one hand, and God and divine commands, on the other. I will argue
that Aquinas's rationalism has more resources for understanding the
relation between God and human morality than is usually allowed
the rationalist. It is often supposed, for instance, that the rationalist
must hold that divine commands should be obeyed only when they
are independently acceptable to human reason and that the human

agent sacrifices his moral autonomy when he obeys a divine command not independently sanctioned by his reason. Aquinas denies both of these claims, and his reasons for denying them illuminate interesting ways in which human morality is dependent on God.

My third contention is that Aquinas's views provide a theoretical account of certain features central to a Christian understanding of the moral life. In section 5 I draw attention to these features and argue that the Christian ought to find Aquinas's rationalism not only a plausible but an attractive basis for Christian morality.

I should say at the outset that I will not explicitly take up the two topics that nearly all recent discussions of religious morality focus on, viz., Euthyphro's dilemma and God's command to Abraham to sacrifice Isaac.[2] The features of Aquinas's metaethical position on which I focus do not by themselves resolve either Euthyphro's philosophical or Abraham's moral dilemma, though they provide resources that will be useful in considering them.

1. METAPHYSICS AND METAETHICS: AQUINAS'S NATURAL TELEOLOGY

In the Greek ethical tradition as represented by Aquinas, rationalism is linked with a kind of universal teleology. Aquinas claims, for instance, that everything seeks its own perfection.[3] He intends this as a perfectly general claim since by 'everything' he means not just all human beings or sentient creatures but all natural substances. When applied to a particular sort of natural substance, human beings, i.e., moral agents, this general claim becomes a part of Aquinas's metaethics, but strictly speaking it is part of his metaphysics, and we need to start there if we're to understand the metaethical claim.

According to Aquinas, a species of natural substances is indicated by their performing a particular kind of activity. Substances of species S are members of S by virtue of having the capacity for performing the activity characteristic of Ss.[4] A particular substance's substantial form is the ontological ground of that capacity; Aquinas calls this ontological ground the substance's first actuality.[5] Thus, in virtue of its substantial form a substance has a specific set of powers and potentialities which constitute its capacity for performing its characteristic activity. For a substance to exercise its specific powers and actualize its specific potentialities is for it to perform its characteristic activity. Aquinas calls the state in which a substance has actualized its specific potentialities the substance's second or final actuality.[6]

On Aquinas's view, the actualities or properties which constitute a substance's final actuality are accidental characteristics.[7] A substance has a given essence in virtue of having a substantial form, so its essential characteristics are only those it has in virtue of having its substantial form, viz., its specific powers and potentialities. But the actualities corresponding to these powers and potentialities are ontologically posterior to the powers themselves, and it is a contingent matter whether a particular substance possesses all of them. Thus, in order to achieve final actuality a substance must acquire a certain set of accidental characteristics. But though these actualities are a substance's accidental characteristics, they form a special subset of its accidental characteristics because they are related in a determinate way to the substance's essence. They are the actualities corresponding to the powers and potentialities which constitute the substance's essence.

Now Aquinas maintains that a substance is completed or perfected as a thing of its species when it has achieved its final actuality.[8] So when he claims that everything seeks its own perfection he means that all natural substances seek their final actuality. Aquinas's reasons for identifying a thing's perfection with its final actuality become clear when it is understood that by 'perfect' he means 'fully actual' or 'complete'. When a substance is in a state of final actuality, when it is exercising the powers and has actualized the potentialities that belong to it by virtue of its being the kind of thing it is, it is completed in the sense that it is fully actual as a thing of its kind; none of its specifying potentialities remain unactualized.[9] So in this primarily ontological sense, a substance's state of final actuality is its state of full actuality, completion, or perfection.

Now, in what sense does Aquinas think natural substances 'seek' their own perfection? Since he thinks that the general teleological claim applies to stones and plants as well as to brute animals and human beings, he cannot think that the sort of seeking at issue requires the formulation of an intention or even consciousness. He thinks that natural substances are endowed with natural inclinations or tendencies, which he calls *appetitus*. Stones, for example, 'seek' their natural place in the sense that they have a natural inclination to fall, and plants exhibit a natural tendency to grow to maturity (by securing appropriate nutrients and environmental conditions) and to reproduce. The natural inclinations of brute animals and human beings, on the other hand, are manifested not only in certain biological tendencies that they share with plants but also in their instinctive behavior—instinctive pursuit and avoidance behavior aimed at survival, for instance—and in conscious end-directed activity.[10] For Aquinas, then, the claim that everything seeks its own perfection is the claim that every natural substance is endowed with a natural inclination directed toward its own completed state or final actuality. The nature of this natural inclination varies with the sort of nature under consideration, and so the sort of 'behavior' expressive of this inclination will be quite different in different kinds of substances.

It is important to see the conceptual link between Aquinas's understanding of a substance's nature as consisting of a set of powers and potentialities and his view of natural inclinations. A substance's natural inclinations are its inclinations toward the exercise and actualization of its specific powers and potentialities. An animal, for example, whose substantial form includes among other things power of perception and local motion, has a natural tendency to exercise those powers and to use them in aid of obtaining food and avoiding harm. Aquinas's metaphysics and natural teleology are two sides of one coin.[11]

Aquinas's claim that everything seeks its own perfection, then, expresses some of the central features of his metaphysics: natural substances, in virtue of their substantial forms (their first actuality), are in potentiality in certain respects and are thereby naturally inclined toward actualizing those potentialities (their final actuality).

What I'm going to call Aquinas's metaethical egoism—his claim that human beings seek their own perfection—is merely a particular instance of his general metaphysical view. Human beings are natural substances whose characteristic activity is determined by their substantial form. The substantial form of a human being, its soul, provides it with the capacity for living, and since what specifies a human soul as human is its being rational, it provides the human being with a capacity for living a paradigmatically human life, that is, a capacity for living in accordance with reason. In virtue of possessing a rational soul a human being is endowed with a complex set of powers and potentialities, including perceptual and intellectual powers, directed toward living rationally. By virtue of possessing these powers and potentialities a human being is naturally inclined toward their actualization, the human being's final actuality. Aquinas calls this natural inclination in human beings rational appetite or will.[12] He calls a human being's state of final actuality its ultimate end, happiness, or the human good.[13]

Thus, Aquinas's natural teleology applied to human beings appears to yield a sort of psychological egoism. According to Aquinas, a human being naturally pursues (wills) its perfection or good (the human good) in virtue of the sort of soul (psyche) it has. He takes the sort of willing in question to be a natural inclination and, hence, to be naturally necessitated.[14] Moreover, it seems natural to assume that what perfects a human being or what a human being's good consists in is what is in that human being's interest. Hence, Aquinas's claim can be reformulated as the claim that human beings always pursue their own interest as a matter of psychological necessity.

Though Aquinas endorses a claim of this sort, he thinks it requires substantial qualification. I think that in the end Aquinas's view is considerably different from the views of modern proponents of psychological egoism, and so I think it is not open to the common objections to modern psychological egoism.[15] But even so it might seem that no metaethics incorporating a psychological egoism of any kind could be a candidate for a Christian metaethics, since Christian morality seems to require altruistic concerns that go beyond those of even the most enlightened egoism. I think Aquinas's egoism can accommodate Christianity's apparent altruism, but we will have to look more closely at his moral psychology to see how.

2. INTELLECT AND WILL: THE WAY IN WHICH HUMAN BEINGS SEEK THE GOOD

The rational soul provides a human being with both cognitive and appetitive powers—intellect and will—and Aquinas's understanding of the relations between these powers requires us to qualify the egoistic claim in important ways. On the one hand, Aquinas's conception of the relation between intellect and will provides an account of the ways in which human willing is necessitated and the ways in which it remains free. This account, which I'll develop in this section, is crucial for understanding Aquinas's egoism. On the other hand, his conception of the human being as possessing intellect is the basis for a careful characterization of the nature of the good that human beings seek, which I'll introduce in this section and develop further in the next.

According to Aquinas's metaphysics, the sort of seeking the egoistic claim attributes to human beings is a natural inclination toward the human good. This natural inclination is the will. But the will does not seek the human good as such; since the will is an appetite belonging to a rational soul, it seeks the human good *as it is conceived by intellect*.[16] Will, as rational appetite, can act only when it is presented with an object by intellect; intellect apprehends an object as good, and will's proper object is the good apprehended by intellect. Now, activity properly characteristic of human beings as such is activity arising from the rational soul; hence, paradigmatic human activity is activity arising from this interrelationship between intellect and will.

Aquinas calls actions arising from intellect and will 'voluntary actions', and so he takes voluntariness to be a distinctive characteristic of human actions.[17] For an action A performed by agent S to be voluntary in the strict sense, the following conditions must be met: (1) the proximate sources of A are internal to S, (2) S apprehends some end E and performs A for the sake of E, (3) S has cognition of the concept of an end, and (4) S has cognition of the relation between E itself and that which is ordered toward E.[18] Aquinas allows that certain behavior of brute animals satisfies conditions (1) and (2), but (3) and (4) are restrictions which only actions of a rational agent can meet.

Only the actions of creatures possessing intellect can satisfy conditions (3) and (4) because these conditions require that an agent be capable of certain sorts of universal considerations available only to creatures with intellect.

The object of the will is the end and the good universally (*in universali*). Hence, there cannot be will in things that lack reason and in-

tellect since they cannot apprehend the universal; but there is in them
a natural or sense appetite determined to some particular good. (*ST*
IaIIae.1.2.ad3)[19]

The souls of brute animals provide them with certain cognitive
powers — powers of sense perception and a faculty of instinctual judgment called the estimative power — and appetitive powers which follow
sense perception. Hence, the dog that digs up a bone in the garden
can perceive the bone, judge it to be a good, and engage in action
aimed at obtaining it. But according to Aquinas, sense perception
is limited to what is particular and, as a consequence, the content
of the dog's perception and judgment are particular. The dog's appetite is determined to this particular good.

 In virtue of possessing intellect, however, human beings can
apprehend universally and hence can apprehend the universal good.
An account of human willing, then, must take into account intellect's ability to present the universal good to will as its object. But
what does Aquinas mean by 'the universal good'?

 Considerations involving the universal good play at least three
distinguishable though closely related roles in Aquinas's moral psychology, and it will be worth keeping them apart. A rational creature's ability to apprehend the universal good (a) implies the rational
creature's possession of a purely formal concept of the good, (b)
implies the rational creature's possession of a general conception of
what it is that instantiates the good, and (c) gives the rational creature reason to will the common good. (a) and (b) are directly relevant to Aquinas's account of voluntary action, so I'll take them up
first and return to (c) in the next section.

 Consider a case superficially similar to the case of the dog's
digging up a bone in the garden: a woman's getting up from her
armchair to get a candy bar out of the kitchen cupboard. As a result
of the woman's ability to apprehend the universal good, the correct
description of this case might be quite different from the correct
description of the case of the dog's digging up the bone. First, though
the woman may act so as to obtain the candy bar in a quasi-instinctive
way, she may also reflect on her particular judgment that the candy
bar is a good, and such reflection might involve her considering her
belief that the candy bar falls under her concept of the good. This
sort of reflection requires that she have a purely formal or abstract,

universal concept of the good. Such purely formal concepts needn't be very sophisticated; Aquinas thinks, for example, that the concept of the good is the concept of what is desirable and the concept of the complete human good, happiness, is the concept of what completely satisfies human desires.[20] Only creatures with intellect possess purely formal, universal concepts of this sort.

At least part of what Aquinas means by condition (3) above, then, is that in order for an action to be voluntary in the strict sense it is necessary that the agent not only act for an end but also be aware of what an end or a good is.

Second, the woman's judgment that the candy bar is good might be guided by her other judgments about what is good, by her long- and short-term intentions and plans. That is, she might attempt to coordinate her desires, judgments, and intentions with respect to the candy bar into some overall, general plan. An overall plan of this sort might be thought of as a general or universal conception of the good, not in the sense that it is purely formal but in the sense that it is broad in scope. Only creatures with intellect can formulate such general conceptions or plans. Such plans will typically be general both synchronically, coordinating a range of present desires and intentions, and diachronically, coordinating present desires and intentions into an overall plan of life. Presumably, a perfectly rational being's general plan will extend to all aspects of her life over the whole course of her life, constituting a conception of a complete, best life.[21]

This is the other part of what Aquinas has in mind in condition (3). In order for an action to be voluntary in the strict sense it is necessary that the agent not only act for an end but also view that end in light of its other immediate and overarching ends, in effect viewing it as part of a more general plan.[22] A human being's ability to guide its actions by considerations of a general plan of the sort I have just sketched is also the basis for condition (4). The woman's ability to view present action as fitting into an overall plan is just the ability to view present ends as ordered toward further ends, either as means to other ends contained in the plan or as particular ways of achieving ends included in but left indeterminate by the plan.[23]

So the intellect apprehends a universal or general good in at least these two different senses: in forming a purely formal concept of the good and in formulating a general, overall plan intended to realize the good. These two different senses of universal or general good are parts of two different distinctions important to Aquinas's account. On the one hand, the good that is universal in the sense of being purely formal is to be distinguished from the concrete or material instantiation of that concept.[24] Aquinas thinks that the formal concept of the complete human good is the concept of the ultimate end, happiness, or the best life. Such a concept is clearly purely formal and uninformative in the sense that it tells one nothing about what constitutes a human being's ultimate end or what life is in fact the best life. Any answer to the question "What does a human being's ultimate end consist in?" or "What sort of life is the best life for a human being?" would be an attempt to say what thing, state of affairs, or sort of life actually instantiates the formal concept of the human good.[25] The first distinction, then, is between a purely formal concept of the good and the thing, activity, or state of affairs which is its concrete instantiation.

On the other hand, the good that is universal in the sense of being an overall plan is itself (a conception of) a general concrete instantiation of the purely formal concept of the good and is to be distinguished from more particular, determinate specifications which are (conceptions of) relatively less general concrete instantiations of the purely formal concept of the good. To hold the view that the life of political power is in fact the best life, for instance, would be to possess a universal conception of the good in this sense, and such a universal conception contrasts with a particular conception which specifies the particular ways in which one intends to lead a life of political power.[26] The second distinction, then, is between a concrete instantiation that is relatively general and one that is relatively determinate.

Thus far I have argued that Aquinas thinks that the possession of intellect explains two important features of practical reasoning: a human being's ability to formulate and use a purely formal, universal concept of the good and its ability to formulate and use more or less general plans, and that Aquinas takes the exercise of these two abilities by an agent as necessary conditions for the voluntariness of the agent's action. But even if one grants that the features Aquinas calls attention to are in fact important features of practical reasoning, why should one take them to be essential to voluntariness?

Aquinas takes these two features of practical reasoning to be necessary for voluntariness because he takes freedom of choice to be essential to voluntariness and he thinks that human freedom is rooted in these two features of practical reasoning. Aquinas thinks that the will is a natural inclination toward the good as conceived by intellect, and as a natural inclination it is naturally necessitated with respect to its proper object. Hence, the will wills the good, of necessity. Aquinas maintains, however, that the will's proper object is the good understood purely formally; that is, the will is necessitated with respect to whatever intellect takes to be the complete and perfect human good. But the intellect is not necessitated in taking any given putative concrete instantiation of the perfect good as the perfect good.[27] Hence, the will is not necessitated with respect to any given putative concrete instantiation of the human good.[28] A human being necessarily wills the best life and, given that its intellect conceives of the life of political power as the best life, necessarily wills the life of political power. But the intellect does not conceive of the best life in this way necessarily. So intellect's role in determining what the human good actually consists in is one root of the will's freedom.

The other root of the will's freedom is intellect's role in specifying or determining general plans. For instance, given one's general conception of the life of political power as the best human life, one needs to determine what particular political activities best constitute the exercise of political power, what means one might take to secure the positions associated with such activities, and so on. Because this one general plan — leading a life of political power — might be realized in more than one way — one might seek the presidency or seek to lead a revolution, one might start by going to law school or by organizing labor unions — the will is not necessitated with respect to such choices. Only when intellect conceives that there is just one way of attaining a given end is the will subject to a kind of necessity: if one wills the end, then one must will what one takes to be the only way of attaining it.[29]

Aquinas, then, thinks that freedom of choice is rooted in intellect's ability to determine (1) what the human good or ultimate end consists in and (ii) alternative specifications of and means for attaining that good. Aquinas calls this function of intellect deliberative reasoning, and thinks that freedom of choice is rooted in deliberative reasoning.[30] An action willed on the basis of deliberation has its sources within the agent in the fullest sense: it arises from the agent's will, acting on the basis of the agent's own reasons. Actions of this sort are voluntary in the strict sense.

So human agents are voluntary agents whose actions are characterized by this tight connection between will and intellect. Because human beings act on the basis of intellect-governed will, Aquinas says that they are masters of their own acts in a way no other natural creatures are; they are paradigmatically natural *self*-movers.[31] Aquinas's conception of human agency, then, includes a strong sense of autonomy. Paradigmatic human action is fully autonomous action, since it springs from the human being's own intellect and will.

This sketch of Aquinas's moral psychology puts us in a position to characterize Aquinas's metaethical egoism more precisely. When Aquinas claims that human beings naturally will their own ultimate end he means:

    (I)   Will is naturally necessitated to will the good conceived purely formally. This means that (a) the will is necessitated with respect to willing what intellect presents to it as the perfect good, ultimate end, or best life, and (b) that whatever the will wills it wills as good.

   (II) Intellect must determine what the perfect good actually consists in (hence, will is not necessitated to will any particular instantiation of the ultimate end).[32]

 (III) Intellect must determine how to achieve the particular instantiation of the ultimate end intended by deciding on a sufficiently determinate specification of it and means for achieving it (hence, will is not necessitated to particular subsidiary ends except where those are perceived to be necessary to the intended ultimate end).[33]

3. INTELLECT AND THE GOOD: THE GOOD THAT HUMAN BEINGS SEEK

I've argued that Aquinas thinks that the possession of intellect allows a human being to apprehend the good from a purely formal point of view and to form a general conception of a life exemplifying the good, but he also thinks that creatures with intellect can apprehend the common good, e.g., the good of the family or state. Hence, intellect apprehends a good that is universal in the sense of extending or being common to many people. Aquinas gives the example of a judge who must render his decisions on the basis of what is good for the community as a whole rather than on the basis of what is good for some individual, and he claims: "The will of some human being who wills some particular good is right only if he refers it to the common good as to an end. . . (*ST* IaIIae.19.10). This is because: right reason . . . judges that the common good is better than the good of one [human being] (*ST* IIaIIae.47.10). More-over, he claims that the more nearly universal (more common) the good, the better it is. Hence, the good of the individual, the fam-ily, the city, and the kingdom are different ends, the former more particular and hence to be subordinated to the latter, more com-mon ends.[34]

It may now seem that Aquinas's claim that creatures with in-tellect apprehend the universal good, when 'universal good' is taken to mean what these last few passages suggest, commits him to aban-doning any sort of metaethical egoism. The good which human be-ings seek by virtue of possessing a rational soul is not primarily their own individual good but the common good; human beings act not exclusively in their own interest but also in the common interest.

But I think one needn't draw this conclusion. Aquinas's remarks about the common good show not that human beings seek something other than their own interest but that their own interest is not nar-rowly individualistic. One might hold that by virtue of their possess-ing intellect human beings have an interest in a good that includes, perhaps even predominantly, the good of others. Hence, when hu-man beings seek the good of the family or the city they seek it as *part* of their own good.[35] Aquinas suggests this view in the follow-ing passage:

> [Happiness] is called a self-sufficient good not because it suffices merely for one human being living a solitary life but also for his parents, children, wife, friends, and fellow citizens, so that it will ade-quately provide the necessities in temporal matters and instruction and counsel in spiritual matters for them too. Such extension is re-quired because a human being is a social animal and its desire is not satisfied in providing for itself; instead, a human being wants to be in a position to take care of others. (*In X Eth. Nic.* Bk. I, L. IX, n. 112)

Aquinas seems to claim that a human being's own desires will remain unsatisfied, and hence its own good will remain unfulfilled, so long as the good of certain others remains unfulfilled. Hence, a human being's good, i.e., the ultimate end that a human being seeks, includes the good of certain others as constituent parts.

There is no clear reason why an egoism of this sort cannot account for the apparent altruistic concerns of Christian morality. Aquinas's egoism is compatible, for instance, with the demand to love one's neighbor and to be concerned about his good.

Now, given this egoistic framework tempered by Aquinas's conception of the relation between intellect and will and intellect's capacity for apprehending the universal good, we can get at the heart of his metaethics. Aquinas holds that human actions, properly so called, are those directed toward the human good, arising from intellect and will; these are actions arising from deliberative willing, or as Aquinas sometimes puts it: actions in accordance with reason.[36] But moral actions are actions resulting from deliberative willing, so moral actions and human actions, properly so called, are the same.[37] Hence, morally right action is action ordered correctly toward the attainment of the universal, perfect human good. Now, given the dual role of intellect in Aquinas's moral psychology (specified by (II) and (III) in section 2 above), a human action's being ordered correctly is a matter of intellect's (i) correctly apprehending the perfect good and (ii) correctly apprehending the relation between the given action and that perfect good.[38] Hence, moral rightness depends on intellect's success in executing its two roles in practical reasoning; or as Aquinas sometimes puts it: the morally right action is the action in accordance with right reason.[39]

4. HUMAN REASON AND DIVINE REASON

Almost everything I've said about Aquinas's metaethics so far could be put in a purely naturalistic framework, so any theological dimension of such a metaethics might appear to be an inessential addition. Moreover, any metaethics that holds that morality is essentially independent of God seems to have at least two consequences unacceptable to the Christian. First, if morality is independent of God, then God seems to be no different from any other moral agent in being subject to the demands of morality. This consequence conflicts with the Christian's belief in God's total independence or aseity since it implies that if God is morally good, he must depend on morality in making moral judgments and be influenced by the demands of morality in acting. Second, provided that human beings can know moral truths, the independence of morality from God implies that God is subject to human moral judgment and that the Christian who wants to be moral (and on a rationalist view, rational) will owe allegiance to two different things—God and morality. These consequences seem to conflict with the Christian's unqualified commitment to God. So it might appear that Aquinas's rationalist metaethics cannot provide an adequate foundation for Christian morality.

In order to see how Aquinas meets these difficulties I'm going to compare his view with that of (what I'll call) a humanistic rationalist. I'll argue that what the Christian has reason to find objectionable is humanistic rationalism and not rationalism as such. A humanistic rationalist believes that human reason is the sufficient and sole criterion of morally right action. According to this view all putative moral precepts, including divine commands, are morally acceptable only if they comply with the dictates of human reason, and the human agent sacrifices his moral autonomy if he acts against the dictates of his reason.[40] Aquinas is not a humanistic rationalist, and in order to see why, we need to look at his view of the relation between human and divine reason.

Aquinas holds that human beings are created in God's image and that human reason is an image of divine or eternal reason. He thinks that to the extent that human beings are capable of reason, they manifest the nature of the divine mind. "Human reason's being the rule of human will, by which [the will's] goodness is measured, derives from eternal law, which is divine reason" (ST IaIIae.19.4). Human reason is not only causally dependent on God but also fills the functional role in human life that divine reason fills in the divine life. In judging what is good and presenting the will with its object human reason's role is an image of the role of eternal law, which is divine reason.

Being a created image of divine reason involves not only being the functional analogue of divine reason but also being finite and in certain respects falling short of it. Human reason and divine reason are not merely different kinds of reason; the former is a necessarily incomplete manifestation of the latter, which is the paradigm of reason. Aquinas believes that human reason is an incomplete manifestation of divine reason in at least three respects relevant to moral theory. First, human reason falls short of divine reason in virtue of not extending to all the matters open to the view of divine reason. Hence, divine reason extends to some moral truths to which human reason cannot attain by its own power. Second, human reason falls short of divine reason in virtue of being subject to error. That is, human reason is subject to making mistaken moral judgments in cases in which it is capable of judging correctly. Third, human reason falls short of the divine in virtue of requiring sustained effort to attain many humanly attainable moral truths. Because of the effort required, human beings might take a long time to attain these moral truths or might never attain them (despite the fact that they are in principle attainable).[41]

So divine reason is the measure of human reason, and human reason falls short of divine reason in these ways. Now Aquinas argues that because divine reason is the measure of human reason, and reason is the measure of human actions, divine reason rather than human reason is the proper measure of human actions.

> In all causes ordered to one another, the effect depends more on the first cause than on a second cause since a second cause acts only in virtue of a first cause. . . . Hence it is clear that the goodness of the human will depends much more on the eternal law than on human reason, and when human reason fails we must have recourse to eternal reason. (*ST* IaIIae.19.4)

Hence, right reason is the measure of right action, and divine reason is the measure of right reason.

This much of Aquinas's view of the relation between divine and human reason is enough to show that Aquinas is not a humanistic rationalist. According to Aquinas, divine reason is the sufficient and sole criterion of morally right action; human reason shares incompletely in divine reason and so is neither the sufficient nor the sole criterion of morally right action.[42]

In Aquinas's view, one of the purposes of divine revelation is to remedy the shortcomings of human reason. In revelation God provides a supplement to human reason intended to allow it to measure up to the rule of divine reason.

> Although the eternal law is not known by us as it is in the divine
> mind, it is made known to us in certain ways, either through natural
> reason, which is derived from the divine mind as a proper image of
> it, or through some kind of revelation which is supplemental [to natu-
> ral reason]. (*ST* IaIIae.19.4.ad3)

The divine commands contained in Scripture are revealed expressions of divine reason added to human reason.[43] This supplement
to human reason remedies its shortcomings by revealing (i) certain
moral truths which are beyond the natural powers of human reason
and (ii) others which are within the natural power of human reason.
God reveals moral truths of type (i) because human reason could
not attain them apart from revelation; God reveals moral truths of
type (ii) despite the fact that they are in principle accessible to unaided human reason because unaided human reason is liable to err
or to find it difficult to attain them.[44] Thus, though unaided human
reason is not a sufficient criterion for morally right action, revelation provides human beings with access to divine law.

 This understanding of the nature of revealed divine law allows
that divine commands overlap considerably with moral judgments
available to unaided human reason. Aquinas's framework allows four
possible relations between a given divine command C and the dictates of the unaided reason of a given human agent S. (a) C might
command what S's unaided reason dictates independently. Aquinas
thinks the commands against stealing and murder (Exodus 20:13,
15), for example, are commands of this sort.[45] (b) C might command what S's unaided reason does not in fact dictate but in principle could dictate given enough time and effort. When this is the
case two possibilities arise: (b1) though S's unaided reason does not
dictate what C commands at the time at which he learns of C, S
subsequently discerns for himself the reason for C, or (b2) S never
discerns for himself the reason for C, though in principle he could.
(c) C might command what S's unaided reason does not and in principle could not dictate. Aquinas thinks that the command against
making graven images (Exodus 20:4), for example, is of this sort.[46]
(d) C might command what conflicts with the dictates of S's unaided reason. Aquinas maintains that when this is the case human
reason is faulty; C is an expression of divine reason, and it is impossible that right human reason contradict divine reason.[47]

Now, Aquinas maintains that in all the cases just listed S ought
to obey C. Hence, he thinks S ought to obey C not only when S's
unaided reason approves what C commands (whether antecedently
as in (a) or subsequently as in (b1)), but also when S's unaided reason neither approves nor disapproves it (as in (b2) and (c)), and even
when S's unaided reason disapproves what C commands (as in (d)).
I'm going to leave aside the other cases and focus on case (d), since
it would appear to be the most difficult case for Aquinas's view. Most
of Aquinas's examples of cases in which human reason might incorrectly dictate some particular action contrary to a divine command
involve the agent's misapplication of some general moral precept to
a particular case. An Israelite, for example, might have (incorrectly)
judged that to despoil the Egyptians during the flight from Egypt
would be an act of stealing and hence morally wrong; yet God commanded the Israelites despoil the Egyptians.[48] According to Aquinas, an Israelite with moral scruples regarding the despoilation would
have been mistaken in thinking that this particular action is an instance of theft; the goods to be taken from the Egyptians were not
their just possession, and so taking them would not constitute theft.

Let's follow Aquinas's example and let C be God's command
to the Israelites to despoil the Egyptians and S be some morally
scrupulous Israelite whose unaided reason dictates that he ought not
to despoil the Egyptians. Aquinas maintains that our imagined Israelite ought to despoil the Egyptians despite the fact that his own
moral reasoning independently dictates that he ought not. One might
object that at this point Aquinas has surely abandoned both his commitment to human moral autonomy and his rationalism. How can
he at once maintain his rationalist metaethics, the claim that S is
morally autonomous, and the view that S ought to obey the divine
command against the dictates of his own unaided reason?

Of course there is a clear sense in which what C commands
is in accordance with reason; it is in accordance with divine reason
even if not with human reason. So Aquinas can maintain a sort of
theological rationalism according to which the morally right action
is the action in accordance with divine reason, and then he can claim
that S ought to obey C because to obey C would be to act in accordance with divine reason. This unqualified theological rationalism
would salvage Aquinas's commitment to rationalism, but it does not
seem to salvage a sense of moral autonomy for the agent who obeys

divine commands in cases of this sort. The obedient agent still seems to obey the command while the only reasons available *to him* count against obeying it.

Aquinas, however, thinks that *S* himself does have reason for obeying the command, and so he thinks *S*'s moral autonomy can be preserved in cases of this sort. If *S* believes God to be a legitimate moral authority and that God has commanded *C*, then *S* can rationally act against the judgment of his unaided reason, which dictates action contrary to obeying *C*.[49] When he obeys *C* out of his belief that God is a legitimate moral authority and that God has commanded *C*, *S* has the reason for his action in himself and remains morally autonomous. In obeying the command *S* does what he believes is the right action, and his evidence for its rightness is its being commanded by God.[50] Of course this is a different sort of evidence than *S* has available in cases (a) and (b1), but it is still evidence and it can provide *S* with internal, autonomy-preserving reasons for obeying the divine command. Thus, the morally scrupulous Israelite who obeys the divine command to despoil the Egyptians because it is a divine command can remain morally autonomous.

The important question for this account, then, becomes whether or not the agent in cases of sort (d) can be justified in taking God to be a legitimate moral authority. There is some reason for thinking that such a belief cannot be justified in this case. One might argue that the judgment that God is a legitimate moral authority must depend on the prior judgment that God's actions and commands are morally right. This latter sort of judgment must be made solely on the basis of unaided human reason, because to invoke God's moral authority at this point would be to argue in a circle. But *ex hypothesi* in case (d) unaided human reason judges the action commanded by God to be morally wrong. Therefore in cases of sort (d) an agent cannot be justified in taking God as a legitimate moral authority.[51]

But Aquinas denies the first premise of this argument. He thinks he can establish God's perfect goodness solely on the basis of arguments from natural theology which make no appeal to God's actions or commands.[52] But even if those arguments were unavailable, Aquinas's view of the relation between human and divine reason would provide him a way of denying the first premise of the objector's argument. The judgment that God is a legitimate moral authority does not depend on a prior judgment by unaided human reason that *every* or *any particular* divine action or command is morally right. The judgment that God is morally good could be warranted inductively if a sufficient number of God's actions and commands were judged by unaided human reason to be morally right. Aquinas's position allows for this possibility because it allows that unaided human reason can achieve moral truth in many cases. Thus, a sufficient number of cases such as (a) and (b1)—cases in which human reason is able to determine the rightness of a divine action or command independently—can provide a strong basis for the judgment that God is morally good. Given a judgment arrived at in this way, one's judgment in some particular case that God is morally good might be non-circularly prior to one's judgment that the particular divine action or command in question is morally right.[53]

Cases such as (b2), (c), and (d)—cases in which the dictates of unaided human reason either fail to validate or actually contradict the divine command—need not be taken as disconfirming the inductively based judgment that God is morally good, because the agent justifiably believes that unaided human reason is both incomplete and fallible. Given the incompleteness and fallibility of unaided human reason, it is possible that it either fail to grasp the moral truth about some action or arrive at a moral falsehood.[54] In a particular case, then, the agent can have reason to suspect the dictates of his unaided human reason.[55] Of course, if unaided human reason systematically disapproved divine commands and actions, then this line of argument would not be open. But that is not the case.[56]

So in claiming that one ought to obey a divine command even in cases in which one's unaided reason disapproves what is commanded, Aquinas abandons neither his view of the moral autonomy of the human agent nor his rationalistic metaethics. Even in cases of sort (d) an agent can act from internal reasons in obeying the divine command and so act in accordance with reason and autonomously.

Thus far my discussion has taken the agent's belief that God has commanded C as given. But of course, the agent's situation might be such that he is uncertain whether in fact God has commanded C, and Aquinas can allow this. In such a case it is at least possible that one's suspicion of the authenticity of the putative divine command is greater than one's suspicion of the dictates of one's own reason, and hence it is justifiable for one to refuse to obey the putative command.[57]

My discussion of case (d) has also presupposed that it is reasonable in such cases for the agent to suspect the dictates of his reason. But Aquinas believes that if in some case the human agent is *certain* that the dictates of his unaided human reason are correct, he cannot have reason to do what contradicts such dictates. Just as Aquinas denies that correct human reason can contradict divine reason, he must deny that it is possible for there to be a case in which unaided human reason dictates with certainty an action contrary to the action commanded by God. Aquinas, then, agrees with the humanistic rationalist in asserting that a human agent ought not to obey a putative divine command when his own reason dictates with certainty that the action commanded is morally wrong. But Aquinas disagrees with the humanistic rationalist in denying that all dictates of unaided human reason are certain; and he is certainly right about this.

Thus, Aquinas's rationalism allows that human beings have independent access to moral truth, but their access is neither infallible nor complete. Hence, human morality is significantly independent while requiring both correction and extension by divine reason. The Christian should not find this sort of rationalism objectionable.

Aquinas also holds that human beings are bound by the dictates of reason, but he allows that human beings can have reason to act against the judgments of unaided human reason. Hence, God is subject to human moral judgment, but human beings nevertheless have reason to defer to God's judgment. The Christian should not find this sort of rationalism objectionable.

Finally, Aquinas holds that the Christian owes allegiance to his reason, but in acting in allegiance to reason a human being is acting in allegiance to divine law, since it is an expression of reason. The Christian should not find this sort of rationalism objectionable.

5. THE ADVANTAGES OF AQUINAS'S THEORY

In the last section I defended Aquinas's position against possible objections against its adequacy as a basis for Christian morality. In this section I want very briefly to draw attention to some virtues of a metaethics of the sort I have sketched that make it attractive as a particularly Christian metaethics.

First, Aquinas's rationalism offers a clear account of the common belief that morality is not a matter of arbitrary choice, whether human or divine. A DCM has notorious difficulties accounting for the truth of this belief.[58]

Second, Aquinas's metaethics allows the Christian to give a plausible account (of the sort developed in section 4 above) of how the Christian can act autonomously and in accordance with reason while acting in obedience to divine commands, even commands that contradict the dictates of unaided human reason.

Third, Aquinas's version of rationalism provides a straightforward account of the Christian's claim that God is good: God's will and actions are entirely in accordance with reason. By contrast, proponents of a DCM find it difficult to provide a straightforward sense for that claim.[59]

Fourth, Aquinas's view accounts for our belief that Christian morality has a great deal in common with secular morality. Christians normally take themselves to be in basic agreement with atheists about very many important moral judgments. When a Christian claims that torturing innocent children just for fun is wrong, she supposes that she is saying the very same thing as an atheist who makes the same claim and that many of her reasons for making that claim are the same as the atheist's. Moreover, when the Christian and atheist disagree about the rightness or wrongness of certain actions, they both normally assume that their disagreement is genuine and that the one is contradicting the other.

Aquinas's rationalistic metaethics renders these facts perfectly understandable. Both Christians and atheists are rational creatures, and it is natural to suppose that they will largely agree about what actions are in accordance with reason. The Christian has no corner on reason, and hence no corner on the moral truth. Moreover, according to Aquinas's theory, when Christians and atheists dispute the moral rightness or wrongness of certain acts they are engaged in a dispute about what is in accordance with right reason, i.e., about what correct reasoning dictates in this case, and hence their dispute is genuine. Of course, in such disputes the Christian may sometimes appeal to facts available only through revelation (sometimes but not always moral facts), but it is an exaggeration to suppose that such appeals always, or even typically, characterize such disputes. Christian and secular moral theory might go quite a long way together, and Aquinas's metaethics allows us to see why that should be so.[60]

Finally, the egoistic component of Aquinas's metaethics provides an explanation of the Christian belief that a life of obedience to God is the most fulfilling life a human being can live. On Aquinas's theory a life in obedience to God is a life in accordance with right reason, and human nature is fulfilled, completed, perfected by the right exercise of reason. According to Christianity, the rational creature achieves his ultimate end in loving and serving God, the *summum bonum*. This is just what Aquinas's egoistic rationalism allows us to say.[61]

REFERENCES

Adams, Robert M. (1973). "A Modified Divine Command Theory of Ethical Wrongness," reprinted in Helm (1981), 83–108.

———— (1979). "Divine Command Metaethics as Necessary A Posteriori," reprinted in Helm (1981), 109–19.

Bratman, Michael (1987). *Intentions, Plans, and Practical Reason,* Harvard University Press.

Feinberg Joel (1964), "Psychological Egoism," in Joel Feinberg, ed., *Reason and Responsibility,* Wadsworth (6th edition, 1985), 480–90.

Helm, Paul, ed. (1981). *Divine Commands and Morality,* Oxford University Press.

Irwin, Terence (1977). *Plato's Moral Theory: The Early and Middle Dialogues,* Clarendon Press.

Kretzmann, Norman (1983a). "Abraham, Isaac, and Euthyphro: God and the Basis of Morality," in Donald V. Stump, et al., eds., *Hamartia: The Concept of Error in the Western Tradition,* Edwin Mellen Press.

———— (1983b). "Goodness, Knowledge, and Indeterminacy in the Philosophy of Thomas Aquinas," *Journal of Philosophy* Suppl. to vol. 80:631–49.

MacDonald, Scott (forthcoming). "The Role of Ultimate Ends in Practical Reasoning: Aquinas's Aristotelian Moral Psychology and Anscombe's Fallacy."

Nowell-Smith, Patrick (1961). "Morality: Religious and Secular," reprinted in Baruch A. Brody, ed., *Readings in the Philosophy of Religion: An Analytic Approach,* Prentice-Hall, 1974.

Quinn, Philip L. (1975). "Religious Obedience and Moral Autonomy," reprinted in Helm (1981), 49–66.

———— (1978). *Divine Commands and Moral Requirements,* Clarendon Press.

Rachels, James (1971). "God and Human Attitudes," reprinted in Helm (1981),
    34–48.
Stump, Eleonore, and Kretzmann, Norman (1985). "Absolute Simplicity," *Faith
    and Philosophy* 2:353–82.
———— (1988). "Being and Goodness," in Thomas V. Morris, ed., *Divine and
    Human Action,* Cornell University Press.
Thomas Aquinas (*ST*). *Summa theologiae.*
———— (*SCG*). *Summa contra gentiles.*
———— (*DV*). *Quaestiones disputatae de veritate.*
———— (*In X Eth. Nic.*). *In decem libros Ethicorum ad Nicomachum expositio.*
———— (*In XII Meta.*). *In XII libros Metaphysicorum expositio.*

NOTES

1. See, e.g., Adams (1973), Adams (1979), and Quinn (1978).

2. For interesting discussion of what I take to be Aquinas's position on these topics, see Stump and Kretzmann (1985), especially pp. 375–76; Stump and Kretzmann (1988),; and Kretzmann (1983a).

3. *ST* Ia.5.1; 62.1; 80.1; IaIIae.1.5.

4. "The nature of each thing is shown by its activity" (*ST* Ia.76.1).

5. "And so the soul itself [i.e., a living thing's substantial form], insofar as it is the subject of its powers, is called a first actuality ordered toward a second actuality" (*ST* Ia.77.1, see also *ST* Ia.5.1).

6. "It is apparent that activity is the final actuality of the thing that performs the activity (thus it is also called second actuality by the Philosopher in II *De anima*), for the thing that has the form can be in potentiality the thing that performs the activity" (*ST* IaIIae.3.2, see also *ST* Ia.5.1).

7. *ST* Ia.77.1.ad5.

8. *In XII Meta.* Bk. IX, L. VIII; *In X Eth. Nic.* Bk. I, L. 10.

9. "Each thing is perfected to the extent that it is in actuality, for potentiality without actuality is imperfect" (*ST* IaIIae.3.2; see also *ST* Ia.5.1).

10. *ST* Ia.59.1; 80.1; *DV* 22.3.

11. *ST* Ia.78.1; 78.1.ad3; 80.1.ad3.

12. *ST* Ia.59.1; IaIIae.6.2.ad1; 8.1; 9.1; *DV* 22.4. I am using the term 'natural inclination' as a generic term meaning the inclination or *appetitus* a substance has in virtue of its nature; hence, will is a natural inclination, since it is the sort of inclination a human being has in virtue of its nature (rational nature). Aquinas, however, sometimes uses 'natural inclination' in a specific sense, meaning by it the specific sort of inclination characteristic of inanimate bodies. In this sense will is not a natural inclination.

13. *ST* IaIIae.1.1–6; 3.2.

14. "[W]ill adheres to the ultimate end, which is happiness, of necessity" (*ST* Ia.82.1-2, see also IaIIae.5.4.ad2; 9.1-2; *DV* 22.5).

15. See, e.g., Feinberg (1964).

16. *ST* Ia.80.1; IaIIae.8.1-2; 19.3.

17. *ST* IaIIae.1.1; 6.1-2.

18. *ST* IaIIae.6.2.

19. See also *ST* Ia.59.1; 59.1.ad1; IaIIae.2.7; 2.8; 4.2.ad2; 5.1; 19.3.

20. *ST* Ia.5.1; *ST* IaIIae.1.5; 1.7; 5.8.

21. In *ST* IaIIae.1.1-7 Aquinas argues that a rational being has a single, all-encompassing ultimate end of this sort; see MacDonald (forthcoming). For an interesting discussion of the role of partial plans in practical reasoning, see Bratman (1987).

22. I do not think that Aquinas intends it as a necessary condition of an action's being voluntary that the agent take account of the action's (or the action's end's) relation to some determinate conception of the best life, only that the agent view the action (or its end) in light of some other ends. I think Aquinas would say that a *paradigm* instance of voluntariness is one in which the agent both has a determinate conception of the best life and orders his actions with respect to it.

23. Thus, the ordered-toward or for-the-sake-of relation includes not only the means-end relation but also the relation between a constituent and the thing constituted; see MacDonald (forthcoming).

24. "[W]e can speak about the ultimate end in two ways: in accordance with the concept (*rationem*) of the ultimate end and in accordance with that in which the ultimate end is found" (*ST* IaIIae.1.7).

25. Having argued in *ST* IaIIae.1 that all human beings seek an ultimate end in the purely formal sense, Aquinas goes on in *ST* IaIIae.2-3 to investigate what the ultimate end actually consists in.

26. The sort of specification involved here includes but is not restricted to specifying means to some end. Assuming that my conception of the best life is the life of political power, I might decide that such a life would be best realized by my holding high political office. As a result of this decision my general conception of the best life becomes more specific—it is now the conception of a life that includes my holding high political office. My holding high political office, however, is not a means to my living a life of political power but what (perhaps partially) constitutes living such a life. I might further specify my plan by deciding to go to law school in order to make myself electable. This would be to decide on a means to a life of political power. Aquinas uses the phrase '*ad finem*' ('for the sake of the end', 'ordered toward the end') to cover both sorts of cases.

27. Aquinas thinks that the intellect is necessitated only by what is certain. Hence, when intellect perceives the self-evidence of a self-evident proposition or the force of a necessary demonstration the premises of which are self-evident, the intellect necessarily accepts the truth of the proposition or conclusion. Similarly, the intellect (and hence the will) is necessitated when it is certain that some candidate for the ultimate end is in fact the perfect good or that some means to an already intended end is the best or only means. Aquinas holds, for instance, that despite the fact that a human being's will is necessitated with respect to willing happiness, and true happiness is to be found only in God, the highest good, a human being's will is not necessitated

with respect to willing God because human intellect does not perceive the necessary connection between happiness and God with certitude (*ST* Ia.82.2; see also note 29 below).

28. "Since the will follows the intellect's apprehension, it happens that some single reality is desired under one description (*uno modo*) but not under another. Therefore happiness can be considered under the description (*sub ratione*) 'final and perfect good,' which is the common concept (*communis ratio*) of happiness, and considered in this way the will naturally and of necessity tends toward it, as has been said. It can also be considered in accordance with other considerations which specify it (*alias speciales considerationes*) . . . and considered in this way the will does not tend toward it of necessity" (*ST* IaIIae.5.8.ad2).

29. For further discussion of Aquinas's account of freedom and will see Norman Kretzmann (1983b) and Stump and Kretzmann (1985).

30. *ST* IaIIae.1.1; 6.2.ad2; 14. Aquinas says that deliberation is only about things *ad finem*. It is a mistake to suppose that he means that deliberation is means-end reasoning only, since for Aquinas '*ad finem*' is broader in scope than 'means' (see note 26 above). That Aquinas intends deliberation to cover both of these sorts of consideration is clear also from the following passage: "Prudence is the ability to deliberate well (*bene consiliativa*) about those things which pertain to the whole life of a human being and to the ultimate end of human life" (*ST* 57.4.ad3).

31. *ST* IaIIae.6.1-2.

32. Aquinas offers arguments intended to reach a determination of this sort in *ST* IaIIae.2-3.

33. Virtually all of *ST* IaIIae beginning with Question 4 and IIaIIae are devoted to determinations of this sort.

34. *ST* IIaIIae.47.11.

35. Notice that the claim that one seeks the good of others as a part of one's own good does not mean that one does not seek the good of others for its own sake but only for the sake of one's own good. One can seek the constituents of one's own good for their own sakes, and also for the sake of the good of which they are constituents. Constituent parts of one's own good, then, will be goods identified by Plato, Aristotle, and Aquinas as things sought for their own sake *and* for the sake of something else. See MacDonald (forthcoming). For an interesting and detailed development of this line in Greek ethics, see Irwin (1977).

36. *ST* IaIIae.1.1.

37. *ST* IaIIae.1.3.

38. *ST* IaIIae.19.3.ad2.

39. *ST* IaIIae.21.1.

40. The tradition described by Rachels as running from Plato to Kant is an example of this sort of humanistic rationalism: see Rachels (1971), section V. I am not claiming that Rachels has characterized this tradition correctly, only that the tradition as he describes it is an example of humanistic rationalism.

41. These three sorts of shortcomings mirror the three sorts of short-comings of human speculative reason. See *ST* I.1.1; *SCG* I.3-8.

42. Nothing I have said about the relation between human and divine reason answers the question of how *divine* reason is related to moral truth. It is compatible with what I've said, for instance, that divine reason appre-hends a moral reality independent of itself. Aquinas's view, I think, is that di-vine reason is identical with moral truth; for a defense of this doctrine and the ascription of it to Aquinas, see Stump and Kretzmann (1985). If one has some other account of the relation between God and objective abstract en-tities, such as the truths of logic and mathematics, that preserves God's sov-ereignty and aseity, it will be compatible with all I've said about Aquinas's metaethics: moral truths can be viewed as objective abstract entities and the relation between God's reason and them will be just the same as that between God's reason and any other such entities.

43. *ST* IaIIae.99.2.ad1-ad2.

44. This view of the content and purpose of revelation mirrors Aqui-nas's account of the revelation of speculative truths. See note 41 above.

45. *ST* IaIIae.100.1.

46. Ibid.

47. Case (d) also admits of two possibilities: (d1) C commands what unaided human reason would approve if it were reasoning correctly and (d2) C commands what unaided human reason would neither approve nor disap-prove if it were reasoning correctly (because the rightness of what is commanded is beyond the scope of unaided human reason).

48. In *ST* IaIIae.100.8.ad3 Aquinas discusses this example together with the examples of God's command to Abraham to sacrifice Isaac and to Hosea to marry a harlot.

49. In this context and for the remainder of my discussion of case (d) the dictates of unaided human reason with respect to a given action should be taken to be the practical judgment about that action arrived at by human reasoning, which does not take into account the action's being commanded by God.

50. Of course, this is not to say that the action's rightness consists in its being commanded by God.

51. Rachels offers an argument of this sort: see his reply to objection (2) (Rachels (1971), 45–46). Quinn thinks Rachels's argument is a good one: see Quinn (1975), 55. See also Nowell-Smith (1961).

52. See *ST* Ia.6 and *SCG* I.28, 37–41.

53. Rachels fails to see this possibility (Rachels (1971), 46).

54. "Eternal law cannot err, but human reason can, and for that reason will which agrees with human reason is neither always right nor always in agreement with eternal law" (*ST* IaIIae.19.6.ad2).

55. Quinn discusses this possibility (Quinn (1975), section III).

56. Rachels argues that one cannot consistently maintain that one's moral judgment is untrustworthy, since one could know this only if one knows that certain actions are morally required and that one fails to judge that they are

morally required (Rachels (1971), 46). But this inconsistency arises only for the claim that one's moral judgment is systematically untrustworthy, and Aquinas's fallibilism (and most versions of moral fallibilism) does not require this strong claim.

57. Quinn discusses this possibility (Quinn (1975), sections II and III). This is the line the humanistic rationalist who wants to preserve the Christian's moral autonomy must take for all cases of conflict between unaided human reason and putative divine commands.

58. Adams argues that his version of a DCM provides for the objectivity of morality, but he defines 'objective' in such a way as to make this claim less interesting than it might appear. According to Adams, morality is objective if its truth is independent of what humans think about it (Adams (1973), 91 and Adams (1979), 113). But of course a morality might be objective in this sense while depending entirely on sheer divine whimsy.

59. For such an attempt, see Adams (1973), section V.

60. Adams devotes considerable attention to trying to dispel the counter-intuitiveness of the claim that the Christian and the non-believer mean something different when they use the same ethical terms (Adams (1973), section VI).

61. I am grateful to Norman Kretzmann and Panayot Butchvarov for comments on a draft of this paper.

Because God Says So

Carlton D. Fisher

> . . . and God saw that it was good . . . and behold, it was
> very good.
>
> Gen. 1:10, 12, 18, 21, 25, 31

I

I have three identifiable purposes in this paper, perhaps one
or two more than is advisable. However, the issues involved are linked
in a way which makes it difficult to express myself clearly about the
central one and resist comment on the others. My primary purpose
is to describe[1] the relationship between God and morality which
1) satisfies the appropriate Christian impulse to affirm the sovereignty
of God, and 2) rejects the divine command theory, which is typically motivated by the desire to affirm God's sovereign control over
his creation. My motivation for making this attempt is found in my
judgment that the horn of the "Euthyphro Dilemma" which suggests that actions are right because of God's commands is unacceptable as a moral theory,[2] and that the other horn—the affirmation
that God commands actions because they are right—does not in fact
make God "subject" to anything to which a sovereign being ought
not be subjected, i.e., not subject to any *thing* at all.

The perceived danger, of course, is that the rejection of divine
command answers to the dilemma appears to some to cut God out
of the moral picture, to make his existence or nonexistence, his will,
commands, and purposes, irrelevant to moral discourse. And this,
rightly, is seen to be unacceptable from a Christian point of view.

No account of morality or ethics could possibly claim to be Christian without agreeing that God, God's will, God's actions, and God's revelation of himself to us in Scripture are importantly related to morality, indeed, foundationally related; and no Christian account could be complete without attempting to say how they are so related. This is such an attempt.

Subordinate to that primary purpose, I hope to shed light on the distinction between epistemological and what I call metaphysical questions concerning the relationship between God and morality, mainly by way of showing that they are distinct. And finally, I wish to show (admit?) that the refusal to explain moral obligations by direct appeal to divine commands does not keep Euthyphro-like dilemmas from arising immediately again, at a slightly different level, nor does it eliminate the eventual need for a final, nothing-more-can-be-said answer. But much more can be said than a direct appeal to divine commands, and some of that is what I hope to say.[3]

II

Let us approach these issues by considering an answer which signifies the crucial relationship between God and morality. The answer: "Because God says so." The question: "Why should I do the right thing?" Or, more specifically, questions like, "Why should I tell him the truth?" "Why should I refrain from sexual intercourse?" "Why should I sign an organ-donor card?" or "Why should I refrain from allowing your left ear to serve as a target for my baseball bat?" The answer—at once both wrong-headed and profound—comes: "Because God said so." I believe it to be wrong-headed because, as usually offered, it suggests that God's relationship to morality is something quite different than I think it is; and yet perhaps it is the best answer when properly understood.

Now it must be noted that the question, "Why should I?" is ambiguous, at least as we are now considering it abstractly, separated from any specific context. The context often makes it clear. When a three-year-old asks, "Why should I?" in response to a parental directive, it is often a clear request for motivation, not for justification or explanation. "Why should I? Who's gonna' make me? What are you going to do if I don't? Persuade me to do as you request." Thus, when we ask, "Why should I?" in response to any statement of moral obligation, we may be asking for motivation. The answer, "Because God says so," might even be an answer to this request. This answer is defective because the motivation for good behavior which seems most honorable does not rely on external forces, whether promises of personal reward or reprieve from personal punishment. On the other hand, when we pause to consider who God is—the all-powerful sovereign creator and sustainer of all that is and ever has been, the designer, creator, and lover of my soul, the one who knows absolutely all there is to know about me and my circumstances and whose care for me is exhibited in the sacrifice of Christ on the cross of Calvary—then to find the source of motivation for action in "Because God says so" is not to act at a three-year-old level, or to sacrifice personal autonomy, but instead can be an indication of deep insight and true maturity.

A second question which can be asked in the words, "Why should I?" is, "How do you *know* that this is what I should do?" This is a question of epistemology, a question of moral knowledge. The first question said, "Persuade me to act; give me motivation." This second says, "Convince me to believe; give me justification that what you say I should do is really what I should do."

Now let us again consider the answer, "Because God says so; I know that you should do this because God says you should do this." This is a terrible answer for several reasons. First, it can't be used in all situations. God has said that you should tell the truth and refrain from sexual intercourse in certain situations. But he has not "said" that you should sign an organ-donor card, or divest yourself of your South African holdings. Indeed, if we interpret "Because God says so" in this context to mean "Because the Bible says so," we are hard pressed to find a condemnation of slavery, to say nothing of apartheid. And what has God said about abortion, genetic engineering, or nuclear disarmament? Second, offering Scripture references to justify claims of moral obligation succeeds in providing such justification only to the extent that one is able to justify the claim that the Bible is a record of what God says, even when appropriate Scripture references *can* be found. And that is surely no simple task. When you tell me that it's going to be a mild winter because that is what the *Farmer's Almanac* says, I will be convinced of your opinion only to the extent that I am convinced that the *Al-*

manac is a legitimate authority on such matters. And this leads to the third difficulty with this answer. In citing as my justification for my moral beliefs, "Because God says so," then, if that is *all* I have to say I cut myself off from fruitful dialogue concerning moral issues with those who either deny the existence of God or who deny that my Bible is an accurate report of what God says.[4]

But—and here is the other side—surely it is perfectly legitimate to believe some things merely on the basis of authority, especially when the one we accept as an authority on a certain matter really *is* an authority on that matter. I accept your report concerning how boring you find this article on the basis of your authority. After all, if anyone knows, you should. I accept the results of the election on the authority of the news media. If anyone would know, they would. And my students accept my evaluation of their exams on my authority, because, after all, if anyone. . . . Well maybe we ought not get carried away! Justification by authority is a tricky matter. Not everyone who says "Believe me" is worthy of being believed. But what about God? If God says that Abraham and Sarah are going to have a baby in their old age, he should know. If God says that we can be forgiven because of Calvary, he should know. If God says that the pure in heart shall see him, that the Christ will come again, and that we shall be like him when we see him as he is, he should know. And, if God says that we ought not to steal, lie, commit adultery, covet, or worship idols, then he—the one who knows all things—should know. There simply is no finer authority to accept than his. "Because God said so"—assuming that he really did—is as good a justification for believing something as any I can imagine. If God has given moral directives—and as Christians we believe that he has—there is no surer justification of moral belief than "Because God said so."

Now we can identify a third question which can be posed in the words, "Why should I?" Why is it that God's *saying so* is such great evidence for its *being so*? God's saying that our faith will be the vehicle for our salvation is good evidence that it will because he will *make* it so. God's saying that the goats will be separated from the lambs is good evidence that they will be because *he will separate them*. And so it is with much of what God says. It is or will be as he said because he made or will make it to be as he said. God could have had Abraham and Sarah adopt a son. But he didn't. And thus when he promised them a son that promise was fully reliable because God would see to it that it would happen.

Is it similar with moral obligations? Is it wrong to steal because God made it wrong to steal? Does God *decide* what is right and wrong? Are our obligations what they are "Because God says so?"

III

Thus the words "Why should I?" can be used to ask a question about the source of moral obligation—not a request for motivation, or even justification, but instead an inquiry about the foundation for obligation, or what might be called the metaphysics of morals. It seeks an explanation of *why* whatever is right is *right,* of why whatever is wrong is *wrong.* And, as with the first two interpretations of this question, the answer is frequently given, "Because God says so. It is wrong to steal because God says that it is wrong to steal. *It might have been otherwise.* But God has commanded us not to steal and thus it is wrong to do so."

Giving the "Because God says so" answer to this question is to affirm some version of what is known as the "Divine Command Theory" of ethics.[5] Plato, in his dialogue known as "The Euthyphro," asked a question, the crux of which has been reformulated in theistic language to be: Is something right because God commands it, or does God command it because it is right? The problems found in affirming either option have resulted in what is called the "Euthyphro Dilemma." Plato's own answer, fitting well with his theology and metaphysical understanding of our world, was that the gods command as they command because *what* they command is right. There is some standard of goodness, independent of our world, independent of the gods, to which the gods appeal in commanding rightly.

This response, however, was not seen as adequate by certain early Christian thinkers. After all, on such a view there exists this standard of goodness, independent of God, to which God is then *subject,* by which God's own actions and commandments are judged. And surely the sovereign Lord of the universe cannot be subject to any such external judgment. Hence, some accepted the alternative, proposed but rejected by Plato: Things are right because God commands them, wrong because God forbids them. "Why should I?" "Because God said so, simple as that."

On one hand, this could be understood as a theory about the meaning of moral words, like "wrong" and "right." Thus "wrong" *means* "forbidden by God" and "right" *means* "commanded by God." But this would have the consequence, unacceptable I believe, that when a divine command theorist and someone else—whether a believer or not—*agree* that applying a baseball bat sharply to your left ear is wrong, their agreement is apparent only, because they *mean* different things by the word "wrong." And that, whatever the meaning of "wrong," is wrong.[6] Further, if "right" means "commanded by God" and "good" means "doing the right things," then when we affirm of God that he is good we would be affirming only that God obeys God's commands, or that his actions are consistent with his will; God does what he wants. And it seems that our affirmation of faith in God's goodness amounts to something more than that.[7]

On the other hand, the divine command theory could be understood as a claim that it is God's commands which are somehow constitutive of the rightness or wrongness of actions. It is divine prohibition which is the true nature of wrongness; divine requirement is the true nature of obligation. God somehow decides what is right and wrong; he creates right and wrong by commanding. God makes up the moral rules.[8]

But this account would force us to accept the following claim: "If God has commanded us to severely torture innocent three-year-olds, then it would have been right to do so." Now this claim is a conditional, and a counterfactual at that. The antecedent is not true, nor will it be. And counterfactuals are difficult to evaluate. In addition, according to very common Christian understanding of God's nature, the antecedent of this conditional is not only actually false, but is necessarily false. This leads many to refuse to be bothered by the claim at all. "So, if he did command that, it would be right. But he didn't. He won't. Furthermore, because of the steadfastness of his good character, he could not have commanded it. So big deal." Nonetheless, I think it is a big deal. Even though it is true that God does not command such torture, even though it may be true that he could not command such torture—and thank God for that—it is still *not* true that *if he did command it,* such behavior would be morally right. No, if he did command it, *he* would be morally *wrong.*[9]

But this leaves us with Plato's view, doesn't it? Can we conceive of God being subject to some external standard of right and wrong which is not of his own making? What about his sovereignty? Doesn't this make God somehow dependent upon morality rather than the other way around?

IV

Let me now try to offer a view of morality which might satisfy both the impulse which leads to a divine command theory and my revulsion at the consequences of such a view, namely that it provides an impoverished account of moral right and wrong and thereby trivializes the claim that God is good.

What is morality, anyway? Isn't it what we might call a human institution? By this I don't mean to suggest, as some would, that it is the creation of human beings, that man is the measure of all things, that something is right because someone or some group thinks it is right, shapes their lives by those views, and advises and criticizes others according to their views.[10] Instead, I mean to say that morality—like the Sabbath—is made for man. We, not God, are the beneficiaries of morality. And when a moral standard is "broken" it is some human being who feels the pain, not the standard.

Suppose that God alone existed. Nothing else. He has not created a thing. Now, what sense would it make to say of him that he is morally good? What does it mean to be good except that there is a certain quality to our relationship with something other than ourselves? My suggestion is that to say of God that he is good is to describe his relationship to something else, his creation.[11] To say of us that we are good is to describe our relationships to something else, those around us. Now what kind of relationships are to be called "good"? Are they whatever relationships God decides will be good?

Consider, if you will, the operation manual for a new car. In it we find instructions to guide our relationship to the car. Don't do this, that, or the other. Do this and that. Commands for behavior. These are the right things to do. Now let's ask Plato's question in this context. Are these instructions right because General Motors commanded us to do them? Or did General Motors command us to do them because they are right? If you will allow me the assumption that General Motors knows what they are doing, I think you will agree that the answer is rather obvious. They so commanded because these are the right things to do in caring for the car.

Now let me ask, in so commanding, was GM subject to some external standard of rightness? Did they, in order to command correctly, have to consider some independently existing code of correct behavior for car care? Of course not. How then were they able to give us the proper instructions? Quite simple: The proper care of the car is derived from the nature of the car itself.[12] If it has solid rubber tires, no instructions would be necessary concerning tire inflation. But, since the tires are not solid rubber, instructions are necessary. And not just any instruction will do. Too little air won't work and neither will too much. And it is the design of the car, the wheel, and the tire, as well as the qualities of the environment in which the car is to operate, that determine the correct instruction. It is GM who writes the manual—not me—because they designed and created the car and thus, other things beings equal, they are in the best position to give advice concerning its proper care.

Let us return to morality and God's relationship to it. God does not decide what rules to make up. Neither does he appeal to some independent and abstract ideal of goodness to which he is subject. There is no such thing. What there *is* is his creation, us. There are people and there are ways of acting which are good for people and ways which are bad for people.[13] God is good because he treats us in ways that are for *our* good; he takes care of us. And he does so wisely. You must know the *thing* in order to know how properly to treat it. God designed us and created us. Hence he is in the best position to write our instruction manual. Nonetheless, he doesn't, nor can he, simply "make it up."

"Ah!" the divine command theorist might exclaim. "So God is *not* in control of morality. He has no power to make things any other than they are. His sovereignty has been sacrificed, not to some independent moral standard, but now to the nature of God's creation! God is subject to his own creation? The bottom line is still that God has no control over the laws of morality."

But that is simply wrong; God is not subject at all, except in a trivial and harmless sense which I will describe in a moment. Right now, let us consider the issue by asking this very simple question: "Could the operating manual that we call morality have been any different than it is? Could some rules be changed, even by God?"

The answer is "Yes." God was fully in control of his creative act.[14] He could have created beings very different from us. (Perhaps he has.) And, if the beings were different, if the *thing* for which the operating manual is constructed were different, so would be the manual.[15] Consider this. God *could have* made it morally right for me to hit you in the left ear as hard as I can with a baseball bat. He could have done so by designing *you* differently than he has. He could have designed you so that such a blow, instead of producing severe pain, and perhaps even more harm, would double your intelligence. If *that* was what you were like, then it certainly would not be wrong for me to bop you one. Or suppose God had designed us and our world so that all we had to do to obtain some material object of our choice would be to think of it, to imagine it. Just the mere thought of a red BMW would result in one materializing before you, complete with keys and title in your name. Now in such a world as that I can see no reason to prohibit theft. No one would need to steal from me. And furthermore, if someone would — perhaps because of unimaginativeness — all I would need do in response would be to think of what was taken and I would have another.[16]

Thus, yes, God is in complete control of the *content* of morality. He is in such control simply because he designs creation, he designs us, and what is or isn't good for us is determined by our design.

But then we can also see the sense in which God is *not* in control of the moral rules. He does not create them by his commands. He creates *us,* but with *us* comes the standard, the operating manual. It is up to God what *we* are *like,* but once we are as we are, it is not up to God to decide what is good for us.[17] Since you are a creature that experiences severe pain whenever your left ear is attacked by a baseball bat, then that behavior is wrong. Simple as that. God can't change that. He could change *you,* but given you as you are, it just is wrong to hit you in that way.[18]

But the objection might be made that this still sacrifices God's sovereignty. After all, this position implies that for God to be good, he *must* care for his creation, he *must* be concerned for the good of his creatures. And, doesn't that limit God in an unacceptable way? Couldn't a sovereign God have it some other way if he wished? Isn't this making him — as Plato would — subject to an external, independent standard?

I don't believe it is, at least not in any sovereignty-subverting way. Consider this. God, in order to be omniscient, *must* know my name. And yours. And a whole lot of other interesting and trivial matters. He must; it's an absolute requirement of any omniscient being. Well, actually, it's not a requirement of the *being*. It is instead a requirement for being correctly described as "omniscient." I don't know whether or not God has the capacity to fail to know my name. But, just as I know that God cannot make round squares (and that this does not identify some lack of ability or control), I know that God can't be *omniscient and* not know my name.

So also I believe that God cannot be good and fail to care for his creatures. Whether or not he could fail to care for his creatures is a different question, one about whether or not he is essentially good. But no matter which position is accepted on that issue, to require that God care for us in order to be good is not so much a requirement on God as it is a requirement on the correct use of the adjective "good." The words we use to describe God have some meaning after all, and, whatever a fully adequate analysis of the word "good" is, it cannot be correctly attributed to one who does not care for the well-being of creatures like you and me. To claim that the truth of assertions about God are subject to the meanings of the words in the assertions and to whether the assertions accurately describe God is, at worst, to endorse a trivial and harmless verbal subjection. It is *not* to make *God subject* to anything. In fact, to reject the claim is to deny the possibility of any meaningful talk about God.

V

Now let me note the ramifications of this view in the area of moral knowledge. How do we obtain information about what is right and wrong? Certainly, if God has revealed some such information to us in Scripture it would be infallibly reliable. He designed us. He created us. He cares for us. He, more than any other, is qualified to write an instruction manual for us. If God has said so, then that is the best possible justification of a moral truth. But is God's manual our only source of moral knowledge?

Returning to our analogy, consider an expert automobile mechanic—uneducated in other matters, but a student of cars with years of experience. New models come his way. He didn't design them or build them. He isn't qualified to write the instruction manual, at least not in the way that the engineers at GM are qualified. But he too knows a lot about cars. And he can tell you much about what you should and shouldn't do in caring for yours. He knows the *thing* — imperfectly to be sure — but to the extent of his knowledge of the thing he too can know what instructions belong in the manual.[19]

The application should be clear. We did not design or create ourselves. We are not expert authorities about ourselves. But that does not imply that we are totally ignorant of what we are like and how we are best cared for. We don't need God to tell us that it is wrong to hit each other in the ears with baseball bats. In fact, we don't even need to believe that God exists, that we are the product of anyone's design and creation, in order to know that. We may not be experts, but neither are we totally ignorant of what we are like and what rules belong in the manual.

The results for the possibility of moral knowledge? Even if the Bible does not condemn slavery or speak directly about euthanasia, we might be able to come to conclusions ourselves. The instructions which *are* in Scripture are there, not because God made them up, but because they *belong* in our instruction manual. With this in mind, we might be able to study explicit commands and uncover underlying principles which can be applied in situations unknown to the biblical writers. Furthermore, since we have access to information about what is best for us independently of Scripture, we might have some evidence for the veracity of Scripture itself, as we find Scripture prohibiting certain behavior which even secular authorities around us are coming to understand as harmful to us (e.g., the psychological danger of unresolved anger or an unforgiving spirit). And, of course, since those of us who accept Scripture as authority are not the only ones with access to information about the *thing,* what we are like, we are not the only ones with access, however imperfect, to an understanding of what rules belong in the operation manual.

Of course this is no guarantee that in our dialogue with nonbelievers we will come to agreement about moral matters. To a significant extent we will; we have. But disagreement will linger, especially so long as there is disagreement between us as to the nature

of the *thing,* human beings. Much moral disagreement rests at that
point. For example, if we could agree as to what the human fetus
is, I suspect we would be much closer to an agreement on the moral
propriety of abortion.

And disagreement between believer and nonbeliever about the
nature of the human being goes deep. It is no slight and trivial disagreement when one asserts that we will survive death and live forever—happily or unhappily—while another claims that this life is
all there is. That disagreement is radical. And it certainly affects the
type of rules which would belong in the operating manual. Hence,
to the extent—which is not small, even though limited—that we
can agree on the nature of human reality, we can cooperate and
even agree with nonbelievers on matters moral. But, since our agreement on the nature of humanity is limited, Christian thought on
moral matters must differ from those around. If the Bible gives us
privileged information concerning the nature of humanity, then any
adequate Christian morality must be based on such understanding.
Because of the importance of human nature and the human environment in determining the moral good, and the importance of Scripture in a Christian understanding of those, Christians can never properly answer the question, "Why should I?" without at some point
saying, "Because God says so."

VI

But what has been gained in the attempt to ground moral obligation, not in God's commands, but in God's creation, in the "thing"
and that which is beneficial to it? How does there arise a moral *obligation* to treat children in certain ways and to refrain from treating
them in other ways simply because the former actions are beneficial
and the latter harmful to them? It is beneficial to my grass to fer-
tilize it and harmful to pitch a tent on it. It is beneficial to my car
to change the oil regularly and harmful to leave road salt on it. But
in neither of these cases do we typically speak of *obligations* to act
or to refrain from acting in certain ways.

Well, I believe that the answer is quite obvious, but leads to
further questions and difficulties. The difference is found in the type
of "thing" under consideration. Some things are due moral consideration; others are not. Some things, we say, have value or are valu-

able; others are not valuable or are less valuable. And, of course, since God is the source of all things, he is the source of all value as well. And now the complications, for here a Euthyphro-like question can again be raised: Are valuable things valuable because God created them? Or, did God create the things he did because they were (would be) valuable? Or again: Supposing that having value is a supervenient property, does it supervene on the property of having been created or on other characteristics valuable things possess?

On a Christian view of things, all of God's creation has value and thus "created thing" and "valuable thing" may be extensionally equivalent.[20] However, having value admits of degrees; being created is all or nothing. And since some things created by God are more valuable than others, being valuable cannot be equivalent to being created. Nor can the value of an object be explained fully by appeal to its creator.[21]

However, one might suggest to the contrary that the explanation of an object's value is to be found in an appeal to its creator, but not in the simple fact that it was created. Instead, its value is grounded in the *attitude* the creator has toward it, in his act of valuing it. It is familiar enough that some things possess value merely in virtue of being valued. This can be because of their usefulness in accomplishing some task which is itself valued — hence the value of this computer I'm now using and the face value of a postage stamp. Or, it can be because a sentient creature, for some reason or for none, chooses to value, places or confers value upon, some object — hence the enhanced value of postage stamps to collectors. This alone could be one account of why my children are so much more valuable than my lawn or my car — I *value* them much more highly.

Christians speak of the value of human beings in both of these ways. First, people are used by God in order to accomplish his purposes in the world. However, it is usually not claimed that God *depends* upon people for the accomplishment of his will in the strong sense that the cooperation of human beings is a necessary condition for God getting things done. Furthermore, God's purpose in the world as understood by Christians is to redeem the world to himself, and the purpose itself presupposes that the world and its people are valuable. Thus the value of human beings as a species cannot be located in the usefulness of some of them in assisting in God's redemptive plan.

Second, Christians sometimes talk as if the value of human beings is grounded simply in the fact that God values us. God, the source of all things, is the source of all value in virtue of the fact that he values — and thus confers value upon — his creation. We are valuable because God loves us. *Why* he values us is a puzzle, but he does, hence we are valuable.

But is it possible to value just anything at all and hence be able to confer value upon anything whatsoever? In some sense, yes. The toddler values the remnant of his blanket (so do the parents in times of need!). The collector can value gum wrappers and pieces of string. But is there nothing else to say about value? When asked, "Is *X* valuable?" is the only appropriate response to search and see if any sentient being can be found which values *X*? Or, could it be that some things are valuable and others not, independently of being valued? Isn't it possible to say correctly, "*X* is not valuable, even though *A* values *X*; *A* is mistaken"? Isn't is possible to say, "*X* is valuable, even though hardly anyone anymore values *X*; they are mistaken; their values are wrong, misshapen, distorted somehow?" Isn't there some objective sense of value such that the *truth* of "*X* is valuable" stands independently of what people value and judges *them,* judges the adequacy of their values according to whether or not they *recognize* the value that *X has*? I do not make human beings valuable by my valuing them. Instead, my valuations are judged by whether or not I value human beings. It seems clear that "valuable" does not mean "valued by me." Nor do I believe it means "capable of being valued," "commonly valued," nor "valued by most."

Could it mean "valued by God"? If it did, that would surely give it the sort of objective content which would allow the truth of "*X* is valuable" to stand as judge over my own valuation of *X*. Furthermore, if God values some of his creation more highly than other of it — which Christians believe he does — then the various degrees to which God values things could account for the various degrees to which things are valuable. On this account, just as human beings are valuable because God values them, so human beings are more valuable than zucchini squash — both created and valued by God, and neither a necessary divine assistant — because God values human beings more than he does zucchini. However, again it seems to me that this is the reverse of the truth. Just as God's moral perfection results in an extensional equivalence between his commands or will and our moral obligations, so it accounts for an extensional equivalence between the things God values and the things which are valuable, and the perfect correspondence between the value of things and the extent to which God values them. I would not want to rule out the possibility that some things are valuable simply because God values them and thus confers value upon them,[22] but it seems more likely to me that most of God's valuations result not from his volition but from his epistemic perfection — he perfectly recognizes value wherever it is found. God's love for us, rather than being the *source* of our value, is *evidence* that we are valuable.

Surely this is reflected in biblical accounts of human value. What is so very special about human beings is not simply that they have been created — so has everything else — but what they are *like*. Or rather, *who* they are like. We have been created by God, yes, but *in his image*. And, being the only part of creation with these characteristics (which include, I believe, the ability to recognize value and moral obligations), we are the most valuable of the creation.[23] So the Euthyphro dilemma can be put into this form: Are things valuable because God values them? Or does God value them because they are valuable? And again I embrace the second horn.

VII

It might be objected that to locate value in other characteristics that an object has is to cut value loose from its source in God and thus to propose a view which is unacceptable within a Christian context. After all, if object X is valuable because it has certain other properties a, b, and c (none of which is the property of being created or the property of being valued by God), then X would be valuable even if it were not created, even if there were no God. Also, if moral obligation stems from the value of things (and what is good or harmful to valuable things), then morality is possible without God; without God, some things *still* would be prohibited. A gulf is opened between God and morality which Christians are want to loathe. And down into that chasm falls all attempts to provide arguments for the existence of God on the basis of morality.

To illustrate, consider a divine command theory. If a moral obligation to refrain from doing X is the result of a divine command not to do X, then one could argue as follows:

(1) There is some action, X, the performance of which would be morally wrong.

Therefore,

(2) God exists.

However, if a moral obligation is not the result of divine activity or volition, but the result of what will benefit or harm a valuable thing, then (1) implies only:

(3) There is some thing which is valuable and which would be harmed if X were performed.

And from (3) one can hardly derive (2).[24]

However, it must be noted that (2) cannot be derived from (1) either. The validity of that inference depends upon the affirmation of the divine command theory. So, the full argument is actually:

(4) Actions are morally wrong because they are forbidden by God.

(1) There is some action, X, the performance of which would be morally wrong.

Therefore,

(2) God exists.

Now I would suggest that the connection between God and morality which is part of a typical Christian view of things is not expressed as well by (4) as by:

(5) Valuable things (other than God himself) cannot exist except for the creative activity of God.

(5) rests easily on the belief that things which existed merely as a result of the chance meandering of atomic particles could not be valuable in the way necessary to make certain kinds of behavior toward them morally obligatory or forbidden and that such is the remaining option once one denies an intelligent and purposive creator.[25]

And now we can exhibit the connection between God and morality in this argument:

(1) There is some action, X, the performance of which would be morally wrong.

Therefore,

> (3) There is some thing which is valuable and which would be harmed if X were performed.
>
> (5) Valuable things (other than God himself) cannot exist except for the creative activity of God.

Therefore,

> (2) God exists.

The nonbeliever, as always when facing such argumentation, has optional responses. He can deny the reality of moral obligations (premise 1) or he can deny the connection between obligation and objective value (first inference) and hence deny objective value (premise 3). But he need do neither, each of which has what seems to me an unacceptably high cost in terms of morality. Instead he can simply deny the claim that valuable things must necessarily depend upon God for their existence (premise 5). He might offer this argument in return:

> (1) There is some action, X, the performance of which would be morally wrong.

Therefore,

> (3) There is some thing which is valuable and which would be harmed if X were performed.
>
> (6) We do not know whether or not God exists and created us.

Therefore,

> (7) God's existence and creative action is not necessary as a ground of moral obligation.

There is an error in this response which we must note. But first we might as well admit that the moral argument for God's existence has little polemic value when addressed to a nonbeliever who affirms the reality of moral obligation but sees no need for a creator God to help make sense of it. Nonetheless, it may be a sound argument. It may indeed be true that only creation, not random collections of atomic material, can produce valuable entities.[26]

Well then, where is the error in the nonbeliever's counterargument? It is in the confusion of epistemic abilities with metaphysical realities. The fact that one who does not affirm the existence and creative activity of God can correctly perceive and affirm both the high value of human persons and the obligation-producing effects of such high value supports a conclusion about one's own epistemic state—valuable things do not require creation *for all I know*—but it does not support a claim that God's existence is not required in order for things to be valuable.[27] The fact is that even the nonbeliever can recognize that human beings are valuable. This is an epistemological point. But the fact that he can recognize the value of humans and at the same time deny their createdness is *not* evidence that human beings *would be* valuable if they were *not* created.

But that is not his most crucial error. His judgment that human beings are valuable is absolutely correct. And he can make that judgment without believing in creation or having any thoughts on the issue at all. I believe that the crucial error of the nonbeliever[28] is in thinking that beings such as we are, complete with all the marvelous characteristics and abilities which make us valuable, could be the product of purely naturalistic nonintelligent forces at all— the rejection of premise 5. He correctly judges us to be valuable, and, in a sense, correctly says that we would be valuable no matter what our origin were, but errs in supposing that beings as valuable as we are could have the origins he suggests we have. *Believing* in God's existence and creative activity is not a necessary condition for recognizing the value of human beings[29] and that is simply because human beings *are* valuable and we—believer and nonbeliever alike— have the God-given ability to recognize that.[30] However, it might nonetheless be the case that God's existence is necessary for such valuable beings even to exist and have such value-recognizing abilities. And this the believer claims.

Thus we can affirm that God is the source of all value without affirming that *what* is valuable about valuable things is simply that they have God as their source. *If* valuable things came from other sources, then, trivially, they would have other sources and other sources would be the sources of valuable things. If there were some other way for me to come to be and to be as I am—namely in the image of God—I would in that case still be valuable and due moral consideration. But the antecedent is false; God is the source of all things.

But still this last assertion, that on which the believer and non-believer strongly disagree, is not required as a point of agreement in order for normative moral discourse to continue. Believer and nonbeliever alike recognize the extreme value of human beings and that that value results in moral obligations.

VIII

So, if God's creation is not valuable simply because it is his creation, if it is not valuable simply because he values it, in what does its value lie? This paper must end, and so must the answering of questions. I think the final answer is found in a description of the creation and the affirmation of certain of the qualities found there that they are the qualities which make things valuable. If we think about the highest of God's creation, it is our ability to love, to think, to act, to value, to plan, to enjoy, to thank, to forgive, to understand, etc. which makes us valuable. As the Genesis account puts it, God, having created, examined his handiwork and *saw* that that which he had created was good. This world and its inhabitants have been created by God and are valuable because of the way that God designed and created them. If we need assurance of that value beyond our own capacities to judge it, we can perhaps find some in "Because God says so." He has made it and it is good because he has made it so. Further, he knows and can testify to its goodness. But it is not good simply because he says so.

Of course, questions can still be asked by the curious or unsatisfied: What is it about these characteristics that makes them constitutive of value? Isn't it simply that they are the characteristics of God? Here again, and finally, I object, and grab the second horn. No, it is God's perfect possession of them which constitutes his supreme value.[31]

NOTES

1. I say "describe" because the persuasive power of most of what follows is located in the coherence of the "picture" rather than in the forcefulness of some argument. Furthermore, I do not claim to have created the picture; only this description is mine.

2. I believe that the traditional objections, centering around claims that

a divine command theory makes morality arbitrary and affirmations of God's goodness trivial, are fatal. More on this later.

3. Recent "modifications" to traditional divine command theory can be seen as laudable efforts to postpone the last word. E.g., William Alston in this volume allows for explanation of divine commands in terms of moral goodness, and then moral goodness in terms of God's character.

4. Of course these objections, as stated, would not hold against one who interprets "Because God says so" much more broadly than as a reference to Christian Scriptures, perhaps speaking of the moral knowledge accessible to believer and nonbeliever alike as some sort of general revelation. Robert Adams, in his "Divine Command Metaethics Modified Again" (*Journal of Religious Ethics* 7, no. 1 [1979]), when admitting that a theory of revelation is necessary in working out a divine command theory, suggests that options include such a broad notion of general revelation as well as biblical literalism, with many options in between. However, the point now under consideration is one of epistemology. Suppose it is God's commanding that creates a moral obligation. Even so, if that divine will is made known to me via my own (God-given, to be sure) moral feelings, intuitions, and careful considerations, then the correct answer to the epistemological question, "How do you know, or how did you discover, that . . . ?" will make reference to those feelings, intuitions, considerations. It will not be, or will not simply or quickly be, "Because God says so." To insist otherwise would be the same as claiming that the correct answer for a believer to give to "How do you know that there is a tree out in the yard?" would be, "Because God said so," in virtue of the fact that God is the source of our sense perception abilities just as he is the source of our abilities to know moral truths.

5. "It might have been otherwise" is not a claim made by *all* who endorse a divine command theory. Indeed some would take as an important task explaining how (1) divine commands are the sole foundation of right and wrong while (2) it (morality) could *not* have been other than it is. Answers are usually found in the quality and steadfastness of God's character or nature.

6. However, this claim that believer and nonbeliever have different meanings for moral terms is made much more plausible than I suggest here by Robert M. Adams in his article, "A Modified Divine Command Theory of Ethical Wrongness," in *Religion and Morality: A Collection of Essays,* edited by Gene Outka and John P. Reeder, Jr. (Garden City, N.Y.: Anchor Books, 1973). Adams has since abandoned the understanding of divine command theory as a theory about the meaning of moral terms.

7. If "God" is being used as a title for the omnipotent, omniscient, omnibenevolent creator of the universe, then the statement "God is good" is both necessarily and analytically true. But I take it that in normal theistic affirmations of the goodness of God, "God" is functioning as a proper name of the being who is the creator, and thus that while "God is good" might still be necessarily true (if God is essentially good), it is not analytic.

8. Again, some divine command theorists would affirm that the true nature of wrongness is found in God's prohibition, but deny that God "decides"

or "makes up" anything. Instead, he is somehow constrained by his nature. But the question then is, "What is it about God's nature which gives his commands their moral force? Is it simply because it is *his,* or because it is *good?*"

9. Of course accepting the divine command theory and then interpreting "command" broadly to mean "will," including what is often referred to as God's "permissive will," has the "advantage" of eliminating the problem of evil—everything that happens is God's will and thus is right. The difficulty we have is simply that we are cursed with defective epistemological equipment when it comes to assessing moral matters. I am always surprised when I have to persuade Christian undergraduates to give up this view.

10. It will become obvious that I have a fairly high respect for our epistemological ability to discern what is right and what is wrong. But it should be understood that this is very different from identifying human opinion as an infallible guide to right or wrong, and entirely unrelated to a claim that human opinion is somehow the source of right and wrong.

11. God could still be morally good apart from creation if it were understood counterfactually as a claim about how he would relate to other beings if there were other beings. This would fit better with a virtue approach to morality, one in which the central moral assessment is of character rather than action. Also, divine goodness might be present in the relationships of the three persons of the Trinity. Thanks to Michael Beaty for this reminder.

12. And, more broadly, the nature of the environment surrounding the car, e.g., laws of physics, amount of oxygen in the air. Also, since part of the nature of the car is its purpose or function as a vehicle of transportation, there are constraints on its design and care so that it is created to be and can remain capable of fulfilling that purpose. But these constraints, again, do not exist "out there" somewhere, but only within the nature of the car and in the goals of its designers.

13. After writing this, I was shown an article by Murray MacBeath, "The Euthyphro Dilemma," in *Mind* 91 (1982), pp. 565–71. In it MacBeath, using tactics which are interestingly different than mine, supports much the same position. He writes, "God, so to speak, decides what to command by reference, not to a moral law independent of himself, but by reference to the interests of sentient beings."

14. The point assumes that God acts freely in creation. It does not assume that God could do evil, that he is not "bound" by the essential goodness of his nature. It simply assumes that God could have done otherwise than he did. Not everyone will accept this assumption.

15. And if GM decides to go into the yo-yo business, to create different things with different purposes, they will have to write new instruction manuals as well.

16. Perhaps heaven will be such a place, that is, a place where most of our earthly moral rules will have no use.

17. The debt to Aristotle in this area should be obvious.

18. This is not to say that there could never be circumstances in which such behavior is permissible, or even required. You may be attacking my wife

with a knife. Those are different issues which can be ignored here. What should be clear, stated more carefully, is that it is *prima facie* wrong.

19. By "instructions" here—and in the domain of morality—I don't intend to presume that *specific* rules of action are always the norm. Tire pressure need not be *exactly* 32 pounds per square inch. Anywhere between 28 and 36 may be fine under normal circumstances. There is looseness in the notion of "that which is beneficial." The commands which are referred to in the divine command theory could certainly be less than precise as well, but I think my position fits better with a sense of morality which does not presume that for every situation there is exactly one course of action which would be morally correct.

20. I say "may be" to allow for the possibility of excluding man-made objects from the class of created things while still affirming their value. This would not be to claim, of course, that their ultimate source of value is to be found other than in God.

21. It seems to me that this error is committed in the art world when an artist becomes so renowned for his talent that *anything* from his hands becomes esteemed as having great merit. Now of course it is true, "God don't make no junk," and in this God differs from the very best of human "creators." But the fact that nothing God makes is junk is a fact about the quality of the products of his work, not an analytical connection between "object of God's handiwork" and "junk."

22. An example might be found in the value someone has because of her role in helping to fulfill God's redemptive purpose in the world. She is not valuable in this way because her help is *required,* but because God allows, accepts, and values her assistance.

23. One great advantage of developing a theory of value within a Christian context is that warrant is found for claiming lesser or greater degrees of value. This can't be done if createdness alone is the source of value, but can be if degree of value is tied to differing levels of God's valuations (which I reject) or to characteristics of the objects themselves which are somehow constitutive of value. While a Christian view does not (when correctly applied) support raping and pillaging the environment for the perceived "good" of humankind, it does support a clear kind of speciesism. Human beings are more valuable than trees. Starving children in Africa do pose a more pressing moral problem than does animal experimentation. And it is no moral tragedy that there is no "Save the Plankton" movement. (Thanks to Gary Larson of "The Far Side" cartoon for that last idea!)

24. At least it is not obvious that you can. I am tempted to think that (3) actually does entail (2), but, of course, that in itself is not enough to make (3) work alone as a single premise in a *convincing* argument for God's existence.

25. Whether or not these two options are exhaustive I'll leave to others now. Some sort of nontheistic Platonist, for example, might think they are not. My thanks to the philosophy department at SUNY Geneseo—where I read an earlier version of this paper—for pointing that out to me.

On the point that moral obligation does not fit well within a materialistic ontology, I recommend George Mavrodes' "Religion and the Queerness of Morality," in *Rationality, Religious Belief, and Moral Commitment,* ed. Robert Audi and William J. Wainwright (Ithaca, N.Y.: Cornell University Press, 1986).

26. Of course it should also be noted that the argument the divine command theorist offers above has little polemic value either. The nonbeliever can affirm premise 1 while denying premise 4 and conclusion 2, and this even if the argument is sound. Premise 4 of this argument has no obvious apologetic superiority over premise 5 of the other.

27. Replacing premise 6 with "God does not exist" would allow a valid inference to the denial that God is necessary for morality. But of course this argument has little polemic value either.

28. Less harshly I could, perhaps should, say, "The central point of his disagreement with me. . . ." I am not here arguing for my position so much as stating it. Here the nonbeliever disagrees and I call that "error." My affirmation of premise 5 and his rejection of it perhaps stem from our differing assessments of arguments from design.

29. Perhaps it *is* for recognizing the *full extent* of their value.

30. I think this is a better way to account for moral agreement between believer and nonbeliever than the claim the divine command theorist must make: "X is wrong because God has forbidden it. The nonbeliever who comes to understand that X is wrong thus has epistemic access to moral truth even though he does not understand the true nature of morality." Instead, I believe that the nonbeliever who knows that X is wrong knows something that God knows and in a sense knows 'what God commands.' However, he knows that X is wrong because he correctly judges X to be harmful to some object which he correctly judges to be valuable. And these truths are the very reasons for God's prohibition of X.

31. Special thanks of my colleague Brian Sayers for his comments and suggestions. Some were even followed.

Contributors

WILLIAM ALSTON is Professor of Philosophy at Syracuse University.

MICHAEL BEATY is Associate Professor of Philosophy at Baylor University.

CARLTON FISHER is Assistant Professor of Philosophy at Houghton College.

JONATHAN KVANVIG is Associate Professor of Philosophy at Texas A&M University.

SCOTT MACDONALD is Assistant Professor of Philosophy at the University of Iowa.

CHRISTOPHER MENZEL is Assistant Professor of Philosophy at Texas A&M University.

RICHARD OTTE is Associate Professor of Philosophy at the University of California at Santa Cruz.

ALVIN PLANTINGA is John A. O'Brien Professor of Philosophy at the University of Notre Dame.

PHILIP QUINN is John A. O'Brien Professor of Philosophy at the University of Notre Dame.

DEL RATZSCH is Professor of Philosophy at Calvin College.

ELEONORE STUMP is Professor of Philosophy at the Virginia Polytechnic Institute and State University.

CHARLES TALIAFERRO is Assistant Professor of Philosophy at St. Olaf College.

STEPHEN WYKSTRA is Associate Professor of Philosophy at Calvin College.

LINDA ZAGZEBSKI is Associate Professor of Philosophy at Loyola Marymount University.